D1206914

A PROGRAMMER'S VIEW OF THE INTEL 432 SYSTEM

Elliott I. Organick

McGRAW-HILL BOOK COMPANY

New York St. Louis San Francisco Auckland
Bogotá Hamburg Johannesburg London
Madrid Mexico Montreal New Delhi
Panama Paris São Paulo Singapore
Sydney Tokyo Toronto

Library of Congress Cataloging in Publication Data

Organick, Elliott Irving, date.
A programmer's view of the Intel 432 system.

Includes bibliographical references and index.
1. Intel 432 (Computer)—Programming. 2. Ada (Computer program language) I. Title.
QA76.8.I267073 1983 001.64 82–24887
ISBN 0–07–047719–1

1234567890 KGP/KGP 89876543

ISBN 0-07-047719-1

The editor for this book was Stephen Guty, the designer was Naomi Auerbach, and the production supervisor was Thomas G. Kowalczyk. It was set in Times Roman by Information Sciences Corp.
Printed and bound by The Kingsport Press.

CONTENTS

PREFACE

Does any technological development of the computer era rival in importance that of the microprocessor? I think not. The first microprocessors, whose short history began just a decade ago, were based primarily on the advances in microelectronic technology, which came much later than and was largely independent of the computer itself. By contrast, today's impressive microprocessor breakthroughs rest heavily on the synthesis of modern computer architecture and operating systems principles and on recent improvements in the software disciplines all of which represent decades of development. The three disciplines: software engineering, programming methodology, and programming languages are heavily utilized in the automation, testing and verification of the microprocessor design itself, and this dependence continues to grow.

From the start, microprocessor designers and manufacturers enjoyed success and acclamation merely by demonstrating that each new design emulated a yet closer "approximation" to a contemporary mini or mainframe computer structure. Observers required no crystal ball to conjecture that if circuit density, speeds, and design automation continued to improve as projected, then microprocessor designs would soon converge to the full power and logic of large minicomputers and perhaps even of mainframe computers.

Most of such conjectures are now realities, However, far fewer observers anticipated that the day would soon arrive when significant advances in mainframe computer architecture would be manifested in the microprocessor. In the highly competitive computer industry it had seemed especially far fetched to imagine that any relatively young semiconductor organization could wrest the leadership in computer architecture from established computer companies. This, too, appears to be happening—and this book is an effort to describe why and how this shift of focus is occurring.

The Intel Corporation has been an acknowledged leader and major contributor in microelectronic technology. In a recent advertisement, this company claims credit for most of the technological breakthroughs since 1971. The advertisement claims that the most recent, and by implication the most significant of these breakthroughs is the new iAPX 432 Micromainframe™ system.[1] The claim is summarized as follows: "1981: with the goal of dramatically cutting software costs, Intel breaks with traditional computer architecture and introduces an expandable multiprocessor system optimized for managing information.'' This succinct assertion should serve as a serious challenge to most of us, for if true, we computer professionals should gain an understanding of the basis of this truth as quickly as possible so that we can seek ways to ''apply'' it. True, or false, the curiosity of many has already been justifiably roused. There will be much serious investigation of this claim.

Already much has been published about the iAPX 432, mainly in literature and analyses provided by Intel itself. Much more is sure to follow from a wider variety of sources as others gain access to copies of the new system, acquire experience in applying it to their problems, and refute or confirm Intel's claim. My effort not only attempts to make the claim of ''breakthrough'' better understood by a wide audience of computer professionals, engineers, analysts, programmers, and students; it also has as its objective providing an introduction to many of the principles and concepts of computer architecture, operating systems, and programming language, which can help potential users of the iAPX 432 become effective users more quickly. The reader profile assumed for this book is a person who is familiar with programming and who is familiar with Ada[2] or Pascal.

[Chapters of this book can serve as case-study text for several traditional computer science courses. I have used drafts of Chapters 2 and 3 for a course in programming languages, sections from Chapters 1, 4, 5, 6, 7, and 9 for a course in computer architecture, and plan to use sections from Chapters 1, and 4 through 10 for a course in operating systems. Other computer science instructors may also find the material useful as text material.]

The book is an outgrowth of my good fortune to be invited early in 1980 by members of Intel's Special Systems Operation group at Aloha, Oregon to begin a study and writing project on the iAPX 432, then in an advanced stage of development. It was immediately clear to me, during the first visit to Aloha, that a major advance in computer architecture was in the making. For a number of years I had been a student of computer architecture, chiefly from the viewpoint of matching computer structures to semantic models of programming languages and of providing support in the architecture for secure and powerful but structurally simple operating systems. The opportunity to study the new Intel system and to write about what I might learn while the system itself was still new and largely unfamiliar to many, even within Intel, would be an exciting but familiar experience. I ''signed on'' with little hesitation.

The study published here represents my understanding of the Intel 432 System as of July 1982. It is primarily a technical description and discussion and should by no means be viewed as a kept-current ''product-description'', even though I was fortunate to receive help from individuals within Intel who were engaged in the design and implementation of the 432 System as a product.

[1]The *The Wall Street Journal,* Wednesday, July 21, 1982, page 5.

[2]Ada is a registered trademark of the U.S. Government Ada Joint Program Office.

A Preliminary Perspective of the iAPX 432 Architecture

Students of computer architecture should be aware that the iAPX 432 represents major technology transfer in four areas of recent advance:

1. VLSI and CAD technology
2. Logical structures (semantics) for hardware systems
3. Logical structures (semantics) for software systems
4. Languages for system implementation

It is no small feat to integrate several technological advances into a new system that offers more promise than can be predicted from the individual advances. Some readers may be interested in background issues related to these individual areas of advance, at least one of which is still considered controversial. For these readers I offer a short analysis in the remainder of this discussion. In essence, application of these advances has led to an architecture that offers an implementation of *transparent multiprocessing* and an *object-based computing and communication environment* reaching new levels of simplicity and efficiency. Chapter 1 fully explains these important objectives and tells why the Intel 432 System was designed to accomplish them. You will no doubt want to understand in greater detail what benefits can be gained from these design decisions. Chapters 2 through 10 address this need and provide sufficient additional detail to permit you to reach your own conclusions as to whether (a) the design objectives are met and (b) the anticipated benefits do follow from reaching those design objectives. The last section of Chapter 1 outlines the purpose of each of the following chapters. The "proper" introduction to this book, therefore, begins with Chapter 1. However, I have been unable to resist the temptation to offer the following four observations as an additional preface to that introduction.

VLSI AND CAD TECHNOLOGY: Intel's leadership in semiconductor technology was clearly demonstrated with the introduction in 1971 of the first (4-bit) microprocessor, the 4004. That leadership has continued. For such a leader, the NMOS semiconductor technology used to produce the 432 chip set would seem today to represent a relatively "simple" extension of previous advances. This advance appears to be primarily in process control, as chip area has been substantially increased with still reasonable yields. At the same time, there appears, superficially, to be no substantial advance over Intel's previous accomplishments in device density, circuit layout, or layering. However, a closer look reveals a significant increase in logical complexity and in the number and size of the required circuit patterns beyond Intel's previous microprocessors.

ordered conceptual levels for description, analysis, and design—from the macrosimulator level (at which macroinstructions of the architecture are represented and understood), to the mask level (at which the basic physical devices that represent abstractions at the higher levels are represented and understood).[3] Software design, analysis, and description tools are built for use at each level. Not only do programs at each level check for consistency within that level but additional programs have been developed to check for consistency between levels. (This methodology is an application of recent advances in computer science and software engineering theory related to formal specification and verification.)

LOGICAL STRUCTURES FOR HARDWARE SYSTEMS: Here I refer to the semantics provided in the computer's instruction set. One can identify two schools of thought among computer system designers regarding the desirability of enriching the semantic content of instructions: those that would keep the meaning of each instruction as simple (atomic) as possible, and those that would select a set of semantically powerful (and more specialized) instructions. The i432 is an application of the state-of-the-art of this second school.

The first school prefers that individual instructions have relatively elementary semantics, each instruction accomplishing a limited function, preferably one that can be accomplished in single cycle of the processor. (For example, given a choice between use of one-address versus three-address instructions, this school would likely choose one-address instructions.) Thus, it is sufficient that the set of available instructions spans all the types of actions that the computer is expected to perform. (One tries to choose a set of instructions whose individual semantics are mutually orthogonal.)

A companion objective for this school is to speed up execution by embedding in pure hardware the (simple) instructions that are most frequently executed and interpreting less-frequently used instructions either in microcode or as macro-instruction subroutines.[4] A corollary design objective is that, as much as possible, a maximum fraction of the processor's logic is "engaged" during execution of each instruction.

For such systems, which have relatively simple logical structure, the computer's resources can then in principle be optimized for the user's benefit, for example through the use of high-quality compilers.[5]

[On the other hand, by increasing the semantic content of individual instructions in the instruction set, it appears to be more difficult to produce a compiler that chooses "best" instruction sequences—and even if this is still possible, best instructions sequences may still not be optimal in terms of overall use of the system's resources. A companion argument is that raising the semantic content preempts the user's opportunity to exploit the special cases that arise and that are recognized in particular situations.

Indeed, this argument carries over to the software/language level. Often the semantics of a chosen programming language and/or its implementation preempts certain representation and functional options that might be specified by a user.[6] Although such preemption may be fine in most cases, it can force selection of inefficient solutions in those cases where the user, who may have more global knowledge of the requirements in a given case, can supply or suggest a better approach.]

[3] "A Methodology for VLSI Chip Design" by Wm. W. Lattin. J. A. Bayliss, D. L. Budde, J. R. Rattner, and Wm. S. Richardson, in *Lambda,* Second Quarter, 1981, pages 34–44.

[4] "RISC I: A Reduced Instruction Set VLSI Computer" by D. A. Patterson and C. H. Sequin in *Proceedings of the 8th Symposium on Computer Architecture,* 1981, pages 443–457.

[5] "The 801 Minicomputer", by George Radin, in *Symposium on Architectural Support for Programming Languages and Operating Systems*, March, 1982, pages 39–47.

[6] "Toward Relaxing Assumptions in Languages and Their Implementations," by Mary Shaw and Wm. A. Wulf; Carnegie Mellon University, January, 1980.

The second school (raising the semantic content of instructions) has included advocates having a variety of motivations, beginning with those primarily interested in matching the hardware to particular high-order programming languages or to particular constructs within high-order languages, such as procedure call, coroutine call and associated context switching, process switching, etc. More recently, a motivation for this approach has come from those wishing to improve the performance, clarity, flexibility, reliability, and functionality of operating systems.

It is from these latter motivations that instructions set semantics have been expanded to include explicitly or implicitly, for example, direct support for data abstraction and object management. In this category are also instructions which involve elaborate mapping steps (access path management and traversal) for controlled sharing of information, data and code protection, controls for processor and storage management (real and virtual), process synchronization, interprocess and interprocessor communication, etc.

This architectural progression can be traced back at least twenty years to the Burroughs B5000. Advances in concepts and implementation strategies have accelerated, especially in the past ten years, as the costs of implementing instructions with higher semantic content, largely with the aid of vertical microprogramming, have come down drastically without significantly penalizing performance. The iAPX 432 represents a technology transfer of the recent ideas and models represented by this approach. In this book I show how the high semantic content of a subset of the i432 machine language instructions strongly influences the behavior and efficiency of the system viewed from the perspective of software development costs and programmer productivity.

LOGICAL STRUCTURES OF SOFTWARE SYSTEMS: Here I refer to the *organization* of the functional elements and the interrelationships among principal support software modules of a system—beginning with the ''inner core'' of the operating system, and extending to the library facility, input output interfaces, and file system facility. I deliberately factor out of this discussion the implementation of particular functions performed by an operating system, such as access control and protection, interrupt handling, etc.

Much has been learned, especially in the past ten years, about operating system principles, some through pure theoretical research, but most through design, implementation, and observation and use of experimental and commercial systems. A good deal of the recent progress is owed to an almost universal recognition that principles of good engineering design and management are applicable to the systems programming phenomenon. The iAPX 432 Operating Sytem (iMAX) is an application of the current state of this software engineering art. Examining several examples of the iMAX structure forms an important part of this book.

STATE-OF-THE-ART LANGUAGE FOR SYSTEM IMPLEMENTATION: The fourth concurrent application of state-of-the-art technology is the choice of Ada as the system implementation language base for the i432 System. Ada is itself the application of the current state of the art in programming languages research and development.[7] Especially important is the emphasis given to the separation of specification from implementation of program units. Ada incorporates the semantic components needed to permit programmer teams to construct and maintain large systems and applications at minimum overall cost.

Ada is also the language target to which a number of specialty languages, such as for database applications, will likely be preprocessed.[8] [Ada is well suited to the packaging, structuring, and isolation of data objects and the procedures permitted to act on these objects.]

[7] ''Introducing Ada'', by Wm. E. Carlson, L. E. Druffel, D. A. Fisher, Wm. A. Whitaker, in *Proceedings of the 1980 Annual Conference,* Oct 27–29, 1980, pp 263–271, Association for Computing Machinery (ACM).

[8] ''Reference Manual for ADAPLEX'' by J. M. Smith, S. Fox, and T. Landers, Computer Corporation of America, January, 1981.

Acknowledgment

This book, as is the computer system it describes, is a result of a large and effective *team effort*. From the beginning, I sought and received participation from and collaboration with key technical personnel at Intel.

The perspective of Nicole Allegre, Fred Dorr, Kevin Kahn, and Justin Rattner provided suggestions for the book's technical scope, level, and for many of its objectives. John Doerr, Barbara Slaughter, Don Ferris, and Justin Rattner coordinated and expedited the interaction between me and the members of the Intel design and implementation teams.

George Cox, Kevin Kahn, Fred Pollack, and Justin Rattner provided me with an initial orientation on many of the system issues they had grappled with in the design of the iAPX 432. Steve Ziegler, Dan Hammerstrom, and Konrad Lai provided more technical assistance when I needed it.

Bill Courington critiqued early drafts of Chapters 1, 2, and 3. T. Don Dennis read, analyzed, and corrected numerous drafts of Chapters 2 through 9 as did Linda Hutchins of drafts of Chapters 2, 3, and 8. Don provided an intense review of Chapters 4 and 9 and Linda contributed heavily to Chapter 8. Jim Morris carefully read and was of great assistance in editing later drafts of Chapters 2 through 6. Jim also helped my assistant Steve Voelker with the compilation of most of the Ada code displayed in Chapters 2 and 3 and in Appendixes C through G. Dave Hubka was a superb critic of Chapter 7 and Steve Tolopka of Chapter 10, after Fred Pollack helped me set the level and orientation for the latter. (The fact is, I received so much excellent assistance from all these generous and able people that I have come to think of myself as their *ghost writer*.)

Justin Rattner not only provided an insightful review of the entire book, but has also coauthored Chapter 1. He, as well as each of the others who toiled with me over each chapter in detail, was always encouraging, offering criticism that was always constructive. Finally, Betty Organick helped by providing constant encouragement.

I am grateful, too, to many other people, both at the University of Utah and at Intel for encouragement and technical and other support. Without all this help, this relatively ambitious book could not have become a reality.

ELLIOTT I. ORGANICK
Salt Lake City
July, 1982

1 TOP-LEVEL VIEW OF THE INTEL 432 SYSTEM DESIGN

coauthored with Justin R. Rattner, Intel Corporation

The term "computer revolution" suggests to all of us computer technology's rapid development and the equally rapid expansion of the applications of computers in our society, our institutions, our businesses and our homes. Even so, computer systems develop remarkably slowly, and according to relatively fixed patterns of logical and physical organization and its related style of use. A computer system's style of use determines in important but often subtle ways how effective and productive its users will be. It is only every few years, perhaps only once in a decade, that a sufficiently innovative computer system is developed to justify a full-length book for describing it and discussing its style of use. In 1981 the Intel Corporation announced such a system and named it the iAPX 432.

Our description focuses on this system's overall structure and functionality from the viewpoint of the programmer who will use it. Our purpose is to help others better appreciate the design of the system and how its developers perceive its promise for improving programmer productivity. In the process of reading this book, a programmer can also expect to learn a good deal about object-based architecture and gain a new perspective about programming itself. To a very large extent, it is the measure of programmer productivity that will determine how effective the Intel 432 System can be for a more productive economy and hence for the general welfare.

This book examines the structure of the iAPX 432 system from three principal but interrelated perspectives,

- its architecture (as exhibited by key elements of its instruction set and by its physical organization),
- its operating system design, structure, and unconventional interface with the user

- its implementation language, which serves not only as a tool for the systems programmer, but is also available to the applications programmer. (The language is really two languages in one. It is Ada, the proposed national and international standard, and it is also a limited number of extensions of Ada that allow the user to make full use of the underlying hardware, should a user choose to do so.)

All three components, the architecture, the operating system, and the implementation language are new; none is carried over from previous bottom-up designs. In the following discussion we shall use the term "i432 System Architecture" to refer to the composite of these three components. (Note that we hereafter substitute the shorter acronym, "i432", for "iAPX 432", the one used for formal reference to the system in publications of the Intel Corporation.)

To open our study we first examine three important concepts in computer system architecture: *multiprocessing*, *object-based design*, and *object filing systems*. The first is a generally-accepted convergence point of modern systems; the second and third are new departures. The principal theme of this book is that the effective implementation of these three concepts, exhibited by the Intel 432 System, provides users with a new dimension for expressive power and productivity for both system software and applications programs.

1.1. Computer Architecture and Multiprocessing

"Computer architecture" is a popular term, understood from many vantage points. Like a rich data base, there are many possible views. Technically, the term *architecture* often refers to the functionality of the system that may be achieved through use of the computer's instruction set (instruction set view). Almost equally often, architecture refers to the physical components of the computer system and their logical, physical, and functional interrelationships (organization and technology view). When a trained computer systems person can gather relevant facts related to either or both views of a candidate system, a surprisingly complete appreciation of a new system can be acquired.

The view we shall take here is perhaps an unorthodox one to the expert, but one that may provide some new insights for novice and expert alike. It is a perspective (actually a bias) begun by trying to track the architectural developments of most commercially available systems. It seems easier to appreciate the advances reflected in the iAPX 432 system using this frame of reference.

1.1.1. Multiprocessor Computer Systems

Most commercially-available systems result from an evolving, cyclic, and bottom-up process, lasting over a many-year span. They appear to their users as part of a series of increasingly better, more general, faster, and more cost-effective models.

The objectives for these systems have varied, but here is a summary, ordered roughly as a *scale of objectives* that reflects known historical development of commercial computer systems:

- run single programs, produced from a variety of assemblers and compilers, with static (later dynamic) resource allocation strategies,
- run several such programs in the same time frame, through time sharing, or multiprogramming resource managers,
- accomplish all of the above while guaranteeing real-time response for some programs executed,
- connect computers to a variety of input/output devices, backing store media, and use external processors (e.g., "channels") to gain overlap of computing and I/O transfer.
- increase computer speeds by making larger programs and data more directly and more quickly accessible through the use virtual memory and cache memory mechanisms,
- accomplish all of the above (though perhaps accepting some limits on performance) and provide controlled sharing of information resources among related tasks (programs) and enforced separation of information resources allocated among non-related tasks—all to achieve protection, security, reliability, and fairness in service,
- accomplish all of the above for increased work loads by providing several processors for sharing the computational load, using some cooperative, processor-pooling strategy.

Generally speaking, the more successful commercial systems have been those which, though begun by meeting one of the earlier objectives, have, through upgrading and other forms of modification, managed to meet a succession of more "advanced" objectives on the above scale. Often, this success has been met within a single computer family. In some cases, however, a family had to be abandoned and a new one started, and in other less fortunate cases the entire computer enterprise had to be abandoned or sold.

In any case, the last objective on our scale, that of a multiprocessor system, most often with a store accessible by all processors, is a popular convergence point in this evolution. In many commercial systems this last point has been reached only after more than a decade of development.

1.1.2. The Multiprocessing Model

No matter what the cycle of product evolution, it seems safe to say that the sharply reduced cost of circuitry, coupled with the need for ever more processing power and diversity of application, has driven architects of general purpose systems toward solutions that involve multiprocessing structures. Thus far, many differences can be perceived in the specifics of these solutions. Even so, one guiding principle or model predominates, that of furnishing a pooled set of processors for execution of a network of interconnecting program units. Sometimes the networks are structured as trees or related groups of trees, but in every case, intercommunication among the asynchronous program units is achieved by some one or group of synchronizing mechanisms.

In its most simplified (and abstract) form, one may view this multiprocessing model as shown in Figure 1-1, which suggests a means for "marrying" processors to tasks that are ready to be executed.

A representation of a Ready Program Unit, such as a message pointing to a "Task Control Block" (to use an older terminology, or to a "Process Object", a term we will be using later), is entered on the Ready Queue in the direction indicated by the arrow. The program unit is then bound to an Available Processor, also representable as a pointer to an appropriate control block ("Processor Object") when each "reaches" the front of its respective queue. This pair of queues may be called a "Dispatching Port".

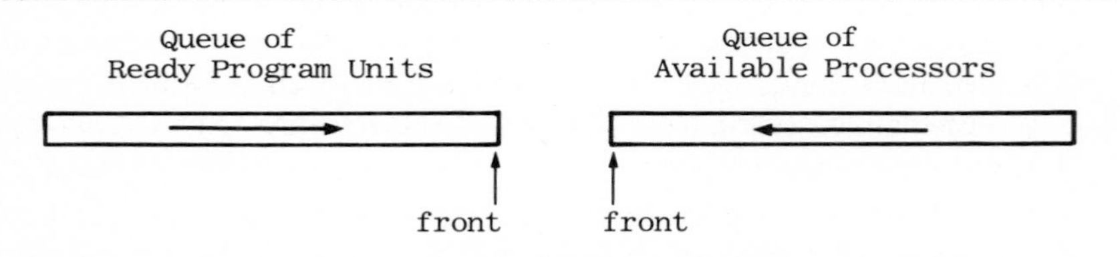

Figure 1-1 Abstraction of a Dispatching Port.

A program unit is executed (i.e., is interpreted by the processor to which it is bound) until a point is reached where the program unit cannot or may not continue to run. (The program has run to completion, a supervisory process has ordered it to be terminated, it has entered a wait state, or its time quantum has been exhausted.) At this point, the program unit is either deallocated or enqueued on some appropriate Wait Queue (not shown in the figure above). The processor, in turn, then reenters the Queue of Available Processors in search of new work to do. When a blocked program unit is again ready to run, it is removed from the Wait Queue and reentered onto the Queue of Ready Program Units.

This multiprocessing model has a number of attractive attributes, among them its essential independence from any underlying semantic model of program structure and execution. It is important to observe that the model is equally applicable, for example, for the multiprogramming of Fortran programs, Cobol programs, Ada programs, including those which have multitasking structures, LISP-like or LISP-based applicative programs, or mixes of these. Moreover, in principle, such a model should behave the same, except for throughput rate, for any number (one or more) of actual processors.

1.1.3. Multiprocessor Memory Organization

Implementing a system based on this model is a major challenge. Should there be one shared (central) store, private per processor stores, or combinations of shared and private stores used in the design? For each selection, access paths from the processors to the stores must be provided with sufficient bandwidth (and in the case of shared stores, with sufficient switching speeds and reliability [55]) to achieve satisfactory performance objectives. Such structures must offer the promise of approximately linear increase in throughput with the number of processors added, at least up to some acceptable number of processors. An equally important set of design choices must be made to determine access paths to secondary stores and to other I/O devices.

The per-processor private store solution is interesting because it offers opportunities for introducing new levels of fault tolerance and improved performance in special purpose systems. We call this organization, the *multicomputer solution*. (The Tandem systems [5] are good examples.) Unfortunately, multicomputer systems have two critical drawbacks when the objective is a general-purpose system. First, it is difficult if not impractical to model and implement shared variable semantics in distributed stores. Unfortunately such semantics are an integral part of nearly all the commonly used high-order languages. Selecting the multicomputer approach seems, therefore, incompatible with the goal of a general purpose system which is to accommodate the needs of a wide class of programmers. Second, code for program units that are to be executed by more than one processor must be copied to the private store of each such processor that executes it. This extra cost seems acceptable for the objective of redundancy to achieve failure tolerance, especially where the amount of copied code can be limited to certain resident operating system modules. However, the frequent extra copying of code is burdensome when the objective is to balance processor loads dynamically, and on a system-wide basis. Furthermore, the private store of any processor in an N-processor system is necessarily limited to 1/Nth the total store available. Therefore, were sharing permitted, there would be a disproportionately greater chance for thrashing when using the individual per-processor stores than in the N-times-as-large shared store.

One shared central store is by far the most frequently advocated solution, even though, for any one switching mechanism used to route information flow between the processors and the shared store, the number of processors cannot exceed some practical limit before traffic congestion in the switch seriously restricts the total processing throughput of the system. (This limit can be determined empirically.) We call this solution the *multiprocessor system*. The i432 system is our prime example.

Multiprocessor solutions may differ greatly in details as to how they execute individual program units. Even so, the architectures of competing large-scale general-purpose systems appear similar. At their highest level of abstraction, they exhibit multiprocessing system *superstructures*. Unfortunately, because many of these systems have been grown "bottom-up", their implementations and modes of use remain, to a variety of users, different in important ways.

1.1.4. i432 Multiprocessor System Organization

Those system architects who can start "from scratch" with a top-down approach, and who are able to profit fully from the mistakes and good ideas of others, have the potential to produce far better implementations. They can begin with the elegance and simplicity of the above-described superstructure (Figure 1-1) and expand to consequent sublevels. Such a development has occurred at Intel with the design of the iAPX 432 system architecture.

A first view of the system structure, showing the relationship between the Computational Subsystem and the I/O Subsystem is given in Figure 1-2. The Computational Subsystem contains three types of elements: processor modules, memory modules, and one or more busses that form a multiprocessor interconnect. The topology may thus become quite complex, consisting of several modules of each type. The processor modules themselves consist of the i432 General Data Processor (GDP) and its associated bus interface hardware. The I/O Subsystem consists of one or more *independent* peripheral subsystems, each interfaced to the Computational Subsystem through an Interface Processor (IP). Multiprocessing is thus an integral part of both computation and I/O in the i432.

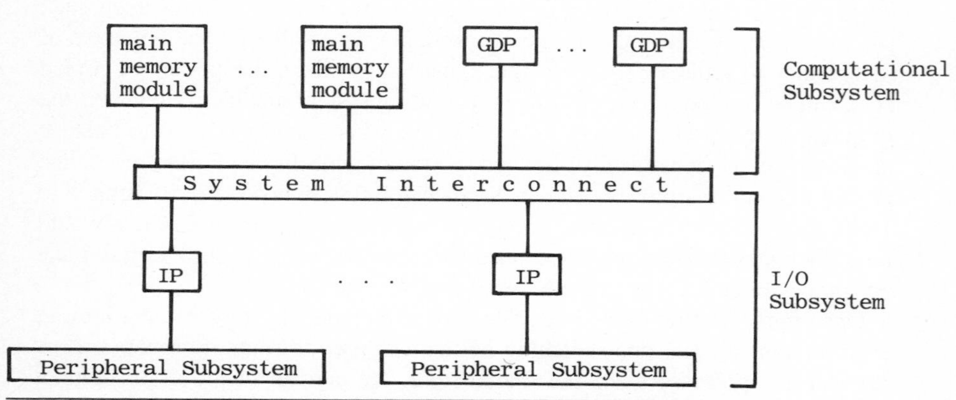

Figure 1-2 A simple i432 system topology.

The actual topology of an i432 System may vary from that shown in the figure according to the particular bus and interconnect circuitry made available and the performance objectives desired. (For a system that is to contain a relatively large number of processors, say more than a total of six GDPs and IPs, an elaborate bus interconnect structure might be required, but we do not dwell on this matter here.)

Through careful attention to multiprocessing issues in the definition of both its system organization and its architecture, the i432 also implements the idea of *transparent multiprocessing*. This simple but important concept means that the number of processors in an i432 system can be increased or decreased without software modification. It is even possible to start or stop a processor at any time without damaging or informing a single piece of software. More importantly, no reprogramming of either the operating system or the application is required to exploit an increase in the number of processors.

It is interesting to note that multiprocessing in the i432 was not strictly motivated by the traditional desire to share the workload among a pool of processors. Somewhat less technical factors were actually responsible for the decision to include multiprocessing in the initial implementation. First, it was felt that competitive architectures would be available in different implementations with a range of cost and performance levels at the time of the 432's introduction. Second, unlike traditional computer manufacturers, semiconductor companies are rarely in a position to provide even a second implementation in less than three or four years. [This is due not only to the relatively small size of semiconductor companies, but also to the fact that they generally have, at any moment in time, only one technology capable of cost-effectively implementing a new architecture.]

These two factors led the Intel designers to seek a design approach that would give the i432 a range of performance from just one implementation. Multiprocessing proved to be a particularly attractive approach for the semiconductor manufacturer because, to achieve increased performance, it relies on the economies derived from replicating the processor circuitry rather than from a complete redesign. Furthermore, multiprocessing also supports the concept of modular, in-the-field, performance expansion either for I/O or data processing with the installation of a simple printed circuit board. The latter gives i432 users a particularly cost-effective way to upgrade their products over time.

1.2. Object-Based Design

The development of a new computer family has frequently been launched with a semantic model of a program structure and a supporting machine language in mind. We may reflect back to the IBM 704, . . . , 7094 series for a good example. This important line of computers, although perhaps not begun with a well-formed model of program structure, was quickly brought into focus with the development of Fortran. Later models in the evolved series added features and components, such as more index registers, higher speed devices, better means of communication with I/O systems, etc., but kept (indeed, were forced to keep) as the principal objective the compilation/execution of Fortran-like object programs. (This series died out before reaching the multiprocessor convergence point.)

Other examples can and should also be cited where the architectural series is rooted to, or influenced strongly by, a view of a particular program structure model. Thus the GE/Honeywell Multics series was strongly influenced by a semantic model of PL/I programs in execution; the Burroughs B5500, B6700, . . . , B7800 series was rooted to the model of Extended Algol programs in execution; that is, Algol60 programs extended to include coroutines, asynchronous tasks, and means for intercommunication among such program components.

Like these earlier architectures, the i432 is also based on a semantic model of program structures. Unlike many of its predecessors, however, the i432 is not based on the model of a particular programming language. Instead, its designers' aim was the direct execution-time support for both *data abstraction* (i.e., programming with abstract data types) and *domain-based operating systems*. The principal insight of the i432 architecture is the fact that both objectives can be supported by a common semantic model, known as the *object model*. In this section, we explain the concepts of data abstraction by describing the emerging object-based programming methodology and review the complementary principles of object-based operating system design.

1.2.1. Object-Based Programming

Object-based programming, in contrast with the more conventional *control-based* style, emphasizes the view that a program largely describes the definition, creation, manipulation of, and interaction among, a set of independent and well-defined data structures called *objects*. The control-based style views a program as a controlled sequence of events (actions) on its aggregate data structures. In both styles, the objective of the program is to transform a set of specified data values from some input or starting form to some specified output or final form. Although the distinction between these two styles may at first appear to be contrived or superficial, there are crucial differences. We attempt to explain why in a very brief way here and distribute a more complete explanation throughout the remainder of the book, giving special emphasis to this matter in Chapters 2 and 3.

In conventional, control-based programming, the programmer finds that, as a program's complexity grows, it becomes increasingly difficult to retain a clear view of the entire sequence (or sequences) of actions that comprise the program. To this end, decomposing long sequences into groups of shorter ones (subroutines) helps a great deal. (In fact, the good programmer never allows a sequence to grow very long in the first place, having the foresight to organize the program, top-down, into a structure of such subroutines.)

Unfortunately, the data operated on by these subroutines is not similarly decomposed into independent entities. Most of the data is represented in global structures that are freely shared by all subroutines; consequently, much of the expected benefit of decomposition into subroutines is never realized. The source of the problem is rooted in the number of subroutines and their mutual dependency on the form and integrity of common data structures. As this number increases, it is often difficult or impossible to arrange the subroutines and the data they operate on into well-matched (isomorphic) substructures—for example, along strict hierarchical lines, even when using an Algol-based language like Pascal.

In object-based programming, by contrast, one begins by associating a single data structure, or instance thereof, with a fixed set of subprograms. The associated subprograms are the only operations defined on that object. In Ada terminology, the data structure is known as an object and its associated set of operations is called a "package". Ordinarily, one set of such "public" operations is defined and made accessible to all components of the program that have access to the data object. These public operations have well-defined input/output specifications; their subprogram bodies and any subprograms on which these bodies may further depend, are factored out and may be totally hidden. The package can also be used to hide the representation of the object, so that subprograms in other packages cannot choose to bypass those public subprograms and manipulate the object directly.

This factoring is called *data abstraction*, and can lead to considerable design simplification; that is, it can make the program more understandable, correct, and reliable. Flexibility (and portability) is also enhanced, because the details of the objects, their representations, and public operations may be changed or replaced by a different set of details.

More formally [26], data abstraction allows us to focus on just those attributes of a data object or of a class of them that specify the names and define the abstract meanings of the operations associated with such objects. We suppress attributes that describe the representation of those objects and the implementation of the operations associated with them in terms of still other objects and operations.

The foregoing concepts, which have since led to the introduction of abstract data types as constructs in modern high-order programming languages, were seeded with the introduction of the *class construct* in Simula 67 [7] [15]. The appreciation of the ideas associated with the Simula class then led to several research contributions and proposals for introducing data abstraction in modern programming languages [3] [36] [39] [62] [63]. The most recent development is the Ada language design effort, whose constructs for data abstraction are built on these earlier contributions.

1.2.2. Object-Based Operating Systems

Concurrent with development of data abstraction, much was being learned about operating system principles. Some of this advance derived from pure theoretical research, but most came through the design, implementation, and observation and use of real systems[9]. The lessons ranged over a wide space. They recognized the importance, for example, of:

- avoiding monolithic, unwieldy structures—a one-time common consequence of early computer designs wherein a computer could execute in one of only two discernably different states, "user" or "supervisor",
- encouraging modular structures that isolate logically distinct functions, and the associated system information (information hiding), so that key properties of the system may be better analyzed and certified, repaired or modified,
- providing for easy interchange (replacement) of logically independent software components (also implying a requirement of low overhead for system recompilation and reinitialization),
- providing for a system's easy extendability, even to the point where ordinary users may participate in the extension,
- identifying and separating policy and mechanism, so that mechanisms may be efficient while policy is easily altered,
- increased failure tolerance by providing the extra code and data structures needed in the initial design (with hardware assistance, as needed),
- providing system and user code debugging aids in the initial design (with hardware assistance, as needed).

The above list is hardly exhaustive, and more lessons are still being learned about how to design and implement better systems. Much of the recent progress is owed to an almost universal recognition that principles of good engineering design and management are applicable to the programming of operating systems.

Given that this list represents an "ideal" set of properties for an operating system, many experimental investigations have focused considerable attention on determining precisely what logical structure is best able to realize these essential system characteristics. Here we use *logical structure* to mean the organization of functional elements and intermodule relationships.

The first attempts at improving operating system organization focused on minimizing the number of primitive functions upon which the system is built, the so-called "kernel" approach, and on ways to "layer" subsequent functions such that the system takes on strict hierarchical structure [18]. [Hardware support for this organization was pioneered in Multics [25].] The observation that not all operating system functions obeyed the same hierarchical relationships led operating system designers to consider multiple, but strictly independent hierarchies called *domains* [57] [58].

[9]A substantial body of literature has been formed, centered initially on papers appearing in the proceedings of symposiums held biannually since 1967 by ACM's Special Interest Group on Operating Systems (SIGOPS).

Almost simultaneously, it was argued [64] that strict hierarchical layering in the design of an entire system would severely limit the flexibility available to high-level users. It was observed that operating system domains were each responsible for the management of particular types of data structures called "objects", which corresponded, in general, to instances of resources (e.g., page, file, and process) in the system. In formal terms, an object was defined [65] as an abstraction of an instance of a resource and thought of as a triple:

```
(unique name,  type,  representation)
```

The *unique name* distinguishes an object from all other objects. Uniqueness of the name can span both space (in which the object resides) and time (beyond the life of the system in which the object was created). The object's *type* defines the nature of the resource represented. An object is an instance of its type which, in a practical sense, defines a set valid operations on objects of that type. The *representation* contains the information content associated with an object. An object's representation may include private data structures as well as references, in the form of unique names, to other objects. Representation also implies certain forms and limits that may restrict the object's content.

The experimental systems proved that organizing the information and physical resources of computer systems so they are represented as objects has a profound effect on the management of these resources. Management schemes are simpler, fewer, and easier to implement and use; individual resources are easier to specify, create (allocate), destroy (deallocate), manipulate, and protect from misuse, accidental or malicious. The ability to hide (and protect against direct access to) unneeded representation and implementation details is an automatic byproduct of the object basis of such systems.

While the experimental studies demonstrated the logical soundness of objects and domains as an organizational model for a modern operating system, they also showed, often in very convincing terms, that without direct hardware support, they were simply too inefficient to be commercially practical. Much of the experimental work in operating systems has moved to other areas in anticipation of the necessary hardware innovations.

1.2.3. Object-Based Computer Architecture

The i432 architectural design began with a commitment to include hardware support for both domain-based protection and data abstraction; in other words, to produce an *object-oriented* architecture. After working on this problem for some time, it was realized that a logical and desirable generalization of this goal would be to use data abstraction as the fundamental design framework of the architecture. This generalization yields what is referred to as an *object-based* architecture.

Although largely intended to overcome the performance problems associated with object-based operating systems on conventional hardware, object-based architecture is actually some twenty years in the making. It is considered to have begun with descriptor-based architectures [11] [30] [31] which pioneered the concept and implementation of segmented virtual memory support. The evolution then progressed with the introduction of *capabilities* and capability-based addressing concepts [13] [16] [20]−[24] [27] [59] [60] to the current view of objects as abstractions of resources, which had its origins in the HYDRA system [64] [65]. A *capability* is an access authorization for a particular object; object managers dispense capabilities for objects to programs units needing to share their use. The i432 architecture models closely, with much hardware support for capabilites, the object structure and object management concepts of HYDRA.

At this point, and in advance of more detailed discussions in chapters 4, 5, 6, and 9, we briefly introduce the nature of the architectural support provided in the i432 System for object-based system design. This support assures that:

- Access to information objects among related program units is effectively controlled.
- Information objects belonging to mutually independent program units are effectively isolated.

  [These two forms of control are achieved because data and program code components are treated as structured objects under hardware and software control at all times. User data and program code units may have arbitrarily defined substructures. A ''capability-based'' accessing scheme provides the underlying mechanism for accomplishing these objectives.]
- The hardware and operating system combine to control the execution of all application programs, including the transfer of information and transfer of control between modules of such programs.
- At all times, the hardware augmented by the operating system serves as a manager of object managers, where the operating system and its user-defined extensions serve as a collection of such object managers. An object manager, also referred to as a *type manager*, is a facility for controlling the creation and use of a data type definition and instances (objects) belonging to a defined data type. Object managers may be composed of more fundamental object managers so as to build up managers for complex databases.
- Certain objects (for example, Context Objects) are recognized by the hardware as belonging to system-defined types; their creation and use is managed in part by the hardware and in part by kernel modules of the operating system.) Other objects are recognized and protected by the hardware as ''extended types'' (user-defined types.) These objects are sensed by the hardware (always) and controlled (managed) by their type managers (which can be easily expressed as Ada packages).

- The instruction set of the processor includes operators that perform or facilitate and control (creation, deletion, and alteration of) objects. These objects include queues, entire program units, their subcomponents such as sets of related instruction and constant objects (known as *domains*), and procedure activation contexts and their subcomponents.
- The important functions of memory management, such as virtual memory addressing and garbage collection, are performed correctly, efficiently, and in conformance with the object-based model.
- Objects are not only a central focus, but a source of consistency and unity. They are the building blocks of program structures. They are atomic units for accessing and protection, for interprocedure and interprocess communication. They transcend hardware, operating system, and application boundaries. Once understood, they are the natural building blocks in models of real world objects.

It is the intent of the i432 designers that the object base of the architecture be used for more than the effective management of the system's configuration and its individual resources (computer administrator view); in addition, it is intended to be used for the general support of data abstraction for its benefits in simplifying program organization (general and system programmers' view). The potentially close connection between system management, on the one hand, and program and data management, on the other, has not yet been exploited fully in other systems. Indeed, it remains an open controversy as to whether this "twinning" effect advanced by the i432 System design is a desirable architectural objective [61]. The view taken here is that providing architectural support that assures exclusive use of objects as just defined (which, in effect, is support for *data abstraction* in programming), automatically provides the address space protection mechanisms needed for the proper management of system resources.

1.3. Object Filing Systems

In traditional filing systems, programmers accustomed to either the conventional control-based programming style or to the newer object-based style have been burdened with unreasonable overheads in dealing with the "intermediate storage" aspects of programs. A typical programmer may be unaware, however, of the magnitude of this burden. By *intermediate storage* we refer to the use of secondary storage for holding interim information between processing stages (compiler passes, for example) or between transactions (data base activity, for example.) We consider a typical data processing scenario to shed some light on this issue:

Intermediate storage is conventionally represented as sequential or indexed files of data which amount to streams of individual values or streams of records. Intermediate steps of the program may then require selection and regrouping of the data into more elaborately structured objects to perform the required analysis, or to permit the required synthesis of results, or both. If copies of these results are to be retained for further processing, however, they must be converted for output as sequential or indexed files into the form of value sequences or record sequences. (Making the file records randomly accessible really adds very little in the way of simplification in the conversion process if the data objects have objects as substructures.)

Reprocessing the linearized or indexed output of one stage of processing requires that the old objects be recreated before they can be reused or modified. Not only is there the burden of processing involved in these repeated transformations, but there is, more importantly, the burden of ensuring that the integrity of these objects is preserved during and in between each ''round trip'' to and from the intermediate and normally non-self-describing form usually selected for the data representation in the file store.

An object-based system design offers the important opportunity to unify the discipline of filing with that of object management and type control, and hence to permit filing to become a natural extension of the addressing and protection model of the operating system. Since objects have unique identifiers and can have lifetimes that span multiple users and uses, it should be possible to view and to treat an object, which retains its type, structure, and other attributes under control of its type manager, in much the same way as files are viewed and treated in conventional operating systems and data-base management systems. With this approach, a file store is merely an extension of the system's uniform address space. This extension of object-based architecture is called an *object filing system* [47].

The i432 Object Filing Subsystem is a planned part of the operating system; it supports the permanent storage of i432 objects in a ''passive address space''. Objects permanently stored are identified and protected in a manner that is consistent with the access control mechanisms over objects in the ''active address space'' of the system. In particular, the identity, type, and structure of objects are preserved whether they reside in passive space or active space.

Recall that objects have names whose uniqueness (theoretically, at least) extends over space and time. The names of i432 objects in the passive address space are unique in the true sense. An object in this space has a name that differs from that of any extant object, any object that existed in the past, or any object that will exist in the future. While residing in the active address space an object has a name that is unique to that space. (At no time are there two active space objects that have the same name.) Since cardinality of the set of active space names is relatively small (2**24) compared with the (effectively infinite) cardinality of the set of names used in the passive space, the Object Filing Subsystem maintains a unique mapping between the two name spaces. In this sense, the set of names in the active space is used as a *cache* of the much larger set of passive space names.

Objects in permanent store are automatically brought into active space when their content is referenced. However, permanent space objects need not be activated to be updated, and two or more programs can attempt to update a data object in passive space without risking inconsistency of the updated object. When two or more programs attempt access to the same shared object in permanent store, the object filing system synchronizes multiple access to the object via implicit calls to the type manager for that object. The synchronizing strategy used is based on the concept of ''Atomic Actions'' [49, 50, 51] and outlined briefly in Chapter 10.

Not only simple objects, but composites comprising a network of simple objects can be filed in the passive store and retrieved as a unit. Individual components of a composite are cross-referenced by capabilities, called *Access Descriptors* in i432 terminology. Relationships among the components of a composite, like a program or like structured data, are preserved by preserving the meaning of the references embedded in the components, independent of the device on which the composite resides. These relationships are also preserved when a composite is transferred to or from the active and passive address spaces.

Among commercial systems only two have offered object filing services, the IBM System/38 [28] and the Plessey System 250 [20]. [There have also been several research implementations, one for HYDRA and one for the CAP operating systems [43]]. Coincidentally, the architectures of all these systems provide capability-based addressing mechanisms. The Multics system, operational since 1969 [44], offers an approximation to object filing. In this system, files are directly addressable; they are represented as single, variable-length segments or linear arrays of same, but there is no distinction between active and passive space, so the system is subject to greater loss of information as a result of system crashes. [The same problem appears to exist for the IBM System/38, where the object also resides in a single space.]

Using an object filing system provides the programmer with the facility associated with a much richer base of support, normally provided only by data-base management systems, a service that is usually built on top of the filing system, rather than in place of it. It now appears that object filing can replace data-base management in many programming situations. Coupling an object-based programming style with the use of an object filing facility is viewed by the i432 system designers as the critical step to be taken by programmers who wish to make quantum jumps in the level of their productivity. Because it provides the tools for practice with object-based programming, and because it provides the object filing system as well, the i432 System may well be the first system of wide availability to convert the potential of the quantum jump in programmer productivity into a broad-based reality.

1.4. Ada and the iAPX-432

Ada is the application of the current state of the art in programming languages research and development. It is the result of a collective effort to design a common language for programming large scale and real time systems [2]. The design work for this language, sponsored by the U.S. Government, Department of Defense, began in 1974 with a series of "requirements" documents that were widely reviewed. A large international community of computer professionals participated in the studies and competitive preliminary designs that led to the final form of the language, which is now being implemented for a variety of computer systems.

Ada's most distinguishing characteristic, when compared with widely-used predecessor languages, is the emphasis given to the separation of specification from implementation of program units. Ada incorporates the semantic components needed to permit programmer teams to construct and maintain large systems and applications at minimum overall cost. Ada will be accepted as a national and international standard language, in large part, because it is designed to enhance portability of programs by providing for a clean separation of machine-independent logical constructs and machine-dependent data representation details.

1.4.1. Ada Program Structures

An Ada program may consist of a collection of packages and one main subprogram (i.e., the initial, or "starter" task) that activates the use of the packages. Structuring the program into such a collection of program units has the advantage that, as the number of program units grows, there is a much better chance that the programmer can maintain an understanding of its meaning (its sequence of actions), since the number of possible interrelationships among the action steps and the data is restricted by the use of the packages—which limit the operations that may be performed on individual data objects, according to the discipline (a kind of algebra) imposed by each package.

In short, a package can serve as the sole supervisor over the creation and use of objects of a given type. In this way, the user is assured that all instances of a given type will always be properly manipulated; that is, that the integrity of each object's "internals" will always be properly maintained, without requiring that the user be concerned with such details, which is the responsibility of the package itself. In this style of programming the user may focus entirely on a data object as a whole or on just those parts of direct concern, or both, when invoking a particular (public) operation of the package. Ada allows the programmer to define an unlimited variety of types of data objects and to delegate the creation and use of data object instances to their respective (and distinct) type managers.

Actually, we have only hinted at a part of the "disciplinary advantage" of an Ada package. More generally, a package may include in its specification part not only a set of valid operations on some (one or more instances of) data objects, but may also contain declarations that define such data objects (type definitions.)

Although the Ada package and its use offers an almost compelling reason to use Ada for subsystems and applications programming, there are still other reasons for choosing Ada. In particular, there is the attraction for decomposing a program into groups of intercommunicating tasks (processes), an idea elaborated first in Chapter 2 and expanded in Chapters 3 and 5. Ada tasks may be created (and terminated) either statically or dynamically. They may be used to gain abstract or actual concurrency by arranging tasks to execute in pipeline or parallel fashion. Tasks may be used to synchronize actions of other tasks and to distribute work to other tasks. Modelling a system as a collection of Ada tasks can lead to greater clarity as well as to faster execution (through concurrency achieved when several processors are available to execute the tasks.)

1.4.2. Ada and Object-Based Programming

The Ada language encourages object-based programming and for that reason was selected as the principal programming language for the i432. Most significantly, programs written in Ada for the i432 may be viewed as compatible extensions of the operating system and the supporting hardware. There is, in fact, no difference between "system programs" and "user programs" as there is in conventional systems. For this reason, we shall begin our detailed study of the i432 System in the next chapter, not with a closer look at the hardware organization or at the operating system, but with a closer look at Ada itself.

To be sure, users are not prohibited from programming in other high-order languages as widely different as Cobol and LISP. Indeed, it is expected that those adopting the i432, be they system manufacturers, independent software vendors, or universities, will develop language processing systems to suit their needs, as is done with other general purpose systems.

To close out this introduction, we remark that Ada relates closely to the i432 architecture:

- Understanding the semantics of Ada programs will allow us to more easily understand some of the most important aspects and innovations of the i432 object-based architecture.
- Once we understand the structure and interactions among the system-defined i432 objects we will gain a better grasp of Ada semantics. From this we can

learn why the i432 is well-matched as a host for the execution of Ada programs.

Our introduction has been a long one—and we are aware that the density may be too much for full ''digestion'' on first reading. Our readers are invited to reread the germane parts as they proceed with the study of the following chapters.

1.5. Remainder of This Book

Chapters 2 and 3 form a primer for readers who are not fully acquainted with Ada or with object-based programming, or both. Our conviction is that, to appreciate the architecture of the i432 System, a reader should first know Ada or a similar language and the way it is intended to be used. Chapter 2 focuses on the use of packages as a basis for the design of a simple Investment Management System, a non-trivial Ada program. This example, which is developed and enhanced throughout the book, also contains several Ada tasks. The structure and use of Ada tasks is discussed at length in Chapter 3. Several alternative task structures for the Investment Management System are discussed, some in considerable detail. The nature of intertask communication, begun in this chapter is revisited in Chapter 5 at greater length.

The architecture study itself is begun in Chapter 4 where a number of topics related to object structures and object addressing are treated. Chapter 5 introduces the hardware and system software support for interprocess communication. Here the i432 Port Objects and port operations, SEND, RECEIVE, etc., are introduced and illustrated. Chapter 6 revisits the architectural and Ada language support for object structures, emphasizing type management and access control. Many features of the supporting operating system, known as iMAX, especially several of its important ''user-interfaces'', are introduced beginning with Chapter 5.

The importance of input-output peripheral subsystems, and their relationship with the central object-based architecture of the i432 system, is recognized by treating this topic separately in Chapter 7. This chapter introduces the reader to the architecture of the i432 Interface Processor and its use as a key component in the Peripheral Subsystem Interface for the Intel 432 System. A message-based model for Input/Output, using this interface is also introduced along with a discussion of abstractions for I/O device interfaces, both asynchronous and synchronous.

The topics of process management, memory management, and object filing, which may be of primary interest to system developers and architects, are treated in Chapters 8, 9, and 10. Each chapter describes the iMAX provided implementations of these services and the user interfaces to these facilities. In the case of process management an iMAX-provided ''template'' is described whose use enables system programmers to implement their own process managers as needed. Chapter 9 describes the extensive memory management facilities of iMAX and the supporting hardware. These include facilities to support the stack and heap memory resources required, for example, by executing Ada programs. In addition, memory management supports an on-the-fly garbage collector, dynamic memory compaction, and, where configured, a virtual memory management subsystem. Chapter 10, as already noted, provides a complete introduction to object filing as it is currently planned.

Another feature of this book is a set of three sets of appendixes.

- The first set (A and B) provided lists of i432-based literature references. These lists are in addition to the more general bibliography for the literature cited in the text proper.
- The second set of appendixes (C, D, E, and F and G) contains a group of compiled Ada program units comprising versions of the Investment Management System developed in Chapters 2 and 3. Readers are urged to study as much of these appendixes as needed in the course of learning Ada through the vehicle of the Investment Management System.
- The third set of appendixes (H, I, J, K, L, and M) comprise the user interfaces to iMAX that are described in Chapters 5 through 10, respectively. Readers are especially urged to read these appendixes as a means of confirming (and expanding) their understanding of the functionality, scope, and flexibility of iMAX.

2 PROGRAM STRUCTURES AND SEMANTICS IN ADA

2.1. Ada—A Top-Down View

When introducing a person to the Ada programming language, one may choose among several views. Frequently, one presents a programming language in a "bottom-up" manner by introducing a series of language constructs of increasing structure and/or semantic richness. Thus, for example, a bottom-up view of Ada might introduce Ada's alphabet, followed by its identifiers, constants, variables, declarations, statements, program units, and finally its programs. This approach is typically followed by authors of language reference manuals. Indeed, a reference manual for Ada, such as [2] is a useful companion piece for this chapter.

Our approach to introducing Ada uses a "top-down" view. At the top-most level, we examine entire Ada programs, regarding them in the general case as networks of interrelated components called modules, or *program units*. Every module has two distinct parts: the module's interface with the remainder of the network (its *specification*), and the module's internal structure and implementation code (its *body*). Although a module's internal structure may itself exhibit a network substructure, we initially ignore this possibility.

This top-down approach is compatible with the view that programming is an explicit intellectual process of system design. A *system* is normally defined in engineering parlance as an ensemble of interacting components (possibly operating concurrently), each of which may have *state information* bound to it. These interacting components constitute a collection of evolving information structures, whose lifetimes span the life of the associated module—which may be, and often is, the lifetime of the system itself.

Ada, more than any other widely available programming language, and in common with several experimental languages [3] [9] [36] [42] [45] [62] [63] encourages the programmer to design and build programs as ensembles of interacting, state-bearing, program units.

An Ada program may be composed of three kinds of program units that can carry (have bound to them) evolving information structures:

- a main subprogram—which may be viewed as the ''starter task'',
- packages,
- tasks.

An Ada program begins execution with a single *thread of control* associated with the main subprogram (starter task.) When a subprogram within a package is called, the thread of control ''moves over'' into the code belonging to the package. Eventually, the thread of control returns to the starter task, much as the thread of control moves about from the main part of a Fortran program (or from the outermost block of a Pascal program) to and from various called subprograms.

At certain program points (for example, during the elaboration of task declarations), new threads of control may be spawned. This spawning process may proceed, recursively, to form a task tree. If the program as a whole ever terminates, it does so only after all spawned tasks have terminated and in reverse order of their activation.

Any task may call a subprogram within another package, but no new threads of control are created as a direct result of such an operation. By a ''package call'' we mean a call on a subprogram, i.e., *operation*, belonging to the *public part* of the package. In the case of a package call, the thread of control may be thought of as being transferred from the code of the caller to the code of the called package, with the reverse effect occurring upon return from the package call.

By contrast, a task ''calls another task'', i.e., issues it an *entry call*, by sending it a message. (The message is implicit in the syntax of the entry call statement and in the matching **entry** declaration of the called task.) As a result of an inter-task call, the caller's thread of control is merely suspended until the called task acts on the message sent to it (completes the acceptance of the caller's message.) If all goes well, the caller is notified that the message has been accepted. When this occurs, the caller resumes execution; that is, the caller's thread of control resumes its execution and the called task proceeds along its separate path of execution.

This protocol, including the temporary suspension of the caller, is referred to as a *rendezvous*. The rendezvous is the only means provided in the language for explicit communication among tasks; use of the rendezvous guarantees that a *structuring discipline*, in the spirit of "structured programming", is applied across tasks.

[The i432 architecture offers the programmer a less structured (but more highly parallel) mechanism for achieving communication between tasks. For example, there are means for explicitly sending messages to one or more tasks without waiting for a reply from any task. To use these i432 facilities, a programmer calls a special package (to be described in Chapter 5). Use of these message communications facilities will make the program more difficult to move to other computer systems. It should be noted, however, that the i432 operating system itself makes full use of these lower-level communication operations to provide the utility packages used by the Ada compiler to implement task facilities.]

When a rendezvous is completed, the calling task may once again execute, possibly concurrently with the called task. In a system like the i432, actual concurrency of calling task and called task is achieved when each task is bound to a distinct (available) processor. In principle, a task tree consisting of m spawned and currently active tasks, including the starter task, could execute with m-fold concurrency if m processors were available.

If one believes the definition of a system—an ensemble of components (possibly operating in parallel), each of which may have state information bound to it—then permitting Ada programs to exhibit rich package and task structures is a significant advance in programming language design. Consider the contrasting situation in Fortran or Pascal. Much of the state information of Fortran or Pascal programs (for example, scalar variables, arrays, records, etc.) is bound to the program as a whole, rather than to any of its subprogram parts. Thus, with the exception of data declared in the outermost block of a Pascal program or in the COMMON blocks and main unit of a Fortran program, all declared information has a lifetime that is limited to a single activation of a block or subprogram. (In Fortran 77 this constraint has been relaxed somewhat with the introduction of the SAVE statement [41].)

A Fortran or Pascal programmer may have difficulty representing a real system to be modelled, or the programmer may have difficulty explaining to those familiar with the real-world model how the program works. This is primarily because the lack of multiple state spaces in Fortran and Pascal inhibits preserving the correspondence between the system to be represented and the program that models the system. Worse still, if some components in the real system being modelled are concurrently active, then the correspondence between the Fortran or Pascal program and the system being modelled becomes even weaker.

The less the behavior of a system corresponds to the behavior of a program that models the system, the more difficult is the chore of verifying this correspondence. Such programs are also more difficult to maintain (modify) as changes are made to the specification of the model (changes to the originating problem or requirements statement). Because *life cycle* costs of programs may be dominated by their maintenance costs, especially for the case of large programs, the importance of preserving a clear structural correspondence between the program and the system being represented should impel us toward a language like Ada.

[When using programming languages like Fortran or Pascal the effort is concentrated in preserving the logical and thereby the functional correspondence between programs and the systems they represent. While this type of correspondence is often sufficient, especially for small programs, the difficulties induced when programs are "scaled up" to realistic size have, in the past, been largely underestimated. Purely functional languages are also being considered as replacements for Fortran and Pascal [4, 11], but they are as yet untested in real applications involving sizeable data bases or in representing models whose components have complex interactions. Moreover, architectures that are especially suitable for such languages are not yet well understood.]

2.2. Ada Packages

The Ada *package* is the construct that the programmer can use to define data abstractions; it is regarded by many experts as the most significant contribution Ada makes toward reaching its software goals of lower costs with higher maintainability, reliability, and verifiability. A package provides us with the means to associate a clear set of specifications for the use of a data structure (or of a class of such data structures) with a particular set of (hidden) implementation details.

Before showing and discussing concrete examples, we identify two important kinds of Ada packages. We refer to them as *transformer packages* and *owner packages*. The transformer packages can be used to implement pure abstract data types, and the owner packages can be used to implement more general kinds of type managers.

- An operation of a *transformer* (or *non-owner*) package can update only the data that is supplied to it through formal parameters(s); the package contains no internal state information bound to it. (That is, there is no data internal to the package that can be updated.) Since a transformer package "owns" no state information, each operation of the package must return its result to its caller. (A transformer package cannot "remember" the effects of preceding calls to it.) An example of a transformer package would be one that creates complex numbers, one that performs operations on complex numbers, or one that does both.
- An *owner package* is "history-sensitive" in that it can "remember" the effects of preceding calls to it. The owner package "owns" some state information; that is, the package contains internal data that can be updated during

the course of the package's lifetime. Thus, an operation of the package may be supplied data on which to operate through its formal parameter(s). In so doing, it may update its state information. An operation of an owner package need not return a result to its caller. An example of an owner package is one that maintains a central table of active files for a compiler.

An Ada package may be used to:

1. specify a set of valid operations on one or more instances of a data type,
2. provide a body consisting of the operations specified in part 1,
3. hide all of the objects, specifications, and implementation details provided in part 2 from the user of the operations specified in part 1.

Thus, for each owner or transformer form of package, there is a *public* and a *private* part (also referred to as the *visible* and *invisible* parts.) The public part is made directly accessible to a user program unit either by:

- prefixing the program unit with an explicit declaration that names the package(s) that are to be made accessible (such a prefix is called a **with** list), or by
- nesting the package within the user program unit, thereby making the package's public part locally accessible (which is done by exploiting Algol-like scope rules).

The first of these mechanisms is an important innovation of Ada-like languages; its use is strongly encouraged. The second of these mechanisms should be discouraged; its use leads to programs that are difficult to read and debug and is a "holdover" from earlier block-structured languages like Algol 60.

In either case, the package's private part is not directly accessible to the user program unit. This information becomes accessible only indirectly, by performing operations that are specified in the interface information of the public part.

Thus, if a package named Shoe_Mgr has an operation OP1 specified, for example, as

```
procedure OP1(x: in string,  y:out string);
```

then this operation may be invoked from the user program unit by

```
Shoe_Mgr.OP1("baby shoes", new_shoe_style);
```

The user-visible specification of OP1 (plus additional commentary about OP1) describes the functional interface to OP1, i.e., describes *what* operation OP1 performs on its input arguments. However, the details of the implementation of OP1 are hidden from the user in the private part of the package, i.e., the methods that describe *how* OP1 does its chore are hidden. Variable data within the package may also be accessible only indirectly. In particular, if Shoe_Mgr is an owner package, there may be in its private part a data base that is updated as a result of invoking OP1. Access to this data base is only indirect, via OP1, or via some other publicly specified operation of Shoe_Mgr.

Because the package structure ensures a clean separation between the public (specification) part and the private part, the private part of a package can be compiled separately from its public part. [Some non-critical details are deliberately glossed over in this initial exposition.] This means that a different private part can be substituted—as better or more correct implementation ideas evolve—without affecting the remainder of the program.

In the next section we provide more motivation and more details concerning packages by introducing the skeletal structure for one realistic application of "packaging." We also motivate the need for a collection of related tasks.

2.3. An Investment Portfolio Manager

Here we describe a hypothetical, but not unrealistic, application that illustrates the structure and use of a group of related packages. The program developed here has direct application in any of several types of organizations that generally rely on the management of a data base.

Type of Data Base	*Managed by:*
Pension funds	banks or trusts
Individual investment accounts	brokerage houses
Personal investments records	home-computer programmer
Investment club portfolio	club officers

In each of these applications, the identity of the person(s) that manage the data base may differ, but from the point of view of program structure all these applications fall into the same category. For this example, however, we select one specific application class so as to allow use of the terminology specific for that class when discussing particulars. We choose investment club portfolios and offer in the following paragraph, for those unfamiliar with such clubs, an indication of the potentially substantial size of this application.

BACKGROUND: The National Association of Investment Clubs, NAIC, is an affiliation of several thousand clubs—averaging about fifteen members each. World-wide, there are thousands more such clubs. [The NAIC is itself a member of the the World Federation of Associations of Investment Clubs!] Each club usually meets monthly to review its respective stock portfolios, listen to reports on new or held stocks, and make buy and sell decisions—usually executed the next day by the club's broker. Normally a club carries a limited number of stocks in its portfolio, since the responsibility for watching held stocks is distributed among the club's membership—typically about one or two stocks per member.

Our example Investment Portfolio Manager program will be austere in its early stages. Later, we will introduce modifications that add functionality to the program; we will suggest alternative methods for pursuing implementations having certain advantages and/or disadvantages. Our initial example illustrates a single-user computer program accessible to the secretary-treasurer of such a club. This officer makes queries of the portfolio (data base) to prepare the monthly report. In addition, she updates the portfolio to reflect buy and sell transactions triggered at the monthly meeting, the results of which are reported to her by the club's broker. Later, we will consider how other club members might be given other types of access to the portfolio.

2.3.1. Building an Ada Program Model to Match a Model of the Investment Club Portfolio System

Our "object-based" program design methodology is a strategy for creating an Ada program model whose structure mirrors a model of the real-world system to be represented. Components of the program structure are chosen to correspond to components of the real-world model.

In this case, the top-level view of the real world system is simple; it consists of two components, the secretary-treasurer (the actor) and the portfolio data base which "reacts" to the actor's initialize, query and update requests. In a corresponding program model, an individual human actor may be represented as a task that interprets the human actor's individual requests and converts them into procedure calls to a program unit representing the portfolio data base. A portfolio data base may be viewed as a data structure, together with a set of procedures for managing it, including procedures that create or initialize it, query it, and update it. A possible program analog for such a view is an Ada owner package (Portfolio_Owner.) Our first view of the program structure can be seen in Figure 2-1.

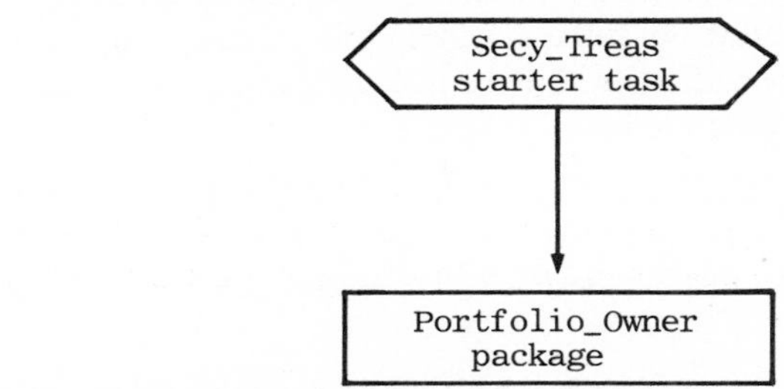

Figure 2-1 Top-level program model for the investment club portfolio management system.

With Figure 2-1 as a starting structure we may then specify the information to be kept in the data base and the set of requests that the secretary-treasurer may make. Once this set of requirements has been confirmed, a representation must be proposed for the data structures of the data base as object structures in storage.

Given this proposal, it is then possible to gauge the ''semantic gap'', if any, between the requests to be posed by the secretary-treasurer and the more primitive object creation, accessing, and updating expressions we think we know how to express in the programming language—in this case Ada. If the gap is considered too great, it may be necessary or desirable to decompose Portfolio_Owner package into a substructure, consisting of several packages.

For example, within a devised substructure of packages, top-level requests may be decomposed by operations in intermediate packages into collections of more primitive requests. These are then forwarded to the package whose operations access the data structures directly. Such intermediate transformations close the aforementioned semantic gap. (We have, in fact, followed this approach in our case study.)

There are other good reasons for decomposing a program unit that represents a data base into a substructure of other program units, even when there is no perceived semantic gap between the requests to be made by a user of the data base and the operations to be defined over that data base itself. Two principles can be applied here.

1. *Data structures should be implemented indirectly through operations (procedures or functions) rather than by direct access to the data structure.* Directly accessing major data structures is considered poor programming practice because it spreads direct, representation-specific references throughout the entire program. In large programs, these direct references to data structures can make alteration of their representation virtually impossible, since there are usually too many places in the program that must be changed to reflect the changes in the data structure. On the other hand, indirect reference through packaged operations ensures isolation of representation-specific references. Later, if there is a desire to change a data structure representation in some manner, this is easily accomplished by changing only the operations within the isolated package; no other part of the program is normally affected.

   This principle is applicable to our portfolio management program because, as we extend the application, we will want to allow a number of program units (in addition to that of the Secy_Treas task) access to the same data base.

2. *Only* those operations required to manipulate the data structure should be made a part of a package that provides indirect access to a major data structure. In our case study, many, but not all, of the operations in the

Portfolio_Owner package would involve access to a portfolio. For example, a user may wish to know the current price of some listed stock, whether or not held in the club's portfolio.

Still other packages may be included in a substructure, either to take advantage of already existing library-level program units that are already available and that shouldn't or needn't be duplicated, or as a means for "segmenting" the top-level Portfolio_Owner package into smaller and more manageable components. Often, in the process of segmenting a larger module, it may be discovered that two or more segments have some part in common, which may then be "factored out" as still another segment of the substructure.

Naturally, this segmenting process may be overdone. Ideally, we would like to see every element in the substructure reflect a particular part of the real world model. In practice, this ideal can only be approximated. (For example, the programmer is likely to encounter the need to include utility packages such as for input-output device operations. Such packages may be only weakly related to components of the system being modelled.)

The graph in Figure 2-2 shows a substructuring that arises as a result of decomposing the Portfolio_Owner package of Figure 2-1 in the manner we have just outlined. We explain this graph by explaining its individual components.

- As mentioned, Secy_Treas is the starter task for this program. Its own internal structure, although not shown here, may be assumed to resemble that of a simple command interpreter, or "shell", that responds to repeated input commands from the *human* user—the club's secretary-treasurer. Each command is translated into a call on the Club_Portfolio package, for execution of one of its public operations.
- Club_Portfolio serves as an interface between its principal user (Secy_Treas) and the portfolio itself. It receives and interprets requests from the user and decomposes them into collections of more primitive requests (operations) that are performed by the Portfolio_Mgr package.

  Club_Portfolio is an owner package. It owns the portfolio instance created with the aid of the Portfolio_Mgr package and defines a set of user-oriented interactive query and update operations over the portfolio. (Club_Portfolio also includes various other operations that do not involve access to the club's portfolio, but do access other library packages.)
- Portfolio_Mgr defines a data structure of type portfolio and a set of operations on instances of that type. Portfolio_Mgr is a transformer kind of package. Its operations include create (to create a portfolio), and many useful query and update operations, more elementary in nature than those in the Club_Portfolio package. These operations form a minimal set necessary to provide access to a portfolio data structure. Portfolio_Mgr is used to isolate within one package all accesses to the portfolio that must be aware of the

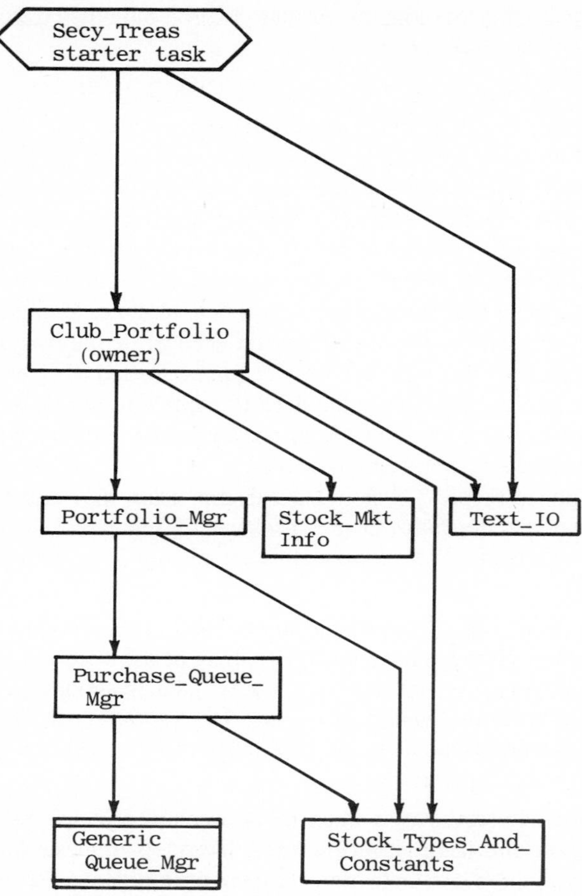

Figure 2-2 Multi-package structure for single-user Investment Portfolio Manager Program.

representation of the portfolio. Outside of the Portfolio_Mgr package, the representation of a portfolio is unknown and not required to be known.

- Stock_Mkt_Info is a library package updated at the close of each market day by a national wire service. To make this scenario more interesting, we assume that this package is accessible to any club affiliated with the NAIC. Initially, we may assume this library package is received daily as a tape or disc and then mounted on an I/O device of the system prior to execution of the portfolio application. In Chapter 7, we consider how the system can be revised to model the situation where data for this package is received by wire in real time.

- Text_IO is a pre-defined Ada library package containing various input-output operations accessible to the user. Text_IO is accessed by Club_Portfolio and also (most likely) by Secy_Treas.
- The three other packages shown in the figure are understood in terms of the details of the Portfolio_Mgr package. The Portfolio_Mgr package, described in greater detail below, maintains information on individual stocks currently held by the club. This information is stored in queues, one queue for each different stock held. When the club decides to sell some of its holdings in a given stock, it may want to sell its longest held shares first, in order to ensure a possible long term capital gains tax benefit. Purchase records for these shares are found at the front of the queue, assuming new purchase records are always inserted at the end of the queue.
  - Purchase_Queue_Mgr. Individual queue data structures are created at the request of the Portfolio_Mgr when attempting to record the purchase of a stock not currently held in the portfolio. Portfolio_Mgr delegates to a subsidiary package, Purchase_Queue_Mgr, the responsibility for performing the operations of create, enqueue, and dequeue for instances of such queues.
  - Queue_Mgr. We further assume that Purchase_Queue_Mgr is itself an instance of a paradigm (or, in Ada parlance, a **generic** package) named Queue_Mgr. Later, we give a more detailed explanation of Queue_Mgr and how it is used.
  - Stock_Types_And_Constants. In Ada, a package may consist entirely of a collection of type definitions, constant definitions, variable declarations, or any consistent combination of these. We place in Stock_Types_And_Constants all those data type definitions, constants, and variables that are common (and hence that should be commonly accessible) to the several packages which are dependent on these definitions.

In Figure 2-2, directed arcs indicate the general relationship "references". The graph

means that A "references" B. Depending on what is being referenced, this "references" relationship can mean several things. If the reference in B is a procedure, then A references B in order to call a procedure of B. If the reference in B is a constant or type, then A references B in order to obtain the constant or type. If the reference in B is a variable, then A references B in order to obtain the current value of the variable.

The implication of the "references" relation has an impact on order of compilation. Ada requires that the specification of a program unit B must be compiled before compilation can occur for any program unit that "references" B. Thus, in the diagram above, the specification of B must be compiled before either part (specification or body) of A that "references" B. [Ada programs are compiled from their individual program units using a set of dependency relationships. These are usually accumulated in a "program library" as the compiler works its way through the units of the program. We will not discuss the technical aspects of "order of compilation in Ada"; for such details, readers are referred to Chapter 10 of the Ada reference manual [2].]

2.3.2. Portfolio Details

For our case study, we assume that a portfolio data structure contains information ordered at three conceptual levels:

- information pertaining to the aggregate of all held stocks, such as:
  - the portfolio name
  - number of different stocks held
  - a stock summary for each held stock
- information in a stock summary provides:
  - corporate name
  - stock exchange where listed and the corporation's acronym on that exchange
  - total number of shares
  - average cost per share
  - a purchase history
- information in a purchase history for a held stock includes, for each purchase whose shares have not all been sold, the following items:
  - date purchased
  - price per share
  - commission paid on the purchase
  - no. of shares remaining from this purchase

With this informal description of the portfolio, we may choose specific representations for the portfolio as a whole and for its components. These choices can be expressed as Ada **type** declarations. We are now almost ready to display and discuss most of the Ada code for this application, but we again request the reader's patience, in order to consider two very interesting extensions.

These two extensions are described in the following two subsections, after which we present and discuss the Ada code for all three versions of this application.

2.3.3. Allowing All Club Members to Query Their Club's Portfolio—Many Single Users

"Ordinary" members of the investment club should also have access to the club's portfolio, provided they are restricted to read-only queries. The model in Figure 2-1 must be amplified, as shown in Figure 2-3, so that there is now an actor (or task) for each club member. We want Portfolio_Owner to accept and respond properly to query requests transmitted by all tasks, but to reject create and update requests transmitted by tasks denoted as "Member" tasks. How should the program structure in Figure 2-2 be modified to provide for such multiple access?

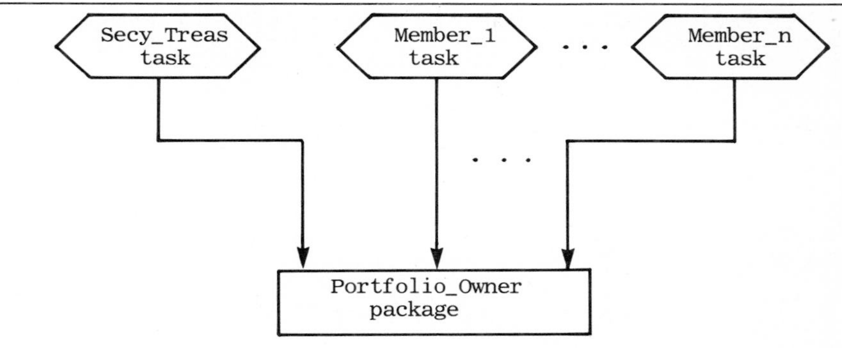

Figure 2-3 Top-level program model for Investment Portfolio Manager program: Second view.

First, we consider a simple solution which assumes that the secretary-treasurer's use of the portfolio will never be concurrent with use by other members. Figure 2-4 shows how we can achieve our objective. Two separate program structures share the Club_Portfolio package and its subsidiary package structure. The secretary-treasurer program structure is unaltered and an additional program structure, representing any other club member, is now provided.

[We make the very strong assumption that no Member task may execute concurrently with the Secy_Treas task—but we do not indicate how this constraint is "policed". We simply presume that this mutual exclusion is achieved by agreement outside the realm of the program. The agreement needn't involve the club members themselves. Proper use of the Object Filing Subsystem, described in Chapter 10, provides one way to provide for the requisite mutual exclusion.]

A Member starter task is able to access Club_Portfolio only indirectly, via a new Member_Ops package (which is accessible to each such Member task.) The Member_Ops package provides access only to the query operations within Club_Portfolio. In fact, Member_Ops is composed only of operations that have exactly the same name as the accessible query operations in Club_Portfolio.

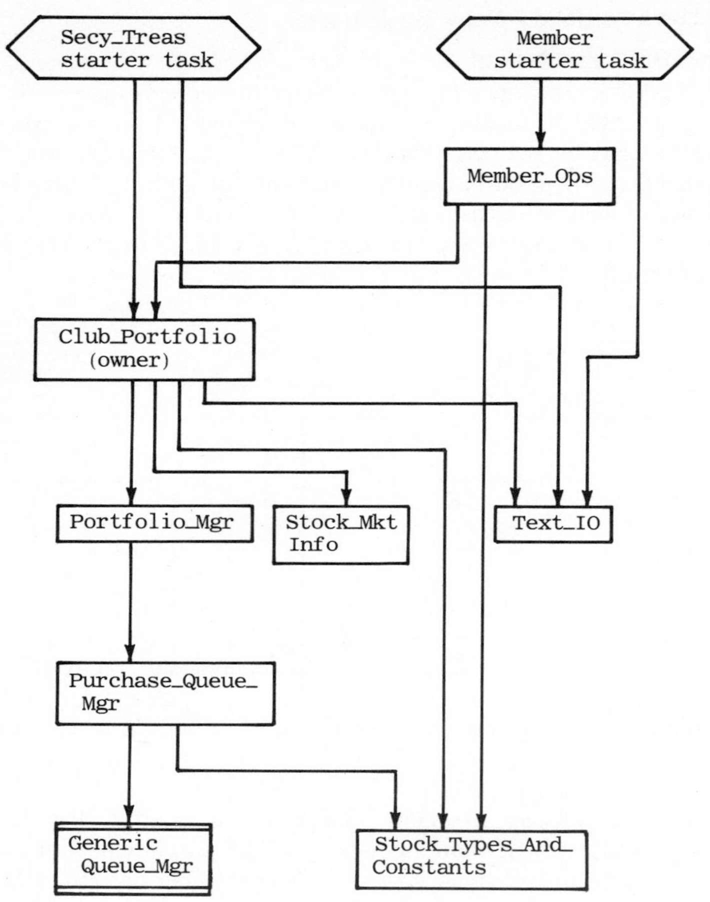

Figure 2-4 Giving a Member task query access to the Investment Portfolio.

The operations in Member_Ops have specifications that are identical with the like-named operations in Club_Portfolio. As we will see when we examine the code, the body parts of the operations in the body part of Member_Ops are merely "identity transformations"; that is, they merely call the corresponding operations in Club_Portfolio. Restricting the Member_Ops package to the query operations of Club_portfolio in this way ensures that a Member starter task cannot update the club's portfolio.

Every unit of an Ada program subject to separate compilation may be prefixed by a **with** list. This list names just those (public parts of) packages that the program unit can access directly. Thus, the **with** list that prefixes the Member starter task will include Member_Ops but not Club_Portfolio, and the **with** list that prefixes Member_Ops contains Club_Portfolio. Inclusion of proper package names in **with** lists in this manner provides the compiler with sufficient information to control access to the appropriate portfolio operations.

The intent here is that the public operations of Member_Ops be a proper subset of the public operations of Club_Portfolio. This subset constitutes what the i432 architects call a "refinement" of the larger set. By utilizing the refinement facility of the i432, Member_Ops can be defined as a physical subset of Club_Portfolio. Special hardware-recognized descriptors can be used to control access to such subsets in such a way that information outside the subset is inaccessible to any program that has access to the subset. Refinements provide the i432 user with the advantage of controlled information sharing without the usual disadvantage of providing too much access. We discuss refinement further in Chapter 4.

2.3.4. Multi-User Solutions to the Investment Portfolio Application

In this subsection, we attempt to relax the constraint that the club's secretary-treasurer not be trying to update the portfolio while other club members are querying it. To do this, we need to move from the case of two or more independent non-communicating tasks (as in 2.3.3) to a set of *mutually dependent* tasks. This can be done by taking advantage of the intertask communication features of Ada.

Our solution involves more control components. We now want a tree of tasks (not a forest of tasks). One such structure is sketched in Figure 2-5. There is only one starter task, which we will refer to as the Task_Master. This task represents the top level (root node) of the tree of tasks. The counterpart of Task_Master in the real world model is an agent delegated to admit club members to a room containing computer terminals, or, more likely, is an operating system that supervises the "login ritual." Task_Master in the program model has responsibility for spawning tasks for club members of a particular "title": president, vice-president, secy-treas, or ordinary member. (An interesting variant is discussed in Chapter 3.)

We now assume there is also a club membership roster (name, title, etc.), established and maintained as an auxiliary data base. Using this roster, we can ensure that a member's access to the portfolio is a function of the member's title. The Task_Master can be coded to spawn one task for each club member when the system is initialized, or to wait to spawn a Member task when the member "logs in".

Since there are now two data bases, several club members may wish to access them without being aware of potential access conflicts and without worrying about preventing unauthorized accesses. The necessary supervision to prevent

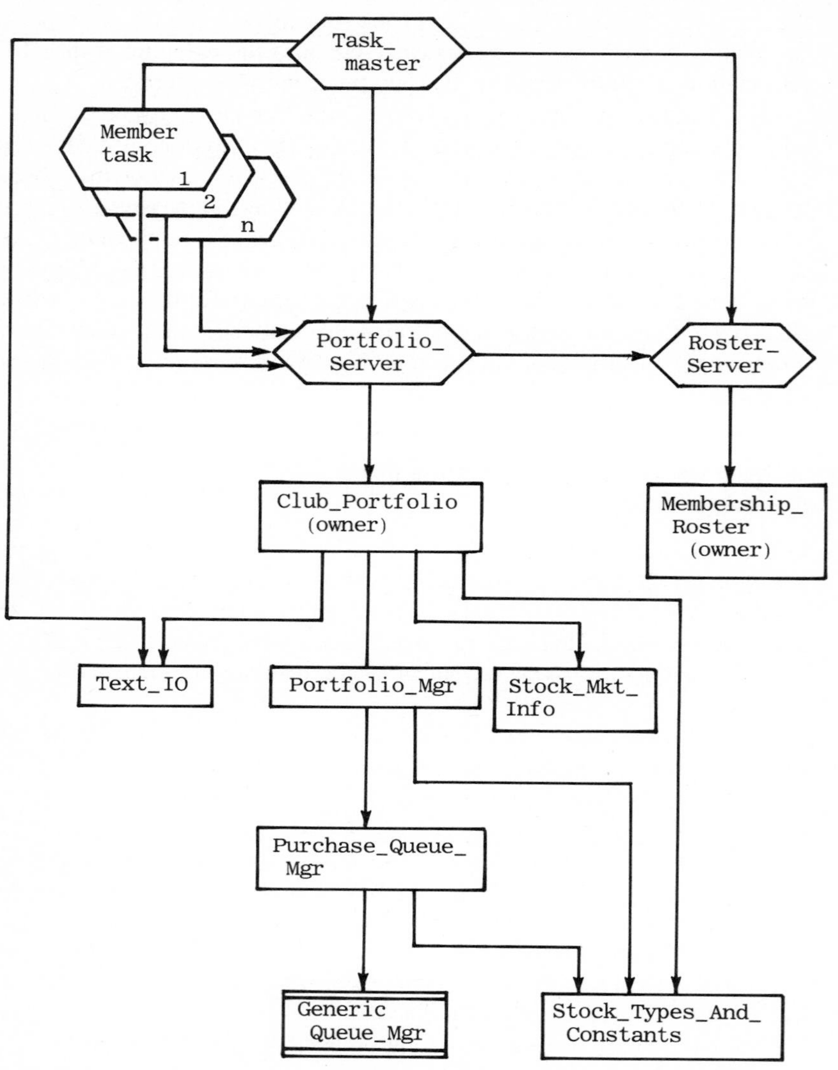

Figure 2-5 Case c. Multitasking structure for Multi-user Investment Club Application Program.

conflict can be delegated to "third parties". For example the club might be expected to designate a "keeper" for each of its data bases, giving each keeper the responsibility for verifying correct and authorized use of one data base. Our program model can easily reflect this added structure.

In the solution of Figure 2-5, the Task_Master spawns two *server* tasks: Portfolio_Server and Roster_Server. Portfolio_Server is given sole access to the Club_Portfolio package. Roster_Server is given sole access to the Membership_Roster package. Individual Member tasks may make concurrent requests to Portfolio_Server, but it will honor these requests only one at a time, thus resolving potential conflicts over use of the portfolio.

Portfolio_Server requests service from Roster_Server to confirm the access privileges of the Member task that requests a particular portfolio service. (Roster_Server acts on these requests one at a time.) Access privileges of the Member task are a function of a member's "title", as checked by Roster_Server. This checking strategy may be carried further. For example, the club's secretary may be the only member accorded access to operations within Roster_Server that involve updating the roster. (We do not outline this embellishment here.)

Given this subsystem structure, we can elaborate the permissions required for various types of portfolio service beyond those we considered in the "many single-users" case of 2.3.3. For example, we can consider incorporating the following controls:

Type of Request	*Requestor(s) Authorized to Receive Service*
query only	any club member
update portfolio	secretary-treasure only
create portfolio	president and secy-treas acting together
delete portfolio	president, vice-president and secy-treas, all three acting together

In the remainder of this chapter and the next one, we display and discuss some of the highlights of the Ada code for the three versions of this system. We relegate complete source listings to Appendixes C, D, and E.

2.4. Highlights of the Ada Code—Figure 2-2 Case

The graph structure of Figure 2-2 serves as a useful guide to the code excerpts we present here and to the code given in Appendixes C and D. We assume the reader is still unfamiliar with Ada and therefore we scan the code bottom-up, that is, we scan the modules in the order a compiler would see them. Accordingly, Figure 2-6 displays code for the Stock_Types_And_Constants package.

The least obvious data types and subtypes in this package are

- The type "dollars" is a non-negative fixed-point type, giving values to the nearest penny. [Note that in the compiled version given in Appendix C, type dollars is defined as integer.]
- The record type "stock_name_info" provides an identification of an individually held stock by its two components: an "external name" that we pre-

```
package Stock_Types_And_Constants is  -- This package has no body.

  subtype long_string  is  string(30);

  type dollars is delta 0.01 range 0.00 .. 1_000_000.00;
                                       -- Maximum is a million dollars here.
                                       -- Precision is to nearest penny.

  type stock_code_pair is
    record
      code:     string(1..4);          -- Abbreviation for listed stock.
      exch:     string(1..4);          -- Abbreviation for stock exchange.
    end record;

  type stock_name_info is
    record
      print_name:       long_string;
      stock_code:       stock_code_pair;
    end record;

  type date is
    record
      day:   integer range 1..31;
      month: integer range 1..12;
      year:  integer range 1900..4000;
    end record;

  type buy_sell_type is (buy, sell);

  type buy_sell_record(buy_sell: buy_sell_type) is
    record
      stock_name:       stock_name_info;
      buy_date:         date;
      num_shares:       integer;
      per_share_price: dollars;
      commission:       dollars;
      case buy_sell is                 -- Record discriminant.
       when sell =>                    -- Extra data field.
        of_buy_date:      date;
       when others =>                  -- No extra field.
        null;
      end case;
    end record;

  subtype  purchase_record  is buy_sell_record(buy);

  subtype  sale_record      is buy_sell_record(sell);
end Stock_Types_And_Constants;
```

Figure 2-6 Code for the Stock_Types_And_Constants package.

viously referred to as the corporate name and an ''internal name'' that we previously referred to as the stock exchange/acronym. The corporate name is of type ''long_string'', representing a string of up to thirty characters. The stock exchange/acronym is represented by the type ''stock_code_pair''.

- The type ''buy_sell_type'' has two values in its universe: ''buy'' and ''sell''. This type is used to facilitate the definitions of the last two types in this package.
- The record type ''buy_sell_record'' is used to define the structure of purchase records embedded as components of a purchase history in the portfolio. A buy_sell_record instance is also used for defining input arguments to operations that update the portfolio. As a fine point concerning Ada, notice that the buy_sell_record comes in two ''flavors'': buy and sell. The sell variant includes an extra field, which specifies the buy date of shares to be sold. When one declares an instance of a ''buy_sell_record'' type, one must supply as the particular discriminant value either ''buy'' or ''sell''.
- In order to avoid having to supply a discriminant value each time one declares an instance of a buy_sell_record to be allocated, the subtypes, purchase_record and sale_record, are also defined in this package. Subtypes are one of several useful data typing constructs in Ada. The subtype declarations are used here merely as a convenient renaming mechanism. [See Chapter 3 of the Ada Reference manual for more details.]

Figure 2-7 provides the skeleton structure of the generic Queue_Mgr package. The complete version of the Queue_Mgr package is given in Appendix C. Parts (b) and (c) of Figure 2-7 constitute the usual specification and body parts of a package. The package is made into a generic package when it is prefixed by a generic clause, as seen in part (a). The public part of the specification part (b) defines a data type ''queue'' holding zero or more items, four queue operations, and an **exception** that designates queue underflow (attempt to remove an item from an empty queue.) An instance of type queue is created by a call on the Create operation. The Is_empty operation determines whether or not a queue is empty. The Add and Remove operations enqueue and dequeue elements from the queue, respectively.

The detailed representation of a type queue instance is declared in the **private** section of the specification part since this representation is of no concern to users of the Queue_Mgr package. The body part of the Queue_Mgr package contains the implementation details of the visible Create, Add, Remove, and Is_empty operations. We look at these details later.

What makes this package interesting is that nowhere in part (b) and (c) do we commit to what is meant by ''item''. The meaning of this identifier has been

```
generic                                   -- generic Queue_Mgr package
    type item    is private;              -- Item is a parameter.
```

(a) Generic clause.

```
package Queue_Mgr is                      -- This package is a transformer.

 -- Declaration for the private type queue goes here.

 -- Specifications go here for:
 --    functions  named:  Create and Is_empty, for
 --    procedures named:  Add and Remove, and for the
 --    exception  named:  underflow.

private

 -- Type declarations that define the queue structure go here.
 -- A queue is a one-way linked list of items with a defined
 -- head and tail.
 -- Structure of a queue instance is provided here:

end Queue_Mgr;                            -- end of specification part
```

(b) Specification part

```
package body Queue_Mgr  is

 -- Specification and body parts of:
 --    functions named: Create and Is_empty and
 --    procedures named: Add and Remove go here.

 -- There are no local procedures needed for this package.
 --    If there were any, their specification and body parts would go here.

 -- There are no initialization steps needed when this package is
 --    instantiated. If such steps were needed, they would go here,
 --    preceded by  begin.
end Queue_Mgr;
```

(c) Body part.

Figure 2-7 Skeleton structure for generic Queue_Mgr package.

factored out of the package. Use of the generic clause makes the identifier item a *generic parameter* of the package.

When we wish to create a particular instance of Queue_Mgr, we must supply a matching argument for this parameter. One can see how this is done in Figure 2-8, which shows the Purchase_Queue_Mgr package as an instantiation of the generic Queue_Mgr package.

The reader should notice the **with** list that prefixes the package instantiation of Figure 2-8. A **with** list directs the compiler to provide access to the objects declared in the listed packages.

```
--------Purchase_Queue_Mgr---------
with Queue_Mgr, Stock_Types_And_Constants;

package Purchase_Queue_Mgr is new Queue_Mgr(
           item    => Stock_Types_And_Constants.purchase_record);

   --
   -- Instantiation of generic Queue_Mgr package to manage purchase queues
   -- formed in portfolio instances by Portfolio_Mgr.
   --
```

Figure 2-8 Purchase_Queue_Mgr package as an instantiation of Queue_Mgr with item bound to purchase_record type.

2.4.1. A Multiplicity of Queue_Mgr Instantiations

The full potential of a generic unit, such as the Queue_Mgr package, is realized when Queue_Mgr is instantiated more than once in the same program with different arguments to match the generic parameter, item. We instantiate Queue_Mgr only once in the example being discussed here, since we only need to manage purchase records for common stocks.

A more complete portfolio, however, might also hold purchase records for bonds, for Treasury bills, for Puts and Calls, for commodity options, etc. For each of these forms of purchase, a distinct record structure might be required. In such a case our application would include a number of Queue_Mgr instantiations. Thus, for the price of implementing a single ''template'' package, we obtain several useful packages.

2.4.2. Details of the Queue_Mgr Package

We are now ready to examine the full details of the Queue_Mgr package. Figure 2-9 shows the specification part of Queue_Mgr. (This is a fleshed-out version of Figure 2-7(b).)

In Figure 2-9, we see the specification for the parameter parts of the three operations Add, Remove, and Is_empty. In Ada, a (formal) parameter is bound to its argument (actual parameter) in one of three modes:

- as an input only parameter, **in**,
- as an output only parameter, **out**,
- as an input-output parameter, **in out**.

An input only parameter may be specified with an initial value. (See, for example, the parameter to_front in the Add operation shown in Figure 2-9.)

```
package Queue_Mgr is                       -- This package is a transformer.
  type queue  is private;
  null_queue: constant queue;              -- Example of a "deferred constant".

  function Create return queue;
    -- Function:
    --   Returns a reference to an empty queue instance.

  procedure Add(
      E:         in item;
      Q:         in queue;
      to_front:  in boolean := false); -- Optional third parameter.
    -- Function:
    --   Adds the input item E to the logical "tail" of the queue
    --   structure referred to by Q, unless to_front is given
    --   a true input argument.

  procedure Remove(
      U:    out item;
      Q:    in  queue);
    -- Function
    --   Removes an item U from the logical "front" of queue structure
    --   referred to by Q. U is an output parameter.

  function Is_empty(
      Q: in queue)
    return boolean;
    -- Function:
    --   Returns false value for instance of non-empty queue.

  underflow: exception;                    -- Raised if Remove is passed an
                                           -- empty queue. Propagated to caller.

private
  type queue_element;                      -- Forward reference.

  type queue_element_ptr is access queue_element;

  type queue_element is
    record
      info: item;                          -- Type item is a parameter.
      next: queue_element_ptr;             -- Link to next queue element.
    end record;

  type queue_rep is                        -- Representation of the queue
    record                                 -- structure at the top level.
      head: queue_element_ptr;
      tail: queue_element_ptr;
    end record;

  type queue is access queue_rep;
  null_queue: constant queue := null;
end Queue_Mgr;
```

Figure 2-9 Specification part of Queue_Mgr package.

For each parameter, we designate both its binding mode and its type. Thus, in the specification for Remove, the parameter Q is specified as:

```
Q: in queue
```

The most common form of binding mode is the ''input only'' mode, designated by the **in** reserved word. This binding mode designates that the parameter is ''read-only'', i.e., cannot be stored into. The Ada compiler normally guarantees that an argument that is bound to an **in** parameter of procedure P is not modified by P. The default parameter binding mode for Ada is **in**, but our programs will usually show the binding mode explicitly.

Since Purchase_Queue_Mgr is a transformer package, a call on the Remove operation to remove an item must designate the queue from which the item is to be removed. The parameter Q is a reference to a queue and as such is not itself modified when performing the Remove operation; hence the binding mode of Q is **in**.

The second binding mode is ''output only'', designated by the **out** reserved word. The Remove operation returns the item that it removes by storing the removed item into its parameter U. For this reason and since U does not provide any input information to the Remove operation, U is designated as an **out** parameter:

```
procedure Remove(
    U:    out item;
    Q:    in queue);
```

Note that although we illustrate the encoding of Remove as a **procedure**, it should be evident that Remove can also specified and implemented as a **function**, for example:

```
function Remove(
    Q: in queue)
  return item;
```

The third form of binding mode for a parameter is denoted by **in out**. This form is used in cases where the specified argument matching a parameter P is a variable V whose value is needed as input for the activation of the called subprogram and where, during the activation, P may be updated (i.e., assigned a new value). If updating of P is performed, then upon return from the subprogram, V will have the last value assigned to P. (We will see only occasional use of the **in out** binding mode in this book.)

[The specific rule for determining when to update an actual parameter V that is matched to a formal parameter P having an **out** or **in out** binding mode, is based on a need to assure the potential for execution efficiency. If V is a scalar or access type, then updating of V is performed only once, upon return from the call that names V as an argument (a pure ''copy-out'' mechanism.'' However, if V is an array, record, or private type, then, depending on the compiler used, each assignment to P can cause immediate updating of V (''reference parameter'' mechanism).]

The data type queue is declared **private** to indicate that users of Queue_Mgr are prohibited from operating directly on components of a queue instance. The only operations allowed on elements of type queue are the equality (inequality) relation and assignment to a variable, including parameter transmission.

The representation of a queue instance is shown in the **private** clause following the visible specifications. Although any human reader of the source code can see how a queue instance is represented, the Ada compiler guarantees that the details of representation given in the private part of a package are visible *only* within the package. From outside the package, another program unit can only know that the type queue exists; it is not possible to determine the representation of a queue.

We see from the **private** part that an instance of type queue_rep is a record consisting of a head and a tail pointer, each pointing to queue elements. In turn, a queue element is a record consisting of an information item (info) and a pointer to the next queue element (next), the latter of type queue_element_ptr. The incomplete declaration,

```
type queue_element;
```

is known as a ''forward reference'' and is used to resolve cross-coupling in mutually dependent declarations involving **access**, i.e., pointer types.

The body part of Queue_Mgr is displayed in Figure 2-10. Writing an Ada subprogram can be illustrated by examining the definitions for Add, Remove, and Is_empty in Figure 2-10. The Add procedure, for example, begins with a (necessarily) duplicate copy of its specification (given in Figure 2-9), followed by the keyword **is**. Following this, the remainder of a subprogram body normally consists of a sequence of local declarations, possibly empty, followed by a sequence of statements. In this case, there is one locally declared object: the variable x. In any case, the statement sequence is heralded by the **begin** keyword and terminated by the **end** keyword.

The Create operation, which has no parameters, returns a reference to a newly-allocated queue having zero elements. The head and tail pointers of this queue are each initialized to the null value, reflecting the fact that the queue is empty. A null-valued head and tail pointer is used by the Add, Remove, and Is_empty operations to detect special queue conditions. A few minutes' reflection will convince the reader that the head pointer is null if and only if the tail pointer is null.

In the Add operation, the local variable x of type queue_element_ptr is assigned a reference to a newly-allocated record of type queue_element. This

```
package body Queue_Mgr is;

  function Create return queue
  is
    return  new queue_rep(head => null, tail => null);
  end Create;

  procedure Add(
      E:         in item;
      Q:         in queue;
      to_front:  in boolean := false)  -- Optional third parameter.
  is
    x: queue_element_ptr := new queue_element(info => E, next => null);
  begin
    case to_front is
      when false =>                    -- Normal case. Add to tail of queue.
        if Q.tail /= null then         -- If the queue is non-empty,
          Q.tail.next := x;            -- add the item at the end of the queue.
        else                           -- If the queue is empty,
          Q.head := x;                 -- place the item at the head.
        end if;
        Q.tail := x;
      when others =>                   -- See code details in Appendix C.
  end Add;

  procedure Remove(
    U: out item;
    Q: in  queue)
  is
  begin
    if Q.head = null then
      raise underflow;
    else
      U := Q.head.info;
      if Q.head.next = null then       -- Is Q.head last queue element?
        Q.head := null;
        Q.tail := null;
      else
        Q.head := Q.head.next;
      end if;
    end if;
  end Remove;

  function Is_empty(
      Q: in queue)   return boolean
  is
  begin
    return Q.head = null;              -- Return truth value of expression.
  end Is_empty;

end Queue_Mgr;
```

Figure 2-10 Full details of package body for Queue_Mgr.

newly allocated record is the new queue_element that is to be entered into queue Q; its info field is assigned the value of the input argument E. Note that the third parameter for Add is assigned the default value "false". The meaning of this construct is that the value "false" is assigned to the parameter "to_front" in the absence of a third argument. Thus, if the subprogram calling Add is satisfied with the default value "false" for the parameter to_front then it need not specify a third argument. On the other hand, an explicitly specified third argument value always overrides the default value. In Figure 2-10 we show only that part of the Add operation that handles the default case. The complete body for Add is given in Appendix C.

The Remove operation is analogous to the Add operation and, in addition, offers us the opportunity to consider two issues of interest: an exception condition and dynamic storage reclamation. If the given input queue parameter Q is non-empty at the time the Remove operation is called, then the output parameter U is assigned Q.head.info, the information item in the head queue element. If Q contains only one element at the time of the call, both head and tail indicators of Q are assigned the value null. If Q contains more than one element, the value of Q.head.next is copied into Q.head. In either case, all references to the removed queue_element are thereby deleted; the ultimate effect of this situation is that the heap space allocated to the removed queue_element is inaccessible and therefore recoverable. On the i432, this recovery is automatically performed by the system's hardware-assisted garbage collector. If the given input queue parameter Q is empty at the time the Remove operation is called, then the underflow exception is raised.

When an exception is raised in a program unit, two actions are possible: the exception is handled locally or it is propagated back to the calling unit. The Ada programmer can supply a local exception handler, in this case, within the body of the Remove subprogram, as suggested in Figure 2-11, or, by choosing not to provide a local handler, can allow the exception to *propagate* back to the program unit that called Remove, perhaps to be handled in that program unit. This propagation continues back through the dynamic chain of subprogram calls until some program unit (ultimately, perhaps, the containing system) accepts responsibility for the exception. (In the absence of local handlers, Ada exceptions propagate according to well-defined rules. [See Chapter 11, the Ada Reference Manual [2] for more details.])

If a local handler is supplied, then upon completing the execution of the handler, control immediately exits the program unit (returns to the caller.) Therefore, whether or not a local handler is provided, Ada semantics state that when an exception is raised, the program unit currently being executed is abandoned.

The function Is_empty returns the boolean value **true** if the head pointer is null; otherwise it returns the boolean value **false**. We see that an Ada function subprogram is, analogous to a procedure subprogram, defined by repeating its specification part and then supplying its body part.

A careful reading of the program and comments of Figures 2-9, 2-10, and 2-11 in the context of the foregoing discussion should be sufficient to persuade a reader new to Ada that such code is relatively easy to understand.

```
procedure Remove(
  U: out item;
  Q: in  queue)
is
begin
  if Q.head = null then
    raise underflow;
  else
    U := Q.head.info;
    if Q.head.next = null then -- Is Q.head last queue element?
      Q.head := null;
      Q.tail := null;
    else
      Q.head := Q.head.next;
    end if;
  end if;
exception
  when underflow =>                  -- Local handler code goes here.
end Remove;
```

Figure 2-11 Local handler inserted in Remove subprogram.

2.4.3. Portfolio_Mgr Code

The specification part of the Portfolio_Mgr package is given in Appendix C. We list in Figure 2-12 the operations defined in this package.

```
Operation name
----------------------
Create

Record_buy
Record_sell

Number_of_stocks
Stock_list
Shares_and_avg_cost
Num_buys
History_of_purchases

Get_portfolio_name
```

Figure 2-12 The public operations of Portfolio_Mgr.

The function of each of these operations is explained in the comments following the specification of each operation; we do not explicitly repeat these explanations here. Rather, we focus our attention on the two private types, stock_summary and portfolio, that are defined in this package. The (private) specification of these types is repeated for convenience in Figure 2-13.

```
private

  type stock_summary;   -- forward reference

  type stock_summary_ptr is access stock_summary;

  type stock_summary is
    record
      stock_name:             stock_name_info :=
                              (print_name => "^^^^^^^^^^^^^^^^^^^^^^^^^^^^^^",
                               stock_code => (code => "^^^^", exch => "^^^^"))
      num_shares:             integer := 0;
      avg_cost_per_share:     dollars := 0.00;
      next:                   stock_summary_ptr := null;
      purchase_history:       Purchase_Queue_Mgr.queue
                                    := Purchase_Queue_Mgr.Create();
    end record;

  type portfolio_ptr is access portfolio;

  type portfolio is
    record
      portfolio_name:         long_string := "not yet named^^^^^^^^^^^^^^^^^";
      num_diff_stocks_held:   integer := 0;
      stock_list:             stock_summary_ptr := null;
    end record;
```

Figure 2-13 **Private** clause of Portfolio_Mgr specification part.

The effect of a call on the Portfolio_Mgr.Create operation is to create an initial ''portfolio'' (drawn from heap storage) and return an ''access'' to it. The structure of a portfolio, given in Figure 2-13, is invisible to Create's caller or to the caller of any of the other public operations. Hence, the returned access (reference) is without rights, forcing the user of this reference to go through Portfolio_Mgr to operate on the portfolio. Of course, nothing prohibits the user from distributing copies of the portfolio_ptr received as an output parameter value. (A more thorough discussion of access control issues is given in Chapters 4 and 6.)

From within the Portfolio_Mgr package, however, we can see that a created portfolio is a record containing a slot for the portfolio name, an indication that no stocks are held, and an empty list of stock summaries. Because the portfolio record type specifies initial values for its component fields, every variable of portfolio type and every dynamically created instance of portfolio type is initialized according to the values given above. This "default initialization" occurs unless there is an overriding initialization when a portfolio type variable is declared or a portfolio type instance is dynamically created.

A major element of a portfolio is the linked list of stock summaries. A new stock_summary is added to a portfolio as a result of a call on Portfolio_Mgr.Record_buy to record a buy of a stock that is not now held. As a result of this new stock purchase, a purchase history is created for the new stock by virtue of creating a new instance of type stock_summary. This new purchase_history gets as its initial value a reference to a queue of purchases that is created by Purchase_Queue_Mgr.Create. (The call on this Create operation occurs for every new instance of stock_summary, because of the default initialization specified for the purchase_history field of a stock_summary.) Thereafter, each new call on Portfolio_Mgr.Record_buy adds another entry to the respective purchase queue instance.

Tradeoffs among alternative portfolio representations must be considered as early as possible by the applications designer. We consider two examples:

1. Our choice of using a queue data structure, rather than a linked list for representing the purchase history for a stock, could well be too restrictive. The queue structure is suitable provided we are satisfied that held stocks are sold only on a first-in first-out basis and provided we are sure that "end users" of the system will rarely be interested in explicitly examining or altering the purchase history entries. If these assumptions are not good ones, then a linked list representation for purchase history records would no doubt be more appropriate; furthermore, an additional set of operations would be required in Portfolio_Mgr so the user of this package could request examination and/or manipulation of records in a given purchase history. (Readers are invited to consider, as an exercise, what is involved in redesigning Portfolio_Mgr and the packages on which it depends to permit such added flexibility.)

2. We may wish to consider letting the portfolio record contain an array of stock summaries (rather than a linked list of summaries), each containing a purchase_queue. The major design tradeoffs here are between the storage management problems that arise (if arrays are used) and the limitations of sequential access (if linked lists are used).

   In our example, a linked list of stock summaries is attractive. As long as the number of stock summaries in a portfolio is of manageable size, sequential searching would be acceptable; thus, an array offers no advantage. On the other hand, by using linked lists, we take advantage of the i432's underlying storage resource allocation mechanisms for adding new list elements when needed. We also take advantage of the i432's underlying garbage collector for recovery of discarded list elements. Furthermore, using linked lists frees us from having to specify arbitrary "boundary conditions" in advance, such as the maximum size of an array.

[If we were to use an array to represent a portfolio, we might declare that a portfolio contains a "tableau" of *size* stock_summarys, where size is a constant given in Stock_Types_And_Constants. A stock_summary would be (initially) a record consisting of an empty stock name, zero shares at zero cost, and a null pointer to a purchase history.

Ada permits the declaration of dynamic arrays (See Chapter 3, the Ada Reference Manual [2]); this permits us to declare the maximum number of stock summaries in the tableau to be a variable whose value is computed at the time each portfolio instance is allocated. Figure 2-14 shows how such a portfolio record might be defined.

```
type portfolio(newsize: integer range 1..600)  is
  record
    portfolio_name:       long_string := "not yet named^^^^^^^^^^^^^^^^";
    num_diff_stocks_held: integer range 0..newsize := 0;
    tableau:              array 1..newsize of stock_summary;
  end record;
```

Figure 2-14 Type portfolio with a variable tableau capacity of up to 600 different stocks.

The identifier newsize is a *discriminant*, that is, a parameter, of the record type. Its actual value may vary from 1 to 600. To create an instance of type portfolio, one supplies a matching argument value in the instantiating declaration, as in:

```
my_folio:  portfolio(newsize => 150);
```

This declaration has the effect of reserving storage for a portfolio variable named my_folio that will contain a portfolio with a tableau capacity of 150 stocks. Once committed to a tableau for a maximum of 150 stocks, however, it would not be convenient to change this "boundary value" during the life of the investment portfolio application.]

2.4.4. Code for the Body of Portfolio_Mgr

When developing the body part of an Ada package, it is not necessary that the body of any operation declared within the package actually be physically present in the body, as was the case for operations declared within the Queue_Mgr package body. Instead, one can elect to supply either a temporary implementation in the form of a **null** statement or a specification *stub*, using the key phrase **is separate**, which declares that the body is physically located in a separate compilation unit.

The most common means of deferral is the use of the **null** statement implementation, but in making this choice the programmer must remember, without help from the compiler, to supply the actual implementation later. Deferral by means of the **is separate** stub may cause more voluminous program listings but has the advantage that forgetting to supply the separate body part will be noticed by the compiler or linker. (No execution will be permitted until such separate parts are supplied.) Figure 2-15 illustrates only the **is separate** method by showing portions of the Portfolio_Mgr body part. We choose this type of deferral throughout this text primarily for ease in organizing our figures.

```
package body Portfolio_Mgr  is  -- Package body begins here.

  function Create(
      folio_name: in  long_string)
    return portfolio_ptr;
  is separate;

  procedure Record_buy(
      folio_ptr:            in  portfolio_ptr;
      buy_info:             in  purchase_record)
  is separate;

  -- Other procedure stubs go here.  (See full code in Appendix C.)

  procedure Number_of_stocks(
      folio_ptr:      in  portfolio_ptr;
      num_stocks:     out integer)
  is separate;

  -- Other procedure stubs go here.  (See full code in Appendix C.)

  -- Locally defined procedures and functions go here:
  function Search_for_stock_code(
      folio_ptr:            in  portfolio_ptr;
      buy_record:           in  purchase_record;
      create_if_not_found:  in  boolean)
    return  stock_summary_ptr;
  is separate;
  --
  -- Function:
  --    Searches portfolio denoted by folio_ptr for presence of stock_code
  --    the same as that given in buy_record. If the stock is found, a
  --    reference to the stock summary for that held stock is returned.
  --    If the stock is not found, the action to be taken depends on the value
  --    of the input parameter create_if_not_found. If true, a new stock
  --    summary is created, initialized, and added to the portfolio, and a
  --    reference to it is returned. If create_if_not_found is false,
  --    null is returned.

begin
  --
  -- Statements to initialize this package, if needed, go here.
  -- (Delete the preceding begin if no statements are needed.)
end Portfolio_Mgr;          -- End of package body.
```

Figure 2-15 Selected pieces of the package body for Portfolio_Mgr.

In Figure 2-15 the function Search_for_stock_code is private (local) to Portfolio_Mgr; it is called only by procedures that are defined within Portfolio_Mgr. A separate compilation unit for Create appears in Figure 2-16.

```
separate(Portfolio_Mgr)                  -- Prefix to indicate to the compiler
                                         -- that Portfolio_Mgr is the context
                                         -- in which the following function
                                         -- is to be compiled.

  function Create(
        folio_name: in  long_string)
    return portfolio_ptr;
  is
    folio_ptr:  portfolio_ptr;           -- Local reference variable.
  begin
    folio_ptr := new  portfolio;         -- Allocates a new portfolio
                                         -- instance and assigns a reference
                                         -- to folio_ptr.
    folio_ptr.portfolio_name := folio_name;
                                         -- Name now assigned to this portfoli
    return folio_ptr;
  end Create;
```

Figure 2-16 Separate compilation unit for function Create. Note the special prefix that identifies to the compiler the context in which this unit should be compiled.

The prefix "**separate**(Portfolio_Mgr)" advises the compiler that the containing context of this unit is that of the body part of Portfolio_Mgr. Another way of stating this is that the prefix advises the compiler that the following body, although given physically here, actually resides logically within the body part of the Portfolio_Mgr package at the point at which the *separate* procedure declaration appears. Similar separate compilation units for Record_buy, Record_sell, and for Search_for_stock_code are given in Appendix D. These examples should be studied by the reader who needs more practice reading and comprehending Ada code. They also illustrate several additional features of Ada including the **renames** feature, a non-local **exception** handler, a **case** statement, and a **while** loop.

[For example, the partially completed subprogram body for Record_sell in Appendix D includes a handler for the underflow exception. This handler would be invoked when the corresponding exception is raised in Purchase_Queue_Mgr and propagates to the point of call in Record_sell. Upon completing execution of the handler,

```
exception
  when underflow => history_underflow := true;
```

execution of Record_sell would be abandoned. Control would then revert to the program point (in Club_Portfolio) following the call on Record_sell.]

2.4.5. Examination of the Club_Portfolio Package

We shift our attention to the Club_Portfolio package, under the assumption that the reader has gained some knowledge of Ada and, in particular, has a good understanding of the Portfolio_Mgr package. The specification part of Club_Portfolio, given in Appendix C, is straightforward. The package defines eleven public operations, as listed in Figure 2-17.

```
    Operation Name
--------------------
 Print_club_valuation
 Print_club_holdings

 Find_stock_code

 Print_individual_stock_summary
 Print_shares_and_value_of_stock
 Print_average_cost

 Print_winners
 Print_losers
 Print_non_movers

 Enter_buy
 Enter_sell
```

Figure 2-17 Public operations of Club_Portfolio.

The Club_Portfolio package serves as an interface between users of the Portfolio_Mgr package and the Portfolio_Mgr package itself. Its primary duty is to convert the machine-oriented information encoded in the portfolio data structure into human-oriented printed matter. All direct access to the portfolio data structure is delegated to the the operations of Portfolio_Mgr, for reasons we discussed in Section 2.3.

Only two operations, Find_stock_code and Print_club_valuation, are value-returning functions. Find_stock_code is called to confirm the official corporate name for a stock and to obtain the corresponding unique internal identifier for the corporate name: a stock_code_pair (defined in Stock_Types_And_Constants.) Find_stock_code is designed such that if the caller provides an approximate corporate name, the response is a printout of all the names that ''closely'' match the given name. A null value is returned as the result of Find_stock_code in this case. If the caller provides a name that is an exact match with the name of a listed corporation, the printout confirms the match and the value returned is the stock_code_pair for this listed stock.

[Find_stock_code is analogous to the operation of opening a file for input/output. Normally, before any operations on a file can occur, it must be opened. An "open" operation is given an external, human-readable name of the file as input and returns an internal, machine-readable file name. From this point on, the user refers to every operation on the file by using the internal name of the file.]

The body of Find_stock_code contains calls to operations in the Stock_Mkt_Info package. This package provides the several lookup functions, including one that supplies a stock_code_pair, given the correct corporate name. The caller of Club_Portfolio can then use this piece of information for subsequent calls whose parameter lists require the stock_code_pair as an argument. An example of such a call, might be

```
Find_stock_price(Find_stock_code
                        ("General Motors^^^^^^^^^^^^^^^^"));
```

where Find_stock_price is assumed to be a public operation of the Stock_Mkt_Info package. (It is also possible for Club_Portfolio to supply Find_stock_price as one of its public operations; in the version presented here, however, this is not done.)

The three operations, Print_winners, Print_losers, and Print_non_movers, are inserted to suggest the possibility of endowing Club_Portfolio with operations that can trigger elaborate computational analyses of portfolio and stock market data.

In the case of these three operations in particular, the invoked analyses are quite simple. The caller supplies a percentage deviation, such as 10%. The response is a list of zero or more of the held stocks for which there has been a net gain over average cost that is greater than 10%, or whose average loss is greater than 10%, or whose net gain or loss does not exceed 10%, respectively.

Public operations that perform more elaborate analyses could be added later. Some embellishments might be added with only minor changes in the specification part. For example, an operation, Print_winners_since could be defined in a way similar to Print_winners, by adding a number_of_months as a second input parameter. Thus:

```
Print_winners_since(number_of_months => 5, spread => 10);
```

could be defined to respond by listing the held stocks for which there has been a net gain greater than 10% over the past 5 months.

The access privileges required to perform the operations of Club_Portfolio depend on the operations themselves. Most operations require only read privilege for the portfolio instance. However, the, Enter_buy and Enter_sell operations involve updating the portfolio and, hence, require write privilege.

2.4.6. Creation and Ownership of a Portfolio Instance

Creation of a portfolio instance occurs as part of the package initialization sequence for Club_Portfolio. This sequence is found at the end of the package body and is repeated here.

```
begin
  our_portfolio := Portfolio_Mgr.Create(
                                "Twenty_cousins_club^^^^^^^^^^^^");
end Club_Portfolio;
```

The call on Portfolio_Mgr's Create operation returns a reference to a newly-allocated portfolio instance named ''Twenty_cousins_club'', which is assigned to Club_Portfolio's local variable, our_portfolio. Thereafter, Club_Portfolio owns (is bound to) this portfolio instance. This binding will endure for the life of the Club_Portfolio package; only one portfolio can be bound to the Club_Portfolio package. [In Chapter 3 we consider for an entirely different reason a modified version of Club_Portfolio. In that version the club's portfolio is not created during the package's initialization; instead, two public operations, Create_folio and Delete_folio are included. These operations enable users of the package to effect explicit creation and deletion of their portfolio.]

2.4.7. Ownership of More than One Portfolio

Programmed in this way, Club_Portfolio owns only the Twenty_cousins_club portfolio. [We assume the availability of system commands that make the entire package structure described in this section a permanent library object whose lifetime is like that of a protected file. We discuss object file lifetimes again in Chapters 4 and 10.]

It is a relatively simple matter to program the Club_Portfolio package such that a multiplicity of package instances can be created for Club_Portfolio, each one owning a different portfolio. This may be done by ''promoting'' Club_Portfolio to a **generic package**. In this case, we could make the following changes to the heading of the package:

```
generic
    folio_name: long_string;   -- parameter of generic package
package Club_Portfolio is
```

By using the generic version of Club_Portfolio, new package instances can be created as needed, each differently named and each having ownership (and jurisdiction) over a different portfolio. For example,

```
package My_Estate is new Club_Portfolio(
                               "Account_45^^^^^^^^^^^^^^^^^^^^");
                        -- "computes" a new package instance
```

or, by:

```
package Her_Estate is new Club_Portfolio(
                                 "Estate_12^^^^^^^^^^^^^^^^^^^^^^");
                         -- "computes" a new package instance
```

It is important for the reader to note here that with the latter set of declarations it is impossible to distinguish My_Estate from Her_Estate at execution time. On the other hand, the concept of ''being able to distinguish a package at execution time'' does not exist in standard Ada since the language does not allow users to form any sort of package ''variable''. In standard Ada, packages are strictly static, i.e., packages are distinguished strictly at compile time.

The 432-Ada language extension to Ada allows users to define package ''values''. Thus, the ability to distinguish package instances at execution time may be important to users of 432-Ada. *Package values* and *dynamic packages* are discussed in Chapter 6.

We are finished discussing the Ada program for the basic package structure of this chapter (Figure 2-2.) In the remaining section, we discuss the Ada coding changes needed to implement the altered structure of Figure 2-4. These changes prove to be minimal. The next chapter discusses the more extensive changes needed to implement the structure changes suggested in Figure 2-5.

2.5. Giving Query-Only Access to an Investment Portfolio

In this section we discuss an implementation that provides ''query-only'' access for a task to a portfolio, as suggested in Figure 2-4. The solution suggested in Section 2.3.3 is elaborated here. There it was suggested that a task which is to be awarded query-only access to a portfolio be given only indirect access to Club_Portfolio, through an ''intermediary'' transformer package called Member_Ops. Here we show the details of the intermediary package's implementation.

Figures 2-18 and 2-19 show a straightforward way to program the specification and body parts of Member_Ops.

As seen in Figure 2-19, the body for each procedure given in the body part of Member_Ops is a simple ''one-liner''. It consists of a repeat of its respective specification part, followed by a call to an identically-named procedure in the Club_Portfolio package, as in:

```
<specification of P>
is
begin
  Club_Portfolio.P;
end;
```

```
--------------------- Member_Ops package, version 1 ------------
with Club_Portfolio, Stock_Types_And_Constants;

package Member_Ops is
  use Club_Portfolio, Stock_Types_And Constants;

  function Print_club_valuation
    return dollars;

  procedure Print_club_holdings;

  function Find_stock_code(
      corporate_name: in long_string)
    return stock_code_pair;

  procedure Print_individual_stock_summary(
      stock_code:      in stock_code_pair);

  -- etc  . . .

end Member_Ops;
```

Figure 2-18 Member_Ops specification specification part.

As shown in Figure 2-18 and 2-19, each call on a public operation of Member_Ops will result in an extra and seemingly superfluous inter-package call on the corresponding operation within Club_Portfolio. By using Ada's ''inline'' **pragma** we can instruct a good compiler to avoid compiling this ''extra'' level of indirection. If each procedure in Member_Ops is declared to be ''inline'' then no extra overhead is associated with the extra level of procedure call. Rather, at the place of calling a procedure in Member_Ops the procedures's body is substituted ''inline'' at the point of call in much the same manner as ''macros'' that are available in some machine code assemblers. In this manner, the extra level of procedure call disappears; the effect is that the call goes directly to the procedure in Club_Portfolio, bypassing the procedure in Member_Ops.

We make two observations about Figure 2-18:

- Notice that the **with** list for Member_Ops enumerates only the two packages Club_Portfolio and Stock_Types_And_Constants. By excluding Portfolio_Mgr, no reference can be made to one of its operations from within Member_Ops. In this way, Club_Portfolio serves as the only channel through which Member_Ops can reference Portfolio_Mgr. Careful use of the **with** list mechanism gives us precisely the form of access control that we desire.
- Observe how we resolve the potential ambiguity in the subprogram bodies within Member_Ops. Each procedure P within Member_Ops contains a call

```
-------------------- Member_Ops body part, version 1 ---------------
package body Member_Ops is
  --
  -- The body of each subprogram declaration given here is a call to
  -- the corresponding procedure in Club_Portfolio.

  function Print_club_valuations
    return dollars
  is begin return  Club_Portfolio.Print_club_valuation;  end;

  procedure Print_club_holdings
    is begin  Club_Portfolio.Print_club_holdings;  end;

  function Find_stock_code(
      corporate_name: in long_string)
    return stock_code_pair
  is begin return  Club_Portfolio.Find_stock_code(
                   corporate_name);  end;

  procedure Print_individual_stock_summary(
      stock_code:       in stock_code_pair)
  is begin  Club_Portfolio.Print_individual_stock_summary(
                   stock_code);  end;

  -- etc . . .

  -- No local declarations and no initialization needed

end Member_Ops;
```

Figure 2-19 Body part of Member_Ops, version 1.

to a subprogram of Club_Portfolio having precisely the same name P and the same parameter list as P. This ambiguity is resolved by using ''Club_ Portfolio'' as a prefix. The prefix is needed to resolve the apparent ambiguity even though we have included the identifier, Club_Portfolio, in the **use** list of Member_Ops. Without the prefix, the compiler will interpret each *intended* call on the P in Club_Portfolio as a recursive call on the P in the Member_Ops package. [For more discussion on this this point, the reader may wish to consult Chapter 8 of the Ada Reference Manual [2], which discusses the visibility rules of the language.]

The **use** clause,

```
use Club_Portfolio, Stock_Types_And_Constants;
```

tells the compiler that, for example, types such as percent, stock_code_pair, dollar, etc., which are not declared in the specification part of Member_Ops, will instead be found in one of the packages named in the **use** list. If the **use** list is not provided, the ''full'' names for each of these types must be used, that is:

```
Club_Portfolio.percent,
Stock_Types_And_Constants.stock_code_pair,
Stock_Types_And_Constants.dollar,
etc.
```

[Readers familiar with Pascal will recognize that the Ada **use** list is somewhat like the Pascal **with** clause, which is also a useful mechanism for factoring out a common context for selected components. The Ada **use** list, however, brackets constructs of broader scope.]

We now show a second way to program the Member_Ops package to indicate that calls on its query operations are to result in calls directly on those of Club_Portfolio. This approach exploits Ada's **renames** feature, as shown in Figure 2-20. Here, the specification part of each Member_Ops operation is replaced with a **renames** declaration; a corresponding body part is not required.

```
------------------ Member_Ops, version 2 -------------------------
with Club_Portfolio, Stock_Types_And_Constants;

package Member_Ops is

  use Club_Portfolio, Stock_Types_And_Constants;
  --
  -- The operations of this package are identical with those
  -- like-named operations in the Club_Portfolio package.
  -- Explanations of these functions are given in that package.

  function Print_club_valuation
    return dollars
    renames  Club_Portfolio.Print_club_valuation;

  procedure Print_club_holdings
    renames  Club_Portfolio.Print_club_holdings;

  function Find_stock_code(
      corporate_name: in long_string)
    return stock_code_pair
    renames  Club_Portfolio.Find_stock_code;

  procedure Print_individual_stock_summary(
      stock_code:       in stock_code_pair)
    renames  Club_Portfolio.Print_individual_stock_summary;

    -- etc  . . .

end Member_Ops;    -- There is no package body in this case.
```

Figure 2-20 Second version of Member_Ops, using the **renames** feature.

To summarize, we see that to extend our application from the structure implied by Figure 2-2 to that of Figure 2-4 simply requires the addition of an intermediate or ''filter'' package, Member_Ops, whose public operations are a proper subset of those in Club_Portfolio. Introduction of Member_Ops into the package structure provides us with the means for specifying that users be granted only query access to a portfolio instance. Use of the ''inline'' or renames feature ensures the absence of unnecessary overhead associated with the extra level of indirection.

As mentioned at the end of Section 2-4, the extensions needed to permit users concurrent access to the portfolio requires major additions to the structure (introduction of server tasks). We devote the whole of the next chapter to this important case.

3 TASK STRUCTURES IN ADA

3.1. Introduction

Early in the preceding chapter we introduced the notion that an Ada task is a program unit possessing its own thread of control and capable of executing concurrently with other tasks in the same program (or system). We suggested that tasks would be useful in applications exhibiting behavior that is most closely modelled by systems that allow for concurrent but controlled access to shared structures, as in the case of the portfolio database. We noted that exploiting the tasking facility of a language is the key to simplifying the design and/or modelling of such complex systems which, like the use of packages, offers a means for reducing the cost of software.

3.1.1. The Analogy between Tasks and Machines

One way to see why the "task" concept is so important in both software and application programs is to perceive a task to be an *abstraction of a machine*. In the same way that real systems are designed and best understood as ensembles of interacting physical machines, software systems can be designed and understood as ensembles of interacting abstract machines. The roles that tasks can play in programs are, with one important exception (to be discussed later), pretty much the same as the roles that machines play in real systems, such as offices, factories, and computer networks.

Consider, for example, the workstations in a factory as a set of such machines. Material flows along certain pre-established paths between the workstations. The paths and the stations can be modeled as the arcs and nodes of a directed graph. Some sections of the directed graph, where two or more workstations are linked in series, represent *pipeline* flow of work, e.g.,

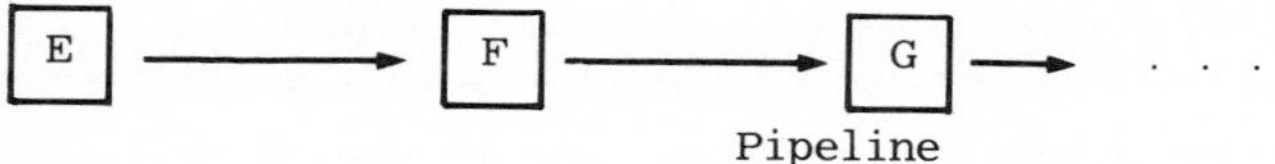

Concurrency, and hence increased throughput, is achieved in the pipeline case when stations E, F, G, . . . are able to perform their respective operations on successive items of work at the same time.

Other sections of the graph, where flow of work forks from one workstation to two or more other workstations, represent *parallel* flow of work, e.g.,

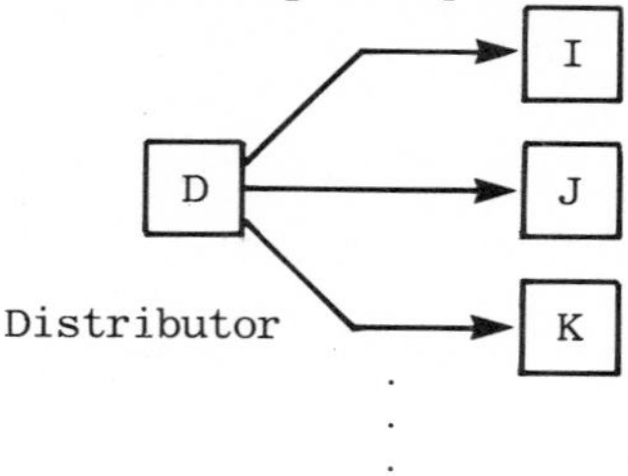

Concurrency, and hence increased throughput, is achieved in the parallel case, when stations I, J, K, . . .,can be kept busy by operating on distinct inputs coming from station D.

The station D serves as a *distributor* of work. (Two non-trivial special cases for D occur when it distributes to no other workstation and to exactly one other workstation.)

Another station C can serve as a collector of work (also regarded as an *arbitrator* or *synchronizer*), e.g.,

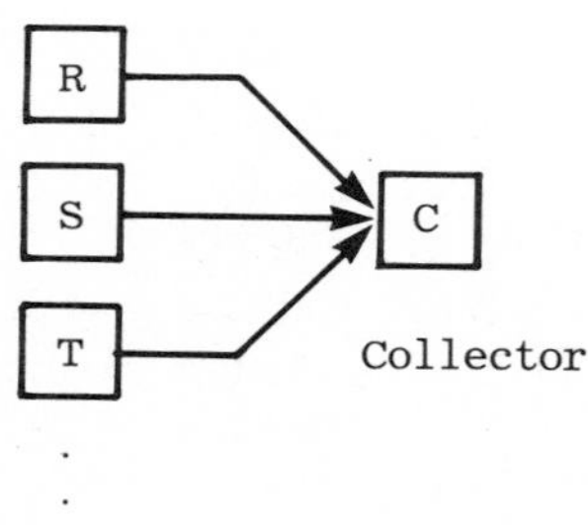

Although our diagrams suggest work flow between related stations in only one direction, for some kind of work (e.g., data to be processed) there is flow in the

reverse direction as well. Also, for each directed arc representing work (or data) flow, there is present, although not always made explicit, some auxiliary control arc(s), such as a *request* and an *acknowledge* arc, to regulate the work (or data) flow.

The foregoing observations allow us to identify four different possible relationships among related workstations, namely: pipeline, parallel, distribution, and collection (arbitration). Correspondingly, individual workstations (also Ada tasks) perform in one of four possible *roles*:

1. as a distributor of work to none, one or more other stations,
2. as a collector of work from two or more other stations—in which case it must perform some form of arbitration to determine the order in which to perform collected work (Alternatively, the function of the collector may be that of synchronizing the forward progress of its predecessor workstations.),
3. as an element of a pipeline, or
4. as an element of an array of stations executing in parallel.

In a more abstract sense, a workstation S that accepts work does so to *perform a service* on behalf of some workstation R that sends work. Hence, we may view S and R as a *server* and *requestor*, respectively. Referring to the preceding structure diagrams, notice that an element of a pipeline, like workstation F, is necessarily both a requestor and a server, whereas workstation D may be a pure requestor and C may be a pure server.

The important conclusion to draw from the above is that it is instructive to classify Ada tasks in the same way that we are able to for machines in general. Accordingly, tasks may be viewed as transmitting messages to other tasks as work (or data) flows between machines or office workstations. Generally, the message information between tasks can flow *in both directions*. This is because a request from a task T1 to a task T2 can involve both outbound and inbound information, by analogy with the **in**, **in out** and **out** parameter modes for a procedure call from P1 to P2.

The concurrency advantages inherent in machine ensembles of real systems are also applicable to programs. The abstract concurrency potential of an Ada program structure is separated from the actual concurrency achieved, which is a function of the number of processors. Thus, an Ada program structured as a collection of m tasks that executes on a general purpose computer having n processors can have as many as $min(m, n)$ tasks executing concurrently. The transparent multiprocessing of the i432 architecture described in Chapter 5 assures that, within a range of n, (where $\{n <= m)\}$, as n is increased or decreased, concurrency is (approximately) linearly increased or decreased—without, of course, any change in the program itself. The opportunity to achieve concurrency in this way is a principal reason to restructure important algorithms, that have heretofore been expressed as purely sequential computations.

The Ada task is, in a very important sense, more powerful than a real machine, which, in general, cannot create other real machines. An Ada task can directly cause the creation (startup, and destruction) of other tasks by exercising another dimension of control not possible with real machines. This new dimension of control leads to the possibility that a task T can *spawn* a set of *n* children tasks, C1, . . . , Cn, setting each into an active state. Under these circumstances, Task T may, but is not required to, function as a requestor of service from its offspring. T's children, in turn, may or may not spawn other tasks, and may or may not function as requestors, servers, or requestor/servers.

3.1.2. A Specific Ada Tasking Structure

It is convenient to regard Ada tasks as having four forms, corresponding to the four roles introduced above. Each role is exemplified in Figure 2-5; its actual form is illustrated subsequently:

- *Non-server/non-requestor task*: such a task does not perform a service for another task and does not request the service of another task (although it may activate other tasks.) Task_Master is an example of a non-server/non-requestor task.
- *Pure requestor task*: such a task requests the service of one or more other tasks (by issuing entry calls on server or server/requestor tasks) but does not itself offer service to other tasks. Requestor tasks do not accept entry calls from other tasks. Each of the Member tasks is an example of a pure requestor task.
- *Pure server task*: such a task has no other role but to wait for and then fill requests for service from other tasks. A pure server task does not issue an entry call for service from another task. The Roster_Server task is an example of a pure server task.
- *Server/requestor task*: such a task plays both a server and a requestor role (and in this sense exhibits the most general structure) by issuing service requests (entry calls) to other tasks in the course of filling service requests (accepting entry calls) from other program units. The Portfolio_Server task is an example or a server/requestor task.

As already noted, a task of any kind can create and activate a task of any kind. For example, the Task_Master has a very simple role to play: This task spawns a fixed set of other tasks, awaits their termination, and then terminates itself. To implement this simple view, we can encode Task_Master so that offspring tasks are created statically (Figure 3-1) or dynamically.

3.1.3. Static Creation of Tasks

In Ada, the static creation of a task by an executing parent task is accomplished in two steps: first, the declaration of a task object within the parent task is elaborated (i.e., resources are allocated for the task object) and, second, the task object is activated. This activation occurs after the elaboration of the declarative part of the parent task has been completed (but before the statements of the parent task begin.) Momentarily we will show the syntactic structures used in elaborating and activating statically-created tasks.

[In the i432 environment, elaboration of a task amounts to the creation of a Process Object representing the task. This object includes a *Storage Resource Object* defining an address space to be used as local storage for this task. Activation of the task is achieved by enqueuing the created Process Object at a Dispatching Port (see Chapter 4), thus indicating that the corresponding Process Object (task) is ready to be bound to an actual processor.]

A task identifier in Ada can be statically declared in a direct manner by declaring the identifier to be a task. Similarly, a task identifier can be declared in an indirect manner by first declaring a task type and then declaring the task identifier as an instance of that task type. In either form of declaration, the program structure of the task is split into a specification part and a body part, just as for procedures.

- All elements declared in the specification part are public. Besides providing the identifier of the task instance (or task type), the specification part supplies, for server or server/requestor tasks, a list of entry declarations specifying the services that this task is able to perform. (An entry declaration is similar in form to the specification of a procedure, but uses the key word **entry**.) For example,

  ```
  entry Print_winners(
      spread:    in  percent);
  ```

  might appear as an **entry** declaration within the specification part of Portfolio_Server. A request for service, i.e., a *task entry call*, must conform to the entry specification in the same manner that a procedure call must conform to the procedure specification.

- The body part of a task is private. It has much the same form as a procedure body. In particular, it can be represented by a **separate** stub and compiled separately. Figure 3-1 shows a possible skeletal structure for a simplified view of the Task_Master.

Alternatively, a task can be created dynamically. For example, the Task_Master need not create a task for member *k* until that member logs in on a terminal and implicitly requests a task to be created. We show how this is accomplished in Ada at the end of this section.

The program structure given in Figure 3-1 is somewhat oversimplified because it does not suggest a workable way in which each individual Member task becomes associated with a person who wishes to gain access to the portfolio. For the moment we gloss over the missing details and assume the following:

The Task_Master executes as a ''log-in responder'' program that responds to ''attention'' inputs from any of several terminals. When a person logs in to a

```
with Text_IO, Membership_Roster, Roster_Types_And_Constants,
              Club_Portfolio, Stock_Types_And_Constants;

use  Text_IO, Membership_Roster, Roster_Types_And_Constants,
              Club_Portfolio, Stock_Types_And_Constants;


procedure Task_Master is             -- Assumes Task_Master is a non_server
                                     -- non_requestor.

  task type  Member_Task;            -- This is the full specification part,
                                     -- assuming that Member_Task is a pure
                                     -- requestor.

  member:  array(1..20) of Member_Task;
                                     -- An array named Member of 20 tasks
                                     -- of type Member_Task is instantiated.

  task body  Member_Task  is separate;       -- Stub.


  task Portfolio_Server is
    -- Entry declarations for this task go here.
    -- Details are given in Appendixes F and G.
  end Portfolio_Server;              -- Instantiation of this task is
                                     -- accomplished upon elaborating this
                                     -- specification and its body part.

  task body Portfolio_Server  is separate;  -- Stub.


  task Roster_Server  is
    -- Entry declarations for this task go here.
    -- Details are given in Appendixes F and G.
  end Roster_Server;                 -- Instantiation of this task is
                                     -- accomplished upon elaborating this
                                     -- specification and its body part.

  task body Roster_Server    is separate;  -- Stub.


begin                                -- All 22 tasks become active here.
  --
  -- Statements, if any, describing the
  -- actions of the Task_Master go here.
  --
end Task_Master;                     -- Await termination of all spawned tasks
                                     -- and then terminate.
```

Figure 3-1 Possible structure of Task_Master.

particular terminal and gives the proper identification, the Task_Master signals a matching Member task (already in execution) that it should take over the job of responding interactively to commands given at that terminal.

According to the structure suggested in Figure 2-5, each input command is interpreted as a request to be serviced either by Portfolio_Server or by Roster. In either case, the command is properly formatted and sent by means of a task entry call to an appropriate entry of Portfolio_Server. The command is treated as follows:

- If the request is a read-only query of the portfolio, the Portfolio_Server issues a corresponding call to the appropriate operator in Club_portfolio. This operator returns a value that is transmitted to the Member task, which eventually causes the appropriate response to be displayed at the user's terminal.
- If the request involves updating the portfolio, then Portfolio_Server first issues a task entry call (request) to Roster_Server to confirm the user's authorization to update the portfolio. Recall from the earlier discussion in Section 2.3.3 that the Roster_Server has sole access to the Membership_Roster owner package, which contains the member name, title, and portfolio/roster privileges.
    - If the Roster_Server's response to the confirmation request is affirmative, Portfolio_Server then issues a call to the appropriate operation in Club_portfolio.
    - If the response from Roster_Server is negative, Portfolio_Server's response to the Member_Task's request is a failure explanation. Eventually, a failure explanation is sent to the Member's terminal.
- If the request involves only querying or updating the membership roster, then Portfolio_Server issues the appropriate task entry call to Roster_Server and merely retransmits the response received to the Member task. In this instance the Portfolio_Server serves only as a "middleman."

After each server task has completed a service request, it is free to accept another one. Service requests may be backlogged while a server task is performing a particular service function or is busy performing some other action, possibly triggered by having completed some service request. A fair amount of concurrency may occur while different Member tasks execute in their respective command loops and formulate service requests and while Portfolio_Server and Roster_Server are busy performing service.

There is also some *blocking* implied with this structure, as a consequence of the "rendezvous" discipline imposed in the semantics of Ada task communication. This blocking could, under certain conditions, prove serious. Upon each task call from a requestor to a server, the requestor is blocked from further action until receipt of the server's response. The delay entailed for this response depends on the structure of the server task, including the means for handling backlogged requests encoded in the task. (We study these details in a later section of this chapter.)

Due to delays inherent in the rendezvous discipline, the response of the system suggested in Figure 2-5 can conceivably prove unsatisfactory under certain sequences of events. Consider, for example, the following scenario:

1. Member(1) issues a portfolio update request.
2. Member(2) issues a portfolio read request.
3. Member(3) issues a request to update the membership roster.

We assume Portfolio_Server acts on these requests in the above order:

In accepting the request of Member(1), Portfolio_Server must first call on Roster_Server and wait for a confirmation response. This response delays acceptance of the request from Member(2) to read from the portfolio, even though Portfolio_Server would be capable of responding to Member(2)'s request without help from Roster_Server.

Suppose Portfolio_Server is now acting on the request of Member(2), which does not require service by the Roster_Server task. Now Member(3)'s request cannot be accepted by Portfolio_Server until completing the current read-only service request for Member(2), even though the third request would not conflict with the use of Club_Portfolio. Thus, during service to Member(2), Roster_Server is forced to idle even though there is a backlogged request that will (eventually) be forwarded to it by Portfolio_Server.

The above scenario illustrates a situation in which delays can be expected for the planned task structure. Other sequences of requests would involve less forced idling. During periods of low "traffic", idling of service tasks is inconsequential.

A system designer is apt to seek a way to eliminate processes that are forced to idle or wait despite waiting requests, especially when these delays are regarded as critical impediments to satisfactory performance. One of several approaches can be taken to remedy the problem:

- One approach is to substitute for the Ada rendezvous mechanism a set of alternative communication operators available in i432 systems. Such operators are given in specially-provided packages; their use results in the execution of the i432 SEND instruction, RECEIVE instruction, and other i432 instructions useful for achieving asynchronous intertask communication. We describe these operators and discuss their use in Chapter 5.

  [In certain applications, it is also possible to model such asynchronous communication within standard Ada. This can be done in various ways. For example, a requestor can use spawned "carrier tasks", each forwarding one request to the server task. This tactic frees the requestor task, permitting it to proceed with its execution even though the carrier tasks may become blocked. The question: how to minimize the waiting time of a requestor task, is also revisited at the end of the next section.]

- A second approach, more in keeping with the desire to conform with the Ada tasking model, would seek an alternative to the structure of Figure 3-1 that provides more pathways between the Member tasks and the two server tasks. One such restructuring is suggested in Figure 3-2.

  Although we discuss this approach further in a later section of this chapter, the reader is likely to deduce the essential idea of this approach rather quickly:

  Club members who have special responsibilities (or privileges) can be associated with tasks in special categories that are distinct from the Member_Task category. Examples are the Secretary, who has responsibility for maintaining the membership roster, and the Treasurer, who maintains the portfolio. Each category of requestor task now transmits its requests to a server via its own package of valid operations on the portfolio and membership roster. These packages make (by private operations) appropriate (though hidden) task entry calls to either Portfolio_Server or Roster_Server, as required. In this way, for example, the club's secretary can be updating the membership roster while another member is querying the portfolio.

  Note that the increased concurrency is achieved by providing independent pathways to the server tasks in order to avoid the "bottleneck" inherent in the previous solution. However, the price paid for removing this bottleneck should be made clear: there is an extra level of indirection in the program structure, analogous to the extra level of indirection that was introduced by the Member_Ops package. This implies an extra step in the access path to the service tasks.

3.1.4. Dynamic Creation of Tasks

As mentioned earlier, tasks may be created dynamically ("on demand") within an Ada program. In the preceding example, all twenty Member_Tasks, the Portfolio_Server task and the Roster_Server task are activated after elaboration of all declarations in Task_Master. Each can be created when and if needed, terminated after performing its function, and recreated later if needed. As the log-in responder, the Task_Master creates a task when a member logs in and deletes that task when the member logs out.

In Ada, an instance of a task type is created dynamically by first declaring an **access** type for the task type, then declaring a variable of the access type, and finally assigning to the variable a pointer to a new instance of the task type. The new instance of the task type is formed as a result of evaluating an *allocator* expression. For example, referring to Figure 3-1, we can replace the declaration,

```
Member:   array(1..20) of Member_Task;
```

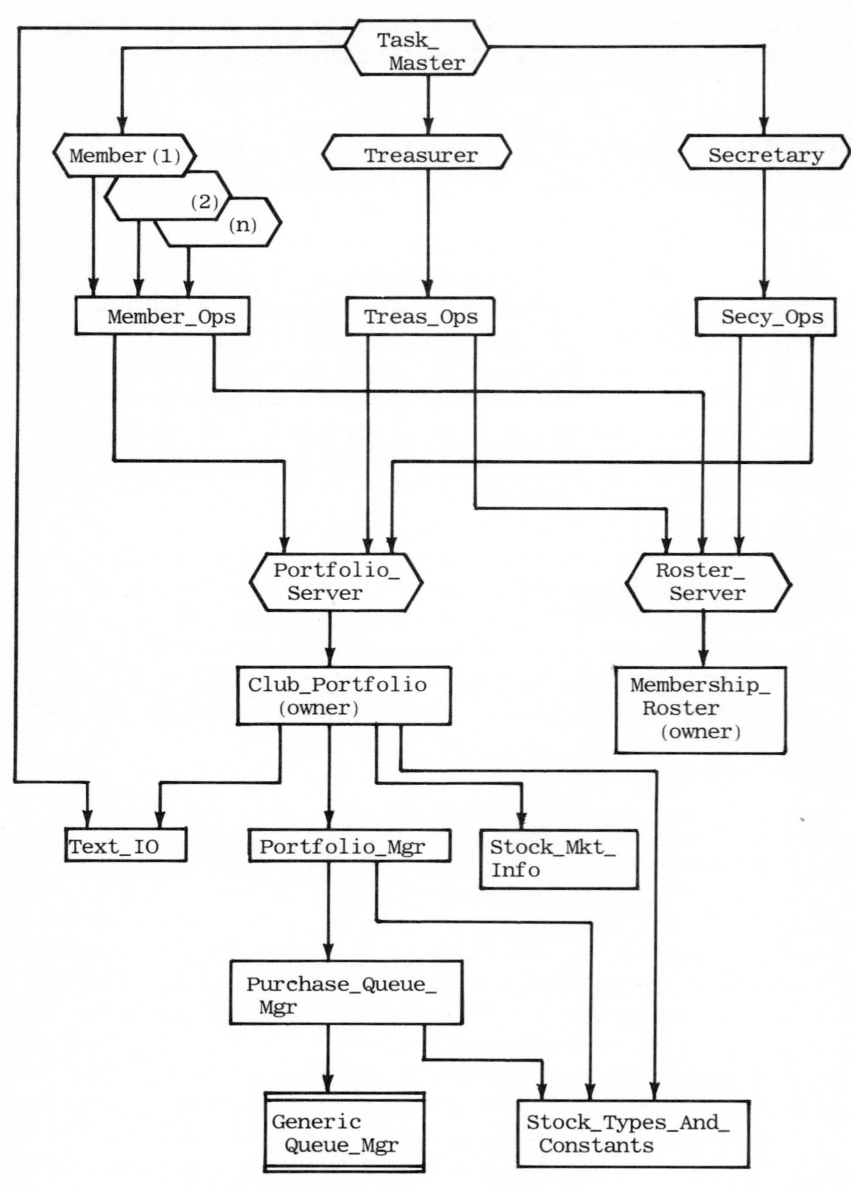

Figure 3-2 Revised Multitasking structure for Multi-user Investment Club Application Program.

with

```
type Member_Ptr  is  access Member_Task;
type Member_Pool is array (1 .. 20) of Member_Ptr;
Member: Member_Pool;
```

thus declaring Member as an array in which each element can be assigned a pointer value to an instance of type Member_Task (an Access Descriptor to a Process Object, in i432 terms.)

A statement of the form

```
Member(k) := new Member_Task;
```

appearing within the scope of the above declarations is executed to create new Member_Task instances dynamically, using the allocator

```
new Member_Task
```

and assigning the resulting pointer value to Member(k).

We shall hereafter assume that Member tasks of our portfolio system are created dynamically by using the scheme just indicated. This being so, we can regard each Member task as a pure requestor task. (Its specification part requires no entries, whereas a statically created Member_Task must have at least one entry to signal the Member_Task that a member has logged in. In the case of a dynamically created task, the fact that a Member_Task has been activated is the indication that a member has logged in.)

For the scheme shown in Figure 3-1, Member tasks require service from Portfolio_Server and indirectly from Roster_Server; there is no significant advantage in creating these server tasks dynamically. Also, because no communication is required between the Task_Master and any of its spawned tasks, Task_Master offers no service (has no entries in its specification part.)

Before moving on to discuss the structure of task *bodies*, we make one last remark concerning Figure 3-2 and dynamically created tasks. In the example of Figure 3-2, we chose to separate members with special responsibilities (e.g., the secretary) from ordinary members by creating separate tasks for club officers. (The code for these special tasks may not be different from that of ordinary members, but their **with** lists will certainly be different!) There is again no difficulty inherent in dynamically creating these separate tasks for secretary and treasurer. Figure 3-3 suggests the type of code that would be inserted in Task_Master.

3.2. Body Structures of Tasks

Task bodies describe the actions of tasks after they are activated. Necessary declarations are listed in the declarative part of the task body, as suggested in Figure 3-4. Such owned resources are private, i. e., not directly accessible to another task or package. A declaration section in a task is optional.

```
-- Secy_Ops and Treas_Ops are added to the with list.

 task type Secy;                      -- A pure requestor.
 task body Secy  is separate;         -- Stub.


 task type Treas;                     -- Another pure requestor.
 task body Treas is separate;         -- Stub.

 Secretary  is access Secy;           -- Pointer variable declared.
 Treasurer  is access Treas;          -- Another pointer variable declared.
--
-- Statements within the   begin...end   part of Task_Master:
--
   Secretary := new Secy;             -- A new Secy task is created and a
                                      -- pointer to it is assigned to
                                      -- Secretary.
--
   Treasurer := new Treas;            -- A new Treas task is created and a
                                      -- pointer to it is assigned to
                                      -- Treasurer.
```

Figure 3-3 Steps in the dynamic creation of Secretary and Treasurer tasks for the structure in Figure 3-2.

```
task body Typical_Task is
  --
  -- If needed, owned resources accessible to
  -- this task are declared here. For example,
  --   type declarations
  --   variable declarations
  --   subprogram declarations
  --   package declarations
  --
begin
  --
  -- Statement sequence(s) to be executed after this task
  -- is activated (and after the resources in the above
  -- "declare" section have been elaborated) go here.
  --
end Typical_Task;
```

Figure 3-4 Skeletal structure of a task body.

As indicated, declarations may include type declarations, variable instances of these or of other types (whose type declarations are listed in modules made visible via the **with** list of this task), etc. All these declarations are locally accessible from statements appearing within the **begin . . . end** section of the task body.

We now proceed to examine the structure of task bodies which, not surprisingly, depend on the role of task at hand:

3.2.1. Non-Server/Non-Requestor Tasks

Any statement sequence allowable within a subprogram body is allowable in the body of a non-server/non-requestor task, including statements that have the effect of spawning other tasks, but excluding statements whose semantics have the effect of requesting the service of other tasks or of providing service to other tasks. When the last statement in the **begin . . . end** sequence of the task body has been executed, or when a **terminate** statement has been executed, the task is made a candidate for termination. If the task has spawned no other tasks or if all its spawned tasks have terminated, then this candidate task is terminated immediately. Otherwise, the task is first put into a *wait state* to await termination of all of its spawned tasks that are not yet terminated. This rule of termination applies to any Ada task, regardless of role.

3.2.2. Pure Requestor Tasks

Bodies of requestor tasks are the same as for non-server/non-requestor tasks, except that entry call statements will appear (also referred to as task calls). An entry call has a syntax similar to that of a call on a package operation. For example, the entry call:

```
Portfolio_Server.Print_winners(spread => 15);
```

issued by, say Member(5) [See Figure 2-5.], is interpreted as a request for service from Portfolio_Server to print the list of stocks, each of which has a current value of at least 15% more than its purchase price.

The caller, Member(5), is then *suspended awaiting rendezvous* with the server until the latter returns the acknowledgement that completes the rendezvous. We introduce the nature and timing of these acknowledgements in the ensuing paragraphs. Upon receipt of the acknowledgement (comparable to, but not identical with return of control from a package call), the caller resumes its execution concurrently with that of the server. In general, each time a requestor issues a task call, it is temporarily suspended (*blocked*) while awaiting rendezvous with the server.

3.2.3. Pure Server Tasks

Server tasks can be called to perform those services listed in the entry declarations (found in the specification part of the server task.) Again, the bodies of server tasks are as for non-server/non-requestor tasks but they include, in addition, at least one **accept** statement. This statement, used by itself (i.e., *exposed*), or nested within a **select** statement (as a *select alternative*), provides the principal means in Ada for the synchronization of tasks. First, we explain the semantics of the **accept** statement when it is exposed, and then we explain its use as a select alternative.

1. Semantics of exposed **accepts**:

   The semantics of the accept statement

   ```
   accept E(...) do S end
   ```

   appearing in a task T can be separated into two cases:

   1. if another task U, currently blocked, has previously performed the task entry call E(. . .) then task T continues execution by performing the statements in statement sequence S or
   2. if no other task has performed the task entry call E(. . .) then task T blocks until another task U does perform the task entry call E(. . .), at which time task T restarts its execution immediately by performing the statements in statement sequence S.

   In both cases task U is blocked from the time that it completes the task entry call E(. . .) until the time that task T completes execution of statement sequence S, at which time both tasks continue execution concurrently. For example, suppose the following **accept** statement appears in the body of Portfolio_Server:

   ```
   accept Print_winners(
       spread: in percent);
   do
     --
     -- Statement sequence to achieve
     -- the required objective.
   end Print_winners;
   ```

   When control reaches the **accept** statement, the enclosed statement sequence is executed immediately if at least one entry call on Portfolio_Server.Print_winners has been issued. If more than one entry call has occurred, the excess entry calls are entered into a FIFO (first in/first out) queue associated with the Portfolio_Server.Print_winners entry. When control reaches the **accept** statement given above, a waiting entry call is removed from this queue in FIFO order. Thus, an **accept** statement always acts on the oldest unserviced pending entry call.

   A requestor task that issues an entry call is blocked in "rendezvous wait" until the issued entry call (possibly queued) has been acted on by completing the execution of the appropriate **accept** statement in a server task. Thus, completing the execution of the **accept** statement completes the rendezvous and unblocks the requestor task so it can proceed with its next step of execution.

   The i432 hardware does not provide explicit hardware support for the Ada rendezvous. However, the Ada compiler does use the i432 message-based communication operations as primitive building blocks to implement the rendezvous mechanism. Based on the above discussion, one can see that the exposed **accept** statement should be used in a server task only when it is acceptable that the server *not* advance past the **accept** statement until the corresponding entry call has been issued. Following is a possible application of this principle, set in the context of our portfolio example:

Suppose that the Club_Portfolio package has an operation enabling deletion of the club's portfolio. Further suppose that the rule for allowing deletion of a portfolio instance is such that three club officers must concur on the deletion by making three independent requests of Portfolio_Server to delete the portfolio. Portfolio_Server is programmed to execute three **accept** statements in series, each for a deletion request from one of the three officers (say President, Vice-president, and Secretary.) The order of arrival of these three requests should not affect the correct execution of Portfolio_Server. Figure 3-5 shows a possible code fragment within the Portfolio_Server task body that implements the cooperative deletion of portfolio instances. By its construction, the last two **accept**s in the series are necessarily *exposed* even if the first one were a select alternative. [The actual code for this fragment of Portfolio_Server's body part can be seen in Appendix F. For this appendix, it is assumed that the Club_Portfolio package differs from that described in Chapter 2 and listed in Appendix C—by having two additional publicly accessible operations: Delete_folio and Create_folio. In this assumed revision, the club's portfolio is explicitly created and explicitly deleted by authorized club members.]

Consider a situation in which the secretary of the club, for example, refuses (or forgets) to issue a deletion request to an activated instance of Portfolio_Server that is attempting to delete a particular portfolio. The task T (e.g., Task_Master) that caused the activation of Portfolio_Server will wait forever for the secretary unless action is taken in task T to remedy this situation. The action taken by T will normally involve placing a time limit on how long Portfolio_Server will be allowed to remain active before T aborts Portfolio_Server, indicating that Portfolio_server has "timed-out." T can use the attribute Portfolio_Server'TERMINATED to determine whether or not Portfolio_Server is still active. If T has no other work to perform other than waiting for Portfolio_Server to terminate, then T can "put itself to sleep" for short periods of time by means of Ada's **delay** statement. This ensures that T does not waste a processor doing "busy waiting" for Portfolio_Server. Finally, if T determines that Portfolio_Server has timed-out, then T can immediately terminate the task by executing the statement

```
abort Portfolio_Server;
```

The approach for coordinating deletion of a portfolio illustrated in Figure 3-5 is motivated by the desire to minimize the blocking of more "important" tasks (President and Vice_president) in the course of issuing their respective delete requests. The extent of such blocking may, however, not be considered critical. Instead, it may be considered more important to *synchronize* all three delete requests to prevent the "forward progress" of any club officer until all have issued a delete request. The **accept** statements used in Figure 3-5 *may be nested* to accomplish the desired synchronization. In general, a nested **accept** structure within a server task permits the server to behave as a synchronizer for two or more requestor tasks.

```
accept President_delete(
    name:          in string_of30;      -- Print name for portfolio
                                        -- instance.
    member_name:   in string_of30;
    check:         out boolean)         -- Check returns false
                                        -- on failure.
  do
    -- Statements to determine and set check with an appropriate value.

  end President_delete;

accept Vice_pres_delete(
    name:          in string_of30;      -- Print name for portfolio
                                        -- instance.
    member_name:   in string_of30;
    check:         out boolean)         -- Check returns false
                                        -- on failure.
  do
    -- Statements to determine and set check with an appropriate value.
  end Vice-pres_delete;

accept Secretary_delete(
    name:          in string_of30;      -- Print name for portfolio
                                        -- instance.
    member_name:   in string_of30;
    check:         out boolean)         -- Check returns false
                                        -- on failure.

  do
    --
    -- Statements to determine and set check with an appropriate
    -- value followed by a statement sequence which has effect of
    -- deleting the given portfolio instance named three times
    -- (in this and previous two entry calls.)
    --
  end Secretary_delete;
```

Figure 3-5 Example use of *exposed* **accepts**: Server-side of protocol for deleting a portfolio instance.

2. Semantics of **accepts** nested within **select** statements:

   Although there are numerous cases, such as illustrated in Figure 3-5, in which a server task is willing to wait (having no other work to perform) at an **accept** statement, this is not always an acceptable policy. Typically, the server may be capable of responding to two or more different requests, or there may be some other action that can be taken by the server in the absence of an entry call for a certain **accept** statement. In either of these cases there is a choice to be made among several alternatives, thereby eliminating the requirement that a task wait for a rendezvous when other work is pending and could be immediately initiated. This type of controlled choice is provided through use of the *selective wait* statement.

Analogous to the **case** statement, a selective wait statement controls the choice among a set of alternative code sequences. Whereas the choice of alternative in a **case** statement is simply determined by the value of a case selector variable, the choice of alternative in a selective wait statement is much more involved. In a selective wait statement, the choice is made by considering a number of factors, including (and most important for this discussion) which of the several alternative **accept** statements, if any, have pending entry calls. Figure 3-6 illustrates the syntax of a selective wait statement within a task body. The structure shown is prototypical for a large class of server tasks.

```
begin
  loop
    select
       {when <boolean guard for Service_1>  =>}
         accept Service_1(...)
           do
             -- Statement sequence.
           end Service_1;
         -- A statement sequence serving as
         -- a sequel to Service_1 may go here.

    or {when <boolean guard for Service_2>  =>}
        accept Service_2(...)
          do
            -- Statement sequence.
          end Service_2;
         -- A statement sequence serving as
         -- a sequel to Service_2 may go here.

    or {when <boolean guard for Service_3>  =>}
        accept Service_3(...)
          do
            -- Statement sequence.
          end Service_3;
         -- A statement sequence serving as
         -- a sequel to Service_3 may go here.
    else
      -- Statement sequence.
    end select;
  end loop;
end;              -- end of task body
```

Figure 3-6 *Selective wait loop* for a task body. [Items in curly brackets are optional.]

The behavior of this type of server task is as follows: After activation, the task enters an endless loop (the **loop . . . end** brackets.) The repeatedly executed selective wait statement is represented by the brackets **select . . . end**. This statement, in turn, specifies a set of alternative actions which must consist of at least one **accept** statement. In the figure, there are four alternative actions: three **accept** statements and their respective (optional) sequels followed by an **else** clause. Any of the **accept** statements may be optionally prefixed by a *guard clause* of the form:

```
when <boolean expression> =>
```

A guarded **accept** statement can be selected for execution if and only if its boolean expression evaluates to true at the beginning of execution of the selective wait statement when the various alternatives are being considered. In Ada terminology an alternative is defined to be *open* (i.e., eligible for selection) if it has no guard or if its guard is true; otherwise the alternative is defined to be *closed*.

The **select** statement chooses a program fragment for execution based on boolean guard conditions and pending entry calls. At the beginning of execution for a **select** statement, each alternative is examined to determine the subset of all open alternatives from which one will be selected for execution. Among the subset of open alternatives, there can be zero, one or many (more than one) alternatives for which unserviced entry call requests are pending. If exactly one open alternative A has a pending request then the program fragment associated with A is executed. If many open alternatives have pending requests then a choice is made among this set of alternatives. The underlying Ada system is responsible for making the choice on a fair and impartial basis in this case. Finally, if no open alternatives can be selected because none have unserviced requests pending, then the **else** clause of the **select** statement is executed.

Other situations can arise which are defined in the semantics of the **select** statement. For example, if one or more open alternatives exist but these have no pending entry calls and no **else** clause has been supplied; the task blocks until the arrival of an entry call for one of the open alternatives. If no alternatives are open and no **else** has been supplied, the task is considered by the underlying system to be deadlocked causing an exception to be raised in the deadlocked task. This exception can either be handled locally within the deadlocked task or propagated to the calling task by terminating or aborting the deadlocked task.

[There are still other possible forms of the **select** statement. The **else** clause may (1) be absent or replaced by either one or more **delay** alternatives or (2) a single **terminate** alternative. Note also that an **else** clause is never prefixed by a guard clause. For more details on these options see Chapter 9 of the Ada Reference Manual.]

As indicated in Figure 3-6, an **accept** alternative can include a *statement sequel*. The actions of an accept alternative may be split into two parts that are executed in sequence:

a. The rendezvous part, consisting of an accept statement to be performed while the requesting task is blocked, and

b. The sequel part following the **accept** statement, executed concurrently with the calling task after completion of the rendezvous part.

Careful use of the rendezvous part and the (optional) following sequel part of an accept alternative allows the programmer to minimize the time that the calling task is blocked in rendezvous. Recall that the calling task is blocked in rendezvous only while the server task is executing the rendezvous part; the calling task and server task continue concurrently at completion of the rendezvous part. Minimizing the time in execution of an **accept** statement follows the hardware analogy of issuing an *early acknowledge* when using a request/acknowledge protocol for message-based communication between asynchronously executing machines.

[A concrete instance illustrating the tactic of early acknowledge occurs in a bank application when a customer makes a deposit or withdrawal. The teller completes the transaction after the customer has departed from the teller's window to do other things. In the corresponding task model the teller and customer tasks communicate (at the teller's window) during the rendezvous part, and the teller completes the transaction during the sequel part (after the customer has departed the teller's window to do other things).]

3.2.4. General Tasks. A more general form of server task is one whose body includes entry calls to other tasks. Thus, the term *general task* is meant to imply a body structure which exhibits both server and requestor behavior. After receiving a particular request for service, the server should be free to "delegate" the work to other server tasks. In Ada, a task call to an entry in some other task is permitted within any sequence of statements. In particular, a task entry call is permitted within the body of an **accept** statement or within its sequel.

A good example of a general task is the Portfolio_Server suggested in Figure 2-5. An entry call from a Member task to the Portfolio_Server task for the purpose of updating the portfolio generates another entry call from Portfolio_Server to Roster_Server. The latter entry call is made for the purpose of verifying the Member's authorization to write in the portfolio (write rights).

Ada imposes no limit on the length of a chain of entry calls, prohibiting only those chains that are cyclic. Thus, Portfolio_Server may not issue an entry call to itself since, due to the blocking nature of the Ada rendezvous, this would result in Portfolio_Server becoming deadlocked.

There is, of course, a practical limit on non-cyclic chains of entry calls; that limit is a function of the negative effect of chaining on Ada program performance. We have illustrated the nature of this negative effect in justifying the more elaborate task/package structure of Figure 3-2.

Although cyclic chains of entry calls are prohibited, a non-chained cycle, in the sense of a "conversation", is not prohibited, and may even be desirable in certain applications. For example, task A calls task B. Task B's response is first to complete the required entry call from A (completing the rendezvous) and then to make an entry call to task A. (Later, A can respond in a like manner until the conversation is complete.)

The option to establish a two-way (or, for that matter, a multi-way) conversation may be useful in a variety of applications, especially those that are transaction- or command-and-control- oriented.

We illustrate by example here a two-way conversation between tasks as a tactic to increase concurrency between the two tasks. In this example, we expand the discussion of the preceding subsection, in which we considered ways to split the requested service into a rendezvous part and a sequel part.

Suppose server task B is required to perform a service requiring lengthy processing that would block requestor task A in a prolonged rendezvous wait. If requestor A can otherwise be doing useful work during this interval, and if a processor is available for requestor A, we can decrease task A's blocked rendezvous interval by the tactic of constructing a conversation between A and B. The protocol that takes the place of a simple rendezvous is as follows:

- Server B completes its **accept** statement (rendezvous part) by copying all the (input) arguments supplied by A into variables locally accessible to B. This releases requestor A from its rendezvous after a minimal period of time, freeing A to continue execution.
- Server B then completes the required processing on A's behalf in the statement sequel.
- When processing in the sequel part has reached the point where output results needed by A have been established, server B now assumes the role of requestor and issues a task call to A at an entry in A corresponding to a preplanned *wait point*, that is, a particular **accept** statement within A. This **accept** statement will appear in A at the point where A cannot do any more useful work without first obtaining its output results from server task B.
- Task A reaches the preplanned wait point and accepts B's call, completing the second rendezvous merely by copying the output results transmitted in the entry call to A by B. This releases task B after a minimal blocked rendezvous interval.

This tactic is cost effective only if the sum of the two rendezvous intervals for the pair of entry calls (A->B, then B ->A) is short relative to the time that would have been required for the single, prolonged rendezvous (A ->B). Figure 3-7 shows a schematic of the Ada program structure for task B's part of the conversation.

```
accept Lengthy_service(
    param_1:  in ...;
    param_2:  in ...)
  do
    local_var_1 := param_1;   -- Copy value matched to param_1
                              -- into this context.
    local_var_2 := param_2;   -- Do the same for param_2.
  end Lengthy_service;        -- First rendezvous completed.
--
-- Statements of the sequel
-- that perform lengthy processing
-- on values of local_var_1 and local_var_2
-- to produce the result the requestor wants.
-- This result is assumed to be stored locally
-- in wanted_result.
--
Requestor_task_name.Lengthy_service_result(
    wanted_result);           -- Call back to requestor to give
                              -- it the value of wanted_result.
-- End of sequel; second rendezvous completed.
```

Figure 3-7 Server-side protocol using two-way conversation for minimizing length of time requestor is blocked in rendezvous.

3.3. Concrete Examples

The preceding discussions have laid the foundation required to understand Ada task structures and semantics. In this section, we examine fragments of concrete examples shown in full in Appendix F. This appendix provides the Ada representation of the Portfolio_Server task and the specification parts of the Roster_Server task and Membership_Roster packages. These program units are designed to conform with the structure in Figure 2-5. [Appendix G provides corresponding program units that conform with the structure in Figure 3-2.

In the program structure implied by Figure 2-5, Portfolio_Server is burdened with a number of extra ''responsibilities''. It must forward a number of task entry calls to Roster_Server besides the entry calls it must convert into operator calls on Club_Portfolio. This dependence on Roster_Server, itself dependent on Membership_Roster, is probably sufficient to immediately reject the structuring strategy of Figure 2-5. Those readers with more experience in concurrent programming may agree already. However, we proceed, in the spirit of an exercise, to illustrate and explain the program structure required for the approach illustrated in Figure 2-5.

Figure 3-8 lists the individual entries that are needed for the Portfolio_Server task. Each of these entries requires an **entry** declaration in the task specification part of Portfolio_Server.

As can be seen in Figure 2-5, Portfolio_Server is directly dependent on the specifications for Roster_Server and for Club_Portfolio. In turn, Roster_Server is dependent on the specifications of the Membership_Roster package.

```
Type of entry                       Entry name
--------------------------          --------------------------
Portfolio queries (9)               Print_Club_portfolio
(Executed as calls on               Print_club_holdings
operations in Club_Portfolio        Find_stock_code
package.)                           Print_individual_stock_summary
                                    Print_shares_and_value_of_stock
                                    Print_average_cost
                                    Print_winners
                                    Print_losers
                                    Print_non_movers

Portfolio update requests (2)       Enter_buy
(Executed as calls on operations    Enter_sell
in Club_Portfolio package after
first making calls on Roster_
server.)

Portfolio create and delete         President_create_folio
requests  (6)                       Vice_president_create_folio
(Executed as calls on operations    Treasurer_create_folio
of Club_Portfolio after first       President_delete_folio
making calls on Roster_Server.)     Vice_president_create_folio
                                    Treasurer_delete_folio

Membership_Roster queries (2)       Lookup_member
(Executed by calls to               List_of_members
Roster_Server.)

Membership_Roster updates (3)       Add_new_member
(Executed by calls to               Update_member
Roster_Server.)                     Delete_member
-------------------------------------------------------------------
```

Figure 3-8 The 22 individual entries of Portfolio_Server used in the Figure 2-5 structure.

A convenient way to proceed in the development of Portfolio_Server is first to develop the specifications of Membership_Roster, then to develop the specifications of Roster_Server, and finally to develop the specifications of Portfolio_Server. This is indeed the way we arrived at the list of entries in Figure 3-8. [Recall that we have already developed the Club_Portfolio package. See Appendix C, but recall that we now assume modifications of this package have been made to provide explicit Delete_folio and Create_folio operations.]

Although our development appears from the above discussion to be strictly "bottom-up", this is not really the case. We find, as a matter of development methodology, it is convenient and "logical" to first design the program structure in top-down fashion, then to design the specification parts for each node of the program structure in bottom-up fashion, and finally to program the body parts of these nodes in top-down fashion. We therefore follow this developmental approach in the ensuing exposition.

We decide that the Membership_Roster package should ''own'' the roster, a private type. The skeletal form of this package's specification part is given in Figure 3-9.

```
with  Roster_Types_And_Constants, Text_IO;

package  Membership_Roster  is

  use  Roster_Types_And_Constants, Text_IO;

  type roster  is private;  -- See definition below.
--
--  There are five operations, as follows (See Appendix F):
--
--    Lookup_member,            -- Returns a copy of current member's record.
--    List_of_members,          -- Prints a list of the information in the roster.
--    Add_new_member,           -- Adds a record for a new member.
--    Update_member,            -- Updates the record for a current member.
-- and
--    Delete_member             -- Deletes the record for a current member.

private
  type roster is array(1..max_num_members) of member_record;
    --
    -- An instance of a roster is (assumed to be) instantiated in the
    -- body part of this package.

end Membership_Roster;
```

Figure 3-9 Skeleton of the Membership_Roster package specification.

The five operations of Membership_Roster are explained in the comments of Figure 3-9. If successful, each of these operations performs the indicated action. The reader can see the full specification of these operations in Appendix F.

Notice that the private type roster depends on the constant max_num_members and on the type member_record. These two items are declared in the auxiliary package Roster_Types_And_Constants, which appears in the **with** and **use** clauses of Membership_Roster. It will be seen later that Roster_Server and Portfolio_Server also depend on Roster_Types_And_Constants. This dependence is explained below.

The Roster_Server task has a total of 9 entry declarations. These declarations are listed in Figure 3-10.

Roster_Server requires access to the representation of type member_record because it must provide responses to the title queries; to do this, it must be able to examine individual components of a member_record instance furnished to it in response to a call on Membership_Roster.Lookup_member. Both Portfolio_Server and Roster_Server forward individual member_records to Membership_Roster in the course of responding to/from roster update requests. For this reason, type member_record cannot be declared **private**.

```
Type of entry                             Entry name
----------------------------              ------------------
Title queries, which are                  Is_president
boolean functions  (4)                    Is_vice_president
(Executed by calls to                     Is_treasurer
Membership_Roster.)                       Is_secretary

General queries of the                    Lookup_member
roster   (2)                              List_of_members
(Executed by calls to
Membership_Roster.)

Requests for membership                   Add_new_member
roster updates   (3)                      Update_member
(Executed by calls to                     Delete_member
Membership_Roster.)
-----------------------------------------------------------
```

Figure 3-10 The 9 individual entries of Roster_Server used in the Figure 2-5 structure.

Figure 3-11 is a skeletal form of the Roster_Server task's specification part, showing the details for three of its nine entries. The full set of entries can be examined in Appendix F.

The use of entries in Portfolio_Server is now illustrated in discussing the protocol for updating the portfolio and for deleting the portfolio. Figure 3-12 is an excerpt from the specification part of Portfolio_Server, showing the **entry** for Enter_buy. Figure 3-13 shows the corresponding **accept** statement in the body part of Portfolio_Server.

The first two parameters of the Enter_buy entry are control parameters. The caller's name must be supplied in my_name; this name should be that of the club's treasurer. The "unauthorized" parameter returns the value true if the supplied member name, as checked by Roster_Server's Is_treasurer entry, does not match that of the treasurer. With this specification for the Enter_buy **entry**, the body of the corresponding **accept** statement for Enter_buy (see Figure 3-13) begins with an Is_treasurer entry call. If this call sets the local variable check_boolean to true, a call on the Enter_buy operation of Club_Portfolio is then made, and unauthorized is set to false; otherwise, unauthorized is set to true.

The final example of this section illustrates the three actions required to delete the portfolio. Figures 3-14, 3-15, and 3-16 show the set of three **entry** declarations in Portfolio_Server that must be called to accomplish the deletion of a portfolio. Figure 3-17 shows the corresponding sequence of three **accept** statements from the body part of Portfolio_Server. Perusal of the comments that accompany the three **entry** declarations in Portfolio_Server should convince the reader that the corresponding sequence of **accept** statements faithfully reflects these specifications.

```
with Membership_Roster, Roster_Types_And_Constants;

task Roster_Server  is
  use Membership_Roster, Roster_Types_And_Constants;
--
------   Title queries:
--
  entry Is_President(
      member_name:  in  string_of30;
      check:        out boolean);
    --
    -- Function:
    --   Calls Membership_Roster.Lookup_member to obtain record
    --   of member_name. Sets check true if member_name matches
    --   name of a member whose title is President, else returns
    --   with check still false.

  entry Is_Vice_president(
      member_name:  in  string_of30;
      check:        out boolean);
    --
    -- Function:
    --   Similar to that of Is_president.

-- Entry for  Is_treasurer   goes here.
-- Entry for  Is_secretary   goes here.
--
------   General queries to the roster:
--
-- Entry for   Lookup_member    goes here.
-- Entry for   List_of_members  goes here.
--
------   Requests for membership roster update:
--
-- Entry for   Add_new_member  goes here.
-- Entry for   Update_member   goes here.
  entry Delete_member(
      my_name:      in  string_of30;
      member_name:  in  string_of30;
      check:        out boolean);
    --
    -- Function:
    --   Calls Membership_Roster.Delete_member to delete all info on
    --   a current member in the membership roster. If deletion is
    --   successful, check is set true before executing the return.
    --   Returns with check false if Delete_member call "fails".
    --   (Can fail if my_name does not match with the name of the
    --   secretary, or if there isn't already a member of the given
    --   member_name in the roster.)
end Roster_Server;
```

Figure 3-11 Skeletal version of Roster_Server specification part.

```
with Club_Portfolio, Roster_Server,
         Stock_Types_And_Constants, Roster_Types_And_Constants;
             -- Not all of these dependencies were shown in
             -- Figures 2-5 and 3-2.
task Portfolio_Server is

  use Club_Portfolio, Roster_Server,
          Stock_Types_And_Constants, Roster_Types_And_Constants;
--
-- Portfolio queries go here. (9 entries)
--
-------      Portfolio update requests:
  entry Enter_buy(
      my_name:       in  string_of30;
      unauthorized:  out boolean;
      purch_date:    in  date;
      stock_code:    in  stock_code_pair;
      num_shares:    in  natural;
      per_sh_price:  in  dollars;
      commission:    in  dollars);
    --
    -- Function:
    --   Determines if member whose name is value of my_name
    --   is authorized to update the portfolio. If not, returns
    --   with value of unauthorized set to true. If yes, sets
    --   unauthorized to false and then calls the corresponding
    --   operation in Club_Portfolio.
--
-- Entry for  Enter_sell  goes here.
--
---------- Portfolio create and delete requests (6 entries)
--
---------- Membership roster requests (5 entries)
--
end Portfolio_Server;
```

Figure 3-12 Skeletal view of Portfolio_Server specification, showing entry for Enter_buy.

3.4. Chapter Summary

In this final section, we tie up some loose ends. First, we return to our supposition that the task-and-package structure suggested in Figure 3-2 is more in keeping with the spirit of modular, concurrent programming than that of Figure 2-5. Second, we consider the broader applicability of our portfolio management case study.

By interposing "specialist" packages, such as Member_ops, Treasurer_Ops, Secretary_Ops, etc., between the tasks representing the interactive users and the two server tasks, Portfolio_Server and Roster_Server, we gain the benefit that the two servers are completely decoupled. In particular, Portfolio_Server is no longer required to communicate with Roster_Server in order to authorize portfolio operations. As a result of this decoupling, each server task is smaller

```
accept  Enter_buy(
    my_name:        in  string_of30;
    unauthorized:   out boolean;
    purch_date:     in  date;
    stock_code:     in  stock_code_pair;
    num_shares:     in  natural;
    per_sh_price:   in  dollars;
    commission:     in  dollars)
do
  Roster_Server.Is_treasurer(my_name, check_boolean);
  if check_boolean then          -- authorized
    Club_Portfolio.Enter_buy(purch_date,
                             stock_code,
                             num_shares,
                             per_sh_price,
                             commission);
    unauthorized := false;
  else
    unauthorized := true;
  end if;
end Enter_buy;
```

Figure 3-13 Showing how the **accept** statement for Enter_buy involves a call on Roster_Server.Is_treasurer.

```
entry President_delete_folio(
    my_name:        in  string_of30;
    portfolio_name: in  long_string;
    unauthorized:   out boolean);
  --
  -- Function:
  --   Calls Roster_Server to determine if member whose name
  --   is value of my_name is the current club President.
  --   If not, returns with value of unauthorized set to true.
  --   If yes, unauthorized is set false and then returns after
  --   recording the portfolio name supplied. Deletion will not
  --   actually be attempted until a sequence of three deletion
  --   requests for the same portfolio name has been received, one
  --   each from the three club officers: President, vice-president
  --   and treasurer.
```

Figure 3-14 Entry declaration for first of three calls to delete a portfolio.

```
entry Vice_president_delete_folio(
    my_name:         in  string_of30;
    portfolio_name:  in  long_string;
    unauthorized:    out boolean);
  --
  -- Function:
  --   Request at this entry accepted if and only if the
  --   most recently accepted entry call was for
  --   President_delete_folio, and that call was authorized.
  --   Determines if member whose name is value of my_name
  --   is the current club vice-president.
  --   If not, returns with value of unauthorized set to true.
  --   If yes, unauthorized is set false and then returns after
  --   recording the portfolio name supplied. Deletion will not
  --   actually be attempted until a sequence of three deletion
  --   requests for the same portfolio name has been received, one
  --   each from the three club officers: President, vice-president
  --   and treasurer.
```

Figure 3-15 Entry declaration for third of three calls to delete a portfolio.

```
entry Treasurer_delete_folio(
    my_name:         in  string_of30;
    portfolio_name:  in  long_string;
    unauthorized:    out boolean;
    check:           out boolean);
                         -- If set true, portfolio has been deleted.
  --
  -- Function:
  --   Request at this entry accepted if and only if the two
  --   most recently accepted entry calls were for
  --   President_delete_folio and Vice_president_delete_folio
  --   in that order, and if both were authorized calls.
  --   Calls Roster_Server to determine if member whose name
  --   is value of my_name is the current club Treasurer.
  --   If not, returns with value of unauthorized set to true.
  --   If yes, unauthorized is set false. The three supplied
  --   portfolio names are checked. If all are not identical,
  --   then check is set to false and a return is executed.
  --   If they do match, then the Delete_folio operation in
  --   Club_Portfolio is called. If this call is successful
  --   (portfolio deleted), then check is set true;  return to
  --   Treasurer_delete_folio's caller is then executed.
```

Figure 3-16 Entry declaration for third of three calls to delete a portfolio.

```
accept President_delete_folio(
    my_name:          in  string_of30;
    portfolio_name: in  long_string;
    unauthorized:    out boolean)
do
  Roster_Server.Is_treasurer(my_name, check_boolean)
  if  check_boolean  then
    local_name_1 := portfolio_name;   -- Save copy of portfolio_name
                                      -- for checking at next accept.
    unauthorized := false;
  else
    unauthorized := true;
  end if;
end President_delete_folio;
--
-- Sequel of two accepts begins here.
--
accept Vice_president_delete_folio(
    my_name:          in  string_of30;
    portfolio_name: in  long_string;
    unauthorized:    out boolean)
do
  Roster_Server.Is_vice_president(my_name, check_boolean)
  if check_boolean  and  local_name_1 = portfolio_name  then
    local_name_2 := portfolio_name;   -- Save copy of portfolio_name
                                      -- for checking at next accept.
    unauthorized := false;
  else
    unauthorized := true;
  end if;
end Vice_president_delete_folio;
--
accept Treasurer_delete_folio(
    my_name:          in  string_of30;
    portfolio_name: in  long_string;
    unauthorized:    out boolean;
    check:             out boolean)
                       -- If set true, portfolio has been deleted.
do
  Roster_Server.Is_treasurer(my_name, check_boolean)
  if  check_boolean  and  local_name_1 = portfolio_name
                     and  local_name_2 = portfolio_name  then
  do
    unauthorized := false;            -- Authorization is OK.
    Club_Portfolio.Delete_folio(portfolio_name, check);
                                      -- Portfolio is deleted if check
                                      -- returned with value true.
  else
    unauthorized := true;
  end if;
end Treasurer_delete_folio;
--
-- End of sequel (end chain of three accepts).
```

Figure 3-17 The sequence of three **accept** statements which must be executed to delete a portfolio instance.

and simpler (has fewer and simpler entries and accepts.) Each task has just those entries that enable it to arbitrate the possibly concurrent use of its related owner package (Club_Portfolio and Membership_Roster.) The program structure required for the decoupled server tasks is shown in Appendix G.

Service requests sent to Roster_Server are guaranteed to be authorized because of the interposed "filtering" packages. Thus, Roster_Server has only the five entries that are in one-to-one correspondence with the operations of Membership_Roster; the **accept** statements of the former are simply calls on operations of the latter.

In a similar vein, but with two notable exceptions, each service performed by Portfolio_Server amounts to nothing more than a call on the corresponding operation of Club_Portfolio. The exceptions are the entries dealing with requests to create or delete a portfolio. The required coding for the chain of three **accepts**, shown in Appendix G, is just a slight amplification of the program fragment given in Figure 3-5.

We trust that enough of the portfolio management system has now been discussed and illustrated in Ada to tempt some readers to complete and test this application. More ambitious readers should also consider the question of the applicability of our case study in a context more general than a single Investment Club. In particular, what changes (if any) from that of the Figure 3-2 structure would be required to apply or extend the system for use in the management of more than one portfolio or with more than one set of authorities granted for accessing and updating the portfolio?

A bank trust department that manages several distinct pension or other funds or a brokerage house that manages numerous investment portfolios would be expected to have more complicated authority structures than is the case for a single investment club. For example, if an account manager is "on vacation" when a buy or sell transaction is requested by an investor, the brokerage house must offer alternative access to the investor's portfolio. Otherwise, an eager or nervous investor may take a dim view of waiting to trade some stock until the account executive returns from vacation.

Is it convenient to express the richer authority structures required in such situations without making substantial changes to the basic program structure in Figure 3-2 at and below the "service tier"? We think so. Also, how easy is it to modify the basic structure to accommodate a multiplicity of portfolios? Again, we think the changes required are minor, but we leave the matter of verifying these conjectures to the reader.

Although we have not made a complete examination of Ada, we have now looked at this rich language in sufficient detail to allow the reader to evaluate it as a useful systems and applications programming language. We are ready, therefore, to consider how programs in Ada map onto the structure of the i432 system architecture. In the next chapter, we look at the execution-time data structures of program units, in order to see how they are represented as i432 object structures.

4 i432 OBJECT STRUCTURES FOR PROGRAM EXECUTION

4.1. Introduction

As alluded to earlier, important advantages arise when the execution time data structure of a program exhibits a close correspondence with the conceptual program data structure it represents. A useful conceptual model that holds for most program data structures is the *directed graph*; most programs (especially systems-oriented programs) make heavy use of directed graph data structures. Nevertheless, few architectures in existence today are able to provide significant support for a directed graph program data structure model; it is usually considered the programmer's task to map his topologically complex data structures onto the relatively "flat" structures of conventional architectures. The i432 architecture provides the user with hardware, firmware, and software support for a directed graph model of program data structure. This is achieved by representing execution time structures as collections of independent address spaces which are *objects*. The correspondence between a directed graph data model and the execution time "object collection" model is: a directed graph node corresponds to an object and a directed graph arc corresponds to a reference (or pointer) to an object.

In this chapter we introduce readers to the details of the i432 execution time object collection model. We will focus primarily on the i432 object structures that arise and that are maintained during execution of programs having single threads of control. Consequently, we limit our discussion to structures that relate to intra-process operations, deferring until the next chapter higher-level relationships having to do with inter-process communication. The following subsection is offered as a review of the basic concepts of "object-oriented architectures", including a bit of historical perspective, that is relevant to this topic.

4.1.1. A Primer on i432 Address-Space Structures

An important problem in the design of modern computer architectures is to achieve acceptable execution efficiency while still providing the memory management and protection facilities required to support the dynamic behavior of objects in a rapidly changing data structure. The early innovative architectures, in particular the Burroughs B5000 (1961) and its sequels did succeed in providing hardware support for address space management. The B5000 memory system exhibited a "segmented, virtual storage". Such systems as the B5000, sometimes referred to as "language-directed architectures", have served as useful early models of architectures with memory management support. However, they were only slowly appreciated by other computer architects, often for good reasons.

For a glimpse at some reasons behind the slow acceptance of earlier architectures, the interested reader is referred to [9] [10] [19] [42] [45]; we will not cover these reasons in detail here. Many complaints about earlier architectures were difficult to dispel because of the relatively slow rate at which hardware, in particular, storage technology had been advancing. However, a more critical reason was the slow appreciation of the significant role played by the "descriptor" (or "codeword") concept [11] [31].

A descriptor is a reference or pointer to the base of a (related) address space. Descriptors and segments can be used to represent complex, directed graph structures: a descriptor represents an arc and a segment represents a node. All segments are independent of each other, i.e. every segment must be referenced through a descriptor and it is impossible to reference any part of segment B through a descriptor for segment A. Segments are variable length, i.e., their size is set when they are created; the size is stored as a part of the descriptor that references the segment. Finally, segments are relocatable, i.e., a segment can be placed anywhere in memory without modification of the segment contents (only the descriptor must be modified to reflect the new segment base location).

Descriptors must be managed carefully if the integrity of an execution-time program data structure (and, more generally, if the integrity of the system as a whole) is to be maintained. Descriptors should also be traversed as rapidly as possible, since descriptors amount to indirect addresses and are often cascaded, lengthening the access path to a target data or instruction component.

The key to efficient implementation of descriptor-based addressing is direct hardware support, i.e., machine instructions that provide descriptor-based addressing at the architectural level. Since descriptors are used very frequently, it is important that they be recognized by the hardware as being different from all other forms of data. In some architectures, for example, Burroughs, a descriptor is recognized by the value in a tag field that is attached to every memory word but is not accessible to the general user, permitting the descriptor to be safely placed within a data segment. In such implementations of descriptors, access rights and storage (address) mapping information are encoded within the same reference word.

The observant reader may have noticed by now that one of the primary difficulties in descriptor-based addressing occurs as a conflict between the desire to store the base address of a segment directly in a descriptor on the one hand and the desire to make segments relocatable on the other hand. When it is necessary to relocate a portion of the run-time structure (such as when segments are swapped back into the main store in a virtual memory system), every reference to the relocated segment (object) must be found and updated to account for the new location of the object. In certain circumstances, the search for these descriptors takes a significant amount of time. For many architects, such costs, related to the management of descriptors, was deemed prohibitive.

A significant improvement on the descriptor concept occurred with the invention and evolution of the *capability* concept [16] [22] [24] [37] [38] [59] [64] [65]. A capability, as we now view it, contains an indirect reference through a mapping table to a segment base, in contrast to a direct reference to a segment base that is part of a descriptor. Every capability that references a segment S does so by referencing the same entry M in the mapping table; this mapping table entry, in turn, directly references the base of segment S. Since all capabilities reference a segment base through the mapping table, relocation of a segment S from base address A to base address B is achieved simply by modifying mapping table entry M to indicate that the segment base address it now references is at address B instead of the old base address A. This one relocation step automatically relocates the segment S referenced by all capabilities that reference mapping table entry M. Thus, a reference to a segment is normally separated into two parts:

1. access authorization and reference to the mapping table entry via a capability
2. mapping table entry

The use of capabilities not only solves the problem of how to achieve efficient segment relocation, but also leads to the solution of the problem: how to control the size and scope of *protection domains*; the latter is based on the observation that different users having different privilege can each be given different capabilities for the same segment, i.e., capabilities with different access authorizations (meaning different *access rights*) for the same segment.

By contrast, protection of individual address spaces in the Burroughs descriptor-based architectures was founded on the assumption that users execute only those programs that are compiled by system-provided high-order language compilers. Users program with "safe languages" only, and they access system services only through "safe interfaces". System-supplied compilers are trusted to generate instruction streams for software or applications programs that correctly manage the creation, distribution, and manipulation of descriptors, thereby assuring the integrity and authenticity of execution-time program data structures, and more generally the integrity of the system as a whole. For those users who wish to have complete access to a processor's full instruction set, or to a wider range of languages and interfaces, or both, the above limitation has seemed too restrictive.

The Burroughs "software" approach to providing system integrity did not solve the general protection problem. Even so, retrospective assessment now suggests that further evolution of the descriptor mechanism with additional hardware support for it, as in architectures like the i432, has indeed led to a solution of this problem.

The failure to solve the general protection problem by prior architectures (descriptor-based or not) has had serious consequences. It has meant, for example, that system software modules must be set apart and explicitly protected from application programs; the former cannot be permitted to *trust* the integrity of in-bound pointer arguments such as descriptors. This disparity has, in turn, made it impractical and unsafe to permit users the freedom to substitute their own versions of selected system modules. A frequent consequence has been that much software within a system tends to be relegated to a small number of very large (monolithic) *protection domains*. This consequence, in turn, leads to high software maintenance costs. We return to this issue later in this section and again in Chapter 6; there we show why and how it is that i432 system solves the general protection problem with the consequent benefit that system software modules are indistinguishable in structure and privilege from user-written application programs. The important conclusion one should draw is that the user's interface to the i432 operating system is significantly different than in other systems built on conventional architectures. In particular, all system modules can, in principle, be safely revised by users or replaced with other versions tailored to specific user needs. Protection domains are usually small, but in any case are type-specific, i.e., related to the type managed within that domain, rather than to a variety of available and possibly ad hoc protection mechanisms.

Before proceeding too much further with our discussion of the i432 addressing structure, we first distinguish between the terms *object* and *segment*. (Later, we drop this distinction.) An object is referenced only by a capability; a segment is referenced only by a mapping table entry. In i432 terminology, a capability, consisting of an access authorization part plus a reference to a mapping table entry, is called an *Access Descriptor*, or just AD. The access authorization part of an AD is referred to as the *access rights* of the AD. Finally, the mapping table is called an *Object Table* and the mapping table entry is called an *Object Descriptor*. We will use this new terminology from this point forward when discussing the i432 architecture specifically.

Normally, an object-based architecture is designed so that the hardware is aware of and maintains the access authorization part of a capability and the mapping table itself. The machine maintains only a single copy of the mapping table entry for a given segment, this being is a crucial restriction. However, there may be multiple copies of the capability, since two or more program components may require access to the same object, possibly with different sets of authorizations.

Processing a reference to an object by a capability is achieved in steps; the ingenuity of the architect/implementor is challenged to achieve these steps as rapidly as possible:

1. Fetch the access authorization part of the capability (the access rights) and check that the coded authorization therein permits access to the object. (The check is based on current state information available to the processor.)

2. Determine the location of the mapping table entry (the Object Descriptor) for the capability by using the logical mapping table entry address encoded within the capability. The *logical address* is usually a (mapping table name, offset) pair. The mapping table name is used to reference a particular mapping table; the offset designates a specific mapping table entry within that mapping table. From the information in the mapping table entry, the base address of the segment can be obtained.

[Speed-up of this two-step process is usually achieved with some kind of caching scheme that relies on a high probability, due to the presumed ''locality of reference'', that the same capability or the same Object Descriptor has been referenced very recently. The i432 provides small, on-chip, storage caches for this type of information. More details may be found by consulting the i432 Architecture Reference Manual.]

Figure 4-1 illustrates, using i432 terminology, the relationships between Access Descriptors, Object Table entries, and segments—hereafter called *objects*. The figure shows two Access Descriptors, containing possibly different access rights, each referencing the same Object Descriptor, which in turn points to the target object.

The structure suggested in Figure 4-1 typically arises as a result of executing ''create object'' operations in the following way: An object T is created. In this creation process, a block of free storage space of the required length is committed for T, and an Object Descriptor providing the physical memory location of the base of T is placed into a table, referred to as an *Object Table*. (An Object Table is simply a directory or list of similar Object Descriptors.) Next, a valid Access Descriptor (or AD) to T (referencing the new Object Descriptor) is formed and deposited into an AD slot specified as an output argument of the ''create object'' operation. In the i432, this entire procedure is accomplished as a single, indivisible instruction. The Access Descriptor for the created object is returned with all meaningful access rights turned on. This Access Descriptor uniquely identifies the object it references; the hardware prevents a user from altering the AD so as to designate a different object. Hence ADs cannot be accidentally altered or forged.

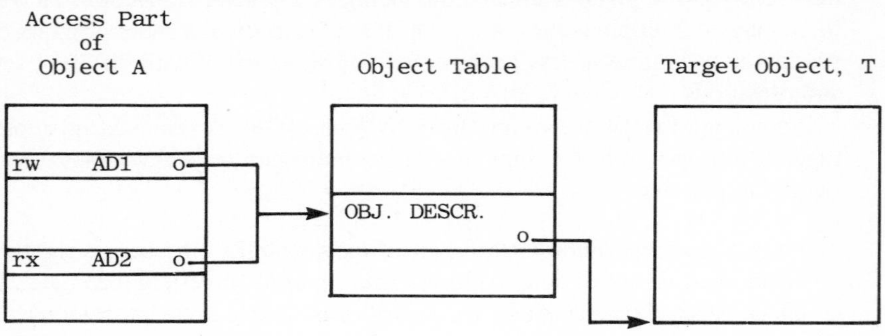

Figure 4-1 A low-level view of the accessing mechanism for a target object, T. Access Descriptors, AD1 and AD2, have distinct access rights to T. Both AD's refer to the same Object Descriptor, which is located in a table of Object Descriptors. (The latter is itself an object whose absolute location may be thought of as determined from a table supplied at system initialization.) Access rights in AD1 are "rw", meaning read and write, Access rights in AD2 are "rx", meaning read only. In the above, "x" refers to a missing right.

Some architectural designs restrict the allowable locations at which capabilities can be stored. This is the case in the i432 architecture, where Access Descriptors may be deposited only in that part of an object known as its *access part*. In this implementation, moreover, only Access Descriptors may be deposited in the access part of an object, as suggested in Figure 4-1.

An i432 object is represented as a contiguous block of storage partitioned into two parts: a *data part* and an *access part*. Each of these parts can contain up to a maximum of 2**16 bytes; each part or both parts can be empty. Later in this section we discuss further the partitioning of i432 objects and the means for controlled access to information in each part of an object.

Associated with every i432 object is a *type*; this type is stored in a location in the Object Descriptor that is known to and accessible by the i432 hardware. The hardware recognizes many of the possible object types as being of special significance; objects carrying one of these special types are known as *system objects*. Most system objects have both a data part and an access part. There are several i432 system objects used to maintain the execution time environment of active programs. For example, Context Objects and Process Objects are both system objects that are used to control the execution of i432 programs. A *Context Object* is used to represent the activation record for a function or procedure. A *Process Object* contains the attributes of a process, e.g., an Ada task, that are required to schedule it, to dispatch it, to perform recovery if it faults, and to allow it to communicate with other processes. A Process Object serves as the root node of the object structure representing an active process.

Note that, although an i432 AD can be copied, it cannot be created, except in connection with the creation of an object of some type T (or of a "refinement" of such an object—as explained later). Also, since an AD cannot be altered to designate a different object than the one for which it is created, a type manager for type T objects can be certain of the integrity of all ADs for objects of type T passed to it as arguments for operations on type T objects. This assurance of AD integrity and authenticity is crucial to the implementation of type-specific protection domains. Chapter 6 completes the presentation of this reasoning along with the necessary details on the i432's hardware support for object access and type control.

We can imagine the genesis of Figure 4-1 as follows: Suppose that the creation of object T results in the creation of AD1 with both *read* and *write* access rights. At some later time, a procedure may be invoked to copy AD1, thus creating AD2. The copied access descriptor (AD2) will have access rights restricted to a subset of the rights of the original Access Descriptor (AD1). Note that AD2 need not be stored into the same object as AD1.

Additional objects may be dynamically created and thus added to the collection of address spaces active during the execution of a program. For example, Figure 4-2 shows how the structure in Figure 4-1, in which AD2 is copied from AD1 minus AD1's *write* rights, might be augmented with the addition of a newly created, second target object. Again, purely for convenience, we show all the Access Descriptors in Figure 4-2 in the same object.

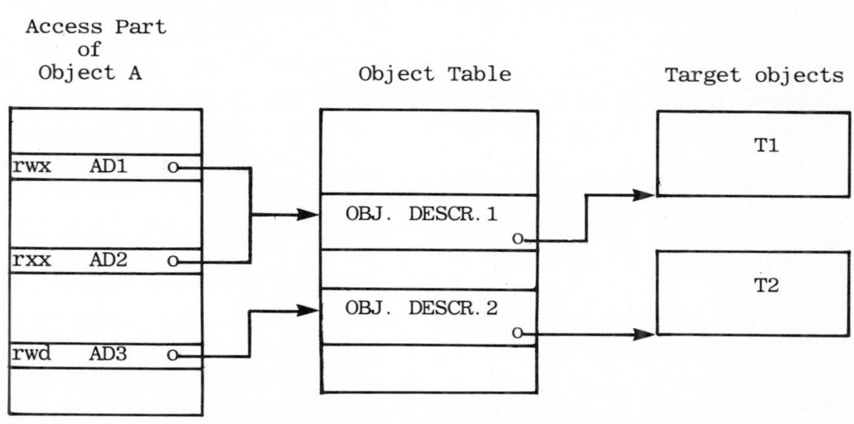

Figure 4-2 Address space structure of Figure 4-1 augmented with the addition of another object whose Access Descriptor, AD3 has *read*, *write*, and *delete* rights.

In Figure 4-2, we introduce "delete rights" as a third access right encoded in an Access Descriptor (*delete* grants the owner the right to delete this AD, i.e., the right to store a new AD (or a null AD) over an AD to be deleted). We see that some access rights associated with an AD refer to the AD itself, rather than to the object referenced by the AD. Thus, *delete* rights refers to a right to delete the AD, rather than to delete any elements in the object referred to by the AD.

As we will see below, a possible side effect of deleting an i432 Access Descriptor, ADx, is the reclamation of the storage space occupied by object T referred to by the Access Descriptor ADx (and, potentially, other objects referenced by T.) The architect must be unusually careful in selecting rules by which Access Descriptors may be formed, copied, moved and deleted. Discovering consistent, useful, and safe sets of such rules has been the subject of intense research for at least ten years [33] [58] [60] [65].

We postpone until Chapter 6 a detailed discussion of rules selected by the i432 architects. Instead, we will mention such rules in passing, as they become relevant in our discussions. For example, a hardware fault is invoked if an attempt is made to delete an Access Descriptor that does not have its delete rights bit set.

It is interesting to note how deletion of i432 Access Descriptors is related to deallocation of objects. The storage space for an object X becomes a candidate for deallocation by the i432 System's garbage collector when X is *unreachable*, i.e., either nowhere are there are any ADs that reference X or all ADs that do reference X reside in objects that are themselves unreachable. [There are several objects that are special and are defined always to be *reachable*; these special objects, recognizable by the i432 hardware, are called *Processor Objects*.] Object T2, illustrated in Figure 4-2, would be a candidate for garbage collection if AD3 were the only Access Descriptor referring to T2 and AD3 is overwritten with another, possibly null, Access Descriptor. In this situation, the i432 System's garbage collector would eventually deallocate T2, resulting in the structure originally given by Figure 4-1. [It is also possible for objects belonging to circular lists to be deallocated, even though there is one Access Descriptor referring to each object in the list. Such a circular list, CL, would be deallocated by the garbage collector when no other Access Descriptor external to CL refers to an object within CL [12].]

In short, at the hardware level a delete right of an AD is simply the right to overwrite it. Exercising the delete right has indirect consequences for object deallocation that must be handled at the software level.

Earlier we indicated that an i432 object is logically and physically partitioned into a data part and an access part. Here we introduce some of the details of accessing and addressing elements within objects. We wish to satisfy the reader's curiosity; and having done so, then use abstractions when they seem appropriate. Figure 4-3 is offered to clarify the structure of an i432 object and the means for accessing information within it.

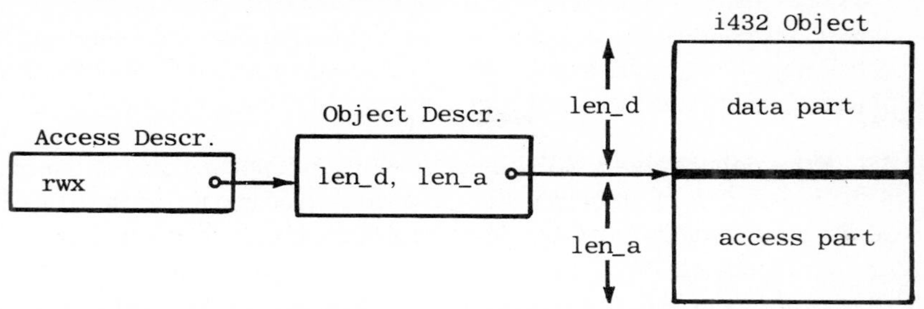

Figure 4-3 First detailed view of an i432 object, showing its data part and access parts. The Object Descriptor contains the base address of the object and the lengths of both the data and access parts, len_d and len_a, either of which may be zero.]

Every i432 instruction fetches its input operands (if any) from some location within an object (in memory) and delivers its output result (if any) back to some location within an object (in memory). This approach is contrasted with almost every other computer architecture in existence today, in which intermediate data registers hold (at least one of) the operands for or the result of an instruction. In these classical architectures the contents of the intermediate data registers are loaded from or stored into memory locations by instructions distinct from the instructions that operate on the data in the registers. An i432 instruction can have zero, one, two, or three operands; each of these operands addresses a location within an object in which the operand resides or will reside.

The i432 processor interprets a *data operand* of an instruction (which is a logical address) as a two-part value, consisting of an *object selector* and a *displacement*. The object selector specifies a distinct Access Descriptor for the object. The displacement is then used by the microcode as an appropriate offset from the base address of the object, as indicated in the object selector, in arriving at a physical address of the target element to be accessed. [Readers wishing more details can find them in the iAPX 432 Architecture Reference Manual that is cited in Appendix B.] Whether the operand reference is to a data value or to an AD, the processor induces a fault whenever the specified displacement into a target object violates the bounds limit given in its Object Descriptor (len_a or len_d, whichever applies.)

Possession of an AD for an object implies the same set of access rights both to the data part and to the access part of the object. *Read/write* access rights for the access part of an object are to be understood as follows: If an Access Descriptor, AD, for a target object, T, has *read* rights, then AD can be used to copy (read) any Access Descriptor in T. If the same AD has *write* rights, then AD can be used to replace (write) any Access Descriptor in T that has *delete* rights.

Before closing this primer on i432 object-space structures, we first introduce certain conventions for indexing into, for displaying, and for discussing structures such as Figures 4-2 and 4-3. We then introduce the concept of Refinement Objects, how they are accessed, and how they may be diagrammed.

4.1.1.1. More details about i432 objects. When referencing an AD that resides in the access part of an object, the specified displacement (measured in 32-bit words) is *subtracted* from the base address of the object. Thus, Access Descriptors are numbered AD0, AD1, AD2, . . . , *downward* from the dividing line between the data and access parts. When referencing into the data part of an object, the displacement of a data field (measured in bytes) is *added* to the base of the object. Part (a) of Figure 4-4 illustrates these relationships.

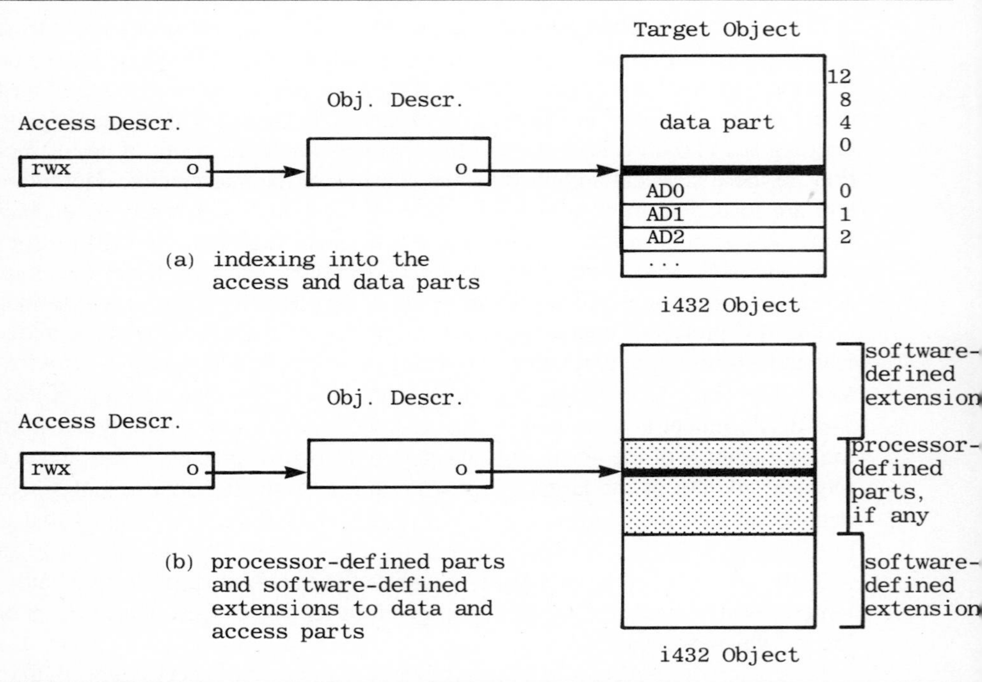

Figure 4-4 A more detailed look at an i432 object.

The lowest-indexed portion of the access part or data part, or both, of an object may be predefined by the various i432 processors. (This is true for all system objects.) For such objects, the higher-indexed regions of the object are regarded as *software-defined* (or user-defined) extensions. We illustrate this key point in part (b) of Figure 4-4. Clearly, deciding what information is to be kept in the processor-defined regions of an object can greatly affect the performance of the system as a whole. This point is addressed frequently later in this chapter.

Access to any target requires traversal from an Access Descriptor, via a particular Object Descriptor, to the target. However, for most matters of interest to us, it is quite unimportant to note this intermediate traversal step. Hence, we may adopt a simpler diagrammatic convention, which shows Access Descriptors pointing directly to their respective targets. Figure 4-5 shows the shorthand equivalent for Figure 4-2. We lose no significant generality with the use of this abstraction for the level of discourse used in most of this book.

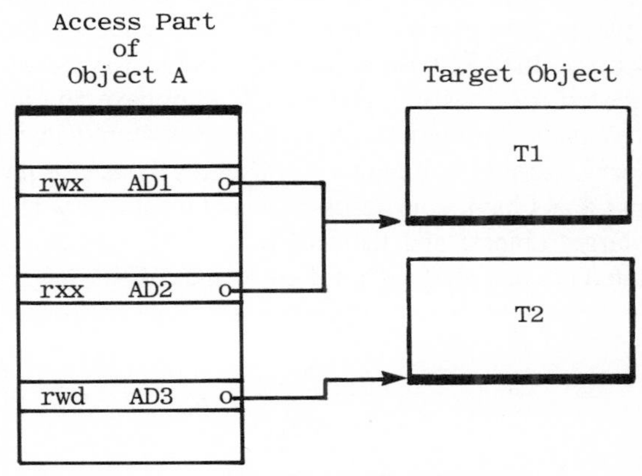

Figure 4-5 Schematic view of accessing structure for objects T1 and T2. The access part of object A holds two different Access Descriptors for T1 and one Access Descriptor for T2.

4.1.1.2. Access paths to Refinement Objects. It is often desirable to create a new object that is, in fact, a physical subobject of another (parent) object. The data part and access part of the subobject must be subparts of the data part and access part, respectively, of the parent object. That the subobject physically resides within its parent object is reflected in the fact that the subobject is defined in terms relative to the parent object. Each part of the subobject is defined to be of some (possibly different) size and to reside at some (possibly different) offset from the base address of the parent object.

For example, one might wish to represent an "actual parameter block" for a procedure call as a subobject within the object representing the current activation record. Each argument that matches a "by-reference" parameter must be represented by an AD that references the actual parameter. (In many cases this AD can reference a refinement of another object representing an activation record.) Such parameters must reside in the access part of the subobject. Any parameters that represent access values (for example, a variable of access type that is passed "by-value") must also reside in the access part of the subobject. Any remaining (data) parameters must reside in the data part of the same parent. Note that we wish to regard the actual parameter block as a single logical object.

The challenge to efficiently represent and control access to subobjects, has an elegant solution in the i432 System. The architecture provides a *Refinement Descriptor* mechanism to efficiently implement the concept of a subobject, as discussed above. A subobject is defined by a Refinement Descriptor which is inserted in the access path between an Access Descriptor and the Object Descriptor for the parent object.

A Refinement Descriptor contains the thirty-two bit data image of the AD for the parent object, a length and an offset value for each of the two parts of the subobject. In i432 terminology, a subobject is called a *Refinement Object*. As suggested previously, a Refinement may have an empty data part or an empty access part. Refinement Descriptors are stored in Object Tables, along with Object Descriptors. Figure 4-6 illustrates the access path to the base of a Refinement Object having an access part and a data part. The offsets (from the base of the target object) and the lengths of each part of the Refinement Object are denoted by the pairs, (off_a, len_a) and (off_d, len_d), respectively.

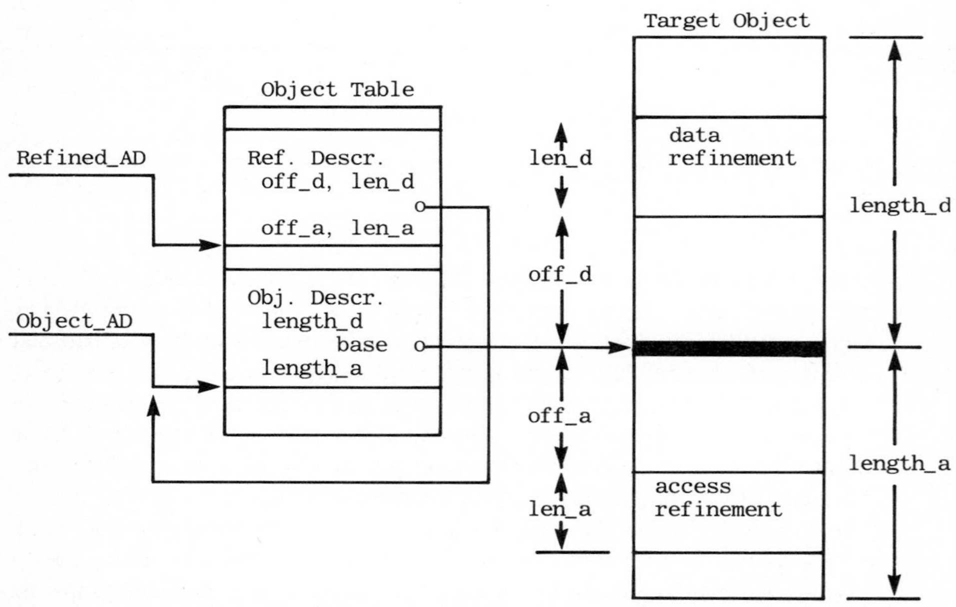

Figure 4-6 Refinement Descriptor as a prefix to an Object Descriptor. Access to the refinement is made using Refined_AD, while access to the full Object is made using Object_AD.

Several important applications of the refinement mechanism are exploited by the 432-Ada compiler. For example, we will see in more detail in Section 4-4 that the public part of an Ada package is accessed as a refinement of a *Domain Object* that represents the union of the public and private parts of the package. The compiler ensures that every external reference to a package has access only to that collection of information accessible via the public part refinement. Thus, the i432 hardware is able to enforce Ada package (i432 domain) privacy. More importantly, by means of refinements the i432 hardware is able to enforce privacy over domains that are created at execution time. This scheme is illustrated in Figure 4-7.

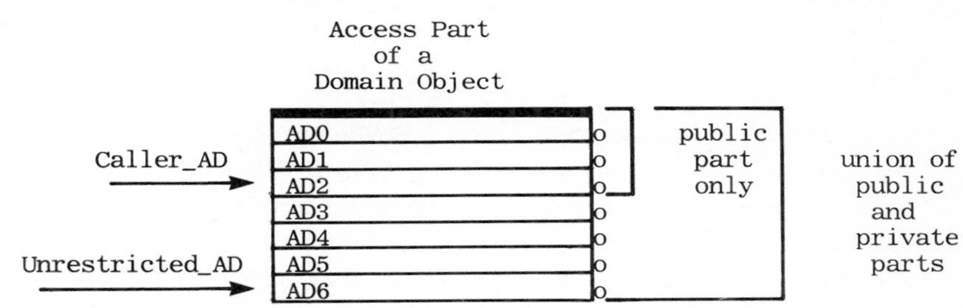

Figure 4-7 Diagrammatic representation illustrating overlapping subspaces within the same object. Here, the subspace accessed by Caller_AD is a refinement of the host object accessed by Unrestricted_AD. The specific application occurs when distinguishing between the public and public-plus-private parts of an Ada package domain.

4.1.2. Run-Time Program Structures

The foregoing preliminaries provide us with a framework in which we can more fully appreciate i432 run-time program structures. We consider here only the execution of single-task Ada programs, such as illustrated in Figure 2-2; we defer until Chapter 5 a discussion of the program structures that arise during execution of multitask programs. First we consider the condition of a program after it has been compiled, and prior to its execution.

A compiled program normally resides in the inactive state in the passive address space of the i432's Object Filing Subsystem [47]. The structure of the compiled program is generally the same as that for the data objects on which the program will operate: a directed graph (grouped into a *composite* within the Object Filing Subsystem). One node of this directed graph is special; it represents the program's root node. The root node corresponds to the object structure that represents the domain in which the program's initial (starter) task must execute. References within this root structure point to substructures, such as, for example, other Domain Objects representing various packages that may be called at run time.

In the case of a program like the one suggested in Figure 2-2, the compiler would notice that the Secretary_Treas starter task and the several packages are not embedded within the starter task, but are rather separate units at the same Ada "library level." The compiler, therefore, generates a separate program structure unit (grouped as a composite object) for each library-level compilation and files it in the passive object space (permanent memory) of the Object Filing Subsystem.

The Object Filing Subsystem permits the protection mechanisms to be extended in the i432 system from "volatile" memory to permanent memory. The Object Filing Subsystem merits a separate study in itself, however, and this is done in Chapter 10.

When a user's program is invoked by the operating system, the various inactive program structure units are activated as needed. By "activated", we mean brought from passive (object filing) memory space into active (i432 virtual) memory space.

As already mentioned, an active program is represented by networks (directed graphs) of *Domain Objects*; this network represents primarily the "static" components of the program unit. A Domain Object consists of a set of ADs and a set of data; the ADs reference Instruction Objects, an object for user-generated literal constants, user AD variables, etc., and the set of data containing domain control information, user data variables, etc. Also, if a package represented by the Domain Object D contains calls to other packages, then D will also contain ADs for the Domain Objects corresponding to those other packages.

Access to a Domain Object D is controlled by the Ada compiler, because the compiler limits the generation of Access Descriptors for D (or for any refinement of D) to those Ada program units that have declared the need to access the corresponding Ada package for D. Ada packages that declare the need to access another package P are those packages that include P in their **with** list.

Domain Objects for Ada library level packages that own variable data, as does Club_Portfolio, are not entirely static in nature. Values of data variables contained in such a Domain Object may vary from one activation of the Domain Object to the next. For example, each separate use of the investment club program may result in an alteration of the data owned by Club_Portfolio. When a program containing an Ada library level package P, represented by domain D, completes, then domain D must be deactivated. This implies that any owned variable values within D that were modified during the time D was active now has to be updated within the older, passive version of D. This assurance is needed so that future activations of D will reflect changes that occurred during the most recent activation of D.

[Notice that it is the responsibility of the Object Filing System to maintain the passive version of Club_Portfolio's Domain Object in a consistent form. Thus, the Object Filing System possesses some of the functionality of a data management system, performing database management at the level of the operating system! (We amplify this important observation in Chapter 10.)]

To execute a program at command level, an operating system module prepares an initial run-time object structure that represents the program. Then, a message, in the form of a reference (Access Descriptor) to this structure, is sent to a *Dispatching Port*, first mentioned in Chapter 1. At this port, the message is bound to a processor for execution. We discuss these details in the next chapter. Here, we focus on what constitutes the initial run-time object structure for the program and what is involved in forming it.

To create an initial run-time object structure, the operating system first creates a Process Object for the program and attaches to it a Context Object, the first of a list of fixed-size Context Objects that are preallocated for the process. The first Context Object serves as the initial addressing environment or activation record needed for execution of an initial procedure. Part of this addressing environment is an AD to the root Domain Object, discussed below. A schematic of this structure is given in Figure 4-8. The reference Process_AD is the message referred to in the preceding paragraph. Note that one such structure is formed for each task, including the ''starter task'', of every Ada program.

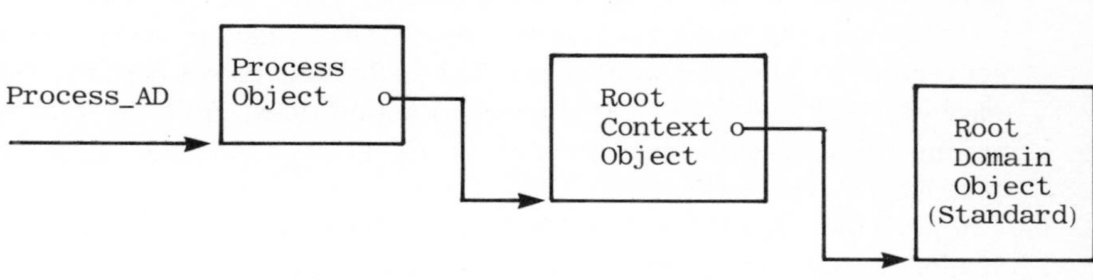

Figure 4-8 Initial Object structure for a program ready for execution—many details still missing.

The domain associated with the initial procedure of a task is called the *root Domain Object*. The root Domain Object was produced earlier by the compiler from an Ada source program and filed in the passive object space. The operating system locates this object via a call on the Object Filing Subsystem, by supplying the program name and relevant directory information. Upon retrieval, the Domain Object is activated and a reference to it (Access Descriptor) is placed in the initial Context Object as another step toward completing the necessary addressing environment. Further steps of this nature are taken to fully initialize the needed addressing environment before actual program execution can begin. Among these is the allocation of a block of free storage space whose size is predetermined by the operating system.

[If a program cannot run to completion with its initial storage allocation, the operating system provides the additional space during execution of the program.]

Each Context Object contains an operand stack and space for local variables. The block of free space is used to allocate a number of other kinds of objects, such as objects for Ada's dynamic arrays. Some of these objects may be automatically deallocated upon execution of relevant RETURN instructions. Context Objects are preallocated by the operating system before a process begins execution. As the process executes, a pointer to the current context moves back and forth through this list of preallocated Context Objects. Thus, Context Objects are not physically deallocated until storage for the process itself is deallocated (by becoming unreachable).

Management of a block of free storage space strictly specific to a process is facilitated by associating with its Process Object a data structure called the *stack SRO*. An SRO, an abbreviation for Storage Resource Object, models a "bank savings account", provided with some initial deposit amount (of free space). An SRO includes a component that models a "bank book." That component is used for keeping track of the balance of free address space available to this process.

The "bank book" component records the beginning and ending addresses of the uncommitted portion of the original block of free storage awarded to the process. A procedure activation may lead to the dynamic allocation of objects needed for use with the current Context Object. Such allocation results in withdrawal of space from the bank book. Return from a called procedure results in recovery of this allocated space (a redeposit in the bank book). Note that storage space occupied by the Context Object is not itself drawn from the stack SRO, but rather is allocated from a *global heap SRO* in much the same manner as the space for the Process Object.

Besides the use of the stack SRO, an executing program may request the creation of other storage bank accounts, called *local heap SROs*. These Storage Resource Objects define pools of storage space from which objects may be allocated dynamically in non-LIFO order, as required by the program in execution. In an Ada program, for example, a local heap SRO is created upon entering a procedure in which types are declared for variables whose assigned values require dynamic allocation of storage space, for example, Ada **access** types. A local heap SRO is created to supply the storage requirements (other than for the Process and Context Objects), for each spawned task. Recovery of local heap objects occurs automatically when the thread of control exits from the procedure activation at which the local heap was created. However, prior to exit from that procedure activation, space within such a heap may be recovered by the System's on-the-fly garbage collector process. (The deallocation mechanisms for local heap objects are described in Chapter 9.)

The process in execution also has access to a global heap SRO, from which objects may be allocated that have *unbounded lifetimes*. These objects are also reclaimed by the same garbage collector when no longer reachable. We expand on this model governing the management of process memory in Chapter 9. See also [34,48].

We are now ready to examine the Process, Context, and Domain Objects in more detail. And, we do this in the next three sections.

4.2. The Process Object

A Process Object, which is created for each process, and hence for each Ada task, has the composite structure shown in Figure 4-9. To gain speed and access control, an internal processor register (Process Object Register) serves as a dedicated pointer to the currently executing Process Object. This register, which is never directly addressable, is loaded when a process is dispatched (i.e., when a Process Object is bound to a processor.)

The offset of each descriptor and data item in the Process Object is fixed, so it can be known to the hardware logic, microcode, software, or to some combination of these. Many of the items we identify within key system objects have offsets that are known to the microcode and to the operating system.

[Preplanning the offsets of individual items within system objects is a non-trivial job that, in theory, carries considerable risk of introducing too much complexity or inflexibility, but which, in practice, offers a high enough payoff in the efficiency of both the software and hardware to be indispensable. Advances in high-level microcode languages, and high-level system implementation languages like Ada, are keys to the success of this approach.]

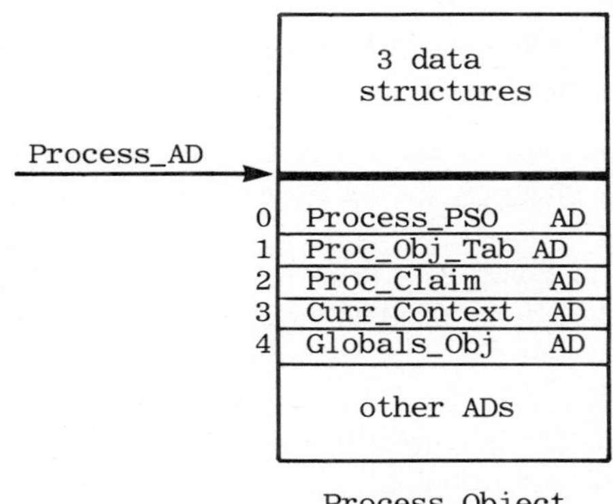

Figure 4-9 First view of a Process Object. Individual parts of the object are discussed in the text.)

The access part of a Process Object, as suggested in Figure 4-9, holds two main sets of Access Descriptors. One set, not detailed here, is related to interprocess message-based communication and dispatching. The other set, detailed in Figure 4-9, is:

0. a reference to the *Physical Storage Object* Component (or PSO) of the stack SRO
1. a reference to the *Object Table* Component of the stack SRO
2. a reference to the *Claim Object* Component of the stack SRO
3. a reference to the *Current Context Object*
4. a reference to the *Process Globals Object*

The data structure representing an SRO contains three principal components. These are the PSO, the Object Table, and the Claim Object. The first three Access Descriptors in the Process Object refer to this set of three components for the stack SRO of the process.

- The Physical Storage Object (PSO), which is the bank book component, holds the set of physical addresses representing boundaries for blocks of unused storage of the SRO.
- The Object Table component holds Object Descriptors and Refinement Descriptors for objects created from the free space controlled by the SRO. For a stack SRO, space for these objects is allocated and deallocated in LIFO (Last-In/First-Out) order, and hence the corresponding PSO component contains only a single pair of physical addresses, namely the beginning and ending points of currently unused storage.
- The Claim Object component holds the value representing the total amount of storage as yet unallocated from this SRO.

The AD in the Process Object that designates the current Context Object is continually changing during the execution of a program as procedure calls are made. At the outset, the current context is the root context mentioned in connection with Figure 4-8. Prior to execution, the operating system initializes a doubly-linked list of Context Objects, headed by the root context, that will normally constitute the local addressing environment for Ada procedures. During program execution, as procedure calls are made, the AD in the Process Object that designates the current context designates different Context Objects in the preallocated list by simply moving back and forth through the forward and backward links of the doubly-linked preallocated list. (There are, of course, mechanisms in place for handling overflow of this list of Context Objects.) Thus, the Access Descriptor for the current context is ''kept current'' in the Process Object; this facilitates restarting a process, in case it was previously suspended for any reason.

[As we will see later, the current Context Object itself contains the instruction and stack pointers which must be reloaded into processor registers before actual resumption of execution can take place. Keeping the Current Context Object AD up to date in the Process Object also facilitates process-level fault recovery.]

An important protection mechanism, related to the creation of objects by a process, is provided in an Object Table entry. When any object is created from an SRO, the level of the current context is recorded in the Object Descriptor as the level number for the created object. (The level number of the current context, or *context level*, is the length of the chain of Context Objects from and including the root context up to and including the current context.) Lifetimes of created objects correspond to their respective level numbers; the higher the level number, the shorter the lifetime. (An object created from a global heap SRO is always given the level number zero.)

The level number of an object is used by the hardware to ensure that no Access Descriptor D references an object of level number j if D resides within an object of level number $i < j$. Such potential *dangling references* are automatically prevented by a hardware prohibition that an AD for an object with a given level number (shorter lifetime) may not be stored into the access part of an object that has a lower level number (longer lifetime.)

The Process Globals Object (PGO) is a read-only object that can be shared by all contexts within a process. A single i432 instruction, executed within any context, is sufficient to place the contents of the Process Globals Object in the directly addressable space of the processor. [We explain how this is done in Section 4-3.]

The particular role of the PGO is left to be defined, usually by the operating system. For example, in the first release of the i432 operating system (iMAX), the PGO is filled in with references to a number of objects that are required by the Ada compiler in the execution of Ada programs. An important purpose of the PGO is to contain a reference to the global heap SRO. This reference is needed when an executing program needs to create an object having an unbounded lifetime, such as one destined to become a passive file. We have more to say about global heap SROs in Chapter 9. More details on the PGO may be found in the iMAX 432 Reference Manual that is cited in Appendix B.

The data part of a Process Object consists of three distinct areas:

1. Process Control Area
2. Process Fault Area
3. Context Fault Area

A brief explanation for each of the above items follows:

1. The Process Control Area includes a collection of information needed for the management of a process. Some values are used for scheduling, while others are used by the hardware or software for process-related storage management and fault recovery. Among the values included here are: the current level number, a process clock value, service period and service count values, the process' own ID, and the process' status. (Process scheduling is a topic discussed at some length in Chapter 5 and again in Chapter 8.)

   All of the above information is prefixed by the Object Lock, which is used by the hardware or software to lock the entire Process Object, when necessary, to guarantee against harmful ''interaction'' with another processor while performing examination or manipulation of any part of the Process Object. [This lock also governs access to all Context Objects associated with this Process Object.]

2. Process Fault Area. When the hardware detects a fault at the process level (a fault such that the process may not proceed until repaired by another process), the hardware deposits certain fault code and state information in the Process Fault Area. Recovery from a process-level fault involves sending the Process Object as a message to another process which is expected to know how to respond to this fault.

3. Context Fault Area. If a context level fault (roughly equivalent to an Ada **exception**) should occur, there is a similar fault information area in the current Context Object into which the processor will deposit the appropriate information. Repair of a context level fault is normally delegated to a procedure within the same process. However, provision must be made for the possible occurrence of another context level fault while attempting to repair the first. This case is handled by depositing the new context fault information in the Context Fault Data Area of the Process Object, thereby promoting this second sequential context level fault to process level. The processor knows when to perform this ''promotion'' from information available to it in an on-chip process status register.

We continue our discussion of Process Objects in Chapter 5. Still more detailed information on Process Objects can be found in the i432 Architecture Reference Manual.

4.3. The Context Object

As mentioned earlier, this object plays a very similar role to that of an *activation record* in stack-based run-time data structures for reentrant programs [40, 44]. [Activation records are often called *stack frames* and sometimes called *contours*, especially when dealing with abstractions of activation records [32, 46].]

Unlike classical implementation strategies for activation record management, each activation record in the i432 is a separate Context Object, with hardware means to protect it from inappropriate access by a processor executing either the current program or any other program. In most classical implementations, activation records are stacked into one contiguous block of storage. Access controls are, at best, maintained for the whole block and not for the individual activation records within it.

Figure 4-10 provides us with our first view of a Context Object. Again, we note that the offsets within the access and data parts are known to the microcode. Moreover, as a means for speeding access to current context information, an internal processor register, the Context Object Register, is provided in the processor to hold an AD for the current Context Object.

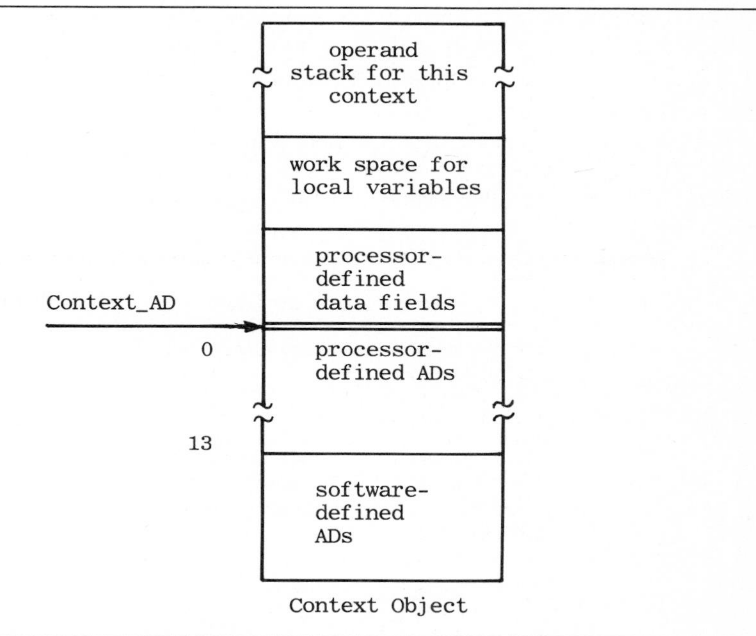

Figure 4-10 Initial view of a Context Object

In the discussions that follow, we will see that a major role of the Context Object is to serve as a receptacle for hardware state information characterizing a program executing in a given procedure activation. Slots of the Context Object designated to hold this information serve as storage images for values in a set of on-chip processor registers. In order to correctly preserve the storage image during each call (return) to (from) a context, microinstruction sequences store (load) processor state information into/from the Context Object.

4.3.1. Details of the Context Object

We begin our discussion of the Context Object by looking first at the key Access Descriptors that lie at the base of the access part. These fourteen descriptors can be grouped into four categories:

1. ADs that define the processor's current addressing environment
2. ADs to key objects of the executing program
3. ADs to relevant messages (intercontext or interprocess)
4. ADs to objects at the "top" of the stack SRO

Table 4-1 lists the individual ADs in each category and the slots to which they are assigned. We give an explanation of each of these ADs in the order listed in the table. The purpose of some of these ADs may be obvious to readers with experience in stack-based architectures. Even so, we present an explanation of the use of each of these ADs. In some cases, the full significance of the reference may not be clear until later. Some of the references are "constants", deposited into the Context Object as part of the procedure entry semantics (ADs 0, 1, 8, and 9.) Some of the others (ADs 5, 6, 7, 10, and 11) are deposited with delete bit reset so that they cannot be modified by the user.

TABLE 4-1. Processor-Defined Access Descriptors in the Context Object

Category	Access Descriptor Target		Slot Index
1	Current Context	(self reference)	0
	Access Environment 1		5
	Access Environment 2		6
	Access Environment 3		7
2	Defining Domain	(current domain)	3
	Calling Context	("dynamic chain link")	8
	Static Link	("static chain link")	13
	Global Constants		1
	Local Constants		4
3	Context Message	(parameter list)	2
	Precreated Message	(argument list)	9
	Interprocess Message		12
4	Top of Descriptor Stack	(top Descriptor)	10
	Top of Storage Stack	(top Object Descriptor)	11

1. ADs that define the processor's current addressing environment.
   - The Current Context AD slot holds a self reference. This slot is assigned a value when the current Context Object is initialized in the course of executing a CALL instruction. (The hardware prevents assignment of a new value to this slot as long as this Context Object remains active, that is,

until a RETURN instruction has been executed from the procedure whose call resulted in the creation of this Context Object.)

The value of the Current Context AD forms the root of the tree representing the processor's current addressing environment. Whenever the processor executes a CALL or RETURN instruction, it loads a copy of this value into its Context Register. Upon executing a RETURN, the processor restores in its Context Register the value of the Current Context AD of the predecessor Context Object.

Upon completion of a CALL, the processor's "on-chip" Context Register also has a copy of the same (new) Context Object AD. The Context Register, which is never directly addressable, is used indirectly as an operand in a variety of instructions that require access to references contained in the Context Object. As we will see, the *current directly addressable* space of the processor is defined in terms of exactly four sets of primary references, one of these being the set contained in the Context Object.

- ADs for Access Environments 1, 2, and 3. The values in these AD slots, which can be set (repeatedly) during execution within the current context, define the other three sets of primary references for the processor. A new value assigned to one of the three Access Environment AD slots has the affect of dynamically altering the current directly addressable space. Such alteration is achieved by executing an ENTER ACCESS ENVIRONMENT (or ENTER GLOBAL) instruction, identifying the Access Environment slot that is to receive a specified AD. The important indirect effect of executing one of these instructions is to copy the same specified AD value into a corresponding on-chip Entry Register.

  [We are now able to explain more fully how the addressability of the processor is controlled. Recall that every operand reference (both data and access references) of an i432 instruction must specify some form of *access selector* that references the AD for the object in which the operand resides. The encoding of an access selector includes a two-bit field that designates one of four environment registers (Context Register, or Entry Registers 1, 2, or 3.) Therefore, the only objects that the processor can access are those whose ADs reside within the objects that are referred to in the four environment registers.]

  Since the ADs for exactly four objects define the directly addressable space, and since the access parts of each of these Objects can, in principle, hold 2**14 AD's and since each object addressed by one of these AD's can have up to 2**16 bytes in its data part, directly addressable data space is 2**32 bytes. Directly accessible AD space is 4*(2**14) Access Descriptors.

  An ENTER ACCESS ENVIRONMENT (or ENTER GLOBAL) instruction indicates by operands specified in the instruction which of the three registers is to be updated and which of the 4*(2**14) directly addressable AD's is to be loaded into that register. Indeed, refreshing the addressable space in this way is the technique which must be used in the i432 when "chasing" a reference chain, some or all of whose AD links are not contained within the 4*(2**14) directly accessible ADs.

When a RETURN instruction is executed, the processor's directly addressable space is restored to that of the predecessor context by restoring into the Context Register and into Entry Registers 1, 2, and 3, the AD values saved in the corresponding slots of the predecessor Context Object. The values in these AD slots also provide important pieces of state information needed to recover from a fault that occurs in a successor context.

2. References to key objects of this program.
   - Defining Domain Object AD. This slot is filled with a reference to the current Domain Object in which the AD for the currently executing instruction object resides. This is the primary Domain Object that will be accessed during active use of this Context Object. The hardware prevents assignment of a new value to this slot.

     Various components within the Domain Object may be needed as part of the processor's directly addressable space. A called procedure can make such a component directly addressable by executing an ENTER ACCESS ENVIRONMENT instruction to copy the value of the Current Domain Object AD into one of the Entry Registers. This step is then followed by a reference-chasing step to "fetch up" an AD for a desired target component accessible via the Domain Object. [The processor has a Current Domain Register. Upon executing a CALL instruction that has the effect of changing domains, this register is assigned a new AD value that points to the base of the private part of the new domain. This value remains valid during intradomain calls and is used by the processor to speed up the interpretation of such calls.]
   - The Predecessor Context AD serves simply as a backward (dynamic) link to the previous context and is used, for example, by the microcode in executing a procedure return instruction. This Access Descriptor is formed expressly without *read*, *write*, or *delete* rights. It does, however, carry a *return right*. Only if *return* rights are *on* within an AD used as a dynamic link can a RETURN instruction proceed to completion.

     A Context Object is given a Predecessor Context AD with *return* rights *off* in cases where objects are allocated (from a local heap) at the same level as that of the Context Object. Upon return from this environment, the execution of the RETURN instruction faults, providing a means for a planned escape to a memory management module of the operating system. This module deallocates objects that were allocated at the level of the current Context Object in effect at the time the RETURN instruction was issued.

After this "cleanup" step, the unfinished RETURN instruction is allowed to resume in normal fashion.

Absence of *read* and *write* rights in the predecessor context AD assures that it cannot be used to access information in the calling procedure's context. This is a key component in the overall security strategy of the i432, a subject discussed at greater length in Chapter 6.

- Static Link AD. Static links are maintained by the i432 in the Context Objects for programs written in languages like Ada that use static binding for block structure semantics [45]. When the static link slots in Context Objects are used properly by a compiler, one can be assured that a called procedure is always invoked from the appropriate environment.

  The Access Descriptor in the Static Link slot refers to the (most recent) Context Object for the subprogram (or block) that *statically encloses* the subprogram (or block) for which the current Context Object has been created. Consider the case in which procedure A and procedure B reside immediately enclosed within procedure C. When A is active, the static link for A references the Context Object for the most recent activation of C, regardless of which procedure called A. If A calls B then the new Context Object for B will reference the Context Object for the most recent activation of C with its static link and the immediately previous Context Object for A with its dynamic link.

  [In languages like LISP, Snobol, and APL, which have dynamic binding semantics, the static link may never be normally used; only the dynamic link is used for the purpose of establishing the proper environment of a called procedure. An exception is the so-called "funarg" mechanism in LISP which would use the static link [50]. In languages like Fortran, Basic, and Cobol whose programs need have only one Context Object, the static links are never used; dynamic links would be used only for calls to system library routines.]

- Global Constants AD and Local Constants AD. Unlike most other machines, the i432 does not provide instruction operands for which the value is given directly within the instruction itself. Thus, no operand value can be stored within an instruction; every operand, including constant operands, must come from an object external to an instruction object. Therefore, when a procedure begins execution, one of its first tasks would seem to be to make addressable some object containing local constants for the procedure. But this is impossible, because the ENTER ACCESS ENVIRONMENT instruction, which is the only instruction that can be used (in this situation) to make an object addressable, itself requires a constant operand! From this discussion it can be seen that the i432 must provide a special constant data object that is made addressable by the CALL instruction itself. Every Domain Object contains an AD for a local data object in which constant data values reside for all procedures in the domain. A CALL instruction copies the AD for the local data object from (a known offset in) the Domain Object to the new Context Object as a result of procedure invocation. Thus, the local data object is addressable when the procedure begins execution. In like manner, the CALL instruction provides an AD to a global Constant Object in the new Context Object. The global constants object contains "popular" constants that are likely to be required in every procedure (e.g. the values one and zero). Every executing process in the i432 uses the same global Constant Object. It is provided primarily to prevent the proliferation of the "popular" constants in local data objects throughout the system.

3. References to relevant messages (interprocedure or interprocess).

   - Interprocedure calls may transmit (accept) information to (from) the caller (callee) by means of explicit Message Objects. The message passing mechanism we describe below is used by a compiler to match an argument list prepared by a caller to a parameter list specified by a callee. Two slots, referred to the as *Precreated Message AD* and *Context Message AD* are used to achieve communication between caller and callee contexts.

     When subprogram P prepares to call subprogram Q by means of a CALL instruction, P places the actual parameters for Q in an arbitrary object which will become the *Message Object*, referenced by Access Descriptor M. Following this, M is copied into the precreated message AD slot. When the CALL instruction begins, the precreated message AD must refer to the Message Object. As part of the semantics of the CALL instruction (P calls Q), the Precreated Message AD of P's Context Object is copied into the Context Message AD slot of the Context Object created for Q. Figure 4-11 illustrates the foregoing concept for the case of a chain of two interprocedure calls (P calling Q with message A, and Q calling R with message B.) Note that message objects need not be separate objects; they may, for example, be refinements of other objects. Thus, Message Object A in the figure could actually be a refinement of the Context Object for P.

   - Interprocess Message AD. The third message slot in the Context Object is reserved for receipt of messages from another process. As we will see in the next chapter, execution of the RECEIVE instruction causes the Access Descriptor for a received message to be deposited in the Interprocess Message AD slot.

4. References to objects at the "top" of the stack SRO.

   The LIFO discipline for the (allocation) stack SRO is achieved by maintaining two ADs in each Context Object that reflect the current "state" of the stack SRO for that Context Object. One of these, the Top of Storage Stack AD, references the most recent Object Descriptor formed in the Object

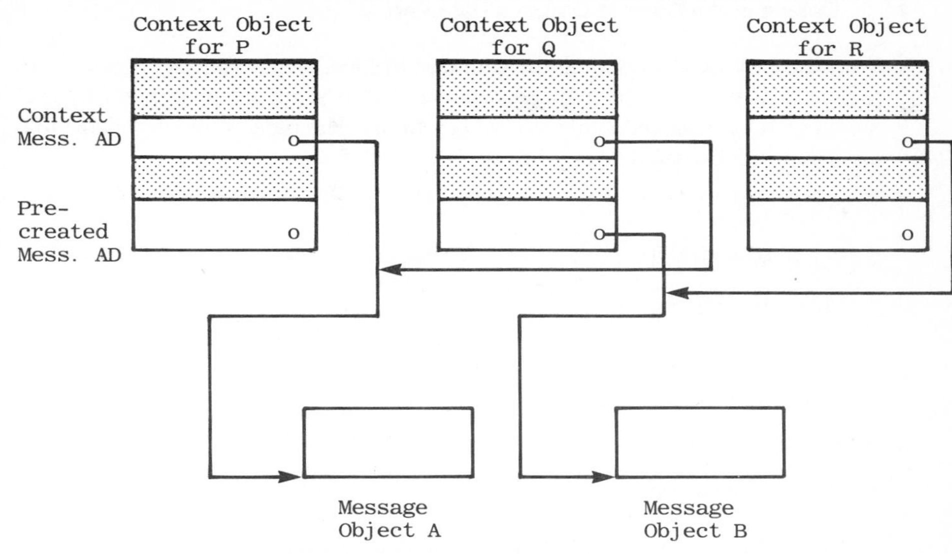

Figure 4-11 Object structures for intercontext message communication.

Table for the stack SRO. The other AD, the Top of Descriptor Stack AD, references the most recent Object Descriptor or Refinement Descriptor formed in the Object Table for the stack SRO. (A Refinement Descriptor is placed in the Object Table for the allocation stack SRO when a refinement is defined for an existing object previously created and allocated from the stack SRO.) The Top of Descriptor Stack AD references the "high water mark" in the Object Table for the allocation stack. The Top of Storage Stack AD references (indirectly through an Object Descriptor) the "high water mark" in allocated physical storage for the stack SRO.

The RETURN instruction does not need to perform any action in order to reclaim storage space and Object Table space from the stack SRO. Since the previous context contains the complete state of the stack SRO in its own Top of Descriptor Stack and Top of Storage Stack ADs and since these two ADs reflected the state of the stack SRO in the previous context at the time of the procedure call, return to the previous context automatically restores the state of the stack SRO for the previous context. (Two kinds of space are recovered using these ADs. The Top of Storage Stack AD is used to recover storage space allocated via the SRO's Physical Storage Object while executing in the current context; the Top of Descriptor Stack is used to reclaim space occupied by Object and Refinement Descriptors formed in the SRO Object Table while executing in the current context.)

4.3.2. Details of the Context Object's Data Part

We now look more closely at the data part of the Context Object. Figure 4-10 indicates there are three major data areas, the first of which is fixed by the architectural design and contains five key fields. The parts of the first data area are listed and discussed briefly below:

1. Context Status
2. Stack Pointer (SP)
3. Current Instruction Object Index
4. Instruction Pointer (IP)—in bits
5. Trace Control Data Area
6. Working Storage
7. Operand Stack

We briefly explain these items in the following paragraphs:

1. The Context Status entry holds two kinds of information:
   a. Fault state information (indicates whether a fault has occurred while executing in this context)
   b. User-supplied processor control codes (for determining precision and rounding modes to be used by the processor during execution in this context). Execution of the SET MODE instruction sets appropriate subfields of the Context Status slot, and automatically updates corresponding control registers of the processor. These registers control the rounding and precision modes for floating point operators. In principle, these mode controls can be turned on and off at any time during execution of a procedure.

2. Stack Pointer (SP). The data part of the Context Object contains the operand stack that is used during the current procedure activation; the SP entry serves as the top-of-stack pointer or offset. SP is initialized, upon entry into the current context to the offset value for the base of the operand stack. This initial value of SP is generated by the compiler and placed in a predetermined slot at the base of the Instruction Object referred to in the CALL instruction. (See next item for more details.)

   When execution in the current context commences, the initial SP value is not only copied into the data part of the Context Object, but is also loaded into a corresponding on-chip processor register. If a processor suspends execution, the processor's SP register value is written into the SP entry in the data part of the current context. Resumption of execution in the context requires the reversal of this information transfer.

3. Current Instruction Object Index. This value is an offset into the access part of the current Domain Object. It identifies the AD of the Instruction Object from which instructions are currently being executed.

   An *Instruction Object* represents the instructions (or a portion of the instructions) that will be executed to perform the actions specified by a procedure. An Instruction Object contains no access part. The data part consists of a set of key data values followed by instructions.

   The data values in the Instruction Object are as follows.

   a. Parameter values to be used in initializing the required Context Object:
      - lengths of the data and access parts
      - offset into the data part used to determine the base of the operand stack
   b. Offset into the access part of the defining Domain Object for this Instruction Object. The slot at this offset holds an AD for the Local Constants Object that is loaded into a slot of the current Context Object as part of the CALL instruction.

4. Instruction Pointer (IP). The IP is a bit offset into the Instruction Object for the currently activated procedure. The initial IP value, like that of the SP value, is placed by the compiler in a slot at the base of the Instruction Object. This value is later copied into the data part of the new Context Object during execution of the CALL instruction.

   The slot in the Context Object reserved for the IP is used to save the processor's copy of the IP during execution of a CALL instruction, or, more generally, for saving the IP whenever the processor suspends execution in this context and needs later to restore the IP to resume execution in the same context.

5. Trace Mode Data Area. The i432 processor supports software debugging and analysis by providing a combination of user-enabled controls and by allocating the special Trace Mode Data Area in each Context Object for use with these controls. This area contains three values, deposited to ''advise'' the processor on the means for resuming normal execution upon completion of any trace action. The saved values are:

   - Instruction Object Index — Denotes the Instruction Object containing the instruction that triggers this trace action.
   - Instruction Pointer (IP) — Identifies the particular instruction whose execution has triggered this trace action.

- Trace Event Code — Encodes the form of resumption of normal execution, if any, that is appropriate upon completing execution of the trace action.

Briefly, the implemented trace control strategy is as follows: First, an i432 processor operates in one of four *trace modes*, as specified in the Process Object of the process to which the processor is currently bound. Second, the AD for an Instruction Object contains *trace* rights which is set *on* to *open* the Instruction Object for tracing. By *tracing*, we mean executing the Instruction Object whose AD is held in slot 1 of the current Domain Object (see the next section) in response to an enabled trace event.

The particular trace event depends on the current trace mode of the processor. The four modes are:

- normal — Tracing is disabled, overriding *trace* rights for individual Instruction Objects.
- fault trace — Perform a trace on the faulting instruction prior to executing the context-level fault handler.
- flow trace — Perform a trace after BRANCHing or CALLing to or from an Instruction Object that is open for tracing and before and after executing a RETURN instruction.
- full trace — Perform a trace prior to executing every instruction in an an Instruction Object that is open for tracing.

More details on these tracing features can be found in the i432 Architecture Reference Manual.

6. Working Storage. The remainder of the Context Object data area is divided between working storage and the operand stack. The working storage area will normally be used to store the current value of data variables local to an executing procedure.

7. Operand Stack. Values are pushed onto and popped from the operand stack during execution of instructions that are used in the evaluation of expressions. It is worth noting that data references to the operand stack in i432 instructions are very short; this means that compiled i432 instruction sequences that make heavy use of this stack are themselves compact. In this book, however, we do not detail further the instruction formats and instruction sequences used in expression evaluation at the i432 machine instruction level. Readers interested in these details should consult relevant chapters of the i432 Architecture Reference Manual.

4.4. The Domain Object

The "permanent" part of an executable program unit is represented by a Domain Object, as indicated in our brief introduction in Section 4-1. Here we elaborate by showing some of the representation details. The reader should note that a Domain Object (also simply called a "domain") is readable and writable; thus any portion of a domain that can be accessed is modifiable, except for slots in which ADs are written that do not possess *delete* rights.

A domain must consist of at least two AD slots that are required by the i432 architecture. The first of these is an AD for the domain's Fault Information Object and the second of these is an AD for the domain's Trace Information Object. These objects provide the processor with the information it needs to intervene and shift the thread of control properly when fault or trace events arise. Information in the data part of a Domain Object may serve any purpose specified by the user (or compiler), as no part of it is required by the i432 architecture.

ADs that reside within a domain D are primarily ADs for Instruction Objects and ADs for other (external) domains that may be referenced while executing within the Instruction Objects referenced by D. In addition, a domain may contain other constant ADs, AD variables and data variables that represent information accessible by all Instruction Objects that reside within the domain. Since a Domain Object is writable, constant information must reside within a physically separate object whose AD resides within the domain. Figure 4-12 illustrates a simple case of a domain that contains only ADs for instruction objects and a single AD for the constant data object.

The access part of the usual Domain Object (Figure 4-12) is logically divided into *public* and *private* parts. Thus, the access path begun with Public_AD leads through a Refinement Descriptor to its target. That target is not a separate object, but merely a "refinement" of the Domain Object. The refinement spans all the Access Descriptors from the one pointed to by Public_AD to the end (highest-indexed slot) of the access part of the host object. The access path represented by Private_AD leads not to a Refinement Descriptor, but directly to an Object Descriptor whose target is the *entire* Domain Object. (That is, at the representation level, the "private part" of the Domain Object is actually the entire Object.) The data part of a domain can be partitioned into a public part and a private part in the same manner as that described for the access part.

Access Descriptors for other domains and for various other objects will normally appear in a domain because of requirements generated by source programs. We give two examples here:

1. Consider the case of an Ada package A containing an operation that calls a public operation in another package B. An AD for B's public part must be included in A's private part to enable A to access B. In general, for any interpackage reference in an Ada program the compiler will provide a corresponding "interdomain link" in the form of an AD residing in the private part of the referencing domain to the public part of the referenced domain. Later in this section we will discuss how the i432 architecture controls such calls.

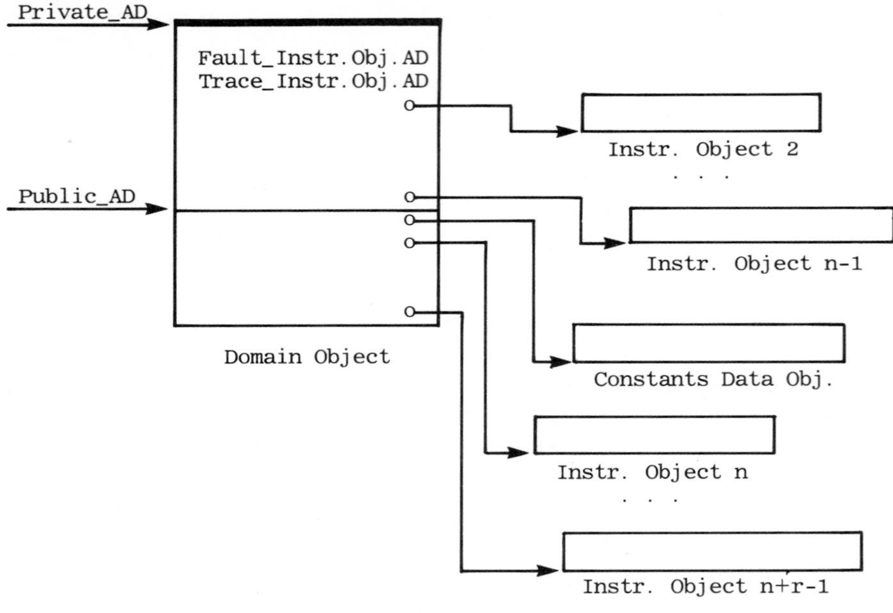

Figure 4-12 Schematic of a Domain Object's access part having *n* locally defined (private procedures) and *r* publicly accessible operations along with one publicly accessible constants data object.

2. In cases where an Ada package owns a set of variables, as in the case of an owner Ada package, the domain will include data locations or AD slots that hold the values of the owned variables. These data locations or AD slots will appear in the appropriate public or private part of the domain, according to whether the owned variables are declared in the public or private portion of the Ada package.

4.4.1. Access to the Public Part of a Domain

A public procedure of an Ada package is called from a given context using either of two instructions: CALL or CALL THROUGH DOMAIN. The CALL instruction is the more general of the two and can be used for all procedure calls if so desired. However, use of the CALL instruction to call a procedure that resides in any domain other than the current domain (an *interdomain* call) is more expensive than a call to a procedure that resides in the current domain (an *intradomain* call). The extra expense incurred is the expense of an extra ENTER ACCESS ENVIRONMENT instruction that must be performed to make the current domain addressable. The current domain must be addressable in order to reference the domain containing the procedure to be called. The CALL THROUGH DOMAIN instruction obviates the need for the extra instruction in an interdomain procedure call if the AD for the domain containing the procedure to be called physically resides in the current domain. The instruction does this by effectively providing one extra AD reference step for a procedure call, i.e., from current context to defining domain to called domain, instead of from (any) directly addressable object to called domain. Besides making interdomain procedure calls more efficient, the CALL THROUGH DOMAIN instruction makes the handling of certain fault and trace events less awkward.

As we will see, a new Context Object will have access to *all* of the new Domain Object. Hence, it is critically important that the new context be inaccessible from the calling context. This is assured because the called context is automatically made inaccessible when control returns to the calling procedure.

The reader may well ask: "How can a calling procedure which possesses only the Public_AD for a Domain Object, provide the processor with the information needed to establish a new context whose *domain of definition* extends over the entire domain specified by Private_AD?" Private_AD is not in possession of the caller and must not be allowed to come into the calling procedure's possession; otherwise the system's protection scheme could be breached.

The answer is surprisingly simple. The microcode for a CALL (or CALL THROUGH DOMAIN) instruction converts Public_AD into Private_AD. To understand how the conversion from Public_AD to Private_AD is done, recall that Public_AD refers to a Refinement Descriptor which, in turn, points to the Object Descriptor for the entire Domain Object. In fact, the Refinement Descriptor contains a copy of Private_AD, as was implied but not detailed in Figure 4-6. This copy of Private_AD is then stored into the defining domain slot of the new Context Object for the called procedure. In short, the hardware executes a controlled *amplification* of the caller's access environment by providing the derived Private_AD for use in the new Context Object. Such amplification is safe because, as was pointed out above, the caller can never gain a copy of Private_AD.

[The i432 has an internal processor register named the Current Domain Register. A byproduct effect of an inter-domain call (return) is to set (restore) the Current Domain Register with the value of Private_AD for the new (antecedent) domain. Of course, only the micro-code has access to this register. Its value is automatically referenced by the micro-code during intra-domain calls.]

After appending a new Context Object to the chain of Context Objects, several AD slots are then filled with information. First, a copy of Private_AD, is placed in the Defining Domain AD slot and also in the on-chip Current Domain Register. In addition, information derived from the newly introduced Domain Object is copied into the new Context Object, as follows: (See also Section 4-3.):

• Current Instr. Object Index	calculated from calling instruction
• Local Constants AD	from the new Domain Object
• Instruction Pointer	a fixed offset value
• Stack Pointer	from called Instruction Object

In the above, "calculated from calling instruction" may require further explanation. By "calling instruction" we mean that the Instruction Object index is imbedded in the CALL (or CALL THROUGH DOMAIN) instruction that invoked the procedure call. By "calculated" we mean that the Instruction Object index given in the calling instruction is (usually) an offset relative to a domain refinement rather than an entire Domain Object. The offset required in the Context Object is the Instruction Object index relative to the entire Domain Object. This must be calculated by the i432.

4.4.2. Use of the Private Part of a Domain

We have just seen that once a call has been completed to a procedure in a new domain, the called procedure has access to the entire domain. We now discuss what is involved in using the full domain. Procedure calls fall into three classes:

- Calls to locally defined private subprograms (intra-domain)
- Calls to locally defined public subprograms (intra-domain)
- Calls to procedures in other domains (inter-domain)

The mechanics of a call to a locally-defined private subprogram provides us with the model for understanding the other kinds of calls.

Let the called public procedure in package A be named Proc1, and let there be a local procedure named, Local_Proc, defined in the body part of A such that during execution, Proc1 calls Local_Proc. Proc1 executes the CALL instruction, specifying the Static Link AD, the value of Private_AD as the domain of definition, and the offset from the base referenced by Private_AD that locates the Instruction Object for Local_proc. The effect of this CALL instruction is to produce a Context Object, newly appended on the Context Object chain, containing Private_AD in the Defining Domain AD slot.

If Proc1 in package A calls another public operation, Proc2 in A, the call from Proc1 to Proc2 is made in exactly the same manner as that described above for Local_Proc as a private procedure contained in A. (It goes without saying that the same intra-domain calling mechanism is used when Proc1 or Local_proc calls itself recursively.)

An interdomain call, from either Proc1 or Local_proc, to an operation in another package B is again straightforward. The Domain Object for package A must contain a Public_AD value for package B or the head of a chain of references leading to Public_AD. The static link, the AD for package B, and the Instruction Object offest are specified in the CALL THROUGH DOMAIN (or CALL) instruction. This has the effect of establishing a Context Object for the called procedure with access to the full domain of package B. [Of course, the compiler of package A has the responsibility for providing the Public_AD for package B, based on the explicit reference to B in the source code of A.]

4.4.3. Processor Registers to Facilitate Domain Access

We have just mentioned that the i432 processor achieves rapid access to the Current Domain Object via the on-chip Current Domain Register. In addition, instruction fetching from the currently executing Instruction Object is, also made highly local to the processor; two on-chip registers facilitate instruction fetch: an Instruction Object Register holds the AD for the activated Instruction Object, and an IP Register holds the bit displacement into this object.

4.4.4. Section Summary

The present and foregoing two sections have focused on the individual forms of the objects required to execute programs on an i432. In the course of these inspections, we have gained some understanding of object creation and manipulation critical to the correct execution of i432 programs. To "put it all together", however, we need to follow an actual execution scenario. In particular, we need to examine a series of execution snapshots for a program having sufficient structure to illustrate and reinforce many of the observations made so far. We attempt to do this in the final part of this chapter by revisiting the investment club program and studying a representative, albeit hypothetical and sketchy, snapshot sequence.

4.5. Some Object Structure Snapshots for the Investment Club Program

We will now attempt to trace the execution of the program structured in Figure 2-1, beginning with the creation of the Secy_Treas starter task and continuing to a call on the Add procedure in the Purchase_Queue_Mgr package while attempting to enter a buy transaction into the club's portfolio. We present and discuss briefly a total of seven related snapshots of i432 execution-time data structures.

4.5.1. Snapshot 1

Figure 4-13 shows the set-up required to begin executing in the starter task. The Process Object (lacking some detail to be investigated in the next chapter), the root Context Object, and the root Domain Object are all displayed. Since the Domain Object represents a starter task instead of a package, it has no public refinement. This snapshot also shows the initial object structure just prior to the call on Club_Portfolio's Enter_buy (public) procedure, including the current context's precreated Message Object.

In the figures illustrating these snapshots, we represent Access Descriptors in the access parts of objects using small open, or filled circles, or the mark "x". An open circle represents an AD that has some (possibly non-null) value, but not one which we wish to illustrate or discuss further. A filled circle will usually have a directed arc emanating from it. (Exceptions to this rule will be explained in connection with a later snapshot.) The mark "x" signifies a deliberate, recognizable, null AD value.

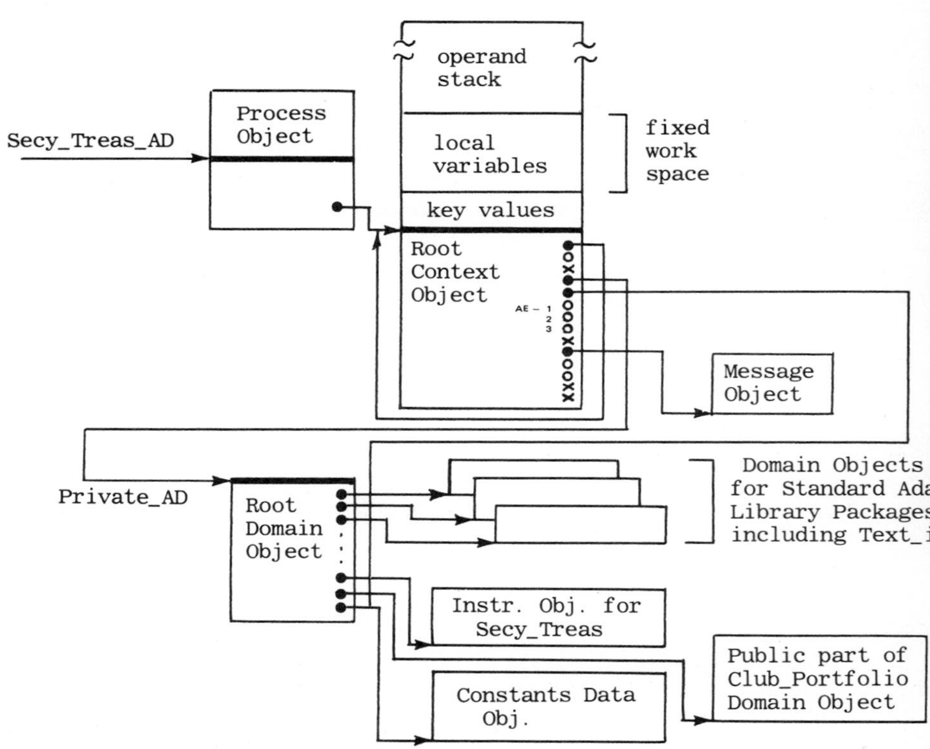

Figure 4-13 Initial object structure ready for execution of code in the Secy_Treas starter task. This figure reveals the object structure just prior to calling the Enter_buy operation of the Club_Portfolio package shows the Message Object used with CALL instructions issued from the root context. (The root Domain Object has no public part.)

We do not attempt to display or explain the role of each Access Descriptor or of each object referenced. However, we do indicate some highlights and some of the more subtle or crucial details. We rely on the reader to use these snapshots in part as exercises, to confirm the partial or full understanding already gained from earlier sections in this chapter. Necessity for some "back and forth" perusing within this chapter and also within the Ada program (Appendix C) is inevitable.

4.5.2. Snapshot 2

Figure 4-14 shows the state of affairs after completion of a call to the Enter_buy procedure. A new Context Object has been linked to the Domain

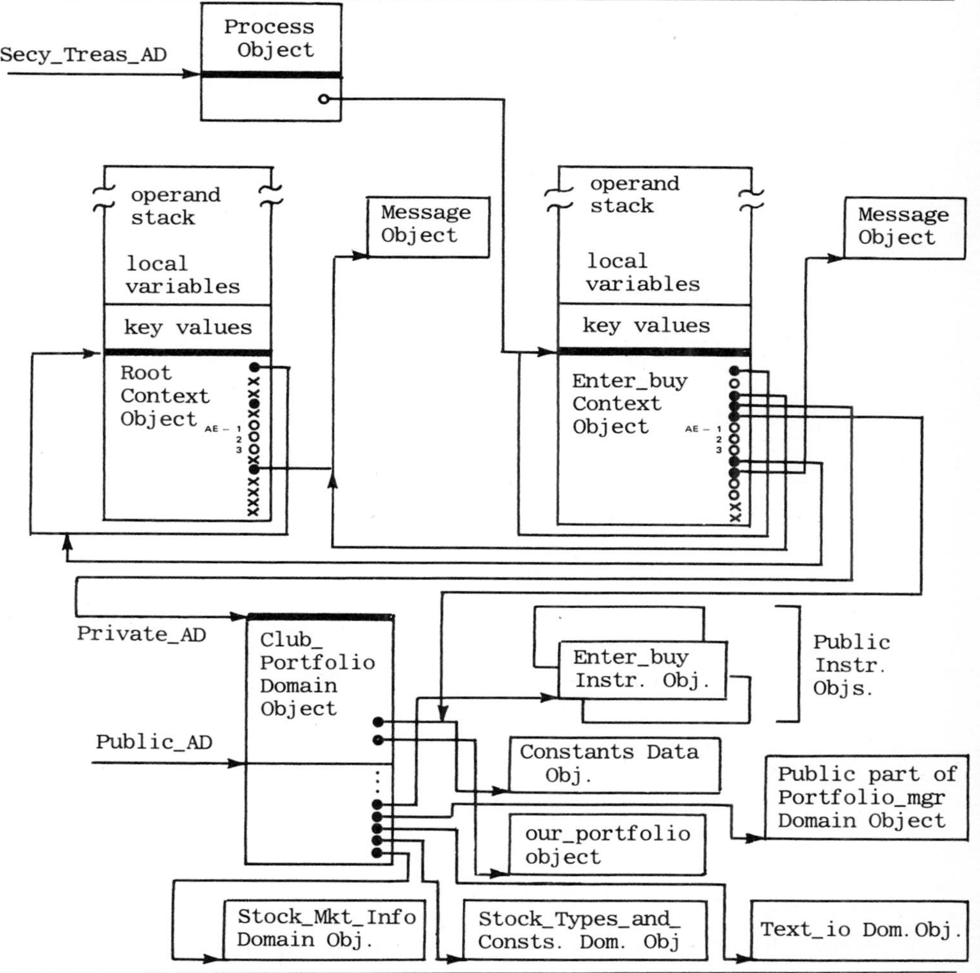

Figure 4-14 Object structure snapshot on entry into the Enter_buy operation of the Club_Portfolio package. Note that the Process Object now points to the new context and that the new context has one pointer into the old context and one into the (received) Message Object.

Object for Club_portfolio. Notice that the Access Descriptor from the Process Object to the root Context Object has been replaced with an Access Descriptor to the new Context Object for Enter_buy. (See preceding snapshot.) The root Context Object has no predecessor context, so its corresponding back-pointer is deliberately null, and marked "x".

The next two bits of detail worth noticing are the AD that references backward to the predecessor context and the AD that references the Message Object associated with the predecessor context. The AD in slot eight is the return AD and serves as a backward link in the "dynamic chain" of Context Objects. It may have *return* rights, but in no case does it have *read* or *write* rights. Thus, it cannot be used to gain unauthorized access to information in the calling environment. The other AD of interest is the Current Message AD referring to the Message Object holding the actual parameters for Enter_buy.

The Domain Object for Club_Portfolio has both a public and a private part. The reader is invited to study the objects pointed to from this Domain Object and to compare them with the objects implied from the Ada program and the discussions earlier in this chapter.

To avoid excessive complexity in this and subsequent snapshots, we adopt the convention of not repeating the display of the Domain Object that goes with the predecessor Context Object. Also, we only display the current Context Object and its immediate predecessor. Static links are ignored. Thus, some of the filled AD circles in the predecessor Context Object have no arcs emanating from them since we do not show their respective targets. Generally, these targets have been displayed previously, so the reader can, if need be, trace backward to determine the actual reference associated with any previously displayed AD.

4.5.3. Snapshot 3

Figure 4-15 shows the state of the object structure reflecting execution of a call on the Record_buy procedure of the Portfolio_Mgr package from Enter_buy in Club_Portfolio. The Process Object now points to the new Context Object for Record_buy.

Access to the Portfolio_Mgr Domain Object, from the new Context Object is via the Private_AD. The reader is urged to check that this part of the snapshot reflects the intent of the Ada program.

4.5.4. Snapshot 4

Figure 4-16 illustrates the situation immediately before a call by procedure Record_buy to the private-part function, Search_for_stock_code. There is only one change shown from the preceding snapshot: Record_buy has copied its input reference parameter (AD for the object instance of our_portfolio) into the new Message Object associated with the Context Object of Record_buy. This

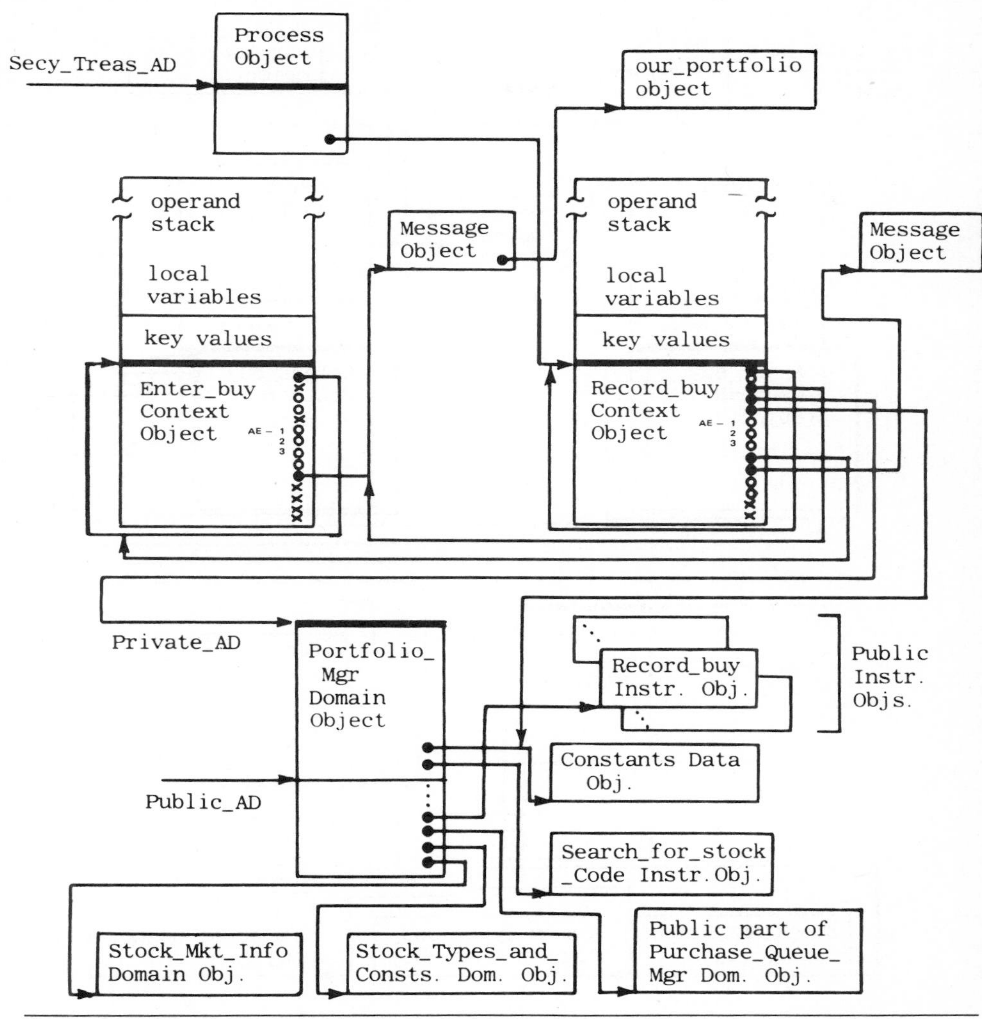

Figure 4-15 Snapshot showing object structure upon entry to Record_buy operation of the Portfolio_Mgr package.

action is necessary for the Record_buy procedure to transmit its actual parameter reference (to our_portfolio) to the Search_for_stock_code procedure.

4.5.5. Snapshot 5

Figure 4-17 shows the object structure for the state that arises as a result of completion of the call to the function Search_for_stock_code. The new Context

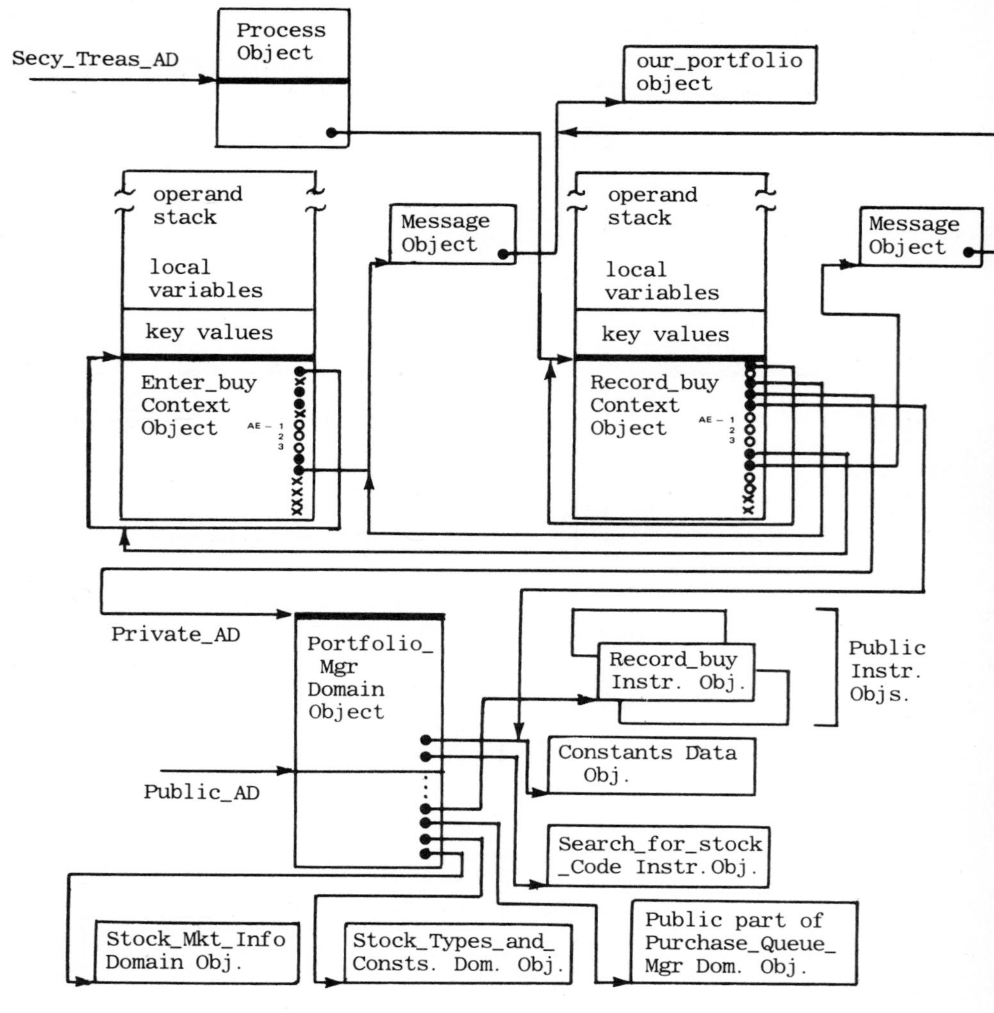

Figure 4-16 Object structure snapshot with Record_buy about to execute a call on private function, Search_for_stock_code.

Object created by the CALL instruction has for its Defining Domain Object AD a duplicate of the value of Private_Ad (the base of the Portfolio_Mgr Domain Object) that is in the Record_buy Context Object.

We assume here that no other subprograms are called from Search_for_stock_code, so we don't bother to display the Message Object for the Context Object of Search_for_stock_code.

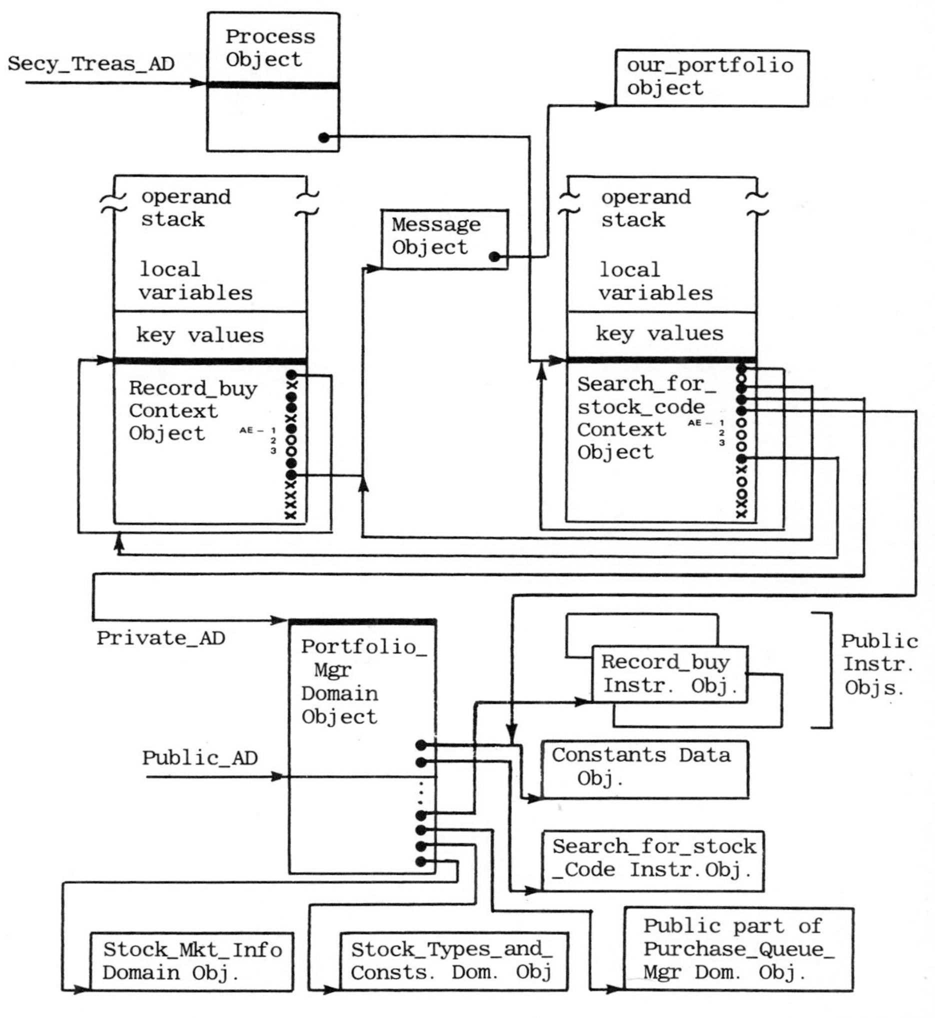

Figure 4-17 Object structure snapshot just after entry to the private function, Search_for_stock_code.

4.5.6. Snapshot 6

Figure 4-18 shows the object structure applicable for the case in which Record_buy has returned from Search_for_stock_code and is ready to issue a CALL on the public Add procedure of the Purchase_Queue_Mgr package.

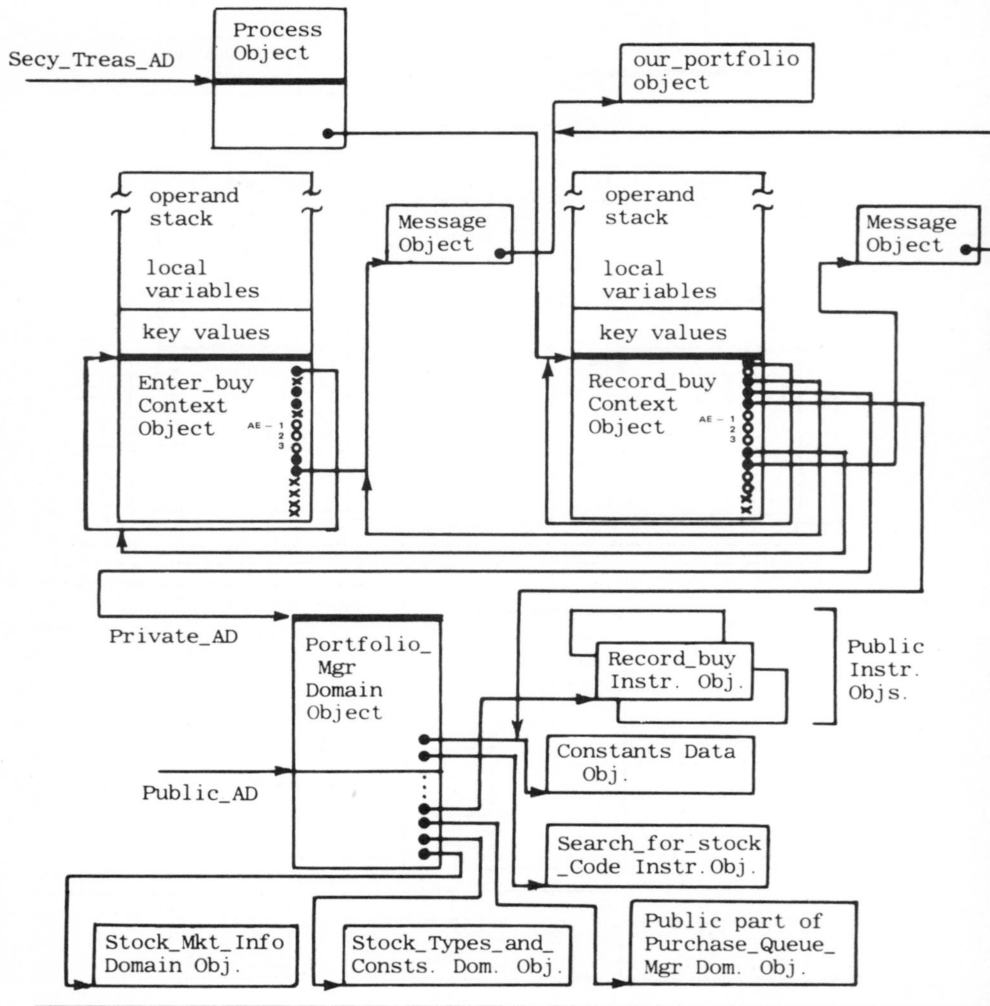

Figure 4-18 Object structure snapshot with Record_buy about to execute a call on the public Add procedure in the Purchase_Queue_Mgr package using a CALL THROUGH DOMAIN instruction.

4.5.7 Snapshot 7

Figure 4-19 shows our final snapshot, revealing the state of the object structure just after entering the Add procedure. The new Context Object is referenced by the Process Object. The new Context Object in turn references the Purchase_Queue_Mgr Domain Object. (There is provision in the private part of this Domain Object for Access Descriptors referring to a queue object and to a queue element.)

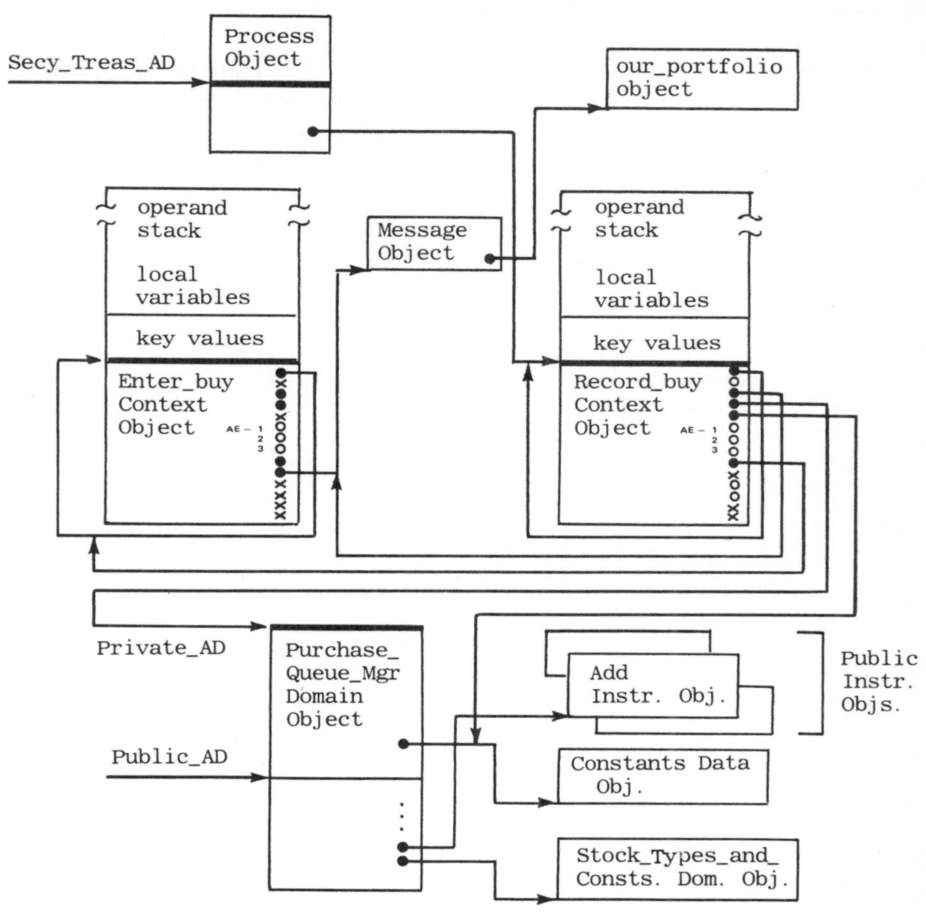

Figure 4-19 Object structure snapshot just after entry into the Add procedure in the Purchase_Queue_Mgr package.

Again, we assume that no other procedures are called from Add, so we choose not to exhibit the Message Object associated with the Context Object for Add.

4.5.8. Section Summary

We have now introduced the "statics" and the "dynamics" of i432 Object Structures for single-thread-of-control processes. We have not looked at all the relevant details, but we have more than scratched the surface. Some of the details left out here have only been postponed until a later chapter. For the rest, the reader is commended to other documents listed in Appendix A, or to actually studying the i432 behavior by running programs and observing their behavior.

We are now well equipped to look at the i432's unifying ''request-server model'', whereby process dispatching and interprocess communication are unified into a relatively simple, effective, and consistent structure. We are also ready to look at the implementation details of this model—and do this in the next chapter.

5 i432 COMMUNICATION STRUCTURES FOR PROGRAM EXECUTION

5.1. Introduction

In the preceding chapter we were concerned primarily with the evolution of an i432 process after it had been created; moreover, we assumed that it was always active. From that viewpoint, the process itself (and its representation as a Process Object) was not manipulable. That approach was taken deliberately, but only to confine the scope of discussion. In this chapter, we are interested in examining the process in the larger scope of a typical operating environment. Here we examine the architectural models and mechanisms for the scheduling and dispatching of i432 processes and the corresponding models and mechanisms and for achieving interprocess communication among i432 processes. (We only view the process after it has been created and defer until Chapter 8 consideration of operating system support structures for process management such as the explicit creation and destruction of processes.) Before taking a closer look at these models and mechanisms, we establish a conceptual frame of reference. In effect, we attempt first a brief review of two major objectives for modern computer systems.

5.1.1. Process Dispatching and Interprocess Communication—In General

The initial and still a major objective of current computer operating systems, whether for uniprocessor or multiprocessor configurations, has been to ensure effective application of the computer to its *workstream*. A workstream is a relative term; its meaning has changed during the several decades of computer and operating system development. For early mainframe computer systems controlled by primitive batch operating systems, the workstream was simply a manually-ordered sequence of computer programs "presented" for execution. Later, related programs, such as compilations followed by execution, were programmatically linked into steps of program sequences called *jobs*. For purposes of resource accounting and control, programs or program sequences were associated with particular users or user groups. Operating system modules computed charges for processor time and memory space utilization by user category for individual user or user group accounts.

When computer systems were implemented with the ability to perform computation overlapped with input/output processing, achieving maximum "throughput" required that more attention be paid to the ordering of jobs in the workstream. Since such jobs could, by then, be maintained on disk and other on-line storage, the ordering process was increasingly delegated to the computer itself through the inclusion of software that could perform job scheduling. Coincidentally, multiprogramming models were developed and implemented that enabled the scheduling of jobs and job steps to become finer-grained; with multiprogramming, one job could be started before another was completed. Moreover, individual job steps of one job could be interleaved with steps of another job. The different priorities and deadline requirements of jobs and their individual program components were then taken into account in the formulation of scheduling policies and their implementation mechanisms. The potential degree of multiprogramming rose with the addition of extra I/O processors and eventually the addition of extra CPUs, which called for more sophistication in scheduling and dispatching algorithms. The superposition of interactive time-sharing requirements, which generally forced ordinary batch processing into a "background" mode of operation, led to the necessity for multilevel dynamic scheduling of workstream components; long-term scheduling was applied to the program components of jobs and short-term scheduling, using *time slicing*, permitted maximum effective interleaving of jobs and job components.

In the models designers used for such purposes, it became natural to exploit hierarchical relationships such as:

```
user class  >  individual user  >  job  >  individual program
```

Finally, as individual programs acquired multitask substructures, the leaf nodes of the hierarchy became individual processes (e.g., Ada tasks). Thus, dynamic scheduling could now be applied to the individual tasks of the same program. The "mix" of work units being scheduled could now include individual tasks or task subsets of different programs, possibly belonging to different jobs.

The workstreams of the modern mainframe computer system frequently depend on moment-to-moment outcomes of previous work units and on new arrivals, some representing predictable real-time demands (for example, in chemical process control applications) and some arising with unpredictable demands and frequency (for example, in business transaction processing). To meet this growth in complexity of workstream, algorithms and implementations for the scheduling and dispatching of work in computer operating environments have tended to grow in complexity almost without control—often leading to disappointing or unreliable performance.

Adding more processors to keep up with growing workloads introduces the need to synchronize processors properly over shared object structures. This usually contributes additional complexity to the problem of achieving good overall resource management.

The evolution of algorithms and structures for solving increasingly complex computer operating systems objectives has guided for several years a similar evolution in the algorithms and structures required to implement increasingly more complex user application programs. Today, application programs, especially those that model real world systems, exhibit many of the structural and functional characteristics of operating systems—vis a vis scheduling and dispatching. [This observation was first made well over fifteen years ago [18].]

As we have seen from Chapter 3, programs are often decomposed into groups of related tasks, not all of which need to run at once. When a task is invoked, it needs to execute. This means the task needs to be put into the workstream (scheduled) so that it can eventually be bound to a processor (dispatched).

Tasks that are not currently ready to execute represent a pool of future candidates for the work stream. While in this future candidate status, tasks must also be monitored to ensure their proper transition to a ready state. Certain events are usually recognized for triggering the transition of a work unit from not-ready to ready. Other events are recognized for triggering other transitions, such as from ready to actively executing (invoked). In the first category, events like the arrival of messages serve as a trigger, while in the second category, events like the freeing-up of a processor may serve as a trigger.

Before a task is invoked, its required input data must be available, often supplied by the invoking task. Before a task completes a particular invocation, it usually must transmit some output data (to some task that may be waiting to receive it). Keeping track of the input and output data streams (the communications between tasks) for a complex structure of tasks, including some that are themselves created dynamically, is usually an overwhelmingly complex intellectual hurdle for a human programmer. (In the past, system architects have attempted to master this complexity primarily through the use of shared data and various synchronization mechanisms; there is very little concurrence today that indicates complexity has been mastered using these techniques.)

5.1.2. Dispatching and Scheduling—A Technical Overview

Positioning a work unit into the main workstream is referred to as *scheduling* that unit of work. Binding a work unit already in the main workstream to a processor, so it can actually run, is referred to as *dispatching* it. The term *short-term scheduling* usually refers to the frequent repositioning of a work unit in the main work stream at the end of a time slice by the recycling scheme just mentioned. The term *long-term scheduling* usually refers to the less-frequent repositioning of a work unit into the main workstream following reassessment analysis; this often involves substantial computation. (In the i432 model, a process P that is removed from the workstream for such reassessment, is said to be removed from the *dispatching mix* and sent to another process S which performs a long-term scheduling function on P.)

The dispatching and scheduling problems of a computer operating system are related closely. Low-level work units in the mix such as individual Ada tasks must be given a fair share of the available processor power, but the decision as to what is *fair* often requires dynamic reassessment of the higher-level resource requirements of the programs or jobs of which such tasks may constitute a small part.

When a process has used up a certain amount of processor time, it is usually *preempted*, that is, forced to become detached from the processor. At this point, either the task is recycled into the main workstream, thus assuring it of a future "turn" (i.e., rebinding to the processor), or it is taken out of the main work stream so that its needs may be reassessed. Various events may trigger the transition of a task (and possibly of the higher level entity of which that task is a member) to and from the main workstream and reassessment status.

Computer architects have faced difficult challenges in designing systems in which dispatching and short-term scheduling efficiency are not sacrificed to the flexibility required for long-term scheduling, and vice versa. As we will see later in this chapter, the i432 design meets this challenge successfully.

Fortunately, the problem is simplified when using an appropriate message-based communication model for expressing the interactions between related tasks. Note that the challenge of managing the execution of a complex program is similar to the challenge of managing the workstream of a general-purpose computer. For this reason, a "bonus" is earned when using a common simplifying model both for organizing the implementation of scheduling and dispatching of jobs and for organizing the implementation of interprocess communication.

It is the availability of a unifying *request/server* model that permits us to embrace a broad objective for this chapter. That is, the model helps us to discuss the full environment of an i432 process as one topic. One panorama, as illustrated in the dual-state diagram of Figure 5-1, allows us to view all the significant states and transitions on processes and processors.

The left and right halves of the model suggested by Figure 5-1 provide a global view of i432 process and processor state transitions, respectively. This chapter examines the details of this diagram and explains the underlying strategies and mechanisms for implementing the model. Important for its appreciation is understanding how and why processes are also treated as data objects;

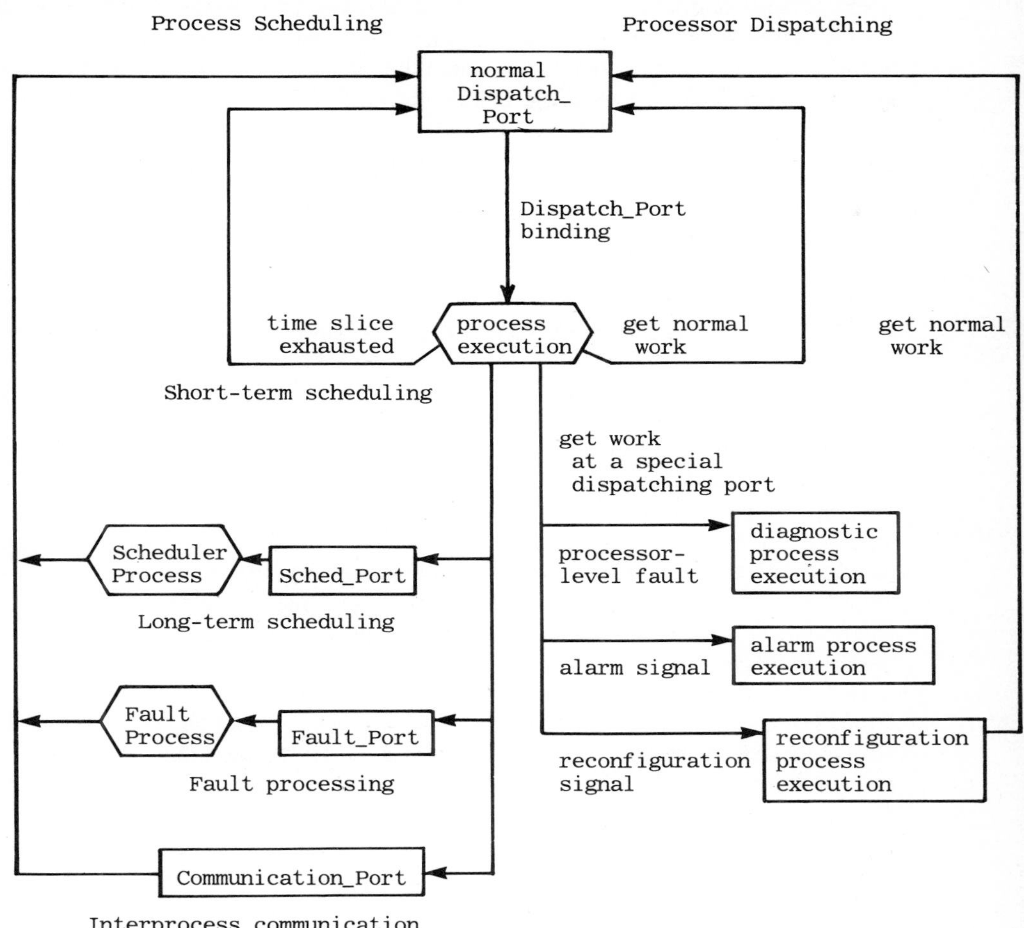

Figure 5-1 Dual state graph of i432 process scheduling and i432 processor dispatching. The left half of the diagram describes states of a process, while the right half of the diagram describes states of a processor.

thus, as a data object, a process can, with the help of the processor, be sent as a message through a port to another process where it can itself be "processed" as needed. If the process is sent to a dispatching port, it is executed; if it is sent to any of the three illustrated communication ports on the right half of the diagram, it is treated as data by the receiving process.

A model like the request/server developed for the i432 system [14] has no doubt benefitted from much earlier research into operating systems principles [8] [52] [56]. We do not, however, need to digress here to review that history as the i432 model is rich enough to explain the implementation details of process management and interprocess communication. The model also serves to explain many key concepts needed by programmers who wish to mount ambitious multiprocess systems applications on the i432.

5.1.3. Plan for Remainder of Chapter

In the body of this chapter, we shall first view a process as a schedulable and dispatchable job. Recall from Chapter 1 we indicated that the i432 initiates execution by binding processes to processors at Dispatching Ports. To see how this is done, we will examine *Process Object*s, introduced in Chapter 4, in relationship to three other i432 hardware-defined system objects, not yet discussed in the earlier chapters. These objects are known as *Carrier Object*s, *Port Object*s and *Processor Object*s.

An abstract view of a *port* reveals it to be merely a queue consisting entirely of service requests waiting for servers or entirely of servers waiting for service requests. In the case of a Dispatching Port, the requests represent ready processes, and the servers represent available processors. In the case of a Communication Port, the requests represent messages that are waiting for the appropriate destination process and the servers represent processes that are waiting for messages.

A more concrete view would show that a Port Object establishes (holds or anchors) a queue of requests or a queue of servers. As a system object, a Port is always locked during use; that is, it is never accessed by more than one processor at a time. As a consequence, at least one queue at each Port, the request or the server queue, will always be empty.

The i432 mechanisms and data structure representations needed to accomplish the binding of a process to a processor at a Dispatching Port will be examined in some detail. In the course of doing this, we will expand our earlier discussion of Process Objects, revealing some of the postponed details. As already mentioned, processes that are ready to run are not necessarily given "full-time access" to processor resources, out of fairness to other processes that may also be ready to run.

In the i432, short-term scheduling (recycling a job on to its Dispatching Port), is made an automatic part of the hardware. On the other hand, the decision, whether or not to so reschedule is based on parameter values inserted by software into the hardware-recognized system objects. The effective separation of policy, as software-managed, and mechanism, as hardware managed—vis a vis scheduling and dispatching—is a major design goal of the architecture of the i432 system.

We next consider programmatic relationships between processes, that is, program structures involving more than one process, as in multitask Ada programs. We examine the i432 architectural support provisions whereby processes can send to and receive messages from one another. The corresponding object structures for achieving interprocess communication are examined.

Once again, hardware-recognized Port Objects, and Carrier Objects are used in conjunction with Process Objects to accomplish the objective of message-based communication. As always, a Port Object is conceptually a queue containing either requests or servers (but never both)—where, in this case, the requests, which are essentially messages, are bound to servers, which are processes. At this point in the exposition, we are able to suggest a possible means for executing some simple Ada task entry calls—and we do this.

After introducing a few further representation details on Port and Carrier Objects, how the i432 hardware instructions use them and how the operating system software augments this planned use, we elaborate the request/server model, and then provide an interim review of the unifying system ideas. All this prepares us to examine some of operating system facilities available to i432 users for constructing relatively efficient systems applications which draw their power and clarity from the use of message-based, inter-task communication. This discussion closes with observations on the equivalence of the Ada rendezvous and the i432 port-based communication operations.

We close the chapter by considering a few simple example applications, and, finally, we revisit the investment club program to consider ways to solve the bottlenecks implied in the multitasking structure of Figure 2-5. This is done by explicit use of the more efficient i432 interprocess communication mechanisms (made accessible to users through operating system modules), in place of direct application of tasking strategies that rely on the Ada rendezvous. At the end of this chapter, the reader should have a better picture of the tradeoffs between the two proposed solutions for the bottleneck problem.

5.2. Processes as Scheduleable and Dispatchable Units of Work

In the conceptual-level introduction for this chapter, we suggested how a process becomes bound to an i432 processor in a two-step sequence; first scheduling and then dispatching. One may wonder if it is really wise to separate these semantics in this way. Is an "overkill" implied here? Could not the system architect identify some shortcut leading to a more efficient means for switching processes? We jump ahead here to indicate a much lower level view of these actions, so that the reader can begin quickly to surmise why it is that short-term scheduling and dispatching can each be accomplished so efficiently within the i432 architecture.

1. Recall that scheduling amounts to placing, at its position of relative impor-

tance, the representation of a process P on the request queue portion of a Dispatching Port. The representation of a process is a Carrier Object that in turn refers to the Process Object representing process P.

The role of a Carrier Object is, at first view, simply a convenient queueing link. However, we have more to say about it later on when we explain how, as a purely hardware action, a process is positioned in a Dispatching Port's request queue.

2. Dispatching is the binding of a request (process) at the head of the request queue portion of a Dispatching Port to a server (processor). Dispatching is a very efficient operation on the i432; it is normally accomplished simply by moving a pointer, extracted from the queue entry of the selected request, to a proper position in the server.

   The request is the representation of a process and the server is a representation of a processor. The pointer (Access Descriptor) for the request is a reference to the Carrier Object for the process, and is copied into a prespecified slot in the object structure representing the processor. In the i432 implementation, a processor representation is, by symmetry, similar in structure, consisting of a Carrier Object containing an Access Descriptor that references a Processor Object) The copied AD is actually deposited in the processor's Carrier Object.

   [Each physical i432 processor is associated at all times with a distinct Processor Object. This object may be viewed as a *storage image*, or virtual processor, that reflects the state of the physical processor. The Processor Object also contains various global control values for use by the processor, such as a set of alternative Dispatching Ports for use when special conditions arise.]

   Dispatching is achieved in the hardware as part of an automatic sequence initiated whenever a processor terminates service for one process (for whatever reason) and is guided, via certain internal control information, to select work (a new process) from some selected Dispatching Port.

Figure 5-2 is a schematic of the Carrier Object and the Process Object that it references. This figure illustrates the structure of a process sent as a request to a Dispatching Port.

The same structure is used to represent an enqueued (or enqueueable) server. Later, we will see how this scheme simplifies matters without loss of performance. Figure 5-3 shows the (symmetrical) representation of a processor server for a Dispatching Port.

The only discernible difference, at this schematic level, between the structure of Figure 5-2 and that of Figure 5-3 is the receptacle slot in the processor's Carrier Object, In_Message_AD, which, at binding, receives a copy of a requesting process' Request_AD. Figure 5-4 shows the relationship between a physical processor, its virtual representation (the Processor Object), and a process currently bound to it.

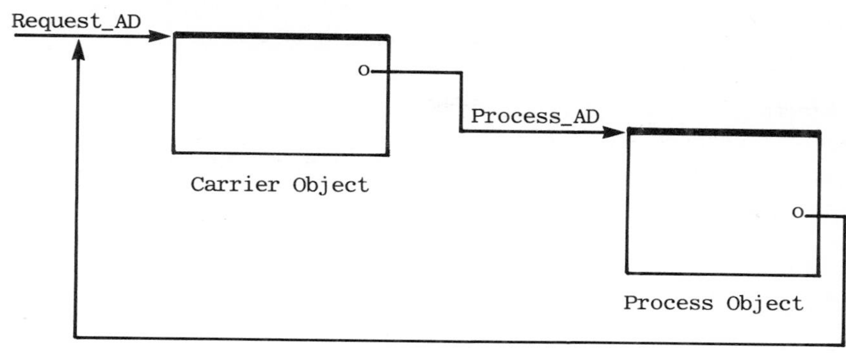

Figure 5-2 Schematic of a (Process Object, Carrier Object) pair. The Process and Carrier Objects are mutually cross-referenced.

[Ports have fixed-length request queues. Until an overflow of this queue is reached, each queue entry amounts simply to a reference to a structure like that shown in Figure 5-2. When more entries are required, the "overflow" is accommodated in a linked list of such request structures, the head element of which is anchored in the Port Object. Links in the chain are embedded in the individual Carrier Objects.

Logically, a Carrier Object may be regarded as an extension of the "carried object", in this case the Process Object. The primary reason for separating a conceptual process into a Carrier Object part and a Process Object part is related to efficient memory management. Carrier Objects are "factored out of" Process Objects in order to minimize the amount of information required to be present in physical store while performing frequent searches of, or manipulations on, enqueued requests or servers.]

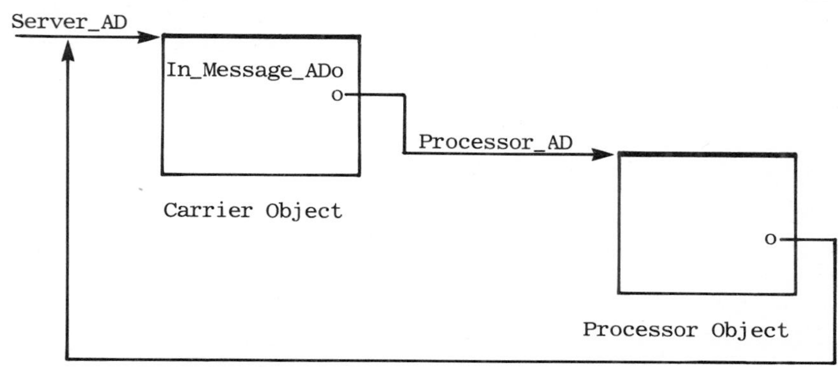

Figure 5-3 Schematic of a (Carrier Object, Processor Object) pair. The pair of objects are mutually cross-referenced. Binding to a request occurs when the slot marked In_Message_AD in the Carrier Object receives a copy of Request_AD.

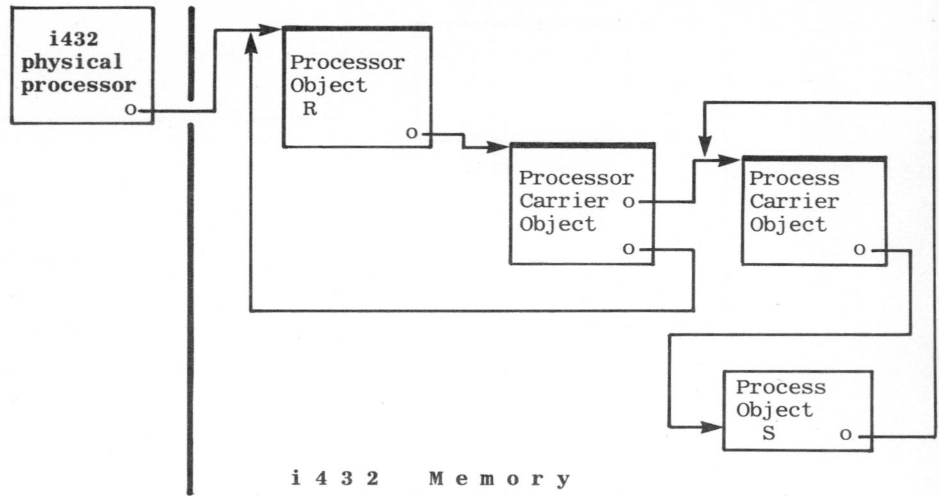

Figure 5-4 An i432 processor and its representation, the Processor Object R bound to a Process Object S through the respective Carrier Objects.

5.2.1. Short-Term Scheduling Viewed as Communication

Short-term scheduling on the i432 is achieved by using exactly the same mechanism that is used for interprocess message communication on the i432. To accomplish the latter, a process sends a message (request) to a Communication Port where the request will eventually be bound to a process (server). Short-term scheduling is accomplished by sending a process (request) to a Dispatching Port where the request will eventually be bound (dispatched) to a processor (server).

5.2.2. Long-Term Scheduling Viewed as Communication

Consider the analogous case of long-term scheduling, where the future claim of some process, call it A, on processor resources is to be reassessed. Here, the message is again the process in question (A). However, now process A is enqueued at a Communication Port where the server is not a processor, but a system process whose responsibility it is to decide on the fate of A. The same communication model serves for both long-term scheduling and short-term scheduling so long as the structure of the server is predefined to contain a receptacle slot for a message AD.

And so, it should not be surprising that the Carrier Object structure for a process and for a processor is actually identical. Although we at first refrained from showing it, there is also an In_Message_AD slot in the process' Carrier Object (see Figure 5-3). In other words, depending on its role at the time, a process structure, headed by its own Carrier Object, may represent a request for service or a server. We will see a number of examples of this symmetry, of interest to application programmers, later in this chapter.

5.2.3. Port Service Disciplines

We have not yet indicated how short-term scheduling is achieved in an efficient manner—in part because we have not yet disclosed details on the *queueing disciplines* associated with Port Objects. We, therefore, digress here to fill in some details on port disciplines.

At the highest conceptual level, a Port Object is simply a queue. Although we sometimes distinguish between Communication Ports and Dispatching Ports, there is really very little difference between these two forms of port on the i432; the only real difference is the form of the requests and servers that are enqueued at a port. Recall that the characteristics of port usage ensures that there will never be both requests and servers queued at the same port. At any instant in time a port is a queue of requests or a queue of servers.

If two or more process servers arrive at a Port before a request arrives, they are always enqueued in FIFO order—on the theory that servers, if more than one, are essentially indistinguishable.

If two or more requests arrive before a server arrives, they are enqueued according to a service discipline for that Port, which is set by system software. That discipline is encoded in the Port as one of four possible hardware-sensed *service modes*. Among these are FIFO-mode (first in-first out) and Priority-mode. [The latter implies ordering arriving requests according to their priority levels, and within a given priority by FIFO. A request of highest (absolute) priority goes at the front of the queue. The priority value of an arriving process request is actually supplied in the request's Carrier Object.]

The discussion in the paragraph above holds only in case the request queue at a port does not "overflow." Every request queue (but not a server queue) associated with a port has a fixed size N that is given when the port is created. After N requests have arrived before the arrival of a server, the next request that arrives (before a server arrives) will cause the request queue to overflow. Instead of this next request being queued in the normal fashion, the carrier of the process that issued the request will be enqueued in a special "overflow queue" associated with the port, and the process blocks.

The service discipline for the overflow queue is FIFO rather than the service discipline associated with the queue. However, overflow requests compete for service as soon as they enter the fixed part of the request queue. Thus, a request arriving after N unserviced requests can never preempt the first of the N unserviced requests, regardless of its priority. Once the first of these requests becomes bound to a server, however, a slot in the fixed part of the request queue is freed up. At this time, the first of the overflow requests is inserted into the fixed portion of the queue in its correct position, according the the service discipline of the queue; this position may well be the head of the queue. After the overflow request is placed into the fixed part of the request queue, the freed process carrier is sent to its specified "second port" which will be a Dispatching Port.

A special service mode is used with Dispatching Ports, called *Priority/Deadline*. In this mode, arriving requests are ordered by priority level, and within the same priority level by a *deadline* value which is a time span (from the present) within which that request, which in this case is a process, must be dispatched.

If a processor tries to service (dispatch) a process from a Dispatching Port and the port is empty, the processor's Carrier Object is enqueued and the processor goes into a "sleep" state. It can only be awakened by an interprocessor communication signal (executed by another processor.) Awakening will occur when a request (Process Carrier) is next sent to that port. At this point, the executed microcode of the sending processor checks if there is a "sleeping" Processor Carrier waiting at the port to receive a Process Carrier request. If so, the executed microcode puts the AD of the incoming Process Carrier into the Processor Carrier Object and then awakens (by a special interprocessor "wakeup" signal) the physical processor associated with the Processor Carrier.

The i432 also defines a fourth kind of port, called a *Delay Port*, that is used with the DELAY instruction. It allows a process to suspend itself for at least some time x, where x is specified in the DELAY instruction.

5.2.4. Scheduling Viewed as Communication

We are now almost prepared to see in more detail how the short-term scheduling of a process is accomplished. One more "piece of the puzzle" must be exposed. When a process is created, not only is its Process Object created, as discussed in Chapter 4, but also its Carrier Object is created and cross-coupled with it in the structure suggested in Figure 5-2. The full structure of the Carrier Object includes a data part and an access part, as in the format of Figure 4-4.

Short-term scheduling is performed automatically by the i432 hardware using the standard model of interprocess communication. Each time the service period (time slice) for an executing process is used up, the executing process is automatically preempted. As part of this preemption, the processor checks whether the period count for the process (a decreasing counter) is still greater than zero. If so, the process is re-sent by the processor as a request to a "second port" specified by the Process Carrier, according to the priority and deadline values found in the process' Carrier Object. Normally, when the period count is non-zero, the "second port" specified by a process carrier is the process' Dispatching Port; however, when the period count becomes zero the "second port" specifies a special long-term scheduling port. This accomplishes short-term scheduling as a hardware operation done in conjunction with the preemption step. The two short-term scheduling parameters, *priority value* and *deadline value*, are placed into the data part of a process' carrier by the operating system. Both the *service period* and *period count* values are scheduling parameters that are placed in the Process Object data part as a consequence of performing long-term scheduling on a process.

Long-term scheduling is performed by the i432 operating system software. Again, the standard model of interprocess communication is used to achieve the scheduling function. Recall that, during preemption, if the period count was detected to have dropped to zero during dispatching, then the "second port" of the Process Carrier is set to a long-term scheduling port. Following this, the next preemption of the process will result in the preempted process being sent to the long-term scheduling port rather than to its (short-term) dispatching port. Eventually the preempted process will be bound as a message to a server process S at the long-term scheduling port. The process S will perform the long-term scheduling of the preempted process based on a reassessment of its resource requirements.

5.2.5. Alternative Dispatching Ports of a Processor

As suggested in Figure 5-1, when a processor-level fault occurs, the faulting processor FP is sent as a message to its *Diagnostic_Port*. A non-faulting processor NFP, alerted to this event, is switched from its normal Dispatching_Port to serve at this Diagnostic_Port. When other unusual system events are detected, a non-faulting processor is automatically switched to serve at one of two other special service ports: the *Alarm_Port* or the *Reconfiguration_Port*. Messages received by processor NFP at these service ports amount to alternative workstreams for NFP. We are now prepared to understand how this switching of a processor from its ordinary workstream to an alternative workstream (at the *Diagnostic_Port*, *Alarm_Port*, or *Reconfiguration_Port*) is accomplished within the framework of the dispatching mechanism already described.

When created by software, each Processor Object is associated with, not one, but four candidate workstreams. These are the three alternative workstreams listed above, together with the *normal* workstream. Each Processor Object has four pairs of prespecified Access Descriptor slots, one pair for use with each of four dispatching ports corresponding to the four workstreams, and one additional Access Descriptor (Current Processor Carrier AD). One AD in each pair refers to the dispatching port, and the other refers to a corresponding Processor Carrier Object. The latter can itself be bound to a Process Carrier representing a process currently bound to the processor via that Port. The Current Processor Carrier AD, which refers to the Processor Carrier that is paired with the currently used dispatching port, is loaded with each change in the processor's "Dispatching Mode."

When one of the hardware events occurs, requiring a processor to switch to a particular alternative workstream (a new Dispatching Mode), an interposed hardware scenario proceeds roughly as follows:

The hardware saves state information of the currently executing process (A) in the Current Context Object and Process Object, as appropriate. Then, the Processor Object's Current Processor Carrier Object AD is loaded with a copy of the AD for the Processor Carrier paired with the AD for the dispatching port to be used next. (Note that the Process Carrier for process A remains linked to the Processor Carrier Object.) The next step taken depends on whether or not the newly-current Processor Carrier happens to be bound to a Process Carrier for some process B:

- If no Process Carrier is currently bound, this means that a new work unit must be found at the corresponding dispatching port. (That is, a dispatching cycle must be entered. The Processor Carrier is sent to the proper dispatching port where it can become bound to a new Process Carrier. If no Process Carrier is currently enqueued at that port, then the Processor Object will itself be enqueued as a server—to await the arrival of a Process Carrier.)
- If there is a Process Carrier currently bound to the Processor Carrier, then the hardware skips the aforementioned Dispatching Cycle, and execution resumes (or commences—as the case may be) in that bound process (B).

We see from the above scenario that preemption of processes from one workstream in favor of processes from another workstream, for whatever reason, is dealt with rather simply by the hardware. The strategy is based on providing in the Processor Object the needed ADs that refer to the preassigned set of Dispatching Ports and to the preassigned and pre-created set of corresponding Processor Carrier Objects.

Those wishing to see more details on the content of the Processor Object may consult the i432 Architecture Reference Manual.

5.2.6. A Second Look at a Process Object Structure

We are now prepared to take a second look at the Process Object in order to discuss the items in it that were left hidden in Chapter 4. This will prepare us for expanding on interprocess communication in the next section. The discussions in this chapter have already provided the motivation for a number of the additional details we discuss here.

In Section 4.2 we described the contents of five of the processor-defined AD slots in the Process Object. As offset from the base of the object, these are: the PSO AD, Object Table AD, Claim Object AD, Current Context AD, and the Globals Object AD. Continuing from here, the additional slots and their functions are:

- Process Carrier AD. Each process has an associated Carrier Object, used when enqueuing the process as a request at a Port. The Process Carrier AD refers to that Carrier Object.
- Dispatching Port AD. When a process is created, system software creates a distinct Dispatching Port object for the process and initializes certain values within this object, for example a set of dispatching parameter values. The Dispatching Port AD refers to this newly created object.
- Scheduling Port AD. A process, upon creation, is also associated with a distinct port for purposes of long-term scheduling. The Scheduling Port AD refers to that port. It is to this port that the process is sent, as a request, when it must be rescheduled.
- Process Fault Access Area. The slots in this area receive copies of key state information, such as the Current Message AD, Current Port AD, Current Carrier AD, and Surrogate Carrier AD. Information is deposited here during execution of an interprocess communication instruction. As we will see in the next section, such instructions require many microcycles to complete and generate more than the usual amount of intermediate state information. If the instruction completes successfully, this area is nullified upon termination of the instruction. If it faults at some point (during some intermediate state), the information in this area is used by the software to complete the instruction.
- Fault Port AD. A process, upon creation, is also associated with a distinct port for purposes of fault processing. The Fault Port AD refers to that port. It is to this port that the process is sent, as a request, when a process-level fault in the process requires processing by a fault-handling process.

5.3. i432 Interprocess Communication

The i432 architecture provides a state-of-the-art set of hardware-supported instructions that accomplish interprocess communication. These instructions represent a richer set than is needed simply for executing intertask communication in Ada programs. Nevertheless, some of the first applications of these primitives to be shown here are those that may explain how some intertask Ada calls may be implemented.

There are six principal instructions for sending and receiving messages, three send instructions and three receive instructions.

```
SEND
RECEIVE

CONDITIONAL SEND
CONDITIONAL RECEIVE


SURROGATE SEND
SURROGATE RECEIVE
```

All send and receive operations are *asynchronous*. For those unfamiliar with the significance of asynchronous operations, we offer the following review. By an *asynchronous send* operation we mean that a process sending a message needn't depend on the speed of execution of a potential receiver process. In general, the sender may send many messages without knowing (or even caring) whether or not any of these messages are ever actually received. The receiver, in fact, may not yet be ready to receive a message at the time the sender issues the send instruction. By an *asynchronous receive* operation, we mean that a process may issue a receive instruction without depending on the speed of execution of the sending process. In fact, the receive instruction may be issued before the corresponding send instruction.

The first two instructions, SEND and RECEIVE, may be taken as the "base" set. The others may be understood somewhat easily in terms of these two. Ada programmers can call (*inline*) procedures within an operating system package that will result in a direct, one-for-one translation of the procedure call statement into one of the six instructions given above. (See: Reference Manual for the Intel 432 Extensions to Ada, as cited in Appendix B.)

5.3.1. The SEND and RECEIVE Instructions

SEND and RECEIVE carry the semantic connotation of "blocking send" and "blocking receive", respectively, because a side effect of each is that the process issuing one of these instructions, is sometimes forced into a "blocked" state, pending completion of the instruction.

- The SEND instruction specifies two operands: a Port Object AD and a Message Object AD. These operands indicate a port at which to enqueue the message as a request. As mentioned earlier, each Port Object incorporates a fixed-length request queue. We consider here two subcases, one that leads to immediate completion of the instruction (fixed length request queue not full) and the other that leads to blocking of the issuing process (fixed length request queue full). For each subcase we assume, for the sake of simplicity, that the governing port discipline is FIFO.
  1. The fixed-length request queue at the designated port is not full. In this case, the designated message_AD object is placed in the fixed length queue in FIFO order, thereby completing the instruction with no further effect.
  2. The fixed-length request queue at the designated port is already full. In this case, the hardware causes the process to become unbound from its processor, and the process' carrier is appended to an *overflow extension* of the request queue. The process that issued the SEND is thereby blocked. The appended request has the structure shown in Figure 5-5. (The freed

processor goes automatically to its normal dispatching port in search of another job.)

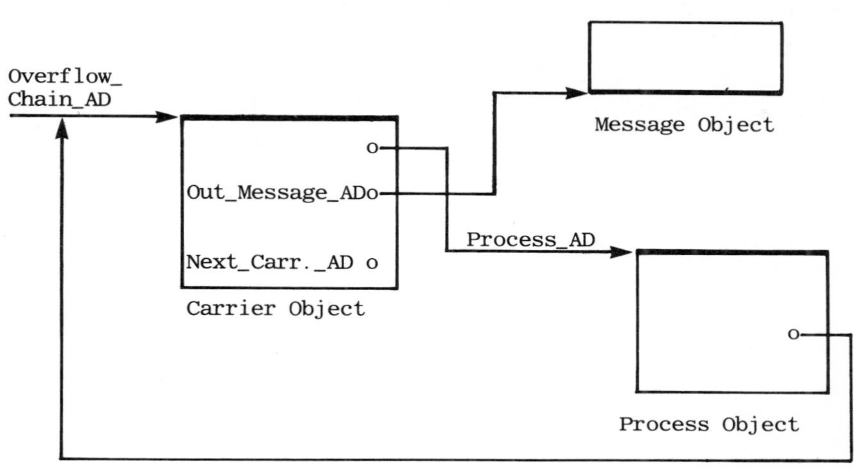

Figure 5-5 Schematic of request structure for a blocked SEND instruction. The message_AD specified in the SEND instruction is moved to the prespecified slot in the Carrier Object, marked Out_Message_AD.

[The data structure details of a Port Object have not yet been described, so the reader may well wonder how this is done. These details are actually not significant for us, but they can be examined by consulting the i432 Architecture Reference Manual.]

If more than one such ''overflow request'' arrives at the same port, then the multiple blocked processes are linked through the Carrier Objects of the blocked processes. The head of such an overflow chain is always anchored to a prespecified position within the Port Object.

When a server arrives at a port, regardless of whether or not an ''overflow'' condition exists, the head message AD entry of the fixed-length queue is bound to the server. This releases a slot in the fixed-length queue. The (always FIFO) first overflow queue entry is then detached from the overflow chain, and the message_AD in the Carrier Object component of the overflow queue entry is extracted and inserted in the freed queue slot of the fixed-length queue. The detached queue entry (a carrier, representing a process) is then forwarded, using the *second_port mechanism*, to the request queue of its proper Dispatching Port (or Scheduling Port), thus *unblocking* the previously queued process.

The second port mechanism is actually a significant (and general) feature of the i432 architecture; it is used to unblock a process that has become enqueued by any send or receive operation. There is a prespecified slot in every Carrier Object, known as the *Second Port AD*. The Carrier Object for a process A has that slot preloaded with a copy of the Dispatching Port AD for process A. And so, when A issues a SEND (or a RECEIVE) instruction and then becomes blocked, the processor can later reschedule A as part of the unblocking operation. No additional i432 instructions need to be executed to accomplish this action. (For the SEND and RECEIVE instructions, the second port specification is implicit. Later, we will see that for the SURROGATE SEND and SURROGATE RECEIVE instructions, the second port specification must be explicitly provided.)

- The RECEIVE instruction simply specifies a port at which to pick up a message. The receptacle slot does not need to be specified because it is implicit in the architecture that a received message_AD is deposited in the prespecified slot of the current Context Object. (This is the slot referred to in Section 4.3.1 as *Message Object AD*.) Again, there are two subcases to consider, one that leads to immediate completion of the instruction (at least one request enqueued at the designated port) and the other that leads to the blocking of the issuing process (no requests at the designated port.)

  1. There is at least one request enqueued at the designated port. In this case, the message_AD at the head of the request queue is extracted from the port and assigned to the proper slot in the Context Object of the process that issued the RECEIVE operation.

     Note that when there is at least one enqueued request at a port there can be no servers also enqueued at that port. This is because there is strict adherence to a locking discipline governing each access of a port, which ensures that only one processor at a time may use the same Port Object. For example, if there is one enqueued request, then only the process that next locks that port can access it. If that process is a server, then it will become bound to the request. Only after that use of the port can another server become enqueued at the port. (Similar reasoning should convince the reader that if there is at least one server enqueued at a port, there can be no requests also enqueued at the same port.)
  2. There are no requests enqueued at the designated port. This condition leads to the blocking of the issuing process. Its Carrier Object is enqueued on a linked list of such servers that is anchored to the Port Object. After enqueuing the current process' carrier, the processor revisits its Dispatching Port for another job. Figure 5-2 illustrates precisely the structure of an enqueued server process awaiting the arrival of a message, so we need not repeat it here. (One has only to change the name of the root AD from "Request_AD" to "Server_AD".)

When the enqueued server entry reaches the head of the server queue, it will become unblocked upon arrival of the first subsequent message. The SEND instruction supplying the new message_AD for that port causes the sent message_AD to be deposited in the Context Object of the enqueued process at the front of the server queue. The enqueued server entry is then detached from the queue and forwarded to its proper Dispatching Port. (This unblocking is accomplished using the implied Second Port AD found in the Process Carrier—as described earlier in the explanation for the SEND instruction.)

An obvious application of the SEND and RECEIVE instructions in the compiled version of an Ada program is for implementing the execution of an "unconditional **accept**" statement within a server task. Recall from Section 3.2.3, that an unconditional **accept** statement is one which requires the task to wait for a rendezvous (indefinitely) in case there are no task calls pending at **entry** E associated with this **accept**. Therefore, implementation of an unconditional **accept** E could be defined as follows: Associate each entry E of a task with a port E-INIT. Issue a RECEIVE instruction for port E-INIT and, upon completing it, perform the body of the **accept** statement. Finally, issue a SEND instruction to port E-RESPOND (to be described below).

A corresponding call of entry E within another task could be implemented as follows: Associate each entry E that is potentially called by a task with a port E-RESPOND. Issue a SEND instruction for port E-INIT and, upon completing it, perform a RECEIVE instruction for port E-RESPOND. Given this implementation of the entry call and **accept** statements, note that port E-RESPOND never contains more than one server. This protocol is suggested in Figure 5-6, where the arrows indicate the direction of message flow.

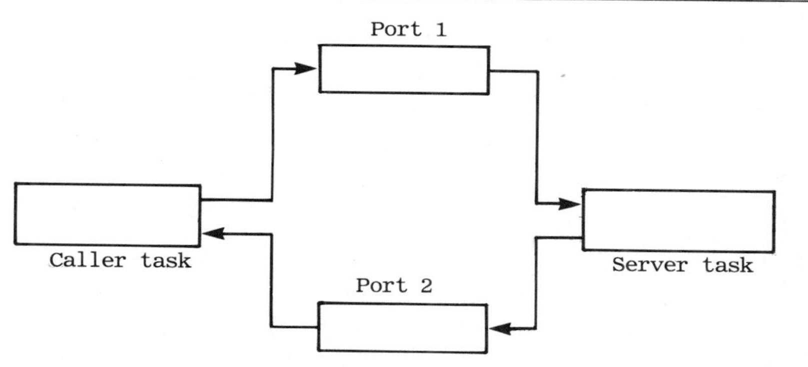

Figure 5-6 Structure of a two-way communication channel between a caller and a server task. The caller task issues a SEND, RECEIVE sequence and the server task issues a RECEIVE, SEND sequence.

Note that the Ada rendezvous semantics suggest that a calling task should be blocked until completion of the rendezvous. Implementing a task call using a blocking SEND, RECEIVE sequence, therefore, harmonizes with this intent.

5.3.2. The CONDITIONAL SEND and CONDITIONAL RECEIVE Instructions

These two instructions are provided to permit a process to avoid becoming blocked during a send or receive operation. Each of these instructions specifies one additional operand, a boolean variable, which is set true if the instruction has succeeded (i.e., message enqueued at port) and is set false if it has failed (i.e., instruction has no effect). In all other respects, the semantics of these instructions are identical with those of the simple SEND and RECEIVE instructions described above.

To decide whether to abort the attempt and set the boolean false, the hardware has merely to test, in the case of the send operation, whether or not the request queue at the specified port is full, and in the case of the receive operation, whether or not the request queue at the specified port is empty. Succeeding instructions can test the value of this boolean to determine the outcome of a preceding CONDITIONAL SEND or CONDITIONAL RECEIVE instruction.

The most obvious application for the CONDITIONAL RECEIVE instructions is for *polling*. For example, when polling one or more ports for a message at any of them, one might use a sequence of CONDITIONAL RECEIVEs.

An interesting application that uses both the CONDITIONAL SEND and CONDITIONAL RECEIVE occurs in the efficient management of a situation in which multiple processors (or processes) are reserving and later releasing objects that are all of the same form. An efficiency problem can arise with respect to the garbage collector if the processes are reserving and releasing the objects at an extremely high rate of speed; in releasing objects the processes can generate garbage so rapidly that the garbage collector falls far behind and the system becomes hopelessly clogged with "garbage" objects. The situation can be relieved somewhat by locally managing a pool of objects that can be reserved for a period of time by one of several processes and later explicitly returned to the pool for recycling.

One can think of this scheme as providing an "object buffer" outside the garbage collection mechanism that "protects" a system from becoming clogged during times of high activity with respect to objects. The scheme works very well in offloading the garbage collector during times of high activity; during times of low activity the garbage collector has no difficulty keeping up with the generation of "garbage" objects. The design challenge is to devise a pool management scheme that functions well during times of high activity, functions well during times of low activity in which the pool may be empty for long periods of time and, finally, ensures that the pool does not grow without bound.

From these requirements, it is easy to see that (1) a process should never wait for the return of an object to the pool if the process requests an object and finds the pool empty and (2) the size of the pool should be bounded.

The management of the pool relies on CONDITIONAL SEND and CONDITIONAL RECEIVE. In particular, the pool is represented by a port with a fixed-length queue size of N. A process that requires an object from the pool issues a CONDITIONAL RECEIVE from the port. If an object exists in the pool (i.e., is queued at the port) then the process is bound to the object and the process continues. If the pool is empty (i.e., no objects are queued at the port) then the process does not block and can request that an object be newly allocated from a heap. When a process wishes to return an object to the pool it issues a CONDITIONAL SEND to the port with the object as the message. If the pool is not full (i.e., less than N objects are queued at the port) then the object is enqueued at the port to be later bound to a process that requests an object. If the pool is full (i.e., the fixed-length queue at the port is full) then the process does not block and can, by destroying its Access Descriptor to the object, ensure that the object will later be reclaimed by the garbage collector.

[Neither the CONDITIONAL SEND nor the CONDITIONAL RECEIVE instruction is sufficient for simulating Ada's conditional entry statement if we use the implementation for the **accept** statement discussed at the end of section 5.3.1. We now proceed to show why this is true. The conditional entry statement was not discussed in Chapter 3; its syntax is as follows:

```
conditional entry call ::=
  select
    entry_call [sequence_of_statements]
  else
    sequence_of_statements
  end select;
```

The informal semantics are: "A conditional entry call issues the **entry** call if and only if a rendezvous is immediately possible" [2].

The use of a CONDITIONAL RECEIVE instruction by a requesting (calling) task cannot be used to implement Ada's conditional entry since this would require that the server (called) task be able to distinguish between its having been called by a conditional entry or an unconditional entry. This requirement would exist because in the implementation given in section 5.3.1, the server expects the requesting (calling) task to begin a rendezvous by sending a message rather than by receiving a message. Neither can the CONDITIONAL SEND instruction be used to implement the conditional entry. This is because the CONDITIONAL SEND instruction succeeds (and therefore initiates an entry) if and only if a slot is available in the fixed-length queue of a port. This does not necessarily ensure that a server is waiting at the port to immediately process the request.]

5.3.3. The SURROGATE SEND and SURROGATE RECEIVE Instructions

The SURROGATE SEND and SURROGATE RECEIVE instructions are among the most interesting and innovative instructions in the entire i432 repertoire. The SURROGATE SEND instruction allows a process to send a message to a port without the risk of itself being blocked. Similarly, the SURROGATE RECEIVE instruction allows a process to wait for a message at several ports without the risk of being blocked at some port before all the waits have been issued. Note that CONDITIONAL SEND (CONDITIONAL RECEIVE) can be used to obtain the effect of SURROGATE SEND (SURROGATE RECEIVE), but the implementation involves polling, or "busy waiting", and is not normally considered an efficient solution to the problems solved by SURROGATE SEND (SURROGATE RECEIVE).

The risk of becoming blocked is avoided by automatically delegating that risk to a *surrogate process*. As a byproduct in studying the SURROGATE SEND and SURROGATE RECEIVE, we can gain added appreciation of the Carrier Object and its potential as an important new data type for computation structures.

Normally, a conceptual process in the i432 is represented as a Process Carrier Object and a Process Object, each cross-referencing the other. However, the i432 also supports the concept of a *surrogate process*: a Carrier Object existing alone, without a corresponding Process Object. Under certain circumstances, to be revealed in this section, a surrogate process behaves exactly as does a process, with all the privileges normally enjoyed by a process. To emphasize its role, we will refer to a Carrier Object representing a surrogate process as a *Surrogate Carrier*. We study the role of a Surrogate Carrier throughout the rest of this section.

With this introduction as background, we are now ready to explain the SURROGATE SEND and SURROGATE RECEIVE instructions.

- The SURROGATE SEND instruction specifies, in addition to a Port Object, hereafter referred to as "First_port", and a Message Object AD, two more operands:
  - A Carrier Object—spawned to serve as a surrogate for the process that issued the instruction, and in doing so to convey the Message Object AD to First_port and to accept the risk of becoming blocked in case First_port's fixed-length request queue is full.
  - A Second_port Object—to which the surrogate will be sent as a message and become enqueued as a request, after delivering Message Object AD at the First_port.

The action of SURROGATE SEND is specified as follows:

The specified Message Object AD and Second Port AD operands are both placed in the Surrogate Carrier object at prespecified slots. The Surrogate Carrier is then treated by the hardware in a manner analogous to how it would be treated if it were the carrier of a process that had executed a SEND instruction to the first port. That is, the Surrogate Carrier either immediately enqueues its Message Object AD in the fixed-length queue of the first port, or is blocked (linked into the chain of other blocked carriers), until it is able to enqueue its message in the fixed-length queue. In either case, a server will (in normal circumstances) eventually accept the message. Finally, after the Surrogate Carrier has eventually managed to enqueue its message in the fixed-length queue of the first port, the Surrogate Carrier is sent as a message to the second port. Recall that the Second Port AD resides within the Surrogate Carrier. The process that issued the SURROGATE SEND instruction always resumes execution at completion of the instruction; a process that issues a SURROGATE SEND instruction is *never* blocked as a result of that instruction. Completion of the SURROGATE SEND instruction is defined as the point at which the Surrogate Carrier has become enqueued as a request in the fixed-length queue of the second port or the point at which the Surrogate Carrier has become blocked at either the first or second port, whichever comes first.

- Once one understands the SURROGATE SEND instruction, the semantics for SURROGATE RECEIVE becomes quite easy to grasp. This instruction specifies, in addition to a First_port, the same two additional operands as specified in SURROGATE SEND, namely:
    - A Carrier Object—spawned to serve as a surrogate for the process that issued the instruction, and in doing so to wait to receive a message at First_port and to accept the risk of becoming blocked in case First_port's request queue is empty.
    - A Second_port Object—to which the surrogate will be sent to deliver itself as a request, with the received Message Object AD embedded within it.

  The action of SURROGATE RECEIVE is specified as follows:

  The Second Port AD operand is placed in the Surrogate Carrier Object at a prespecified slot. The Surrogate Carrier is then treated by the hardware in a manner analogous to how it would be treated if it were the carrier of a process that had executed a RECEIVE instruction from the first port. That is, the Surrogate Carrier either immediately receives a Message Object AD from the fixed-length queue of the first port, or is blocked (linked into the chain of other blocked carriers), until it is able to receive a message from the fixed-length queue. In either case, the Surrogate Carrier will (in normal circumstances) eventually receive a message. At this point, the Surrogate Carrier, carrying the message that it just received, is sent as a message to the Second Port. Recall that the second port AD resides within the Surrogate Carrier. The process that issued the SURROGATE RECEIVE instruction always resumes execution at completion of the instruction; a process that issues a SURROGATE RECEIVE instruction is *never* blocked as a result of that instruction. Completion of the SURROGATE RECEIVE instruction is defined as the point at which the Surrogate Carrier has become enqueued as a request in the fixed-length queue of the second port or the point at which the Surrogate Carrier has become blocked at either the first or second port, whichever comes first.

Useful applications of i432 SENDs and RECEIVEs, including the SURROGATE instructions, are bound to be numerous. One can use these instructions directly by issuing calls to (inline) procedures implemented within a special, system-supplied Ada package. Calls to these procedures are compiled as i432 SEND and RECEIVE instruction forms. In Section 5.5 we show how this is done. Here we merely sketch one or two possible applications for the SURROGATE instructions.

In the remainder of this subsection we choose an instructive application for each of the SURROGATE operations.

- For SURROGATE RECEIVE we choose as the application a simplified model of the Ada **select** statement.
- For SURROGATE SEND we choose as the application a user-tailorable priority message system.

Although the instructions generated by the i432 Ada compiler to represent a particular Ada **select** statement includes SURROGATE port operations, the model of implementation is more complex than we wish to consider here. (The full semantics of the **select** statement is surprisingly complex.) Hence, we choose to simulate here only a simple and special case. In particular, we consider the case where none of the **accept** alternatives are guarded by **when** conditions, where **delay**, **terminate**, and **else** alternatives are absent, and where applicable entry calls are unconditional only.

For this restricted example, each of the alternative **accept** statements that constitute the **select** statement (numbered, in order, as 1, . . . , k, . . . , N for reference) is associated with its own ACCEPT_k port. In addition, a single R_QUEUE port is used as a "junction box" for enqueuing each rendezvous that has occurred for the various **accept** statements within this **select** statement. The entry calls associated with each rendezvous may originate from any of several tasks. Figure 5-7 shows this message flow structure for three **accept** statement alternatives. Later, we will discuss the return flow structure for routing of return messages that behave as end-of-rendezvous signals.

The Ada compiler performs a select statement elaboration for each select statement that occurs within a task. This elaboration is performed as part of the initialization of the task. The elaboration is accomplished by the task issuing individual SURROGATE RECEIVE instructions, one for each **select** statement alternative. For example,

```
SURROGATE RECEIVE(ACCEPT_1, Carrier_1, R_QUEUE)
SURROGATE RECEIVE(ACCEPT_2, Carrier_2, R_QUEUE)
SURROGATE RECEIVE(ACCEPT_3, Carrier_3, R_QUEUE)
```

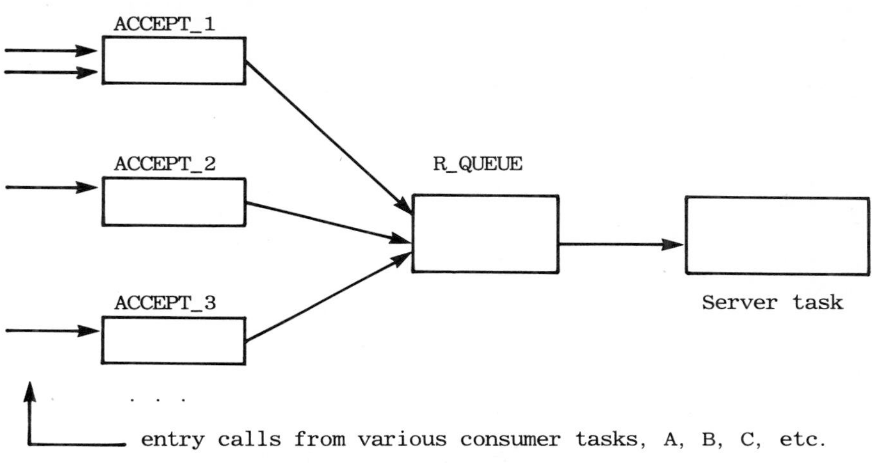

Figure 5-7 Structure of forward message flow to an Ada server task.

Each of these instructions is a request to pick up a single message at an ACCEPT port and deliver it as a request to R_QUEUE. If these instructions are followed by the instruction,

```
RECEIVE(R_QUEUE)
```

then the **select** statement will eventually receive a carrier from R_QUEUE that contains a message indicating that a rendezvous has commenced for one of its constituent **accept** statements.

The enqueuing of incoming rendezvous requests into R_QUEUE uses the queueing discipline of R_QUEUE, so that the **select** statement merely picks the head rendezvous entry of the R_QUEUE port. (This implies that the Carrier_k sent to its ACCEPT_k port must contain appropriate priority information for select alternative k.) By examining the carrier associated with this rendezvous entry, the server task can determine all it needs to know to process the selected **accept** statement and any succeeding statements within the alternative. This is because the AD for each received Surrogate Carrier is unique (as is any AD), and so the carrier can be correlated to the **accept** statement with which it is associated. An important additional assumption made here is that the received message within the carrier associated with the rendezvous will also contain information that can be used to identify the calling task. This information is needed to specify a target port for the end-of-rendezvous message and is supplied by the compiler in the generation of the message sent by the calling task.

When the **accept** statement completes (the rendezvous completes), the executing task must perform two functions before it can continue:

1. it must respond with an end-of-rendezvous message to the calling task and
2. it must ensure that the **select** statement is re-initialized.

Responding to the calling task is carried out in almost exactly the same manner as the case of a simple rendezvous discussed earlier. An end-of-rendezvous message, including the result values for any **out** or **in out** parameters, is sent to the calling task's E-RESPOND port. Re-initializing the **select** statement ensures that the alternative just selected will be given another opportunity to cause a rendezvous in case the **select** statement is executed again. Consequently, if the carrier associated with the rendezvous is Carrier_k then the **select** statement is re-initialized by executing the instruction

```
SURROGATE RECEIVE(ACCEPT_k, Carrier_k, R_QUEUE)
```

The calling task is not aware that it is intended to rendezvous by means of an unconditional **accept** statement or an **accept** statement within a **select** statement. Consequently, the action of the calling task is the same in both cases. This action was discussed in section 5.3.1.

After the termination of a task containing one or more **select** statements, there must exist a finalization sequence of instructions that "cleans up" the apparatus currently pending for **select** statements. We leave such details, if of interest, to be pursued by the reader.

The foregoing has been an extended example, which in essence has merely illustrated the use of SURROGATE RECEIVE instructions to implement what is commonly termed a "multiple wait" paradigm, familiar to many system programmers. The example was deliberately couched in the Ada setting so readers can appreciate what may be involved in implementing a **select** statement. We have not considered a general solution to this implementation problem, but one can see how much machinery is involved. Without hardware support, such as provided in the i432, execution of the **select** statement might be too slow for frequent use.

We now turn to our second example, the user-tailorable message priority system from Cox et al. [14], to illustrate the application of the SURROGATE SEND instruction. In this system, process PRODUCER sends a potentially infinite length stream of messages of varying priorities to process CONSUMER. The PRODUCER process cannot depend on the CONSUMER process' rate of message consumption, and the CONSUMER process cannot depend on the PRODUCER process' rate of production.

Surrogate carriers are needed, not only to prevent process PRODUCER from becoming blocked while it issues its stream of messages, but also to ensure that each message sent is inserted into its proper position within the queue of messages not yet consumed by process CONSUMER.

For the remainder of this example we assume a priority queueing discipline at any ports in question and we refer to the information needed to place an object into its proper position within a port as its *priority*. Note that when a process sends a message to a port using a priority queueing discipline, the priority of the message is taken from the Carrier Object that holds the message. Therefore, when a process sends a message using a SEND instruction the priority is taken from the carrier of the process that sends the message. But, of course, this can't be what we want for the above application. Not only does the priority of the process have nothing to do with the priority of the messages it is sending, but every message will have the same priority if the process' priority doesn't change—and this is clearly not what is intended.

In order to be able to attach a priority to a message that is sent to a port, the SURROGATE SEND instruction must be used. The priority of the message to be sent is placed into the *priority slot* of the Surrogate Carrier that is specified as an operand to the SURROGATE SEND instruction. Since the Surrogate Carrier is the carrier that holds the message when it arrives at the port, it is the priority of the Surrogate Carrier that will be used to enqueue the message. For example,

```
SURROGATE SEND(First_port, message_ref, my_carrier, Second_port)
```

will cause the message_ref to be delivered by my_carrier to First_port. Assuming First_port's service mode has been set to Priority-mode and assuming that my_carrier has its priority value set as desired, then the message will be inserted in priority order when my_carrier arrives at First_port.

After delivery of the message, my_carrier is enqueued at Second_port (FIFO queueing discipline), where it can be picked up by process PRODUCER and reused in sending another message of the same or different priority value. Until needed however, the my_carrier may remain enqueued at Second_port, which serves as a pool (or ''parking garage''). The pick-up of a ''parked'' carrier may be done with an ordinary RECEIVE or with a CONDITIONAL RECEIVE. For example:

```
RECEIVE(Second_port)
```

will render the first available Carrier accessible for reuse in another SURROGATE SEND. The above scenario is illustrated in Figure 5-8 which diagrams the flow of messages of the several send and receive operations as directed arcs joining process and port objects.

5.3.4. Modelling Asynchronous Send/Receive Operations in Standard Ada

We have now examined the i432 architecture's facilities for support of asynchronous interprocess communication. In Section 5.5 we will examine how these facilities can be invoked explicitly by the user at the Ada level. It seems useful at this point to consider, as an alternative approach, how equivalent asynchronous intertask communication can be expressed in standard Ada, i.e., without direct appeal to the underlying i432 port-based operations.

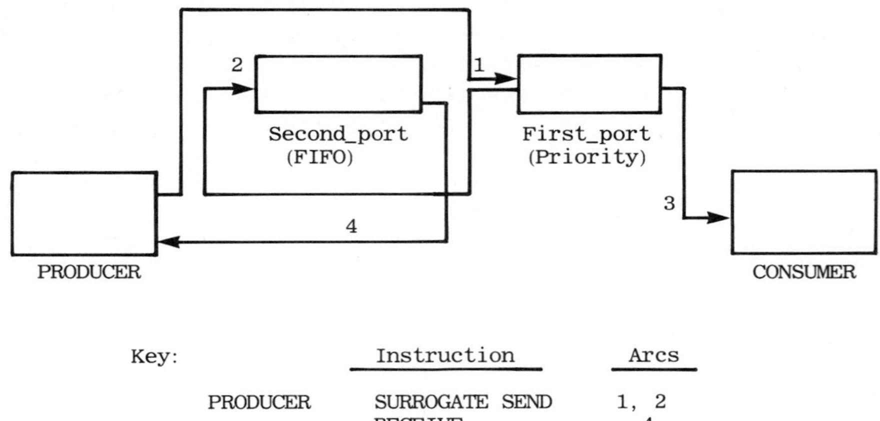

Key:

	Instruction	Arcs
PRODUCER	SURROGATE SEND	1, 2
	RECEIVE	4
CONSUMER	RECEIVE	3

Figure 5-8 Request flow graph for implementation of a user-tailorable message priority system to illustrate use of the SURROGATE SEND instruction.

Recall that the Ada rendezvous mechanism forces synchronization of the task caller (sender) and the server task (receiver). Even so, it is possible to model asynchronous communication, and thereby to eliminate performance delays in certain common situations. This may be done provided the programmer is willing to interpose "intermediary" tasks between the sender and receiver tasks. For example, if an Ada task A only sends information to another task B (i.e., if task A does not need to wait for completion of the associated **accept** statement in task B), then we can simulate an asynchronous send operation using the technique mentioned in Section 3.1 and amplified below:

Suppose a third task Q is interposed between A and B so that A does a rendezvous with Q. Then either:

a. Q does a rendezvous with B, forwarding to it the message received from A. Since Q can immediately accept the message from A, the time A is blocked in rendezvous with Q can be minimized. Note that B blocks only if Q is awaiting rendezvous with A.

or

b. if A is expected to send a sequence of messages, Q, after accepting each message from A, spawns a new task and does a rendezvous with that spawned task, forwarding to it the message received from A. Each of the spawned tasks then does a rendezvous with B. Each spawned task terminates after completing the rendezvous with B. In this case, B blocks only if no spawned tasks are awaiting rendezvous with it and A blocks only if it sends another message to Q before Q can complete the spawning of a new task for relaying an earlier message sent by A.

We illustrate alternative (b) as follows: Suppose A would ordinarily have made the entry call

```
B.Some_entry(k);
```

and B accepts by

```
accept B.Some_entry(k: integer) do
    -- statements that include k;
  end  B.Some_entry;
```

With task Q interposed, however, the call by A becomes

```
Q.Relay_to_Spawned(k);
```

and the **accept** statement in B remains unchanged. A new task Q is defined at the same scope level as that of tasks A and B as follows:

```
task Q is
  entry Relay_to_Spawned(k: integer);
end Q;

task body Q is
  task type Spawned is
    entry Relay_to_B(k: integer);
  end Spawned;

  task body Spawned is
  begin
    accept Relay_to_B(k: integer) do
      B.Some_entry(k);
    end Relay_to_B;
  end Spawned;          -- This task terminates upon completion
                        -- of this accept.

type ref_to_spawned is access Spawned;
Spawned_Task: ref_to_spawned;

begin
  loop
    accept Relay_to_Spawned(k: integer) do
      Spawned_Task := new Spawned;
      Spawned_Task.Relay_to_B(k);
    end Relay_to_Spawned;
  end loop;
end Q;
```

Under this scheme, each spawned task operates very much like the surrogate carrier of an i432 SURROGATE SEND instruction. (Observe that the variable Spawned_Task is reused in Q. This means that earlier spawned tasks become unreachable by Q, so that after each of these spawned tasks terminates it becomes a candidate for garbage collection. Also note the task Q can be redefined as a **generic** package having a generic parameter that designates the structure of the relayed information.)

The above scheme seems attractive because it relies on no special packages, such as those we will describe in Section 5.5 for use of i432 ports. On the other hand, the cost in performance may well be prohibitive, unless the underlying architecture can support the Ada rendezvous with efficiency comparable to that of the equivalent i432 port operations. Moreover, if the sender task (task A) is dependent on receipt of a response correlated with each sent message, additions to an already complicated task structure may be needed. We pursue this line of reasoning no further here; these matters should be left as open questions, to be answered when more experience has been gained with the use of Ada and with the i432 System.

5.4. The Unified View Offered by the Request/Server Model

We next want to illustrate the user-interface provided for the i432 architecture's interprocess communication facility, and we attempt this in the next section. There, we show how operations of interprocess communication can be made a direct and useful part of applications programs. However, before doing so, we can gain some useful perspective if we pause here to take stock. A few observations are in order concerning the models and mechanisms introduced in this chapter thus far.

- We have seen the merit of i432 architects' design choice to make scheduling and dispatching of processes fit into a message-based communication framework following the request/server model. Policies, which are best left to software derivation, are neatly separated from the mechanisms of dispatching and scheduling, which are best done as swiftly as possible, and hence best done with as much hardware support as possible.

  An example of policy is the determination of which process to dispatch in a set of processes that are waiting for service. Dispatching decisions may vary greatly between applications; depending on the system environment, such decisions may be changing on a second-to-second basis. (One of the biggest dangers in transferring operating systems functions from software into hardware is that failure to properly separate policy issues from mechanism issues can result in policy decisions creeping into hardware, where they cannot be changed on any short-term basis.)

- The model and the mechanisms, some newly invented in the i432, and most arrived at as a direct consequence of the object-based addressing and access controls of the architecture, lead to an efficient interprocess communication facility. The latter is not only general purpose, but in fact extends the state of the art. This extension is embodied in the SURROGATE SEND and RECEIVE operations and, in turn depends on the innovation of the Carrier Object used in a uniform way for *sends* and *receives*, whether explicit or implicit, and whether for dispatching and scheduling or for more general process-to-process interaction.

The special invention that appears to stand out above the rest is the Carrier Object used as a surrogate. Its full utility is probably yet to be determined, however at the "top level" we see that it provides a process a simple and direct way to exercise control over whether or not it blocks in sending and receiving messages. Certainly there are many applications in which a process must have this kind of control over its own destiny. Other relevant ideas concerning surrogates are:

- In explaining the role of the Surrogate Carrier, we have used the analogy of a *surrogate process*, but there may be better explanations, or at least some useful supplementary explanations. For example, Cox et al. [14] have referred to the Surrogate Carrier as a "self-addressed, stamped envelope". In a SURROGATE RECEIVE operation, such an envelope is sent to the First_port and left there, pending the arrival of the expected message. When the message arrives, it is stuffed into the envelope and "mailed". Since it is addressed, the envelope can reach its ultimate destination, Second_port. Since it is stamped, it has the necessary "potential" for travel through the mail system to arrive at its destination.
- The envelope analogy also holds for the SURROGATE SEND, but with a new "twist" required in the interpretation. Here one must understand that the envelope bearing the message, has significant value in its own right—much like the sturdy metal cake box, whose see-through top effectively alerts postal workers to its perishable and fragile contents, which may be more valuable than the cake it contains. The box must be returned to "grandmother", if another cake, on another birthday is to be forthcoming.
- When models like the request/server, and analogies, like surrogate processes or stamped return envelopes, help us grasp and perceive as simple, mechanisms that would otherwise appear formidable and complicated, they serve as critically important tools. Use of them may make the difference between broad use of an innovative and powerful facility or broad shunning of it. This is why we can foretell wide use for message-based communication operators of the i432 architecture.

- Asynchronous communication and synchronous communication are both available as modes of communication. There are many applications in which one or the other of asynchronous or synchronous communication is the most desirable method of interprocess communication. The i432 provides completely asynchronous communication through, again, the utility of the surrogate carrier object. Synchronous communication can always be accomplished by establishing a protocol (like the Ada rendezvous) between sending and receiving processes. Such a protocol requires that a process S, which sends a message to a process R, wait for a received acknowledgment message from R before proceeding.

- Education of users to the potential of multiprocessing applications is a major challenge. Real-world applications are in many cases difficult to express with clarity without use of an underlying and unified communication model. The i432 communication model may well provide the needed catalyst.

5.5. Ada Programmers' Interface with iMAX for Interprocess Communication

An Ada programmer can use all of the i432 features for interprocess communication described in Section 5.3 as an alternative or supplement to the Ada rendezvous facility. The i432 features are accessed by using either or both of two user-accessible Ada packages supplied by the iMAX operating system. These packages are:

- Typed_Ports
- Untyped_Ports

The Typed_Ports package fulfills most user needs for i432 interprocess communication by permitting the programmer to create and use ports requiring messages of a specific type. A typed port is thus a constraint of a port that allows an Ada programmer to send (receive) messages of only a single, specified type to (from) a port. This constraint is checked at compile time. The use of a typed port has the advantage that it follows the spirit of Ada's strong type-checking objective by allowing the Ada compiler to verify that the typed port is used correctly. We have provided the Ada specification for the Typed_Ports package in Appendix H. The reader is referred to that appendix if more details are desired.

The second package, Untyped_Ports, is useful for lower-level applications, where it is essential to relax the one-port/one-message-type constraint. An untyped port can be used to transmit a message of any (Access Descriptor) type.

The primary disadvantage of Untyped_Ports is that compile time checking of message types is impossible. The primary disadvantage of using Typed_Ports is that a programmer must create an individual instance of a generic package for each distinct message type required. For very large applications, this may produce many generic instantiations that may, in turn, produce programs that require excessive memory space. However, for most applications, this disadvantage is far outweighed by the convenience and built-in safety features offered by Typed_Ports.

Our objective in this section is to demonstrate the use of the Typed_ports package to allow an Ada programmer to gain access to the i432 communication model. First, we look at the key components of Type_Ports. Then we illustrate their use by revisiting the examples introduced at the end of the Section 5.3 and by showing how they may be coded in Ada. The section closes with observations on the equivalence of the Ada rendezvous and the iMAX Typed_Ports facility and on some tradeoffs between the two approaches. In the next and last section of this chapter we revisit the investment club program to see how Typed_Ports may be used to advantage.

5.5.1. Structure and Main Features of Typed_Ports

Typed_Ports is an Ada library unit package that contains three generic packages named:

- Simple_Port_Def
- Carrier_Def
- Surrogate_Port_Def

The Typed_Ports package is structured as three generic sub-packages so that programmers can choose to instantiate any of the three generic packages individually, thus minimizing, in appropriate cases, the size of instantiated packages. Thus, for example, in an application not requiring SURROGATE SENDs and RECEIVEs, a programmer will create only instances of Simple_Port_Def. This will provide the capability to create and use ports with either FIFO or Priority service disciplines in SEND, RECEIVE, CONDITIONAL SEND, or CONDITIONAL RECEIVE operations. The skeletal structure of Typed_Ports is given in Figure 5-9. Excerpts from the code for Simple_Port_Def are given in Figure 5-10.

Examining Figure 5-9 first, we note that Typed_Ports depends on iMAX_Definitions. Actually, the iMAX_Definitions package is only the "tip of the iceberg." Other iMAX packages on which iMAX_Definitions is dependent (and on which Typed_Ports is indirectly dependent) are responsible for all the low-level storage, descriptor, and extended-type management that make interprocess communication at the user interface safe and easy to apply. We defer discussion of these topics until Chapters 6 and 9.

Suppose a programmer wishes to establish simple communication between two tasks, A and B, by sending messages of type "memo" from A to B and messages of type "response" between B and A (assume that types memo and response have already been declared.) According to the Ada specification in Figure 5-9, the following declarations would instantiate the packages required to achieve this communication:

```
with iMAX_Definitions;
package Typed_Ports is
  -- Function:
  --   Typed_Ports consists of three packages which provide the user
  --   with a high level (Ada typed) view of ports, carriers and other
  --   operations.

  use iMAX_Definitions;

  generic
      type user_message is private;       -- All messages that this package
                                          -- deals with are of this type.

  package Simple_Port_Def is
    -- Function:
    --   This package provides definitions and operations that enable
    --   the user to create ports, and do simple operations on those
    --   ports involving only messages of type "user_message".
   .........
  end Simple_Port_Def;

  generic
      type user_message is private;       -- Type of message as
                                          -- specified by the user.
      type user_carrier_id is private;    -- Type of carrier_id as
                                          -- specified by the user.

  package Carrier_Def is
    -- Function:
    --   Definitions and operations on carriers are provided in
    --   this package.
   ..........
  end Carrier_Def;

  generic
      type user_port     is private;      -- Port capable of handling
                                          -- user_messages.
      type user_message is private;       -- Type of messages as
                                          -- specified by the user.
      type user_carrier is private;       -- Carrier capable of
                                          -- carrying user_messages.
      type user_carrier_port is private;  -- Port capable of handling
                                          -- user_carriers.

  package Surrogate_Port_Def is
    -- Function:
    --   This package contains surrogate port operations.
    --
   .........
  end Surrogate_Port_Def;

end Typed_Ports;
```

Figure 5-9 Top_level structure of the iMAX Operating System package, Typed_Ports.

```
with Typed_Ports;
          ...
package Memo_Port_Def is new Typed_Ports.Simple_Port_Def(memo);
package Response_Port_Def is new Typed_Ports.Simple_Port_Def(response);
```

5.5.2. The Simple_Port_Def Package

In Figure 5-10, we reveal another layer of the Typed_Ports package; in particular, we reveal the specification of the generic sub-package Simple_Port_Defs. By looking at this specification and understanding the semantics of the operations in the package, we can determine how to create ports and how to use them once they are created. Before proceeding to illustrate this use, we digress here to observe some fine points of Ada that we will exploit below.

Note that the Create function in Typed_Ports returns an object of type user_port. To create a particular port, named my_memo_port, for transmitting objects of type memo, one can use the following declaration in any program unit that "imports" Memo_Port_Def:

```
my_memo_port: Memo_Port_Def.user_port  := Memo_Port_Def.Create(15);
```

The declaration above specifies that my_memo_port is a port having a fixed-length message queue capacity of 15 messages of type memo, having a default service mode of FIFO, and whose storage is allocated from the global heap.

By noting that the Create function returns an object of type user_port, the experienced Ada programmer would realize that a subtype declaration may be used as a renaming device to make the above declaration more compact. Thus, the given subtype declaration:

```
subtype memo_port is Memo_Port_Def.user_port;
```

The declaration and initialization of the variable my_memo_port can be written as follows:

```
my_memo_port: memo_port  := Memo_Port_Def.Create(15);
```

or, even more succinctly, as:

```
use Memo_Port_Def;
 ...
my_memo_port: memo_port  := Create(15);
```

The ports to be shared by processes A and B must be created by the common parent of A and B, using, for example, the set of declarations shown in Figure 5-11.

From examination of Figure 5-11, we learn how processes A and B would take advantage of the created ports for transmission of messages. For example, process A could send messages using:

```
generic
    type user_message is private;           -- All messages that
                  -- this package deals with are of this type.
package Simple_Port_Def is
  --
  -- Function:
  --    This package provides definitions and operations that enable
  --    the user to create ports, and do simple operations on those
  --    ports involving only messages of type "user_message".

max_message_count:  short_ordinal := 1000; -- Max number of messages
                  -- in a port's message queue.

type user_port is private;                  -- Ports of this type
                  -- can only be used with type user_message.

null_user_port: constant user_port;

type q_discipline is  (
    FIFO,        -- First_in_first_out, also default q_discipline.
    priority);   -- Within same priority, FIFO is used.

function Create(
    message_count:     short_ordinal range 1 .. max_message_count;
                 -- Max number of messages in the port's message queue.

    port_discipline:  q_discipline := FIFO;
    sro:              storage_resource := null)
  return user_port;                         -- User port that is created.
  --
  -- Function:
  --   A user_port with the specified message_count and the specified
  --   message queue discipline is created. The SRO used in the
  --   creation defaults to the default_global_heap_SRO.

procedure Send(prt: user_port; msg: user_message);
  --
  -- Function:
  --    The specified user_message is sent to the specified
  --    user_port.

procedure Receive(prt:  user_port; msg:  out user_message);
  --
  -- Function:
  --    A message will be received from the specified user_port.

end Simple_Port_Def;
```

Figure 5-10 Excerpts from the generic package, Simple_Port_Def.

```
package Memo_Port_Def is new Simple_Port_Def (memo);

subtype memo_port is Memo_Port_Def.user_port;


package Response_Port_Def is new Simple_Port_Def (response);

subtype response_port is Response_Port_Def.user_port;

  ....

use Memo_port_Def, Response_Port_Def;

  A_to_B_memo_port:       memo_port       := Create (15);

  B_to_A_response_port:   response_port   := Create (15);
```

Figure 5-11 Ada code to instantiate two differently typed port-definition packages, one for memos going from A to B and one for responses going from B to A, and to create a single instance of each of these ports.

```
declare
    ...
  my_question:    memo;
  the_answer:     response;
    ...
begin
  Send (A_to_B_memo_port, my_question);
    ...
  Receive (B_to_A_response_port, the_answer);
    ...
end;
```

Because of Ada's strong typing and overloading features, it isn't necessary to use the longer forms Memo_Port_Def.Send and Response_Port_Def.Receive in the procedure call statements given in the example above. Based on the type of the actual parameters to Send (Receive), the correct target procedure for each call can be correctly resolved by the compiler (if no ambiguity exists).

The specification of Simple_Port_Def given in Appendix H indicates that conditional versions of Send and Receive are also available in Simple_Port_Def, and hence in Memo_Port_Def and Response_Port_Def.

The hardware's ability to check on the validity of a Port Object argument includes being able also to check whether the caller's argument (which is an Access Descriptor) has *send rights* for a call on Send or on Cond_send, or has *receive rights* for a call on Receive or on Cond_receive. We defer discussion of such rights checking until Chapter 6.

5.5.3. Carrier_Def and Surrogate_Port_Def Generic Packages

In order to use the surrogate send and receive facilities, a programmer will have to create tailored instances of the Carrier_Def and Surrogate_Port_Def packages in addition to any Simple_Port_Def instances. Consider the message priority system example of Section 5.3, in which process Producer is to be programmed to send a stream of "reports", of varying priorities, to process Consumer.

For this application, a pool of Surrogate Carriers will be needed, each tailored to carry messages of type report. To create these carriers, it will be necessary to instantiate a tailored version of the Carrier_Def generic package. Two ports must also be created: a priority port that is sent surrogate carriers containing messages of type report and a FIFO port that is sent recycled carriers as messages. To create these two ports requires two new instantiations of Simple_Port_Def. Finally, there must exist an indication that the two newly instantiated ports are related, i.e., that one of the new ports is the first port and the other new port is the second port for a surrogate send operation. Specifying this relationship is a necessary prerequisite to using the surrogate send opera-

```
package Report_Port_Def is new Simple_Port_Def(report);
                    -- Instantiates Simple_Port_Def for reports.
subtype report_port is Report_Port_Def.user_port;
                    -- Renames user_port.

package Report_Carrier_Def is
        new Carrier_Def(
                report, id: integer);
                  -- Instantiates Carrier_Def
subtype report_carrier is Report_Carrier_Def.user_carrier;
                    -- Renames user_carrier.

package Report_Carrier_Port_Def is
        new Simple_Port_Def(report_carrier);
                    -- Instantiates Simple_Port_Def for surr. carriers.
subtype report_carrier_port is Report_Port_Carrier_Def.user_port;
                    -- Renames user_port.

package Report_Surrogate_Port_Def is
        new Surrogate_Port_Def(
                report_port,                  -- Message port type.
                report,                       -- Message type.
                report_carrier,               -- Carrier type.
                report_carrier_port);         -- Carrier port type.
                  -- Instantiates Report_Surrogate_Port_Def.
      . . .

use Report_Port_Def,           Report_Carrier_Def,
    Report_Carrier_Port_Def, Report_Surrogate_Port_Def;
      . . .
```

Figure 5-12 Declarations for instantiating packages, ports, and carriers for implementing program to send a stream of reports of varying priority from process A to process C.

tion. In all, four generic package instances must be instantiated for this particular application.

Figure 5-12 shows a set of declarations that would create the package instances. The declarations can be understood in terms of the explanations in the preceding section and in terms of the details of Appendix H.

Creation of the two needed ports and a pool of Surrogate Carriers can be made part of an enclosing package, called Send_Reports, which also includes the operation to send a report. The body of this package, which follows the plan suggested by iMAX Operating System implementers, is shown in Figure 5-13. (See also the iMAX 432 Reference Manual as cited in Appendix B.)

```
  package body Send_Reports is

    first_port:     report_port   := Create(10, priority);
                      -- Creates a port having a capacity of 10 items
                      -- of type report and with priority service mode.
    second_port:    report_carrier_port := Create(10);
                      -- Creates a FIFO port having a capacity of 10
                      -- messages of type Report_carrier.
    spare: report_carrier;

    procedure Send_a_report(
        rpt:            report;
        priority:  short_ordinal)
    is
      b: boolean;
    begin
      Cond_receive(second_port, spare, b);
                      -- Get spare carrier from
                      -- carrier_pool (second_port).
      if   b  then
        Set_carrier_priority(spare, priority);
                      -- Update spare carrier's priority value.
      else
        spare := Create(0, priority);
                      -- If carrier pool is empty then create
                      -- a new carrier with proper priority.
      end if;
      Surrogate_send(first_port, rpt, spare, second_port);
                      -- After sending new report to first_port,
                      -- carrier will be returned to the pool
                      -- at second_port.
    end Send_a_report;
begin
  --  Initialization of this package starts here.
  --  Builds an initial pool of five carriers.
  for i in 1 .. 5 loop
    spare := Create(0);          -- Create a new carrier with 0 as id
                                 -- and a 0 default priority value.
    Send(second_port, spare);   -- Place spare into the pool.
  end loop;

end Send_Reports;
```

Figure 5-13 Package body for a user's priority-message system

The reader should have little trouble following the implementation shown in the body of the Send_Reports package. This package body is a good illustration of the usefulness of an initialization section for a package. In this initialization section, five carriers are created and sent to the "pool", i.e., to Second_port. All the carriers in the pool are "nameless"; that is, they have no useful id values. In addition, they do not initially acquire any distinguishing priority value. When Send_a_report is invoked, a carrier is fetched from the pool, given the desired priority value, and sent off with a given Report value. This is accomplished by using the Surrogate_send operation of the Report_Surrogate_Port_Def package.

In the event the receiving task runs more slowly than the sending task, the pool of carriers can become empty. This will happen if, for example, Consumer falls fifteen messages behind Producer at first_port. In this case, ten messages will be enqueued in the fixed-length queue at first_port and five carriers will be enqueued in the carrier queue at first_port. If Send_a_report is invoked to send a sixteenth message before Consumer can process a message, then Producer will find the carrier pool empty. If this occurs, Send_a_port simply creates and uses a fresh carrier.

[At this point a reader may wish to review our earlier discussion of carrier pool management (in Section 5.3.2) where we considered a way to keep the pool from growing too large by using a CONDITIONAL SEND instruction. One may enhance the carrier management scheme used in Send_Reports (Figure 5-13) in a similar way by taking advantage of the Cond_send operation.]

We close this section by considering how, with the aid of Typed_Ports, we can implement the message flow structure diagrammed in Figure 5-7 (multiple waiting). We shall consider the case where senders deposit messages in a fixed number of letter_boxes (three in our case). The single receiver fetches letters from a central_box by issuing Surrogate_receives from each of the letter_boxes and blocking Receives to the central_box. Each of the letter_boxes is a simple port that transmits messages of type letter. On the other hand, central_box is a port that transmits messages of type letter_carrier.

By contrast with the preceding example, the number of letter_carriers required in this example is fixed. Exactly one letter_carrier for each letter_box is sufficient, since a carrier can shuttle back and forth between its respective letter_box and the central_box. Furthermore, the receiving process could not process the received letters any faster if there were more letter_carriers available. All of the ports in this example have FIFO service mode.

The declarations for instantiating the required generic packages from Typed_ports are identical with those shown in Figure 5-12, except that the word "Letter" replaces the word "Report" uniformly throughout the figure. Figure 5-14 shows a fragment of a program unit that uses these packages to create the required ports and carriers and to process letters received from other tasks. (Again, the structure of this program fragment follows that given in the iMAX 432 Reference Manual.)

```
declare

  use Letter_Port_Def,          Letter_Carrier_Def,
      Letter_Carrier_Port_Def, Letter_Surrogate_Port_Def;

  letter_box: array (1 .. 3) of letter_port;
                                    -- Letter_box capacities
                                    -- set individually during
                                    -- initialization below.
  central_box:  letter_carrier_port := Create(3);
                                    -- Letter_carrier capacity = 3
  letter_bearer: array (1 .. 3) of letter_carrier;
                                    -- Id values of carriers are
                                    -- assigned during initialization below
  bearer:         letter_carrier;      -- Carrier variable.

  ltr:  letter;    -- Type definition for letter assumed accessible.
  id:   integer;

begin
  -- Initialize capacity values for individual letter_boxes.
  letter_box(1)  := Create(8);         -- Letter capacity =  8
  letter_box(2)  := Create(12);        -- Letter capacity = 12
  letter_box(3)  := Create(4);         -- Letter capacity =  4

  for i in 1 .. 3 loop
    letter_bearer(i)  := Create(i);    -- Id of ith carrier
                                       -- is made value of i.
    Surrogate_receive(letter_box(i), letter_bearer(i), central_box);
                 -- Ith letter_bearer sent to ith letter_box to
                 -- await letter and bring it to the central box.
  end loop;
  -- Initialization ends here.

  loop
    Receive(central_box, bearer);        -- Recover carrier from pool.
    Get_carrier_message(bearer, ltr); -- Extract message and put in ltr.
    id := Get_carrier_id(bearer);        -- Extract carrier's id.
    Surrogate_receive(letter_box(id), letter_bearer(id), central_box);
                 -- Recycle letter_bearer to get another message.
    -- Process letter in ltr.

  end loop;
end;
```

Figure 5-14 Ada code for a multiple wait message structure.

A few points about the program fragment in Figure 5-14 merit explanation.

- The capacities chosen for the letter_boxes (8, 12, and 4) are problem dependent, selected according to the expected frequency with which other processes send letters to those boxes. On the other hand, the letter_carrier capacity of the central box need not be larger than 3, since there can never be more than three letter_carriers enqueued at the central_box.

- When a letter_carrier arrives at the central_box, its id value and its message are extracted. The id value is used to identify the letter_box that received the letter. Using this id value, another Surrogate_receive is issued to that letter_box. The letter_carrier from which the letter was extracted, having performed its duty, can now be sent back to its letter_box of origin to wait for another letter.
- After the letter_carrier is recycled to its letter_box of origin, the most recent (FIFO order) letter received from the central_box is processed.

5.5.4. The Equivalence between Ada Rendezvous and iMAX Typed_Ports Facility

A discussion focusing on the equivalence between the two ways to express interprocess communication, namely: use (a) of *Ada rendezvous* statements and (b) i432 Port Objects and port operations, is now timely and perhaps overdue. We do not have in mind a definitive analysis of the two approaches, in part because to do so would require a much more thorough study of the Ada rendezvous syntax and semantics than has been given in this book. Even so, some observations, based on what has been learned so far, are in order. In what follows, we abbreviate ''i432 Port Objects and port operations'' as ''i432 ports facility''.

Two questions should be answered.

1. Are the two approaches equivalent? That is,
   - can Ada rendezvous semantics, i.e., those of the Ada *entry call*, *conditional entry call*, *entry declarations*, **accept** and **select** statements, be fully implemented using i432 ports facility?
   - can all i432 port operations be represented in terms of the Ada rendezvous?
2. Given a choice, which approach should be used? What special portability problems, if any, might be expected when transporting to and from ordinary Ada environments and the i432 Ada environment?

In response to the first question, Intel compiler writers are in the process of implementing the full Ada rendezvous semantics in Ada using the underlying i432 ports facility. The success of this enterprise will demonstrate that the i432 ports facility is at least as expressive as Ada rendezvous. The converse, expressing the semantics of the i432 ports facility (as expressed, for example by Typed_Ports) using Ada generic packages and Ada rendezvous statements, actually a straightforward exercise, would imply that the Ada rendezvous semantics offers at least the same expressive power for interprocess communication as the Typed_Ports package. This being so, the equivalence proof rests solely on demonstrating each of these two mappings. The first mapping is to be demonstrated by Intel in due course and the second, hereafter called the

Typed_Ports_By_Rendezvous, is left as a challenge for the reader.

Given the aforementioned equivalence, programs using either approach fall under the category of standard Ada, and the choice between the two approaches becomes a matter of pragmatics and style. For executing multitask programs on the i432, it is expected that, for many practical applications, the efficiency advantage of the Type_Ports operations will dominate the decision process. Transporting such programs to non-i432 Ada environments will simply require including in the new environment a copy of Typed_Ports_By_Rendezvous as a library-level package. (Nor will standard Ada programs transported to the i432 from a non-i432 Ada environment require any change. To run more efficiently, however, it may pay to map certain time-critical rendezvous operations into i432 port operations.)

5.6. Explicit Message-Based Communication for the Investment Club Program

In Section 3.1, we promised to consider substituting explicit message transmission for the Ada rendezvous in order to avoid the bottlenecks inherent in the program structure outlined in Figure 2-5. We do this here. Recall, several solutions were to be considered. One was to restructure the program as in Figure 3-2. That solution permits each Member task to call either the Portfolio_Server or the Roster_Server task, but only via a package (Member_Ops, Treas_Ops, or Secy_Ops) that acts as a "controlling switch", or "filter".

[Another possibility for eliminating performance delays was to use spawned intermediate tasks for relaying requests from Portfolio_Server to Roster_Server. However, we have already examined what is involved in pursuing this approach (See the end of Section 5.3). It is not especially attractive, especially because each of the messages sent by Portfolio_Server (in the form of an entry call) requires the generation of a response (in the form of a result value) by Roster_Server.]

Deciding to replace the relatively high-level Ada rendezvous as the only means for inter-task communication, by substituting in its place Send and Receive operations available through Typed_Ports, opens up a large space of possible solutions. We consider only one of these here. In this alternative, we keep the structure of Figure 2-5. The strategy to be used may be summarized as follows. Each Member task communicates its request directly to the Portfolio_Server task. Three subcases are then recognized:

- The request requires service only from Roster_Server. Such a request is forwarded to the latter intact. In this event, Roster_Server's response will go directly to the originator of the request, and not to Portfolio_Server.
- The request is such that no confirmation is required from Roster_Server. Portfolio_Server immediately processes the request and sends a response directly to its originator.

- The request requires confirmation from Roster_Server. In this case, Portfolio_Server places an Access Descriptor for the member's request in a new message sent to the Roster_Server. The latter's reply message to Portfolio_Server, whatever the outcome, always includes this same Access Descriptor. Whether the response from Roster_Server signals confirmation or denial of authorization, Portfolio_Server will have sufficient information to process the member's original request and send that member an appropriate reply.

Figure 5-15 illustrates the message flow graph implied in the above strategy. In this figure, ports are depicted as nested within tasks merely to suggest that the containing tasks execute Receive operations on those ports.

[There is no intention to imply, for example, that such ports must be declared within the contained tasks. Such nested declarations are not ruled out, however.]

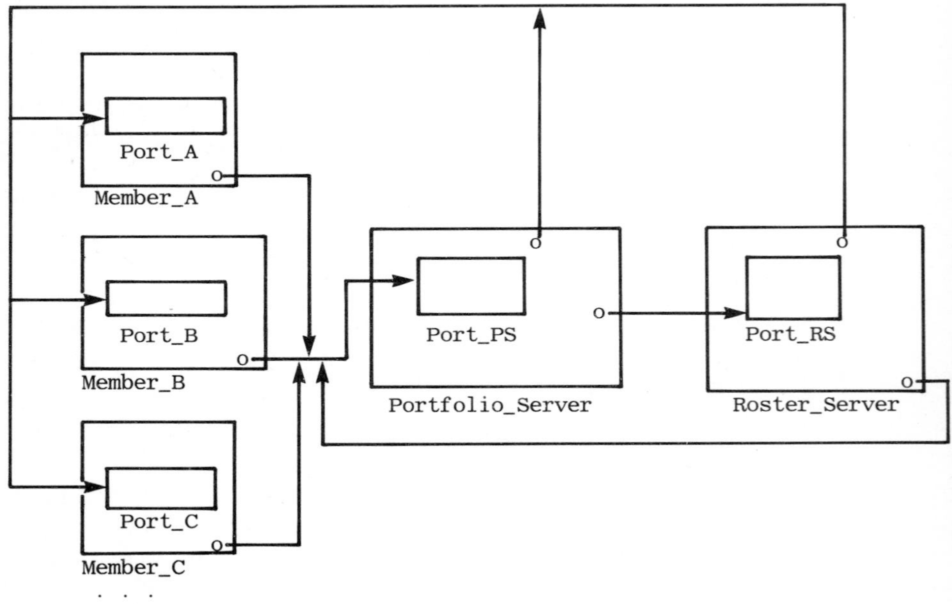

Figure 5-15 Message flow graph for explicit message transmission between member tasks (including officers) and the portfolio and roster server tasks.

No Surrogate operations are needed in implementing this strategy, and so only Simple_Port_Def must be instantiated. To keep the number of such instantiations to the minimum of one, each message implied in Figure 5-15 must be formed as an instance of the same data type. In addition, each message should carry the identification of the sending task, so that the response may be directed to that sender. It should be fairly easy for the programmer to adhere to these two constraints. The following is an example of a message_type which may be used for all messages:

```
type message_type is
  record
    command:       integer;         -- Code representing particular request.
    reply_port:    user_port;       -- If message is a reply, value is null,
                                    -- else value  refers to the port
                                    -- to which reply is to be sent.
    sender_id:     string_of30;     -- Same as member_name, except
                                    -- in case of Portfolio_Server
                                    -- and Roster_Server.
    message_body:  dynamic_typed;
                                    -- A predefined type representing
                                    -- any Access Descriptor. See
                                    -- Section 6.3 for rules governing use
                                    -- of this type.
  end record;
```

The command field encodes the kind of request (and is equivalent to the **entry** identifier it replaces), such as Enter_buy, Enter_sell, etc. The reply_port field, which would be null for a reply message, explicitly specifies the port to which a reply message for this request is to be sent. [The value of this field may be considered an alternative to the sender_id when one can be inferred from the other.]

The sender_id would be the same as a member's my_name argument. In case the sender is Portfolio_Server or Roster_Server, the name would simply be "Portfolio_Server" or "Roster_Server", respectively (and padded with trailing blanks as required). [Sender_id may be the null string when the sender is Roster_Server and the receiver is a member task.] Message_body would be an Access Descriptor for an object that contains all the **in** and **in out** (actual) parameters of the replaced entry call—but not including my_name, which is of course already provided as the sender_id. This object would be expressed as a record structure. For example, message_body in an Enter_buy message to Portfolio_Server would be an AD to an instance of the following record type:

```
type Enter_buy_send_type is
  record
    purch_date:    date;
    stock_code:    stock_code_pair;
    num_shares:    natural;
    per_sh_price:  dollars;
    commission:    dollars;
  end record;
```

Responses from Portfolio_Server and from Roster_Server must also be formed into instances of message_type. For example, the message_body part of Portfolio_Server's response to a member's Enter_buy request might be an instance of the following one-component record type:

```
type Enter_buy_answer_type is
  record
    unauthorized: boolean := true;
  end record;
```

Only one component is needed here, but we retain a record structure because we want message_body to be an access type, and the allocation of a new record instance (using the **new** operator) assures us that the compiler will provide the wanted Access Descriptor. A declaration and a statement like the following might be used to create a response record for the Enter_buy performed by Portfolio_Server.

```
my_response: message_type;
  . . .
my_response := new message_type'(10,
                                 Port_A,
                                 "Portfolio_Server'^^^^^^^^^^^^^^^",
                                 new Enter_buy_answer_type'(false));
```

Any response from Roster_Server that goes as a message to Port_PS, the same port to which messages from members arrive, must contain "Roster_Server" as the value of sender_id, but must also include a copy of the originating sender_id value as one of the components in the message_body instance. Therefore, when Roster_Server sends back a response for the Is_treasurer inquiry requested by Portfolio_Server, the formulated response requires a two-component message_body component, for example,

```
type Is_treasurer_answer_type is
  record
    sender_id:    long_string;       -- Originating member name.
    check:        boolean;
  end record;
```

In the context of the Roster_Server, a statement like the following might be used to formulate a response to the Is_treasurer inquiry:

```
my_response: message_type;
  . . .
my_response := new message_type'(3,
                                 Port_PS,
                                 "Roster_Server'^^^^^^^^^^^^^^^^^",
                                 new Is_treasurer_answer_type'(
                                              "Jones^^^^^^^^^^^^^^^^^^^^^^^^^"
                                               false));
```

To be sure, for some categories of the incoming messages, the same record types may be used. Even so, there are enough differences to require a significant number of distinct record types, as just illustrated. Defining and keeping track of all the sender_id's and message_body types and properly using them in place of the argument lists in the eliminated entry calls is one of the major prices a programmer will pay to use direct message transmission in place of Ada entry calls.

We do not take this example much further, but only outline a few of the points that may be considered were one to implement the changes needed. Readers will find it instructive, however, to complete the exercise of converting the two server tasks given in Appendix F for direct message transmission.

- The steps to be taken are those we illustrated in the preceding section. To make matters simple, both Portfolio_Server and Roster_Server may be coded to assume that the single instantiation of Simple_port_def and all of the created ports are accessible within the respective tasks.
- As a reminder, all the ports will have FIFO service modes, else it would be necessary to use Surrogate send operations as in the user-tailorable message priority system detailed in the preceding section. (It would, in fact, be reasonable to consider making Port_PS a Priority port, if one wished to give special priority privileges to requests initiated from, say the club's Treasurer. This ''enrichment'' would serve as another useful exercise.)
- Blocking Sends and Receives should be suitable for all types of message operations. Member_tasks should issue requests of Portfolio_Server as Send, Receive pairs—an important disciplinary requirement that is no longer handled for the user automatically, as when issuing task entry calls.
- We preserve in the body part of both the Portfolio_Server and the Roster_Server the primary **loop** . . . **end loop** structure, which now consists basically of issuing a Receive call and then performing the indicated processing that leads, at the end, to the issuing of a ''matching'' Send.
- We have already outlined the strategy to be followed by Portfolio_Server following the issuance of a Receive call. The strategy followed by the Roster_Server after receiving a message is even simpler: just process the request and send a matching response either to Port_PS or to the receiving port of the member task that originated the request.

6 i432 OBJECT ACCESS AND TYPE MANAGEMENT

6.1. Introduction

In Chapter 1 we outlined the roles played by the the i432 hardware and operating system in support of access control over objects. It was suggested that the hardware and operating system form a partnership in providing a facility for the typing of objects and for enforcing the intended use of objects, according to their respective types. Moreover, we said that this typing facility is extended to the user, who can define new object types and specify how the system should control access to instances of typed objects. The main purpose of this chapter is to elaborate these concepts and to explain the details of object type management and object access control.

We also suggested that part, but not all, of the provided type management facility could be exploited within the framework of the Ada language. It must be recognized, however, that Ada was designed for programs that execute in relatively static environments. This implies that an Ada program is expected to execute in a host system having a relatively fixed configuration. If there is to be a change in the host execution environment, an Ada program may have to be altered "off line", recompiled and then reloaded. The Ada language does not include linguistic constructs permitting an Ada program to adapt itself to on-going changes in the system in which it is embedded. This constraint may be explained in part by a desire to ensure that Ada programs are as machine independent (and as portable) as possible.

The i432 System architecture is itself more "dynamic" than Ada in this regard. Programs can run on the i432 that are adaptive to on-going changes in the environment, such as dynamic changes in the attributes of external I/O devices. To achieve this additional adaptability at the Ada level of interface to the i432, one may use certain extensions of Ada that expose the dynamic aspects of the i432 system. In particular, one can define variables that contain packages as their values. This is achieved by extending Ada to allow packages to be declared as types, just as with integers, boolean, arrays, etc. Different package values (instances) can then be stored into a package variable at execution time, thus achieving a dynamic, adaptive instance of a package. This is in contrast to standard Ada, in which an Ada program must be modified, recompiled and reloaded in order to achieve a different implementation of a package.

Provision for the invocation of an alternative implementation of a given (abstract) data type, selected at run time, is not an entirely new proposal [54].] Moreover, we have already alluded to this language extension in connection with a suggestion in Chapter 2 for dynamically invoking different instances of the package Club_Portfolio, and we expand this idea in the ensuing discussion.

An Ada programmer is able to express a wide range of access control over typed objects without use of any Ada language extension. As we will see, the architecture, the iMAX operating system interface, and the Ada compiler "cooperate" to let the programmer express such controls either implicitly, through judicious use of **private** declarations and pragmas placed in type manager packages, or explicitly, by means of calls to operations of the iMAX interface.

The i432 System has the ability to control appropriately structured user-defined objects in the same way that it controls access to instances of *system objects*. When such user-defined objects are allocated, their respective Object Descriptors are encoded with a system type, "extended type", which is a system-recognized type. (These objects are called *Extended Type Objects*. In Intel parlance, such objects are also referred to as *Dynamic Typed Objects* for reasons which will become more clear when we discuss 432-Ada later in this chapter.) Ada users of the i432 can refer to Extended Type Objects as instances of Ada **access** types.

Unlike instances of system objects whose types are recognized as special only by the architecture and operating system, the type of a user-defined Extended Type Object is specified by the programmer and is compiled into a system-defined object known as a *Type Definition Object*. After creation, each Extended Type Object contains, in its associated Object Descriptor, a reference to the Type Definition Object, which contains a user-defined set of attributes. This reference is readily accessible from 432-Ada by use of the *type_value* attribute; it may be used in various operations on the object, and also for performing run-time type checking.

Our intent is to describe in more detail the respective roles played by the architecture, the operating system, and the compiler for achieving the desired controls on Extended Type Objects. It should be realized that it is precisely these controls plus access rights that are required to implement type managers—and which the i432 System makes available to its users. Before closing this introduction, we provide some additional motivation for examining the Ada-level type management facility offered to the i432 user.

Consider our portfolio management application. One officer, the club secretary, is to be given sole authorization to update the membership_roster object. It is to be kept in mind that, over the life of the club, secretaries may come and go. Ensuring that no ex-secretaries retain unauthorized access to the portfolio implies that *write* access rights must be dispensed under control beyond what was indicated in Chapter 3. In section 6.4, we revisit this problem to see what program changes are required for accomplishing objectives of this sort. In particular, we will see how treating the roster as an Extended Type Object permits us to solve this access control problem.

Another challenge related to the portfolio management application arises when providing for the use of more than one portfolio-owner package (Club_Portfolio). This need could arise in the case of a bank's Trust Department that manages a number of distinct portfolios for its clients. Each trust officer of the bank would need *write* access rights to the several portfolios managed by that individual, while several officers and staff members of the bank might require *read* access rights to each portfolio.

Earlier in this chapter we suggested an extension of Ada that would "promote" a package declaration to a type declaration (that is, declare a class of packages), thus promoting a package from a program unit to the status of an Ada object. Individual variables could then be declared of a package type. Different versions of the package body could, by appeal to a "manager" package, be selected and instantiated as needed and assigned dynamically to a (different) package variable. For convenience, we may name this new level of manager package Club_Portfolio_Mgr and assume that its Create operation returns an access to a distinct instance of Club_Portfolio each time Create is invoked.

This "package type" extension to Ada serves well for dealing with the multi-I/O device problem. The challenge here is to compose a program that can continue to run in spite of dynamic changes in the set of available I/O devices and their respective functionalities.

One way to achieve this measure of device independence is to make accessible an abstraction for each candidate I/O device. This abstraction might take the form of a particular instance (implementation) of a package whose contained procedures are I/O operations. Each call on an input or output routine causes the appropriate I/O operation in the desired I/O package instance to be invoked. The ability to select dynamically the desired I/O package is possible with the "package type" language extension, because a package instance is promoted to the status of an Ada value that can be passed as an argument for a subprogram.

The use of package types is crucial to the implementation strategy in iMAX for the i432's Input/Output subsystem. The details of this particular application are examined in Chapter 7.

It seems important to reiterate that the i432 architecture and the "package type" extension of Ada combine to transcend Ada's static limitations in safe and efficient ways. In particular, the extended Ada language and the i432 in combination leads to a greater degree of effective dynamic control over the transmission of functions and their functionalities than has been possible in most predecessor systems.

Note first that Standard Ada explicitly rules out subprograms that have procedures (or functions) as parameters. (Other high-order languages, such as Fortran and various "Algols" do permit subprogram parameters provided, however, that they are treated as constants and not variables.) The reasons why such parameters are forbidden in Ada are now obscure. A possible explanation is that permission to pass only procedure constants (and not procedure variables) as arguments to other procedures would violate a "completeness principle" in language design (and to allow procedure variables as well would too greatly expand the scope of Ada.) If procedure (or function) constant parameters were permitted in Ada, it would be no "hardship" for a modern compiler to fully check each subprogram call to ensure that the input/output characteristics (i.e., the *functionality*) of a supplied procedure (or function) constant argument matches that of the corresponding procedure (or function) parameter. Such compile-time checks are especially important for programs that execute on computers having conventional architectures, since fully-general run-time type checking is not convenient or feasible.

A different situation arises for programs written in the "package type" extension of Ada that are to execute on the i432.

- First, the execution-time environment of the i432 provides relatively simple and safe mechanisms for passing procedures (or functions) as arguments and for performing fully general run-time type checks of the functionality of such arguments. In fact, passing of procedural arguments is generalized at little added cost, since what is passed in the Message Object for an i432 CALL instruction is a Domain Object AD, rather than an individual Instruction Object. (That is, one may pass as a single AD in the Message Object a reference to the entire collection of subprograms implied by the domain AD.) The types of objects *input* to a called subprogram and the types of objects *output* from a called subprogram can be completely checked at run-time by taking advantage of the underlying type definition facilities for *system objects* and *Extended Type Objects*. Relatively small overhead is associated with these type checks.
- Second, the compiler for the "package type" extension of Ada takes full advantage of these underlying i432 object access and type control mechanisms.

We are now ready to examine the relevant i432 System details provided in support of object access and type management. Section 6.2 reviews the hardware mechanisms while Section 6.3, 6.4, and 6.5 review the user-accessible iMAX services and companion Ada-language extensions.

6.2. Hardware Support for Access Control and Type Management

The need for dynamic control over types in running programs can arise in at least two kinds of applications:

- Multiple-user environments. The various users come and go and they have changing needs and authority over the lifetime of a single application.
- Multiple-I/O device environments. Peripheral devices of different attributes (functionality) are added to or deleted from the system during the lifetime of a single application.

Recent experience in operating systems development has shown that in a multiple user situation it is imperative to provide satisfactory protection mechanisms for the controlled management and sharing of information objects. The general problem faced is to provide a means for the creator (or owner) of an object, X, to dispense restricted access privileges for X to other modules. For any object, X, the variety of accesses that might be, or should be, dispensed will naturally vary according to the particular level of the application (that is, its proximity to the hardware.)

Determining what is a useful set of dispensable access rights has not been an easy problem for the system architect. It must be ''complete'' in a practical sense, so that any particular combination of access controls may be expressed. Moreover, the controls should not be circumventable, so that the system can remain secure.

Trying to predict in advance the different forms of access control over all possible kinds of objects is hopeless. Architects of the i432 System have resolved the dilemma by applying the following three-step strategy:

1. Establish a set of *base rights* (and companion hardware controls), that can be applied to access any object, such as *read* and *write* rights. For example, the owner of object X should be able to give to another module Y an Access Descriptor for X that contains *read* rights only, with the assurance that Y cannot modify that descriptor (amplify the rights) to include, for example, *write* rights as well.
2. Augment the base rights with an additional set of *type rights* applicable to every system object and provide companion controls that permit proper interpretation of these rights for such system objects. (Type rights are interpreted relative to the system type of the object; this interpretation may vary for objects of different system types. Base rights have the same interpreta-

tion over all objects.) For example, X may be a Port Object whose owner may wish to dispense to some Ada task M an Access Descriptor for X, allowing task M to have only *receive* rights at that port. Denied *send* rights to X, a relatively unreliable task M cannot then use port X in its complete role as a local message queue. [The task M might otherwise attempt to Receive a message from X before Sending one to X, or attempt to Send too many messages to X (and cause an overflow of X's fixed-length message queue.) The first behavior would result in a blocked Receive and the second would result in a blocked Send—and either one would then result in deadlock for task M.]

Implementing hardware-supervised type rights for system objects turns out to be an essential requirement for achieving security in the i432 system. We show why this is so later in this section.

3. Beyond providing base rights for all objects and additional type rights tailored for specific system objects, provide a type definition mechanism for arbitrary new (user-definable) typed objects, called Extended Type Objects, together with a general mechanism for control over access to these objects. Users are given access to these two mechanisms through a suitable 432-Ada language and operating system interface.
Since the hardware cannot know about user-defined types, *a priori*, a special representation, common to all such user-defined types, is required so that the hardware can recognize objects belonging to these types. In some "tagged architectures", each object instance is paired with its type encoding to make the object instance self-describing [Gehringer 79]. The i432 architects have taken a related approach.

To understand this approach we explain the use of the *system type* field in an i432 Object Descriptor. This field contains a tag that encodes the type of the object referenced. The encoding, which is set at object creation (for the life of the object), is subdivided into three principal categories:

1. generic	The referenced object has no special attributes assigned either by the hardware, the operating system, or the user.
2. system	The referenced object is a particular member of the set of predefined *system objects*, such as Process Object, Port Object, Domain Object, etc., whose attributes are predefined, partly by hardware and partly by stored definitions accessible to modules of the operating system.
3. extended type	The referenced object has a special set of attributes assigned by the user. This set is usually deduced by the compiler and assigned to the associated Type Definition Object (see below) to represent the type of the object.

Thus, an Extended Type Object is one which is recognized by the hardware as belonging to category three. An Extended Type Object itself contains a *Type Definition Object* AD in its associated Object Descriptor. This format, which relates the object to its type definition, is shown in Figure 6-1.

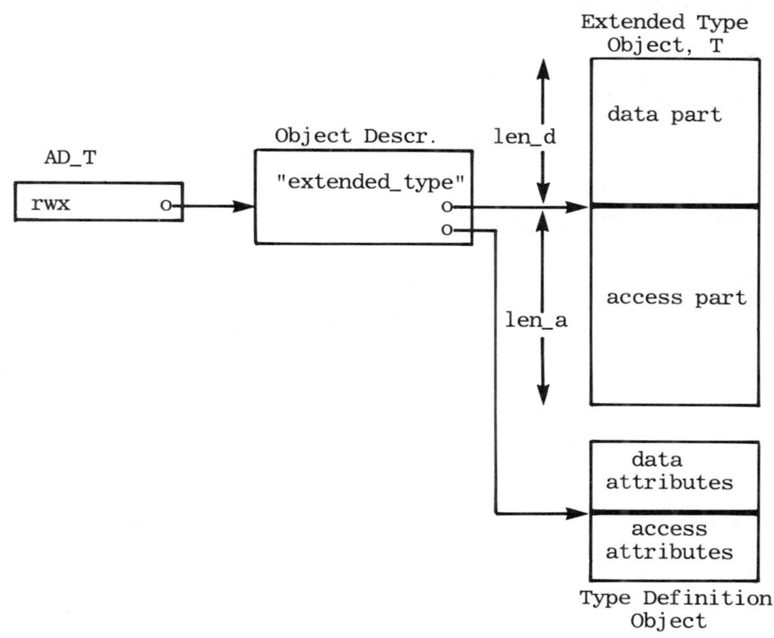

Figure 6-1 Structure of an Extended Type Object, T, and its related Type Definition Object (TDO). The type of T, "extended_type", is encoded in T's Object Descriptor. The particular set of attributes for this type is found in the TDO, referenced by the AD also found in T's Object Descriptor. The TDO generally contains a set of type-specific data and access attributes.

[A similar treatment is used for each class of i432 system objects. The hardware recognizes the particular system type as encoded in the Object Descriptor. Additional type definition information for each system object class is found in the Type Definition Object, which is referenced from the TDO AD placed in the Object Descriptor.]

We see that Extended Type Objects are interpreted as instances of the type specified by the object's *Type Definition Object* (TDO). The format of an Extended Type Object T differs from that of a generic object only in two key respects: (a) its Object Descriptor marks it as being of type "extended_type", and (b) its Object Descriptor slot contains a reference to its Type Definition Object. Since each TDO is unique, the reference to it in the Object Descriptor is also unique and hence identifies T as being an instance of a unique type. If two or more Typed Objects are intended to be of the same type, their Object Descriptors must contain the same Type Definition Object AD. The i432 architecture does not specify the mechanism by which a system for the i432 preserves the uniqueness of TDOs.

6.2.1. Object Creation Instructions

Objects are created using one of two i432 instructions. These are:

- CREATE OBJECT
- CREATE TYPED OBJECT

A generic object is created by executing the CREATE OBJECT instruction, and an object of system-recognized type, including "extended type", is created by executing the CREATE TYPED OBJECT instruction.

Briefly, the CREATE OBJECT and CREATE TYPED OBJECT instructions specify the lengths for the access and data parts of the object to be created and an access selector for the destination slot that will receive the Access Descriptor for the created object. The CREATE TYPED OBJECT instruction also specifies an AD (which must have *create* rights set) for a system object known as a *Type Control Object*, or TCO. This object, as suggested in Figure 6-2, contains the information needed by the hardware for encoding the system type of the created object and for encoding the rights fields (base and type rights) in the AD for the created Typed Object. A TCO used for creating an Extended Type Object provides the type encoding in the form of a reference to the type's TDO; a TCO used for creating a system object provides, in addition, a distinct system type code. (As might be expected, TCOs for i432 system objects have formats that are identical with those of Extended Type Objects.)

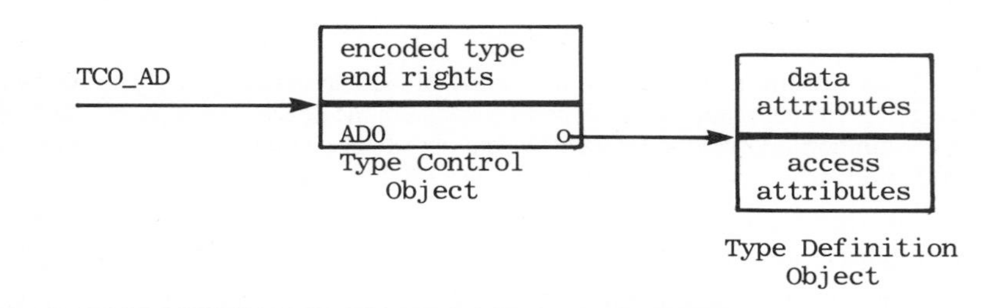

Figure 6-2 Structure of a Type Control Object

A TCO contains the encoded type, e.g.,"extended type", and also, in its zero-th AD slot an Access Descriptor (TDO_AD) for an object (the TDO) whose system type is "Type Definition Object." A duplicate of the TDO_AD is placed into the Object Descriptor for the created Extended Type Object.

There are two distinct levels of control that can be expressed (exercised) with respect to Typed Objects:

1. Control over creation	Who is permitted to create a Typed Object.
2. Control over access	Who determines the access rights to be placed in an AD for a Typed Object.

Control over creation of non-generic objects is governed by possession of an AD having *create* rights set in the AD for the Type Control Object associated with a particular extended type. The TCO for a *system object* would normally be created by the operating system on behalf of a type manager; the operating system would supply to that type manager an Access Descriptor with *create* rights for that Type Control Object (TCO_AD). The type manager would then use TCO_AD during each activation of its Create operation to create an Extended Type Object on behalf of the type manager's caller. Ordinarily, this TCO_AD would be kept private to the type manager.

Control over access to a previously created Extended Type Object, T, is governed merely by possession of an AD (with appropriate access rights) to T. When the Create operation within T's type manager returns an AD for T to the caller of Create, the decision as to what access rights to supply in the AD for T is the responsibility of the type manager. The AD for any newly created object always includes both *read* and *write* rights. If rights to T are to be restricted, then the type manager's own local object creation operator must "strip off" such rights in any copy of the AD for T that is passed back to Create's caller. A type manager will normally reserve for itself control over the amplification of rights to T.

Any rights stripped off the AD for T when the AD is issued to the user can be reinstated by the type manager when the same AD is later presented to the type manager as an argument to another of its operations. Rights restriction and amplification are accomplished by taking advantage of the i432 RESTRICT RIGHTS and AMPLIFY RIGHTS instructions. The latter instruction can be executed only when the appropriate TCO_AD, maintained privately within a type manager, is specified as an argument. These details are elaborated later in this section.

We now divide our discussion here into two parts. First we examine the "inner layer of access control" provided through the base and type *rights* fields of Access Descriptors, the base and system *type* fields within Object Descriptors, and the control functions that arise through the hardware's interpretation of these fields. These mechanisms form the foundation on which the system's security rests and also the foundation on which the extended type management facility is built.

In the second discussion we examine the security strategy—which, is based, in essence, on denying the programmer the freedom to manufacture Access Descriptors and on controlling Typed Object creation and amplification of rights to these objects.

6.2.2. The Inner Layer of Access Control

An Access Descriptor may be thought of as having a hardware-sensed record structure with three primary components:

- logical_address — Consists of two subfields: directory index and object index. These specify the referenced Object Descriptor (See Figure 4-1.)
- control_info — Consists of the valid bit, delete rights and unchecked copy rights, none of which is discussed here.
- rights_field — Has two parts: *base rights* and *type rights*

We limit our discussion here to the rights_fields component, consisting of two parts: base rights and type rights. (Base rights are also called *representation* rights.)

- Representation rights, consist of *read* and *write* rights. These are interpreted by the hardware according to the position of an object as a source operand or destination operand within the operator (instruction) being performed. The representation rights bits are interpreted independently of the type of object on which a read or write is attempted. As mentioned in Chapter 4, representation (or base) rights apply to both access and data parts

  For example, both the LOCK OBJECT and UNLOCK OBJECT instructions have operands that specify an AD for the object containing the lock. If that Access Descriptor has no *write* rights, the instruction will not be executed, and a context-level fault will occur. A similar circumstance occurs if an instruction attempts to read an Access Descriptor with write-only access. Any attempt to execute, say, a MOVE instruction that specifies a source AD having only *write* rights will induce a read fault.
- The *type rights* field of an AD is interpreted according to the system type of the object referenced by the AD. The system type of the object is, in turn, encoded in the Object Descriptor referenced by the AD. We say more about Object Descriptors below. Figure 6-3 lists the processor-interpreted type rights for i432 system objects. A reader who wishes more details should consult the i432 GDP Architecture Reference Manual.]

For the following discussions, it is useful to recall that there are two kinds of descriptors that can be referenced by an Access Descriptor: an Object Descriptor and a Refinement Descriptor. Let us assume that the target of the logical_address given in an Access_Descriptor is an Object Descriptor, and

System Object	Type Rights
Context Object	Return
Instruction Object	Trace Create a context
Port Object	Receive Send
Carrier Object	Use as a Surrogate
Processor Object	Send an interprocessor message Broadcast an interprocessor message
Storage Resource Object	Create
Type Control Object	Create typed object Refine typed object Amplify rights
Type Definition Object	Create Retrieve
Object Table Object	Create (an Access Descriptor)

Figure 6-3 System Objects on which type rights have been defined

now glimpse at its internal structure. An Object Descriptor can be thought of as having three principal components:

- physical_address_info — The base physical address of an object or a secondary address of a non-memory resident object.
- memory_mgr_control_info — A collection of items used in storage management, including garbage collection.
- object_type — There are two subfields:
  system type
  processor class

We are concerned here only with object_type, which has two components that contribute to the classification of the described object.

- The system type subfield qualifies each object according to its system-significant or user-defined function, if any. If an object has no system-significant function or user-defined function, its system type subfield is encoded as ''generic''. The availability of non-generic system types permits the hardware to detect a variety of object access faults that occur when an operand of an attempted instruction maps to an object whose system type is inconsistent with the semantics of that instruction.

For example, an attempt to execute a RECEIVE instruction whose operand does not specify a Port Object will lead to a process-level fault. There are a large number of hardware detected faults of this kind. Those who wish more information about these faults can find it in the published in the i432 Architecture Reference Manual.

- The processor class field may further categorize the system object, according to the kind of processor that is permitted to operate on this object. Currently, there are but two kinds of i432 processors, but in the future this number could increase.

  For example, the system's Interface Processor (IP) operates with a Processor Object that has a different format and content than the Processor Object associated with the General Data Processor (GDP), whose architecture we have been describing thus far. A processor-level fault will be caused when there is an attempt to bind a processor P to a Processor Object encoded for a different kind of processor Q. [The IP, of which there must be at least one in every i432 System, plays a critical role in interfacing the i432 with an I/O subsystem. The IP and the I/O subsystem are described in Chapter 7.]

  Not all object types are or should be associated with a particular kind of processor. For example, generic objects are treated alike by both GDPs and IPs (even though the GDP's richer instruction set allows it to do more with such objects.) For this reason the processor class marked "all" is provided. It is used for objects that may be processed by the union of all kinds of processors extant in the system.

  [The i432 architects have laid the groundwork here for the eventual inclusion of a variety of other kinds of processors that may be co-attached through the system's general interconnect structure. As more experience is gained with use of the i432, it will be tempting for the system architects to design and add to the system other special-function processors besides the IP. A special purpose Garbage-Collector (GC) processor is one conceivable candidate; a specialized LISP language processor may be another.

  Because different kinds of processors will have different instruction sets, it may be desirable that, even for identically formatted system objects, different type rights should be defined for different processors. Since the number of different kinds of processors that can be included in an i432 System is intended to be open-ended, the processor class field may play an especially important future role in the lifecycle of i432 Systems.]

6.2.3. i432 Security Strategy

Key to the i432 System security is a guarantee that every information object must be accessed via an Access Descriptor. All i432 processors satisfy this constraint. It may not be clear from a casual examination of the instruction set of the GDP that a programmer is incapable of fabricating and using Access

Descriptors to gain access to any (and ultimately to every) object. What prevents the clever programmer from "fooling" the hardware into using an arbitrary AD to reach other objects?

Put another way, if a programmer can manage to manufacture even one Access Descriptor with an arbitrary logical_address component, then the system is fundamentally insecure! A necessary condition for the system to be secure, therefore, is to deny any programmer, including any system programmer (except the person responsible for the system's initialization), freedom to manufacture Access Descriptors in an uncontrolled fashion. This has been achieved, as the following discussion attempts to show. [Some not-so-curious readers may wish to skip the rest of this discussion.]

In the normal course of events, Access Descriptors are created only as a byproduct of object creation. Once created, an Access Descriptor can be copied and parts of it altered, but only under controlled conditions. The logical_address part part of an AD can never be individually altered, i.e., without altering the entire AD. It seems sensible, therefore, first to examine the details of object creation. In the course of doing so, we will complete our exposition of the role of the Type Control Object.

Objects can be created only by executing one of two i432 instructions. These are:

- CREATE OBJECT

  Creates a generic object of specified lengths for its access and data parts (each of which may be zero) from a specified SRO and returns an Access Descriptor for the created object in a specified AD slot of another object.

- CREATE TYPED OBJECT

  Creates a non-generic object of specified lengths for its access and data parts (each of which may be zero) from a specified SRO and a specified TCO, and returns an Access Descriptor for the created object in a specified slot of another object. The created Object Descriptor and Access Descriptor are respectively encoded with system_type and rights_fields copied from the specified Type Control Object. An AD for the object's TDO, copied from the TCO, is also placed in the created Object Descriptor. The AD for the specified TCO must have *create* rights.

Common to both of these instructions is the fact that creation of an object involves the creation of an Object Descriptor and an Access Descriptor that points to that Object Descriptor. The created Object Descriptor is placed in the Object Table associated with the specified SRO operand. The created Access Descriptor is assigned to a slot in the access part of the "destination" object specified by the destination AD (which must have *delete* rights itself). The hardware ensures that the created Access Descriptor cannot be placed in a slot in the data part of a destination object. Moreover, the hardware determines the encoding of the created Access Descriptor and Object Descriptor.

In the case of the CREATE OBJECT instruction, created Object Descriptors have generic system types. An object created by CREATE OBJECT can initially inherit no special or privileged attributes. Only the use of the CREATE TYPED OBJECT instruction affords the opportunity to create an object that is encoded as a *system object*. But to successfully use this latter instruction, the programmer must specify, as an additional operand, an Access Descriptor for a Type Control Object. The TCO is, in essence, a template containing the system attributes (e.g., system type codes and rights) that will be "conferred" on the created object and the returned AD.

How are TCOs for *system objects* created? A Type Control Object is a system object also. To create a TCO requires an Access Descriptor for an appropriate Type Control Object. If the reader has followed the line of reasoning to this point, all the earmarks of a "catch 22 situation" seem to be in evidence. It should be clear that there is no way for a programmer to create a *system object* unless at least one Type Control Object (along with its Object Descriptor and an associated AD (with *create* rights) is deposited in memory at some known location at the time the system is initialized. TCOs for other types of system objects can be constructed from the initial TCO. If the system program that is loaded at the time of system initialization is sufficiently reliable, and if the operating system code loaded subsequently is also reliable and sensitive Type Control Objects are hidden in the private parts of system packages, it should be possible to deny all users access to all Type Control Objects used by the system. This is the sufficient condition that is needed to guarantee the system security in the i432.

By analogy with TCOs for *system objects*, users who program Ada type manager packages can create TCOs for Extended Type Objects with the aid of the operating system. These users are then responsible for control over the distribution of ADs (having unrestricted rights) to these TCOs in securing their own subsystems.

Our study of the i432 System's security strategy is not yet complete. We have examined the instructions for creating objects, and the controls governing the use of these instructions, but we have not yet introduced the AMPLIFY RIGHTS instruction (and its companion RESTRICT RIGHTS instruction). If the use of AMPLIFY RIGHTS were uncontrolled, this instruction would certainly be a weak point in the System's "security armor."

- The AMPLIFY RIGHTS instruction allows a programmer to add base and type rights to a specified Access Descriptor for an object T, but only if the instruction specifies an AD with *amplify* rights for the Type Control Object that "governs" rights amplification for T. In addition, other conditions explained below must be satisfied. When a suitable TCO is specified in the AMPLIFY RIGHTS instruction, the processor ORs the base and type rights of that TCO with those of the Access Descriptor to be altered.

The additional conditions to be satisfied are as follows:

a. if the specified TCO is for a system typed object, then the object type encoded in the Object Descriptor for target object T must match the object type encoded in the TCO.

b. if the specified TCO is for an Extended Type Object, then the TDO_AD encoded in the TCO must match the TDO_AD value in the Object Descriptor for target object T.

Since the operating system denies users access to TCOs for system typed objects (and since an application subsystem user should not be able to gain access to a TCO for an Extended Type Object residing in a private area of an application program), there can be no *system* security risk here (and there should be no *application* security risk here either.)

- Nor is the RESTRICT RIGHTS instruction a security risk. This instruction allows a programmer to remove base and type rights from an Access Descriptor (presumably before making it available to a less privileged "friend".) For this instruction, a Type Control Object must also be specified, but here, no controls on it are demanded. In fact, a TCO may be fabricated and specified as a refinement of an ordinary generic object. The Access Descriptor that references this TCO need have no special rights beyond *read* rights. The critical issue here, however, is that the restriction of rights is done by the processor, logically ANDing the base and type rights found in the TCO to those of the Access Descriptor to be altered. Since it is not the programmer but the hardware that performs the ANDing of rights, there is no chance that the RESTRICT RIGHTS instruction can be used for rights amplification instead.

The last point to be made about the i432 security model is that, by careful plan, there is no way a user can manufacture and then use an Access Descriptor to access a "forbidden" target. Access Descriptors are constructed by the system only in connection with the creation of objects and refinements. Thereafter, only the rights fields of the AD can be altered—with amplification strictly controlled, as we have just seen. A user can destroy an Access Descriptor D that contains *delete* rights, but only if the user holds an AD with *write* rights for the object in which D resides. Moreover, such "destruction" is always controlled: either D is replaced by another valid and legal Access Descriptor, or D is replaced with a *null* AD—a descriptor that is marked *invalid* and hence never usable. Since the processor fetches ADs only from the access part of an object, it is of no use for a user to implant a manufactured (imitation) AD in the data part of an object with the expectation of "fooling" the processor into using it.

What might appear as an obvious way to breach the system's security is for a user to acquire and use an AD with *write* rights for an Object Table. To do this, the user could first create an object in some SRO, thereby obtaining an AD for that object with full rights. Then, having *write* access to that SRO's Object Table, the user could modify the Object Descriptor for that created object to represent any desired system type, for example, a Type Control Object for any kind of system type. However ADs for SROs made available to users by the operating system have *read* and *write* rights removed, so a user cannot succeed with such a plan.

In summary, the foregoing has been presented as an informal proof that the capability-based system implemented in the i432 architecture is a sufficient foundation for a secure system. The system is secure to the extent that its operating system prevents users from gaining access to TCOs for system typed objects and from gaining possession of an AD with *write* rights for the Object Table of an SRO.

6.2.4. Instruction-Level Use of Extended Type Objects

The last instruction to be discussed in this section is RETRIEVE TYPE DEFINITION. This instruction is used to retrieve the defining TDO_AD for an object A whose AD is currently accessible. The object A can be either an Extended Type Object or a system typed object. The RETRIEVE TYPE DEFINITION instruction takes two operands. The first specifies the Access Descriptor for the source object (A, as discussed above), and the second specifies the slot to receive the requested TDO_AD. The set of rights in the returned TDO_AD includes only *read* and *write* rights, but either or both of these can be removed using the RESTRICT RIGHTS instruction.

We illustrate the use of the RETRIEVE TYPE DEFINITION instruction in a situation in which we are given an AD for an object R of some alleged type S, and we wish to verify that R actually has this type. An i432 instruction sequence like the following might be used:

```
RETRIEVE TYPE DEFINITION(R_AD, unknown_TDO_AD)
                                          -- TDO_AD for R is deposited
                                          -- in unknown_TDO_AD.
EQUAL ACCESS(unknown_TDO_AD, type_S_TDO_AD, truth_value)
                                          -- Sets truth_value to true
                                          -- on equal compare of two
                                          -- given ADs, else sets
                                          -- truth_value to false.
BRANCH FALSE(truth_value, Not_S)          -- Branch to label Not_S
                                          -- if truth_value is false.
-- Steps to be taken if object R is of type S.
      . . .
```

The actual content of a Type Definition Object is not specified in the i432 Architecture. For many applications it may be sufficient for the TDO to be empty because the AD for it serves as the type's unique identifier. As we will see, however, in Chapter 10, Type Definition Objects may contain references useful to modules of the Object Filing Subsystem for determining how to file typed objects in the passive, long-term store of the system.

[One can easily conceive of an application in which a TDO is a Domain Object that refers to a set of operations (attributes) that may be performed on (associated with) a type. Such an application would differ from one controlled by a standard Ada compiler in the sense that the set of operations (attributes) defined for a particular extended type could be varied dynamically, as required.

This form of dynamic typing is used in languages like LISP for which there is a *property list* associated with each variable. Properties and property values on such lists may be altered dynamically. In a database application, to choose a more familiar example, the access rules for typed records would be referenced indirectly from associated Type Definition Objects. These rules could be altered dynamically, by some supervisory module of the program.

Certain applications in computer graphics also suggest themselves. For example, some spatial objects must be displayed under potentially changing display rules. These objects can also be represented as Typed Objects. One can see that the number of useful applications for Typed Objects appears to be open-ended.]

In the next Section, we look at the more ''benign'' user interface provided by iMAX for gaining access to the architecture's Extended Type facility.

6.3. iMAX Interface to the Extended Type Facility

The iMAX Extended_Type_Manager package, provides the user-level interface for managing objects with extended types. We have already introduced the reader to this package in Section 6.1, and we have explained the underlying hardware mechanisms on which the package depends in Section 6.2. Therefore, the reader should now have no difficulty understanding the Ada specifications for this package (given in Appendix I). In this section, we quickly go over the highlights of these specifications and then show how a programmer would use the package for managing Extended Type Objects.

In the context of this discussion, we may ask, who is the ''user'' of this iMAX package? It seems fair to say that systems programmers, such as those working for *original equipment manufacturers* (OEMs), including compiler writers, and some interpreter writers, will be the typical users. Applications programmers who choose to program in Ada, who generally prefer to work at a higher level, should not need to use the iMAX package directly. We attempt to show why this is so later in this section. We first discuss the lower-level, or direct, use of the iMAX interface. We then show how the equivalent operations are expressed within Ada.

The iMAX interface package offers six operations, as listed in Figure 6-4. Each of these corresponds to a key i432 hardware instruction whose semantics we have previously described.

```
Operation Name                  Applicable i432 instruction
---------------                 ----------------------------
Create_type_definition          CREATE TYPED OBJECT
Create_type_control             CREATE TYPED OBJECT
Create_extended_type            CREATE TYPED OBJECT

Retrieve_type_definition        RETRIEVE TYPE DEFINITION

Restrict_rights                 RESTRICT RIGHTS
Amplify_rights                  AMPLIFY  RIGHTS
```

Figure 6-4 Operations of the iMAX package Extended_Type_Manager.

We now suggest how one can program a type manager package, S_Mgr, that manages objects of some type S. This package would make calls on the iMAX Extended_Type_Manager to obtain a TDO for type S, to obtain a governing TCO, and to create Extended Type Objects typed by S (which we hereafter call "Typed_S" objects.) In addition, S_Mgr might offer its users a predicate for determining whether a given typed object is a Typed_S object. We will also see that, unknown to the user of S_Mgr, the latter might perform Restrict_rights and Amplify_rights calls on Extended_Type_Manager. In short, a typical user-written type manager package is likely to make use of all the operations listed in the iMAX Extended_Type_Manager package. We explain this idea further below where, for simplicity, we assume that S_Mgr is a transformer package, rather than an owner package.

As suggested, the public operations of S_Mgr would include the two basic operations to create a Typed_S object and to verify that a given object is of type S. See Figure 6-5.

```
with  Extended_Type_Manager     -- and other packages, as needed
                                ;
package S_Mgr is
  use Extended_Type_Manager;

  function Create_typed_S(len_d, len_a: short_ordinal)
    return typed_S_ref;

  function  Is_type_S(unknown_typed:  dynamic_typed)
    return boolean;

  -- Other function and procedure specifications that are
  -- particular to type S go here.

end S_Mgr;
```

Figure 6-5 Skeleton of a low-level Type manager.

Also included but not shown would be declarations of types and variable instances of these types, either public or private.

Create_typed_S returns an AD for a Typed_S object, given as arguments the lengths of the access and data part. The base rights supplied in the returned AD depend on the application. Thus, if S_Mgr's callers are regarded as "unreliable", both *write* and *read* rights would be withheld. (We see later that such a case corresponds to an Ada **private** access type.) The caller of Create_typed_S supplies neither a TCO argument nor an SRO argument. This is because the attributes of type S are known to the programmer of S_Mgr. Thus, when that package is initialized, references for both the TDO and TCO for type S are obtained by a (single) call on the Create_type operation of the iMAX package.

The function Is_type_S returns a boolean value true if the supplied reference is an AD for a Typed_S object and false otherwise. (In the implementation of Is_type_S, S_Mgr makes a call on the iMAX operation Retrieve_type_definition to obtain an AD for the TDO of unknown_typed.)

In the event S_Mgr has removed *read* and *write* rights, or both, when returning a reference for a created Typed_S object, then upon receiving subsequent calls, S_Mgr by the user might need to call on the Amplify_rights operation of the iMAX package. This would be done in order to restore the rights needed by S_Mgr so that processing of the call can continue. When processing is completed, S_Mgr may wish to call on the Restrict_rights operation of the iMAX package to again remove the restored rights if, for example, the AD was supplied as an argument of an **in out** parameter.

To be more concrete, let us suppose that S_Mgr includes the public operation

```
procedure Update_typed_S(
     -- param1: in        . . . ;
     -- param2: in        . . . ;
        param3: in out  typed_S_ref)
```

If rights for Typed_S objects are not initially withheld from S_Mgr's caller, then the implementation of Update_typed_S uses param3 directly as received, and returns the same AD value after possibly modifying the object referred to by param3. If, however, base rights to Typed_S objects have been withheld, then the implementation of Update_typed_S would first issue a call like

```
Amplify_rights(
                    ext_type       => param3,
                    tco            => typed_S_tco_ref);
```

if both *read* and *write* were needed for updating the Typed_S object specified by param3. Just before completion of the update procedure, a corresponding call to restrict the rights in param3would also be issued:

```
Restrict_rights(
                    ext_type      => param3,
                    read_rights   => 1,
                    write_rights  => 1,
                    tco           => typed_S_tco_ref);
```

In both of the above calls, the value passed to the parameter "tco" is a variable that is strictly private to S_Mgr.

The direct use of the iMAX interface package permits the management of Extended Type Objects within a "spectrum" from fully private to fully public. If the type manager removes (supplies) all rights to Typed Object ADs before handing them to the user, such objects are clearly fully private (fully public). A fully private object models a real world object that is *sealed*. One cannot unseal it (to find out what is in it or to use what is in it) for lack of a key. A fully public object models a real world object that is open for inspection or manipulation.

Intermediate points on the spectrum running from fully public to fully private are also possible. Suppose, for example, the user of a returned AD having both *read* and *write* rights for a Typed_S object chooses to further restrict certain dispensed copies of the AD by stripping off these rights. Further suppose that some of the operations of S_Mgr, like Is_type_S (or Update_typed_S) are re-specified to require *read* rights or *write* rights, or both, and that exceptions are raised by S_Mgr when such rights are not provided with **in** or **in out** Typed_S references. In this situation, a much richer set of management controls can be exercised.

A particular kind of intermediate level of control governs the provision of the right to verify the type of a Typed Object. Possession of a reference with *read* rights to an Extended Type Object can be used to model possession of an access to a "trademark" on that object. We can think of the Type Definition Object that is associated with a Typed Object as the object's *trademark*. Having access to the TDO permits verification that the given object is an authentic instance of some type (assured by checking the object's trademark).

The ability to check for the expected trademark on a Typed Object in modelling real-world systems can be regarded as a useful *user-defined right* that can be dispensed to those modules that need it. For the case where a type manager dispenses (at least) *read* rights to a created Typed Object, we can easily implement such a scheme. It is only necessary to specify the Is_Type predicate of the type manager such that the caller must supply *read* rights in the in-bound reference to the Typed Object. (To be specific, suppose module E is given exclusive access to the manager package T_Mgr. Suppose subprograms in E get ADs to created Typed_T objects with *read* rights. This right can then be retained in copies destined to some of E's callers but stripped off of copies destined to others, thus dispensing the right of trademark-checking to some and withholding it from others.)

6.3.1. Implementation of Ada Access Types

The extended type facility (architecture and iMAX interface) described in the foregoing text forms the foundation for the i432 Ada compiler's implementation of Ada access types. Every access type variable of type T in an Ada program is an AD that references an Extended Type Object if and only if

```
pragma Enable_Dynamic_Typing(T);
```

is specified in the same unit in which T is declared.

Declaring an access type T that references a **limited private** type (hereafter referred to as a *private access type*) and specifying the pragma Enable_Dynamic_Typing(T), directs the i432 Ada compiler to form sealed references for all instances of T, whether allocated statically or dynamically. *Sealed references* are ADs that have no base rights. Furthermore, when such instances are subsequently supplied as arguments to operations of the package in which the type T is declared, the compiler automatically generates the necessary calls on operations of Extended_Type_Manager to amplify base rights on in-bound arguments and to restrict these same rights on out-bound arguments. Rights amplication and restriction is made invisible to the user.

This direct match made between the high-level concept of an Ada private access type and the i432/iMAX mechanisms for support of type managers has significant implications for the improvement of security and software productivity. Benefits accrue mainly because local as well as system-wide security is automatically gained for the data of Ada programs declared using private access types. Since the achievement of total security is implemented simply by the use of the private access type feature of Ada, application programs need not be augmented with or encapsulated in code to invoke special system routines for achieving the same level of security. By avoiding such ''embellishment'', programs can be simpler and easier to understand—hence the expected increase in software productivity.

The benefits outlined above are gained at some cost in space and execution speed for an executing Ada program. For some Ada access types, a user might prefer that the compiler choose an untyped representation, thereby avoiding the costs of extra object creation and rights amplification and restriction (and assuming the implicit security risks as well). For this reason, the 432 Ada compiler default specifies that untyped representation should be used for access types and that sealing should be inhibited.

We now consider in somewhat greater detail the implementation of Ada **access** types and their use. Consider the following Ada program fragment:

```
type R is
  record
    --
    --
    --
  end record;

type R_ref  is access  R;

pragma Enable_Dynamic_Typing(R_ref);
  --  Compiler generates code to produce a TDO for type R (TDO_R)
  --  and a TCO  (TCO_R_ref) that contains an AD for TDO_R.
```

A subsequent program fragment may contain steps to declare an instance of type R_ref and to allocate a new value for R:

```
X:   R_ref;         -- Compiler generates an association between X and
                    -- the AD for TCO_R_ref already obtained.
--
--
X := new  R'( . . . );
                    -- Compiler generates, either directly or indirectly,
                    -- a CREATE TYPED OBJECT instruction that
                    -- specifies the AD for the TCO_R associated with
                    -- variable X, thereby creating a Typed_R object
                    -- and assigning the returned reference to X.
```

The object structure resulting from executing the above assignment statement would appear as in Figure 6-6.

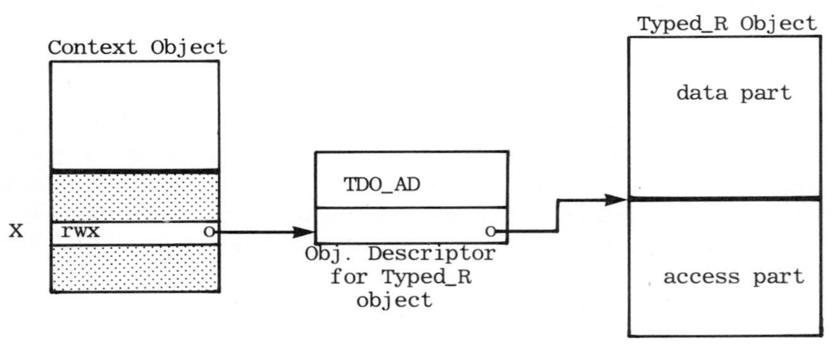

Figure 6-6 Data structure snapshot immediately after assigning to X a reference to a new Typed_R object. It is assumed that variable X has been allocated a slot in the access part of the current Context Object.

6.3.2. Compile-Time and Run-Time Type Checking

Since instances of Ada access types can be created dynamically as well as statically, it is useful to review the kind of type checking automatically provided by the Ada compiler at compile time and/or run time. Such type checking is an essential building block in the security structure for all i432 application programs.

First, we need to review the Ada concept of *type conversion* to see how it applies to access types. Second, we need to appreciate how run-time checks are provided in those cases in which type conversion involves the special i432 Ada type *dynamic_typed*. A variable of this type can contain any Access Descriptor and is used in important ways when interfacing with the iMAXOperating System. [Type *dynamic_typed* is a predefined type in the SYSTEM package supplied with the Ada compiler system and as such can be regarded as an extension of Ada.]

Ada permits the programmer to specify the conversion of an expression value from one type (and representation) to another "related" type (and representation). For example, if types X and Y are related types, then one may convert a value of type X to type Y or vice versa using the following syntax:

```
declare
 first:  X;
 second: Y;
begin
  . . .
 first  := X(second); -- Converts value of type Y to value of type
                      -- X and assigns it to first.
  . . .
 second := Y(first);  -- Converts value of type X to value of type
                      -- Y and assigns it to second.
  . . .
end;
```

By *related* types we mean X and Y must belong to some common category. For example, both types must be numeric, or both types must both be arrays of some conformable dimensions and have related element types. More importantly for this discussion, Ada also allows conversion between *derived* types, that is, between one type, A, derived from another type, B, *and vice versa*. [A reader may wish to consult Chapters 3 and 4 of the Ada Reference Manual for more details on type conversion.] For example, type A is said to be derived from type B if type A is declared in the declaration:

```
type A is new B;
```

or, in the declaration

```
type A is new B constraint;
```

In the second example, the constraint simply limits the domain of values that type A can have to a subset of those B has. For example,

```
type mid_week is new day range tue .. thu;
```

Following the same principle, all access types are related, as they may all be considered as having been derived from the "generic type" dynamic_typed. This means we can express the conversion of one particular access type to another using the same type conversion syntax as just described.

The special, predefined dynamic_typed type has been introduced to provide a simple way for programs to manipulate reference (AD) values whose referenced types are unknown at compile time. We have encountered but not yet elaborated one such example in Section 5.6, in which the record type "message_type'' contained the component message_body, of type dynamic_typed. In this case, the sender must assign an access value of some particular type to the message_body component of the message and the receiver, in order to use the message_body, must convert this value of type dynamic_typed to some particular and meaningful access type.

Consider the following situation, in which we have three access variables A, B, and C, and where the value of one is to be assigned to another:

```
type R_ref is access R;

pragma Enable_Dynamic_Typing(R_ref);

A:       dynamic_typed;

B, C:    R_ref;              -- A particular access type.

A := dynamic_typed(B);       -- Passes a compile-time type check.

B := R_ref(A);               -- Run_time check is generated by the compiler

C := A;                      -- Illegal without invocation of
                             -- Unchecked_type_conversion on
                             -- right-hand side, as explained below.
```

The first assignment ''A := dynamic_typed(B)'' is determined at compile time to be legal since a value of any access type can be assigned to a variable of type *dynamic_typed*. The second assignment ''B := R_ref(A)'' supplies the information needed by the compiler to generate machine code for a run-time type check. This check is executed as follows: The system type that is encoded in the object descriptor for A is checked for equality with that of B. If not equal, a type fault exception is raised. If equal, and if the system types of neither is ''extended type'', then the check succeeds. If both types represent ''extended type'', then a further check is made for equality of the governing TDO_ADs. One of the TDO_ADs is stored within the Object Descriptor for the current value of object A and the other TDO_AD is that for type R_ref, which is B's correct type. Recall that the governing TDO_AD for A is found in the Object Descriptor for object A and the governing TDO_AD for type R_ref is stored within the TCO associated with type R_ref. The assignment completes normally if the check succeeds; a type fault is raised if the check fails.

To understand why the assignment ''C := A'' is determined by the compiler to be illegal, we briefly review the key Ada rule governing assignment of values to variables.

If the type of the name on the left hand side of an Ada assignment statement is not (resolvable at compile time or run time to be) equivalent to the type of the expression on the right hand side of the assignment, then Ada semantics requires that the generic function Unchecked_Conversion must be applied to the right hand side expression. This precaution provides the compiler with the opportunity to guarantee that the user is *aware* that he is stepping outside the bounds of Ada's type checking system. If Unchecked_conversion is not specified and the two sides of an assignment statement are of incompatible types then the compiler can safely imply that the user has committed an unintentional error.

```
with Unchecked_conversion;
  . . .
   type some_access is access  . . . ;

   function Convert_any_to_some is new
                           Unchecked_conversion(source => dynamic_typed;
                                                target => some_access);
                                      -- Declares a specific instance of
                                      -- the generic library subprogram,
                                      -- Unchecked_conversion.
   X: some_access;
   Y: dynamic_typed;
   . . .
   X := Convert_any_to_some(Y);       -- The function call on the right-hand
                                      -- side specifies the target type.
                                      -- No run-time check occurs.
```

[Adherence to these rules was implicit in the discussion we had in Section 5.6 concerning the sending (and receiving) of messages in which values of different access types were to be assigned to (and read from) the message_body component of various messages transmitted through the same typed port. For those interested, the required use of Unchecked_conversion is defined in Chapter 13 of the Ada Reference Manual in the section entitled, "Unchecked Programming."]

We can invoke Unchecked_conversion to transform the illegal assignment "C := A" of the earlier example into a legal assignment. The Ada program fragment would be changed in, for example, the following manner:

```
with Unchecked_conversion;
  . . .
  type R_ref is access  . . . ;

  function Convert_any_to_R_ref is new
                         Unchecked_conversion(source => dynamic_typed;
                                              target => R_ref);
                              -- Declares a specific instance of
                              -- the generic library subprogram,
                              -- Unchecked_conversion.
   pragma Enable_Dynamic_Typing(R_ref);

   A:      dynamic_typed;
   B, C:   R_ref;              -- A particular access type.
   A := dynamic_typed(B);      -- Passes a compile-time type check.
   B := R_ref(A);              -- Run_time check is generated by the compiler.
   C := Convert_any_to_R_ref(A);
                               -- The assignment is legal (although unsafe)
                               -- even though there may be a mismatch
                               -- between the current type associated with A
                               -- and the type of C. No run-time check occurs.
```

6.4. Sealing the Membership Roster

In Section 6.1 we suggested that another look at protection of the membership roster in the portfolio management application program would be in order after gaining an understanding of the i432 security system. Our expectation is to improve security by preventing a person from masquerading as the officer authorized to update the membership roster, and thereby gaining improper authorization for updating the portfolio.

One can understand the security problem most easily by a review of the program structure in Figure 2-5.

A portfolio update request to Portfolio_Server (Appendix F) is first confirmed by a call to Roster_Server, which is sent the name of Portfolio_Server's caller. A simple name is not hard to forge, so let us assume that we have already "improved" Roster_Server by requiring that a password be supplied along with the person's name. That name and password must be checked by Roster_Server (Appendix F.) Only the club's current Secretary is permitted to write new names (and passwords) in the membership roster. The weak link in the security plan is that no provision has yet been made to prevent a person from "impersonating" the Secretary and thereby gaining the power to alter any and all other passwords in the roster. (Many useful systems rely on passwords as the basis for maintaining security, but, in this case, we shall assume that passwords are deemed insufficient.)

We now consider how the *sealing* facility for i432 objects can be used to control system security. Recall that a sealed object of type S is a Typed_S object under control of a type manager whose operations dispense ADs (for Typed_S objects) that never contain base rights. Recall also that the i432 Ada compiler guarantees that transformer type managers for objects reached via private access type variables dispense only sealed objects to users. It would appear that a straightforward approach to the use of seals for this problem might proceed as follows:

At first glance, one might think that the owner package Membership_Roster, which creates the roster during its initialization, should be changed to a transformer package and given a public Create operation. The Create operation would then return a reference to a sealed membership roster.

However, there is another potential security problem associated with this approach. In principle, any module that can access the package can also access this Create operation. Use of the Create operation would permit the imposter to populate an entirely different membership roster (using the Add_new_member operation) in which the imposter installs himself as the secretary. Having installed a fraudulent roster, the imposter could now issue entry calls to Portfolio_Server, supplying it with a reference to a "proper" member name along with a "proper", though fraudulent, membership roster. Roster_Server, called for confirmation by Portfolio_Server, would be duped into responding with a message confirming that the imposter is, in fact, the club secretary, thereby providing authorized access to the portfolio itself.

A solution to this problem is to hide the Create operation, by letting it become part of the initialization sequence of the Membership_Roster package—which is the approach we had taken in the first place. Pursuing this idea further, let us suppose that in addition to steps required to create the membership roster, performed during the initialization of Membership_Roster, additional steps are executed that have the effect of transmitting to Task_Master a reference to the sealed roster.

Transmitting the roster reference from Membership_Roster back to Task_Master presents a bit of a problem, as the reader will see in the following discussion. For the moment, however, let us postpone the question of how the requisite information is returned to the Task_Master, and instead pursue question: What will Task_Master be expected to do with that information?

We propose that Task_Master provide a reference to the newly initialized membership roster to Portfolio_Server after it is started up, and also to the Secretary task, after it is started up. Thereafter, when Portfolio_Server accepts an entry call requesting update of the membership roster, Portfolio_Server can check (for an exact match) of its copy of the roster reference against the one supplied as an argument in the call. Here we presume that the specification of each operation in Portfolio_Server to update the roster has been modified to include the proper roster reference as an additional reference argument. This reference does not, of course, contain base rights.

Central to this solution is the assumption that the Secretary task can be "trusted" not to send out copies of the roster reference it receives from Task_Master. This trust is well placed if the Secretary task is written by the same programmer who writes Task_Master, or who, at least, is not the same as the person who is the club's secretary.

There is one more ingredient to the security strategy that should be discussed before we return to the postponed question of how the Task_Master receives the roster reference. How is an orderly "change of the guard" effected when the job of club secretary is passed to another individual? One simple solution would be to have either the retiring or the incoming secretary update the roster entries appropriately to reflect the change of duties.

At first glance, this proposal seems to be a bit naive. In fact, however, it is naive only if it is to be assumed that the outgoing secretary is untrustworthy. Otherwise, there is no reason to believe this approach will not work. A trustworthy secretary would, as a "last act of office", alter the membership roster to reflect the change of guard. Thereafter, only the new secretary would be able to log in and attach to the Secretary task.

More sophisticated solutions for the change-of-guard problem also come to mind. For example, Task_Master could be coded to receive from the Secretary task a message, sent by an outgoing secretary, telling Task_Master to abort that Secretary task and to start up a new Secretary task to be used by the incoming secretary. It is not clear why or when this more elaborate approach would be required.

We can now resume consideration of our postponed question: how should the reference to the created roster, produced by Membership_Roster during its initialization, reach Task_Master? Four solutions are suggested, in increasing order of soundness.

1. The information reaches Task_Master via shared storage. This approach is unattractive. The shared storage approach is possible only if Membership_Roster is statically nested within Task_Master. It is preferable that Membership_Roster be an Ada library-level package, but this approach is precluded if the package is nested within a task.

2. The information is transmitted as the result of an Ada task entry call (after the membership roster is initialized) from the initialization part of Membership_Roster to Task_Master, using the rendezvous mechanism. But a task entry call from Membership_Roster to Task_Master will result in a deadlock situation, because only one thread of control is involved. (The package which Task_Master is in the process of activating, has called an entry in Task_Master; this is a circular deadlock situation.)

3. The requisite values are transmitted by explicit i432 message-based communication. (The deadlock problem in the preceding solution is avoided.) The steps to be taken are as follows: After completing its initialization of the membership roster, but before returning to its caller, Membership_Roster issues a Send of the requisite message (containing the initialized membership roster) to a Port that is commonly accessible to both Task_Master and Membership_Roster. When control returns to Task_Master, following the initialization of Membership_Roster, the former can issue a Receive for the membership roster message at the same Port. (Readers are referred to Chapter 5 for the explanation of Send and Receive steps.)

4. Very likely the best solution, one that is wholly contained within the Ada rendezvous mechanism, would be to engage two distinct tasks in the activity of transmitting the information produced during initialization of Membership_Roster to Task_Master. Such a solution could be accomplished, for example, by having the Task_Master start up an auxiliary task, Masters_Helper, that has no other responsibility but to instantiate Membership_Roster, which is now respecified as a generic package.

   A task entry call from Membership_Roster to Task_Master after the former's initialization of the membership roster is in full harmony with the

Ada rendezvous mechanism. Task_Master would, of course have to be programmed to accept such a call.

At this point Task_Master will have acquired the requisite reference to the membership roster. Membership_Roster will have been properly initialized, and Task_Master can now send to Portfolio_Server the information that the task needs to protect itself from receiving a bogus membership roster.

To summarize, we have outlined, using the seal facility, a plan to strengthen significantly the security of the portfolio management program structure of Figure 2-5. The increased level of security is as good as the security of the sealing mechanism itself, and is in turn as secure as the i432 architecture and operating system—which, as has been argued earlier, is indeed secure.

We do not intend to show further security solution details for this program structure. Instead, we leave these details, and the full satisfaction of producing them, entirely to the reader. We leave as yet another exercise for the reader the matter of deciding whether a comparable effort is required to increase security for the portfolio management program structure of Figure 3-2.

6.5. Access Control Using Dynamic Packages

In earlier discussions of Extended Type Objects we commented on the potential for dynamically (and efficiently) altering the attributes of typed objects. This alteration is made possible because the user can obtain, using the iMAX Retrieve_type_definition operation, an AD with full base rights for the Type Definition Object for a given Typed Object. It is true that we have not given a concrete example, but nothing prevents a systems programmer, such as a compiler writer, from exploiting extended Type Definition Objects more fully.

The Intel 432-Ada compiler has also attempted to expose the dynamic character of 432 Domain Objects at the level of the Ada programming language (as well as other i432 features) by slightly extending the language. This has provided an extension whose use offers the programmer, at a high level of abstraction, dynamic control over the internal data and access components of individual Domain Objects. To be more concrete, an Ada extension is provided that permits a package specification to be declared as a *dynamic package*. Making such a declaration implies a class of possible instances, any one of which may be selected either statically or dynamically before an operation of the package is applied. Dynamic selection of a governing package instance, for example, may be achieved simply by declaring variables to be of the given dynamic package type and later assigning a particular package instance to that variable. The particular package instance so assigned is a value formed by elaborating a package body (instance) declaration. This value must, of course, be accessible in the current context of the assignment to the package variable. A dynamic package is implemented as a standard Ada **generic** package that is instantiated at execution time rather than compile time.

The Club_Portfolio package of Chapter 2, for example, could be redeclared as a dynamic package. The specification part is identical to what we have already seen (in Appendix C), except for the "package heading" line, which now changes from:

```
package Club_Portfolio is ... end;
```

to

```
generic package Club_Portfolio_Pkg is ... end;
```

augmented with the type declaration

```
type Club_Portfolio is access Club_Portfolio_Pkg;
```

Variables of type Club_Portfolio may then be declared, as in:

```
His_Estate: Club_Portfolio;
```

Thus, in any scope in which both His_Estate and the dynamic package type Club_Portfolio are visible, one can provide (that is, declare) a particular package body instance for Club_Portfolio, such as Volunteers_Portfolio.

[This may be done using the declarations:

```
Volunteers_Portfolio: constant Club_Portfolio :=
                                 new Club_Portfolio_Pkg;
package body Volunteers_Portfolio is
     -- Declarations and statements for the body
     -- of this version of the Club_Portfolio_Pkg
     -- package go here.
end Volunteers_Portfolio;
]
```

It is then permissible to assign (the constant package value) Volunteers_Portfolio to His_Estate. Thereafter, one can make calls to operations of Volunteers_Portfolio (Club_Portfolio) by prefixing its operation names with His_Estate. Several distinct package constants can be declared. By assigning distinct package constants to a particular package variable, the package can, when initialized, acquire a distinct portfolio instance or have operations with different implementation details, or both. (As an illustration of the latter, different averaging rules might be used for the Print_average_cost operation in two different versions of the package body.)

Suppose, for example, a subprogram, P, is being executed and that within the scope of P, both His_Estate and package Volunteers_Portfolio are visible. Then, within the body of P, we may have the following statement sequence:

```
His_Estate := Volunteers_Portfolio;
. . .
His_Estate.Print_average_cost(
                    His_Estate.Find_stock_code(
                           "General Motors^^^^^^^^^^^^^^"));
. . .
```

In this sequence, His_Estate is first assigned the package value, which is a particular implementation of Club_Portfolio. Then the call is made to display the average cost of the General Motors holdings of the portfolio owned by the package assigned to His_Estate.

We make several closing observations concerning the increase in expressive power gained when using the dynamic package facility. Subprogram P may call another subprogram Q, passing it His_Estate as an argument. Thus, Q could be defined to accept as a parameter any matching package (that is any value of the specified package type) as an argument. We will see a convincing application of the passing of package type arguments in the next Chapter. The facility would not be possible were it not for the fact that, with the dynamic package extension, users of Intel's extended 432-Ada language can declare variables of some particular package type. Other uses of package variables arise where it is necessary to select dynamically a particular package implementation, according to data- or data-representation dependent decisions. The full syntactic and semantic definitions for the dynamic package extensions to Ada, as well as more complete examples, are explained in the Reference Manual for the Intel 432 Extensions to Ada, cited in Appendix B.

Another use of the dynamic package is passing a function to a subprogram as an actual parameter. (Some readers may wish to skip over the following bracketed discussion which shows the details.)

[Our example, repeated from the reference manual just cited, demonstrates how a function can be passed to an integration procedure. The function is passed inside an actual parameter which is a package value. See also Figure 6-7. The function that will be the integrand function is the only element of the package named Integrable_Function_Pkg. The integrand function is specified as a parameter to Integrable_Function_Pkg so that many different packages can be created, differing only in that each carries a different integrand function. Any of these packages can later be passed as an actual parameter to an integration procedure named "Simpson_integrate". (This integration procedure uses the function that resides within the actual parameter package as its integrand function.)

The creation of a package value is realized by using the standard Ada allocator expression, extended to allow the type name to be a package value name. Thus, for example, to create a package that is passed to the Simpson_integrate shown in Figure 6-7, one may write

```
function   sine(x:  in real) return real;
  ...
function cosine(x:  in real) return real;
  ...
answer1 := Simpson_integrate(
               left, right,
               new Integrable_Function_Pkg (sine));
  ...
answer2 := Simpson_integrate(
               left, right,
               new Integrable_Function_Pkg (cosine));        ]
```

```
type real is digits 8;
  ...
generic
  with function Function_parameter(x: in real)
    return real;
package Integrable_Function_Pkg is;
  F(x: in real) return real renames Function_parameter;
end Integrable_Function_Pkg;
  ...
type Integration_Pkg is access Integrable_Function_Pkg;
  ...

function Simpson_integrate(
    a, b: real;
    p:     Integration_Pkg)
  return real
is
  ...
  x, h, area: real;
  ...
begin
  ...
  area := area + h*p.F(x);       -- This is the heart of the integration
                                 -- algorithm.

  ...
end Simpson_integrate;
```

Figure 6-7 Illustrating how an integrand function, F, can be passed as a parameter to the Simpson_integrate procedure. Note that F is locally defined in Integrable_Function_Pkg. It is the only public operation of Integrable_Function_Pkg and renames the generic formal parameter, Function_Parameter.

The 432-Ada compiler writers have implemented the dynamic package facility in the following way. The value assigned to a package variable, P_v, of type T and body T_instance, is simply a reference (Access Descriptor) to a Domain Object, which is the representation of the package body T_instance.

Readers will find that other interesting and potentially useful Ada extensions, including the means for specifying specific i432 instruction sequences, are described in the reference document on i432-Ada. (The package operations to include i432 instruction sequences are specified in the Reference Manual for the Intel 432 Extensions to Ada.) In most cases the objective of added high-level facility is to provide the user a better opportunity to take full advantage of the hardware architecture as "completed" by the iMAX operating system.

432-Ada directly allows programmers to specify refinements to objects at the Ada level. (For example, a programmer can specify a refinement to a package.) Recall that Refinement Descriptors provide the underlying facility for controlling access to subblocks of data and access parts of objects. At the level of 432-Ada, a programmer can, by the use of the extended Ada refinement declaration, create (declare) aliases to existing Domain Objects, including subsets of the operations of a given package. These declarations, which are discussed in Chapter 7, are directly supported by the i432 architecture through use of the refinement mechanism and the pertinent iMAX interfaces.

Our account of the Access Control and Type Management in the i432 system is now complete. We have skirted several related topics that could have been included here. Among these are the low-level mechanisms for converting data references in i432 instructions to accesses into the data and access parts of target objects, touched on only briefly in in Chapter 4. Indeed, we have entirely skirted discussion of i432 instruction formats, their rich and variable structure, and the formats of the data reference components of the instructions. This topic is an interesting one, but is well covered in the GDP Architecture Reference Manual.

Nor, have we yet examined other control information that is encoded in Object Descriptors that relates primarily to memory and object file management. We do this, however, in Chapters 9 and 10.

7 i432 INPUT/OUTPUT

7.1. Introduction

Input/Output control programs and their supporting hardware are known as *I/O Control Systems*. They have evolved over a span of some twenty-five years. These control systems, which originated as key modules of early operating systems, were often composed largely of software and were monolithic in structure (to achieve objectives of protection and throughput.) Over time, as the objectives of I/O control became better understood, hardware and software architectural support has become modularized and distributed out and away from the central core of the computer system.

The earliest objectives of I/O Control Systems were to achieve input/output of multiple data streams at high rates, in such a way as to permit the central computer system to remain as free as possible to continue the processing of "compute-bound" functions, thus gaining overlap of computation and I/O transfer. About the time that it was learned how to achieve those objectives, a rapidly-expanding variety of I/O devices was becoming available, shifting the focus of the system designers to a new and more challenging objective, namely: How to help the user run programs having a maximum of device independence. Reaching this objective has often been painful and costly, especially since that objective was generally incompatible with previous I/O Contol System designs.

A number of architectural schemes have been tried. Perhaps the most comprehensive strategy is that represented by the Multics I/O System, whose objectives and structure serve as a principal ancestor of the scheme adopted by the i432 System architects. That ancestor, ahead of its time, still serves as a paradigm for many modern conventional I/O Systems. [To better appreciate the i432 I/O System, one may need to compare it with more conventional approaches, and hence the reader may find it useful to read Chapter 8 of "The Multics System" [44].

We do not base our discussion of i432 I/O, however, by initially showing it in juxtaposition with conventional structures. (We assume most readers are already familiar with the structure of some I/O system.) Instead, we adopt a bottom-up approach. First, we examine the architectural support for I/O (unique to the i432 System). We do this in the remainder of our introduction. Then, we examine the iMAX Operating System's user interfaces which rest on that architecture (Sections 7.2 through 7.4). The flexibility of the provided interface also depends strongly on the 432-Ada extensions for *package refinement access types* illustrated later in this chapter. (See also Appendix B, Reference Manual for the Intel 432 Extensions to Ada.) These Ada extensions exploit the i432 hardware operators that create and control access to refinements (in this case to refinements of Domain Objects). Having examined the i432 I/O structures and mechanisms, we make some higher-level observations and also identify advances made in the i432 I/O structure beyond that of more conventional systems (Section 7.5). At the end of this chapter (Section 7.6), we again revisit our portfolio management information system to apply some of what has been learned about i432 I/O to that program.

7.1.1. System Organization Revisited

Figure 7-1 reviews the i432 system structure introduced in Chapter 1. In this simplified diagram we treat the multiprocessor interconnect as a single *System bus* and show the physical relationship between the Computational Subsystem and the I/O Subsystem.

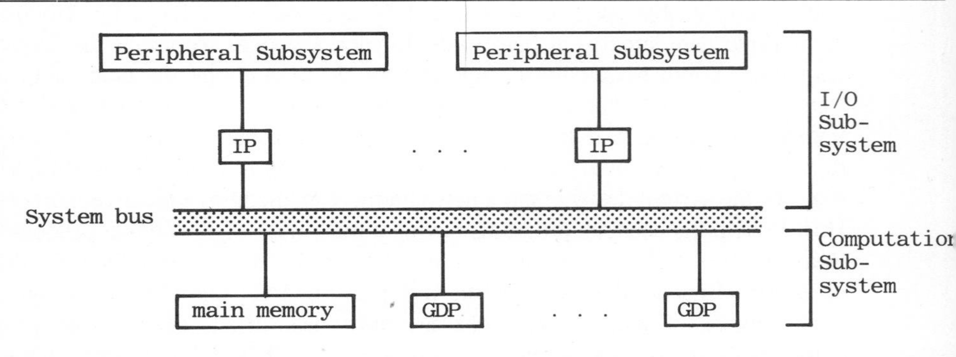

Figure 7-1 A simple 432 system topology.

As mentioned in Chapter 1, the I/O Subsystem consists of one or more *independent* peripheral subsystems, each interfaced to the Computational Subsystem through an Interface Processor (IP). [Although their roles are different, both GDP and IP processors access the same object-structured main memory through the common System bus. Indeed, an essential role of the IP is to provide the means for a Peripheral Subsystem to access the object-based 432 memory.]

7.1.2. Architectural Support for Input/Output

Our main learning objective for this chapter is to understand how the Computational Subsystem executes the input/output steps of programs. A necessary sub-objective is to understand, at least in an abstract sense, the architecture of a Peripheral Subsystem and how it functions in cooperation with the Computational Subsystem. (Since individual Peripheral Subsystems are logically mutually independent, it is sufficent to assume the presence of only one of them—and we do so in subsequent discussions.) A final objective is to learn how a user of the i432 System may take advantage of the operating system interface software provided for the programming of input/output operations. Because the underlying framework for specifying input and output operations is that of interprocess communication, the mechanisms outlined in Chapter 5 are directly applicable.

An overriding goal of the total system architecture is to adhere to a modular design philosophy in hardware as well as in software. This translates into the objective of preserving a clean separation between subsystem components at each level, so that one component may be designed, implemented, and function (and possibly later modified) as independently as possible of another component. These objectives imply clear separation of roles among subsystem or subsubsystem components and the hiding of implementation details within individual components. Keeping these objectives in mind is especially helpful for learning how input/output works in this system.

Some of the direct design consequences of these objectives are:

- Interaction between the Computational Subsystem and a Peripheral Subsystem is accomplished entirely by message-based (normally asynchronous) communication. The Computational Subsystem operates without interrupts from a Peripheral Subsystem.
- New input/output devices and code to drive them may be developed and brought on-line over the life of the system without shutting it down. (Devices may come and go.)
- The disparity between the object-based storage organization and operating behavior of the Computational Subsystem and the record- or stream-based organization and real-time behavior of a variety of conventional and nonconventional I/O devices is bridged by a ''smart interface'' composed of hardware and software. Hereafter, we call this the Peripheral Subsystem Interface (or sometimes simply PSI). [Part of the software for this interface

resides in 432 memory and (the larger) part resides in the memory of the Peripheral Subsystem.]

A prototypical Peripheral Subsystem and the Interface Processor to which it is attached, has a top-level structure as shown in Figure 7-2.

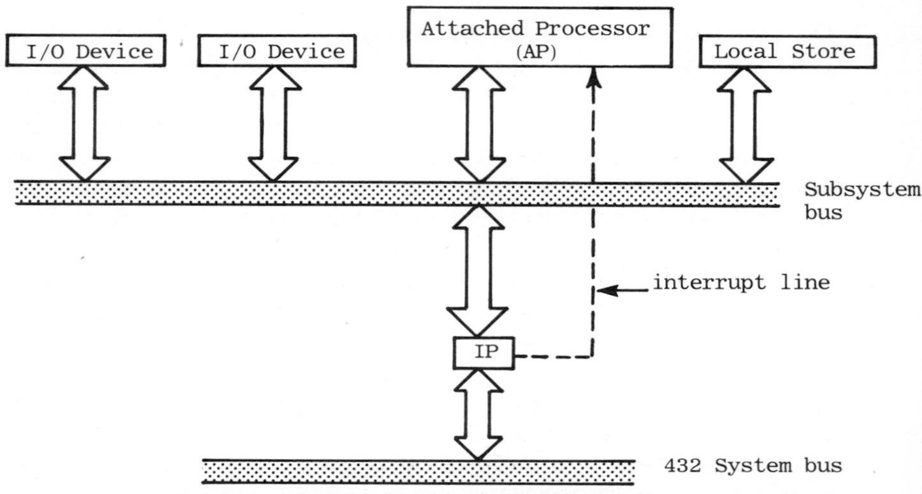

Figure 7-2 Structure of a Peripheral Subsystem.

The Interface Processor (IP) ''takes orders'' from the Attached Processor (AP) to perform functions for communicating with the Computational Subsystem. These orders are carried out in a 432 environment. In particular, the IP is represented by a Processor Object and each order that it executes is accomplished in a specified process environment defined by a Process Object and a Context Object. These system objects, although somewhat specialized for the I/O interface, are comparable to those outlined in Chapters 4 and 5. Within the Peripheral Subsystem Interface, the AP and IP intercommunicate in ways familiar to those acquainted with *memory mapped* I/O subsystems.

[A memory-mapped I/O structure is based on the idea that a dedicated block of the processor's address space represents not actual memory, but rather a mapping to a set of I/O devices. That is, writing into a particular word (or word group) within this block of *pseudo* addresses is interpreted as an I/O command to a corresponding device. The I/O command is sent over a local bus directly (or through some intermediary controller hardware) to the mapped device, which then executes the command.

Commands for reading from the device or writing to the device usually refer to specific buffer areas, also within the computer memory—writing into the buffer in executing a *Read* command, and reading from the buffer in executing a *Write* command. Upon completing a command, the device sends back a report to the processor by (a) writing status information into one or more words within the same word group of computer memory locations from which the I/O command was sent out, and (b) sending an interrupt signal to the computer. The notified processor may then read the status information to decide what to do next.]

The Attached Processor controls the Interface Processor much like an ordinary processor drives a memory-mapped I/O device. That is, the IP responds to function requests, hereafter termed *orders*, as does a memory-mapped I/O device, by executing or attempting to execute the requested order, by sending back status information, and by sending an interrupt to the AP when finished with an order. The order and returned status information are mapped from a dedicated block within the AP's address space onto a predetermined block within the data part of the IP's (single) Processor Object. Specification for this mapping is referred to as a *Control Window*. (The IP's Processor Object and its included Control Window are generally set at the time the system is initialized.)

Other orders which can be issued by the AP to the IP include those that have the effect of setting up correspondences (maps) between buffer areas within selected dedicated blocks of the AP's address space and portions of the data parts of specified i432 objects. A total of four such maps, here called *Data Windows* may be established dynamically. (See Figure 7-3.) Each IP order, such as one to establish a Data Window, is written through the Control Window to a dedicated area in the data part of the IP's Processor Object known as the *Function Request Area*. Once a Data Window is established, the AP can execute an arbitrary sequence of Read or Write instructions from or to addresses that fall within an established Data Window, thereby causing direct transfer of bytes between the data part of the mapped i432 Object and, depending on the instruction set of the AP, either into designated registers within the AP or into other memory cells accessible to the AP.

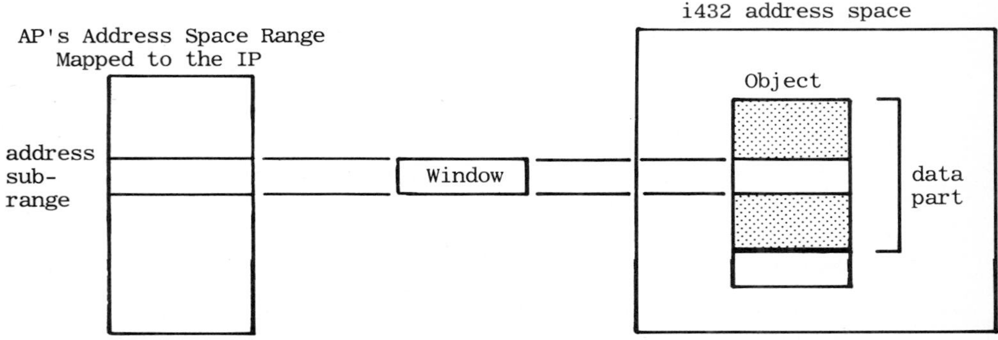

Figure 7-3 IP Window Mapping. A range of peripheral subsystem address space (i.e., a 64K byte section of the AP's address space) maps to the IP. A subrange (of this section) is mapped to a selected section (of equal size) in the data part of an i432 object.

All such transfers are under hardware control of the parameters specifying the operative window; thus, any transfer that would copy data into or from sections of an i432 object that falls outside the bounds implied by the window will induce a fault. Notice of this fault is, in turn, transmitted to the AP by an interrupt.

[For especially fast I/O operations, Data Window 0 may be used by the AP or by a Direct Memory Access (DMA) controller for "block transfer" kinds of Read and Write instructions. For such operations, Data Window 0 is placed in "block mode" and supplied with a "byte_count" parameter that specifies the size of the block to be copied into or from an i432 object. The IP architecture supports such high-speed block transfer by providing a small on-chip FIFO data buffer whose use helps to balance the speed and duty levels on the 432 System bus and I/O Subsystem bus. Further details on use of the two window modes, random and block transfer, in the iAPX 432 Interface Processor Architecture Reference Manual listed in Appendix B and hereafter referred to as the "IP-ARM".]

Upon completing an IP order, the "result", if any, and certain status information for that order are deposited by the IP at predetermined offsets within the Control Window; therefore, the AP can execute follow-up Read instructions to fetch this information. This is done by specifying as operands in Read instructions the addresses in the AP address space that correspond, by virtue of the Control Window, to result and status information in the Function Request Area of the IP's Processor Object. [The Control Window opens on a block of storage within the data part of the IP's Processor Object. This block, whose default size is 256 bytes, but which may be set to a larger value, contains a number of key data structures, including specifications for the five windows and the Function Request Area into which each IP order is transferred before it is executed. The Control Window may also contain a buffer area used in the execution of an OPEN MESSAGE order about which we have more to say later.]

We can already see, however, even from this limited overview that the IP is quite different from an ordinary memory-mapped I/O device in that the orders it performs are not explicit input-output data transfers but rather operations that extend the capablility of the AP for communicating in a controlled way with the Computational Subsystem. Some of the main examples of such orders (functions) are introduced here:

- Functions that establish or disestablish correspondences (mappings) between specified sections of the AP's memory address space and data portions of specified i432 objects. The technical term used to describe these functions is *Opening* (*Closing*) *a Window*.

  As already suggested, opening a Window enables data transfers in either direction through the opened window. Once a Window is Opened, the AP (or, for that matter, any other processor attached to the same Peripheral Subsystem bus) can execute transfers to or from the mapped portion (in the data part) of an i432 object.

  Full i432 access control is exercised in completing an order to open a window. Thus, the order to open a window must specify an AD for the i432 object that is to be viewed through the window; that AD must have appropriate *Read* or *Write* rights, or both, depending on the intended direction and nature of the data transfer through the window being established. The "entry state" operand supplied in the Open Window order indicates "read intent", "write intent", and "block/random mode". If block mode is specified, then exactly one of "read intent" and "write intent" can be true; if random mode is specified, then either "read intent" or "write intent" or both can be true. *Read* rights, *Write* rights, or both are checked by the hardware, according to which intent(s) is (are) specified.

- Functions that perform interprocess communication (RECEIVEs and SENDs) to and from a 432 process and an IP process. Including such orders in the repertoire of the IP permits i432 processes running on GDPs to drive the Peripheral Subsystem without being subject to hardware interrupts when the Peripheral Subsystem completes input/output orders on behalf of the i432 process. From the viewpoint of an i432 process, execution of an I/O operation is achieved entirely via message-based communication, thereby freeing the i432 process of the real time synchronization requirements for certain I/O devices.

  A (blocking) RECEIVE order causes a specified IP process to fetch a message from a designated port in i432 object space. (The reference for the received message is then placed in a predetermined slot of the Context Object for that IP process in strict analogy with the way a RECEIVE is executed in a 432 process.) A (blocking) SEND order causes a specified IP process to deliver a message to a designated port in i432 object space. CONDITIONAL SEND and RECEIVE orders and SURROGATE SEND and SURROGATE RECEIVE orders are also included in the order list of the IP.

- Special functions that reduce windowing overhead associated with messages representing I/O requests and replies. Without these special functions, then when a message representing an I/O request is RECEIVEd from a request port, the AP might be required to inspect its *command* component before it can process its *data* component. To do this, AP would first have to open a data window on to the command component of the Message Object and then read and interpret this command information; only then could the AP always know how to open a data window on to the data component so as to perform the proper sequence of read or write instructions. This high windowing overhead might be prohibitive for certain kinds of frequently used block transfers, such as in frequent movement of small objects to a swapping store.

  Use of the high-level OPEN MESSAGE and CLOSE MESSAGE orders greatly reduces the effort to process data from a RECEIVEd message. If the RECEIVEd message object is of the IP_Message system type, then the OPEN MESSAGE order copies the command portion message object directly into a buffer positioned in a dedicated area of the Control Window section of the IP's Processor Object. Thus, the command information from the GDP process that is making the I/O request becomes immediately accessible to the IP. This command is then used, together with other operands supplied in the OPEN MESSAGE order to open a data window on to the data component of the I/O request. The successful completion of this window opening is indicated by returning a true result for the OPEN MESSAGE order (alternatively false).

Similar IP-AP speed-up, and corresponding simplification of AP-side software, is achieved by using the CLOSE MESSAGE order to transfer desired status information after the transfer indicated by the I/O request has been completed. CLOSE MESSAGE not only closes a (data) window specified by an operand but also performs the equivalent of a CONDITIONAL SEND of a specified message object to an i432 reply port. (Readers wishing to learn more about these powerful OPEN and CLOSE orders should consult the IP-ARM.)

- A function that performs interprocessor communication, permitting the AP to send control signals to GDPs and IPs (individually or collectively, by broadcast). During normal operations, the Computational Subsystem will drive the Peripheral Subsystem, but during system startup, maintenance, emergency shutdowns, and other special occasions, the AP must drive other processors attached to the 432 System Bus. Including interprocessor communication operations in the order list of the IP accomplishes this system control objective.

Understanding how IP RECEIVE and SEND orders are implemented helps explain how the AP and IP cooperate to create the effect of a high-level interface for message-based communication between i432 processes and AP processes. We provide some of these details here:

- Whenever execution of a SEND (or RECEIVE) order causes an IP process to become blocked, this fact is recorded in the Function State field of the Function Request Area; the AP, reading this state information, can learn that the process is blocked. The IP is itself able to execute other orders; and so the SEND or RECEIVE order is regarded as completed. (The IP issues a completion interrupt signal as a second means of informing the AP of this event.)
- Whichever way the AP learns about the blocked process, the AP can then select another IP process to execute the next order. Selection of another IP process is done by simply writing the index for that process into the appropriate field in the IP's Function Request Facility Area through the Control Window. The new order is then issued by writing it into still other predetermined fields of the same Function Request Facility Area.
- When a blocked IP process becomes unblocked, it can be "re-used" by the AP in the execution of other IP orders. The scenario that explains how the AP learns of the unblocking may be described as follows:

- When a blocked IP process becomes unblocked, it is forwarded to the IP's Dispatching Port (by following the "second port mechanism" described in Chapter 5). An IP process, regarded as a message, is removed from the IP's Dispatching Port as a consequence of the AP issuing the IP a DISPATCH order. The AP issues such an order when it knows that the IP should (must) wait for the unblocking of one of the IP processes.
- The effect of a DISPATCH order is that of a Surrogate Receive instruction. That is, the IP's Processor Carrier is sent to the Dispatch Port. The IP receives the enqueued IP Process as a message if one is enqueued there; otherwise the IP's Processor Carrier is itself enqueued as a server. The IP is itself not blocked and is free with one exception to execute subsequent orders issued by the AP; the exception is another DISPATCH order which cannot be executed because the IP has only one associated Processor Carrier. Subsequently, upon forwarding an IP Process Carrier to the IP's Dispatching Port, an "assisting" GDP will determine that an IP Processor Carrier is enqueued there as a server, will bind the Process Carrier to the IP Processor Carrier, and will then send that IP an IPC (interprocessor communication) message to notify the IP of the received IP process.
- The notified IP will send the AP an interrupt to indicate completion of the DISPATCH order. The AP must then read the "Selected Process Index" field, also through the Control Window, to determine which IP process has been dispatched.

7.1.3. A Higher-Level View of I/O in the i432 System

Our purpose in introducing the foregoing low-level view of the interaction between the Computational Subsystem and the I/O Subsystem is to establish the basis for a more abstract model of I/O operations in which the Peripheral Subsystem Interface plays a key role but whose details can now be suppressed without risk of a "credibility gap." A single example, discussed in some depth seems sufficient for our purpose. We consider the case where an Ada task executing as an i432 process is programmed to issue a series of print requests (to print single lines of data on a line printer). Each such print request is forwarded across the Peripheral Subsystem Interface (PSI) to a process that is executing on a processor of the Peripheral Subsystem. The scenario is introduced with the aid of Figure 7-4 and detailed further with the aid of Figure 7-5. (In what follows, we use the terms *task* and *process*, respectively, to distinguish between program units viewed as *Ada tasks* executing in the i432 object space from program units viewed as *non-Ada processes* executing in the Peripheral Subsystem address space.)

We assume that task A issues a stream of print requests at a rate which is roughly independent of the printer device's ability to print lines under control of process C. For this reason, we imagine that for each print request to be formed, task A draws a new message object from a pool of such objects found in the Print Reply Port. (It is likely that this pool is intialized with some predetermined number of message objects, but we ignore such detail here.) After receiving a message object by executing an i432 RECEIVE instruction from the Print Reply Port, task A then writes into the message object a new request and SENDs it to some other port that the IP process, controlled by the AP, knows about. In Figure 7-4, this port is called the Print Request Port. The AP process executing within the Peripheral Subsystem Interface issues an IP RECEIVE order to obtain access to the message object and then transfers the message information into the AP address space to form a new version of the message object understandable to process C. Multitasking software on the AP side is assumed to use "mailbox" operations similar to the i432 port operations for intertask communication. Hence, the AP mechanisms of the PSI are assumed to forward print requests to process C by transmitting messages to the Print Order Mailbox.

Each time the printer device completes a print request, status information is returned to process C, which in turn transmits a reply message to the PSI (via another mailbox) to indicate the outcome of a print request. The PSI (AP process cooperating with the IP) then issues an IP SEND order to return the original i432 print message object to the pool maintained in the Print Reply Port. The returned message object is presumed to contain a version of the status information forwarded by process C that can be interpreted by task A.

Notice that the pool of message objects in the Print Reply Port will be maintained within some acceptable bounds so long as the rate of "production" of print requests and the rate of their "consumption" by the printer device is reasonably balanced. (Examples in Chapter 5 have already discussed ways that the number of messages in such a pool can be explicitly increased or decreased whenever appropriate.)

Notice also that Figure 7-4 also hides the details of interpreting the message sent by task A (a program abstraction of a print command) and the details of transmitting that interpretation to process C in a form the latter can "understand". The reverse interpretation, namely, converting process C's response into a form that can be understood by task A, is also hidden. All these hidden details are assumed to be subsumed as the responsibility of the PSI.

For this abstraction, we place no limit on the richness of this Peripheral Subsystem. For example, its I/O control software may be decomposed into modules such that control over individual devices is distributed to *driver processes*, like process C, which have access to the attributes of the specific devices they drive. Also, this Subsystem may be assumed to execute under supervision of a multitasking operating system.

Under such a structure, the process that distributes work to a device driver, like process C, is the one that controls the IP. This process is not shown explicitly in Figure 7-4. (It must execute on the AP.) In most cases, the processor that executes process C will also be the AP. However, we do not rule out cases

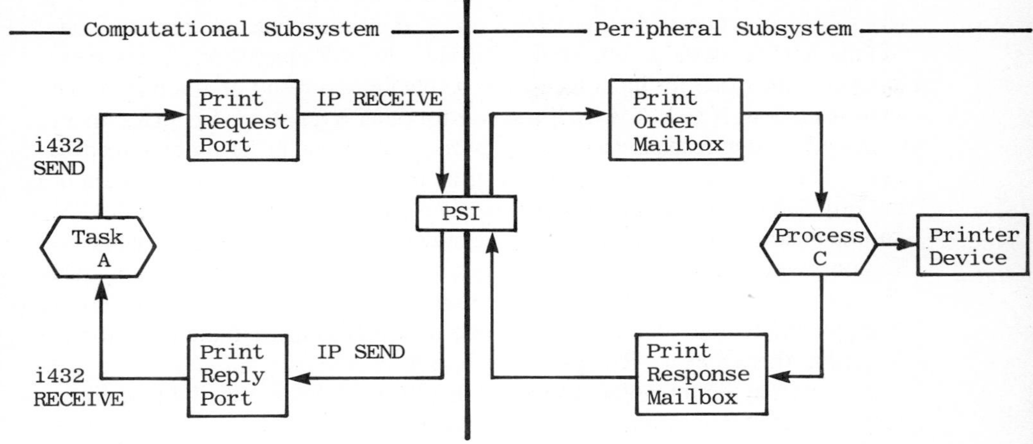

Figure 7-4 Model of the role played by the Peripheral Subsystem Interface, PSI. A is a user's Ada task running on a GDP formulating and sending line printer requests to a process C, which is a printer device manager program running on a processor of a Peripheral Subsystem, e.g., the AP. The language and representational gap between task A and process C is bridged by the PSI.)

where a Peripheral Subsystem has several processors jointly sharing local memory and intercommunicating on the Subsystem bus.

At the other extreme, a much more simple Peripheral Subsystem may have only one processor, the AP, with no provision for multitasking. In such a case, the AP process that controls the IP would also drive every I/O device within that Peripheral Subsystem.

The important observation to be made here is that regardless of the structure used to implement a Peripheral Subsystem, the interface it presents to i432 tasks that need to drive it can be precisely the same. Thus, task A can follow a simple (and constant) protocol for executing I/O operations. To print a line, record, or file, it sends the appropriate message to the appropriate port (Print Request Port) and may then expect a reply, telling of the outcome of the print request, at some other port (Print Reply Port). It is totally unnecessary, however, that the i432 task wait for such a reply. In the model suggested by Figure 7-4, task A is actually free to ignore status information in the reply messages. Even if such status information is not ignored, its recognition can be ''offset'' from the I/O request that induces this status information by some pre-determined number of I/O requests. [Readers familiar with conventional *buffered I/O* schemes will recognize that the use of a pool of *m* message objects simulates an I/O buffer whose size is a multiple *m* of I/O blocks, where each block holds command, data, and status for one I/O operation.]

The model in Figure 7-4 is also applicable to the case where task A issues a series of input requests. In this case, a series of message objects, this time containing input requests, is sent to the PSI via a Read Request Port. These messages contain space for input records to be obtain as a result of completing the input operation. If task A is itself a server for other requesting i432 tasks, then, to provide faster response to its requestors, task A might be programmed to issue a series of input requests as part of its initialization and in anticipation of any originating input requests that it receives as a server. In any case, the PSI communicates with process C, now regarded as an input device controller. Response messages forwarded by process C to the PSI now contain data obtained from the input device and also status information. The PSI then deposits these packets into i432 message objects and SENDs them to the Input Reply Port from where they are RECEIVEd by task A.

We see from the foregoing discussion that the model in Figure 7-4 is applicable for either output or input. This asynchronous model can be used as the basis for an even higher-level interface, in particular, for the benefit of programmers who wish to view I/O requests as purely synchronous actions. Indeed, iMAX provides a synchronous I/O interface superposed over the asynchronous interfaces illustrated in Figure 7-4. This synchronous interface is described in Section 7.3.

As promised, Figure 7-5 suggests some of the details for a possible structure of the Peripheral Subsystem Interface. All AP subprograms that directly control the IP or that execute Read or Write transfers through IP windows are collected in a single module called the *IP Controller*. A set of individual AP processes that communicate with specific device driver processes also form part of the PSI. (These AP processes know how to issue calls on the routines within the IP Controller module and hence know about the IP architecture. However, they are unaware of I/O device details. The device driver processes, on the other hand, know a great deal about the I/O devices they drive but need know nothing about the IP.)

Below, we give a very brief account of the logic of the two server processes in the PSI that support Printer Process C.

- The Printer Request Process executes an endless loop receiving messages from the Print Request Port. Since each of these messages exists in i432 object space, the data part of the object that represents each message must be associated with a section of the AP's memory address space to become accessible to the AP. Getting each message and making it accessible is achieved by issuing first an IP RECEIVE order and then an Open Window order (officially called ALTER MAP AND SELECT DATA SEGMENT), or alternatively by using simpler and faster OPEN MESSAGE / CLOSE MESSAGE sequences.

  Once the message has been placed in the window, the Printer Request Process can properly interpret the message and forward it—in this case to the

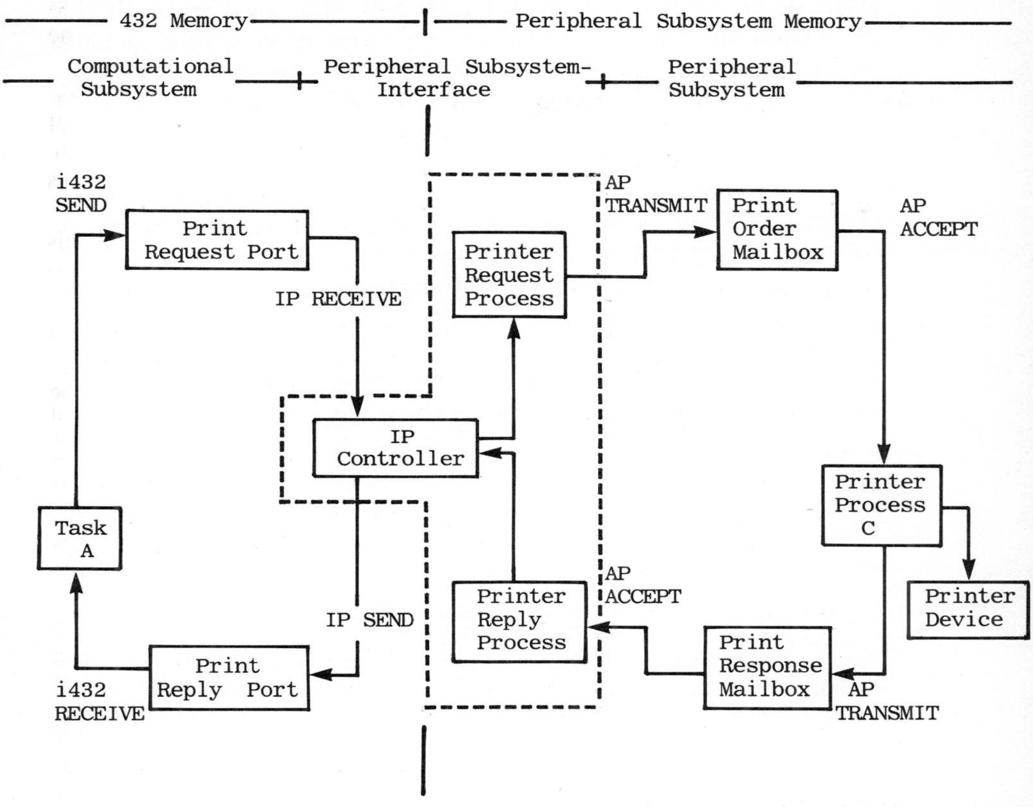

Figure 7-5 Exposing some details of the Peripheral Subsystem Interface for the Print Example of Figure 7-4

Printer Process (Process C). This forwarding may also be done by message-based communication similar to that which goes on in the 432 Subsystem, but internal to the Peripheral Subsystem.

To distinguish between the two message systems, a distinct notation is used for describing message flow in the Peripheral Subsystem. Here, messages are said to be *TRANSMITted* and *ACCEPTed* through *mailboxes*, rather than SENDed and RECEIVEd through ports.

- The Printer Reply Process operates as a server in a similar endless loop, accepting return messages, sent by the Printer Process, via the Print Response Mailbox, and forwarding a corresponding reply message to task A. The original print request message can also serve as an adequate reply message; that is, no new information other than returned status codes need be created for return to Task A. Hence, forwarding is done simply by issuing a SEND order to the IP, specifying the destination port in the i432 object space. (If only status information needs to be sent to the reply port, the reply code portion of the message object must be updated. This can be done in one of several ways: For example, an INDIVISIBLY INSERT SHORT ORDINAL order can be executed to write into the message object followed by execution of a SEND order. Alternatively, and more simply, a CLOSE MESSAGE order can be executed, accomplishing the same effect. Recall that this order writes specified status information into a specified message object and then performs the equivalent of a CONDITIONAL SEND to the proper reply port.)

As indicated in Figure 7-5, task A will RECEIVE the forwarded reply message via the Print Reply Port; the message itself is identical with the original print request message except for the inclusion of returned status informaton. Task A may then "refill" the reply object with a new value and reSEND it as a new print request, via the Print Request Port.

The Printer Driver Process (Process C) also executes in an endless loop. In this loop, it accepts a message from the Print Order Mailbox, issues the corresponding print command to the Printer Device, and, after fielding the received interrupt signal indicating completion (or other) outcome, transmits a reply message, via the Print Response Mailbox to the Printer Reply Process.

[In the example of Figure 7-5 we showed as a possibility two AP processes within the PSI, both of which are in communication with Printer Driver Process C. In an actual implementation, the two PSI server processes would probably be combined into a single PSI process. In addition, the PSI would include (at least) one such server process for each I/O device driver process in the Peripheral Subsystem. Such specific details are to be found in the iMAX 432 Reference Manual cited in Appendix B.]

We have now completed our scenario illustrating the intended role and possible software structure of the Peripheral Subsystem Interface. We propose now to turn our attention away from this part of the system architecture and focus for the remainder of the chapter on the i432 user's higher level view of input-output processing. Space in this book does not permit including more of the interesting details of the IP architecture and its AP-side support software, but these are well presented in the IP-ARM.

The next section explains the design strategy and intended use of the iMAX I/O interface packages made available for users. Later sections illustrate possible uses of these packages, including application to our portfolio management system.

7.2. The iMAX I/O Interface

Our introductory view of the I/O system reveals how the (central) 432 Subsystem is "screened" logically and physically by the Peripheral Subsystem Interface from the detailed structure and operation of the device drivers. This permits I/O functionality to be seen on the 432 side of the Interface, while hiding I/O implementation on the other side. The iMAX I/O Interface exploits this separation further. Its use permits a programmer to "see" particular I/O devices, actual or simulated, from any of several different perspectives—from most generic in nature, and hence least device-dependent, to fully specific.

A direct benefit of this approach is that it becomes especially easy to implement connections to purely logical I/O devices; that is, what is syntactically expressed as an I/O request can be executed entirely as an internal transfer of data between co-resident i432 objects. When two objects are "connected" in this way, one serves as a source and the other as a sink. Such a connection forms what is referred to in other operating systems as a "pipe". (Two-way channels can be established between pairs of i432 objects using a pair of I/O connections.) Even though the implementation of logical I/O devices represents an important special-case application of the iMAX I/O Interface described in this section, our discussions will primarily assume we are dealing with the general case, i.e., where the I/O device is a real one that resides on the AP side of the peripheral subsystem interface.

Whatever the current perspective of a given device, the user of iMAX has the choice of specifying a given I/O request either in the form of a synchronous I/O call (e.g., Read or Write) or in the form of an asynchronous action by invoking a Send or Receive procedure (in which the I/O request is supplied as a message argument). That is, the user may call an operation of the "synchronous interface" or of the "asynchronous interface"; iMAX provides a pair of such interfaces, one for each device. The iMAX implementation of a synchronous Read or Write amounts to a call on the appropriate operation of the asynchronous interface (e.g., Send or Receive.)

A synchronous interface provided by iMAX is implemented so as to provide input/output buffering; this assures that, typically, control will return from a call on Read or Write to an actual I/O device without having to wait while the generated I/O request message makes a round trip through the Peripheral Subsystem Interface and back again. The model provided in Figure 7-4, applied to either input or output, is useful for seeing why this is so. The necessary buffering can be provided merely by ensuring a that a sufficient pool of (input or output) message objects is enqueued at the Reply Port accessible to the task executing the Read or Write call.

A programmer may choose to "bypass" the provided synchronous interface and access the Peripheral Subsystem Interface directly by issuing calls on the provided asynchronous interface. In this case the programmer is obligated by protocol to deal with lower-level matters, such as managing buffers, checking for replies, and handling error messages.

7.2.1. The I/O Device Abstraction Hierarchy

The basis for the multiple-view objective is the concept and use of a set of *I/O device abstractions*, which specify public I/O operations having varying degrees of device dependence. The iMAX I/O Interface provides a set of these abstractions, a paradigm by which the Ada programmer may create new device abstractions, and a rationale and means for selecting among them. Moreover, by using 432-Ada, selection of an operative device abstraction may be accomplished dynamically.

I/O device abstractions are thought of as forming a hierarchy. Proceeding toward the root of the hierarchy takes one to a more generic, and hence to a more device-independent view. The most generic view provides a small set of I/O operations common to all devices. Each successive (descendant) view includes more I/O operations, but these are common to successively smaller subclasses of devices. (Clearly, program units that can use a more generic view of a device, in expressing demands on it, will more easily survive changes in the actual device used.)

A useful strategy to be followed is this: when I/O operations are to be performed that are more device dependent, steps of the program are first executed to change the current level of abstraction, that is, shift the view, to one that is less generic. After such operations are completed, execute steps to shift back to the earlier, more generic, view of the device.

Adhering to such a strategy can isolate (and hence minimize) the number of program units that are subject to revision; only the isolated program units would require change when one I/O device is replaced by another of differing specific characteristics. Indeed, one can imagine many applications for which use of certain generic I/O device abstractions is sufficient, allowing (entire) programs, for all practical purposes, to be device independent.

Consider, for example, these three levels of I/O device abstraction. At the root level, we have only operations that are independent of any specific I/O device or device type. In this category are examples like, querying the identification and characteristics of the device, resetting it, or, if applicable, closing it.

Abstractions at the next level in the hierarchy, are those that remain independent of particular devices but dependent on particular device types. At this level, for example, we have abstractions for a class of printers, a class of input devices, a class of storage devices, or a class of terminals. Each of these classes may be understood in the general sense as *sink*s, *source*s, *store*s, or some combination of these. For example, any printer device is first to be viewed as a sink for a data stream, and hence has a *write* operation in addition to the operations "inherited" from the more generic view of that device. (A particular printer may indeed have other output operations, like skipping two lines, but such operations may not be sufficiently common to all printers to be included in this view (in this level of abstraction).) In a like manner, we may assume that the generic class of all input devices, such as card and paper tape readers and read-only discs, have a generic *read* operation in addition to operations like query and reset.

Abstractions at the next level would include operations that are specific, not just to a particular device class, but also to a particular device itself. For example, a particular terminal device, viewed in more generic terms as a *terminal sink*, may include an operation to display a second window, another to move the cursor from one window to the other, and so forth.

Adhering to the hierarchical view of device abstractions, we see that an abstraction at level *k* includes all the operations in the abstraction of its immediate parent node, at level *k*-1 in the hierarchy. Apart from its conceptual elegance, the idea of a device abstraction tree offers certain practical implementation benefits, especially when the underlying architecture is that of the i432.

For example, thinking in terms of Ada packages, the set of applicable operations corresponding to a device abstraction at level *k* may be implemented as a domain refinement of a less generic abstraction (descendant node in the abstraction tree) at a level greater than *k*. Shifting view from one device abstraction level to another, along a path in the hierarchy, is a matter of changing refinements. As we will see in the next section, shifting a view along such a path involves a call on Transform_interface, a special function made available in every refinement of a synchronous device interface.

7.2.2. Synchronous and Asynchronous Interfaces

As mentioned earlier, the iMAX I/O Interface "architecture" is intended to provide users the facilities for issuing either synchronous or asynchronous I/O requests. These facilities are called *I/O device interfaces*. The initial version of iMAX 432 provides device interfaces having generic I/O operations (Generic_Source, Generic_Sink, and Generic_Store) and simple terminal I/O operations. The iMAX packages that specify these I/O device interfaces are paradigms for all such interfaces. Studying them helps us understand not only how these interfaces are intended to be used, but also how interfaces for other device abstractions would be structured and used.

A synchronous interface for a device abstraction is represented as a *package refinement access type*, hereafter mildly abbreviated as "pkg-ref access type". The particular device viewed with that abstraction is represented as a refinement instance of that pkg-ref access type. As suggested at the end of Chapter 6, there may be any number of package instances for a particular pkg-ref access type. Package instances may be declared, assigned as values to variables of that type, and passed in procedure calls as actual parameters.

The pkg-ref access type for a device abstraction provides the specifications for all operations germane to its level of abstraction and to the levels of all parent abstractions. There is no practical need for a pkg-ref access type representing the root node itself, which would contain the three common functions, Interface_description, Reset, and Close and two common utility functions, Transform_interface and Get_asynchronous_interface. Instead, these operations are absorbed into the three immediate offspring abstractions, as shown in Figure 7-6.

Operations of the Package Refinement Access Types for Generic Abstractions

Source	Sink	Store	
Interface_description	Interface_description	Interface_description	
Close	Close	Close	
Reset	Reset	Reset	Basi
			I/O
Transform_interface	Transform_interface	Transform_interface	Inte
Get_asynchronous_ interface	Get_asynchronous_ interface	Get_asynchronous_ interface	fac
Read	Write	Read	
	Flush	Write	
		Flush	

Figure 7-6 I/O Operations for the three generic abstractions: Source, Sink, and Store

The operations listed for each generic abstraction would also appear at the head of the list of operations in a descendant abstraction. For example, the pkg-ref access type, Terminal_Source contains the specifications, in the order shown, for all the operations of Source, followed by the two additional operations: Get_terminal_characteristics and Set_terminal_characteristics. These additional operations may be used, for example to examine and then reset the baud rate of the terminal to one of the allowed rates.

The two utility operations listed in Figure 7-6, Transform_interface and Get_asynchronous_interface, are of especial interest for this discussion.

- Transform_interface is called to obtain a new view of the I/O interface, either an expanded view (more device dependent), or a restricted view (more generic). If the new view is valid for that interface, the function returns a different refinement of that interface (actually a typed domain refinement). Use of Transform_interface is illustrated in Section 7.3.
- Get_asynchronous_interface returns a reference to the *connection record* that is implicitly created when the synchronous interface is itself created and initialized. The connection record is a data type declared in the asynchronous interface package which is itself a set of definitions and operations used by all synchronous interface packages. A connection record defines the I/O channel used for sending and receiving I/O request and reply messages.

  In particular, to use any of the Send or Receive (or Cond_send or Cond_receive) operations of the asynchronous interface, one must specify the proper connection record. By supplying Get_asynchronous_interface as a public operation, the user (as well as implementer) of the synchronous interface package is able to issue calls directly on the operations of asynchronous interface package.

The Asynchronous_IO_Interface package may be used for transmitting I/O operations at any level of device abstraction. (Hence, only one such package is needed for use with all device abstractions.) We amplify our remarks on the use of Asynchronous_IO_Interface in Section 7.4, where we take a closer look at the structure and content of a *connection record*.

7.3. Structure, Acquisition, and Use of Synchronous I/O Device Interfaces

We give a more detailed view of iMAX synchronous I/O interfaces in this subsection. To streamline our discussions, we provide in Appendix J listings of some relevant iMAX packages for ready reference.

A key data structure belonging to any device interface is the *query record*, whose representation, query_record_rep, is defined in the package, IO_Definitions, listed at the beginning of Appendix J. This record type has several fields used to identify the device and the Peripheral Subsystem to which the device is currently attached. The record also contains an array of abstraction descriptions, which is a list of valid views that can be supported by this device interface—and to (from) which the interface may be transformed. (It is this array that is consulted by the Transform_interface function.)

Scanning the package Synchronous_IO_Interfaces is instructive. This package hosts three package refinement (pkg-ref) access type declarations named Source, Sink and Store. They are preceded by declarations for the exceptions that may be raised during activations of operations in instances of the three pkg-ref access types. Also, three subtypes are declared that define the buffer areas used in Read and Write operations of the pkg-ref access types. Explanations provided in the listing for the exceptions and the buffer area subtypes require no further amplification here.

Following the exception and subtype declarations, there is a set of comments representing a paradigm of the basic, but non-existent root node device abstraction. This paradigm is referred to as "package access Basic_IO_Interface". A copy of it is inserted into each of the succeeding pkg-ref access types: Source, Sink, and Store. The paradigm provides specifications for the five operations: Interface_description, Close, Reset, Transform_interface, and Get_asynchronous_interface. [The function Interface_description returns a reference to the instance of query_record_rep for the particular device interface.]

In the next two subsections we briefly overview the acquisition and then illustrate the use of synchronous device interfaces.

7.3.1. Acquisition of a Synchronous Device Interface

Before the I/O operations of a synchronous interface can be called, a user process must acquire an Access Descriptor for the desired interface (refinement). To do this, the user process must appeal to a type manager that controls access to synchronous device interfaces. This manager package would have direct access to the package that defines the particular synchronous I/O device interfaces. A call on the operation of that type manager package returns a reference to the wanted synchronous device interface refinement. For some kinds of device interfaces, such as for disk files, activation of the Get_interface operation can in the process lead to a (dynamic) instantiation of a specific device interface package. In any case, what is returned is a refinement of a package, pre-existing or newly created.

For example, the i432 system provides both a Terminal_Manager and a File_Manager package. A Terminal_Manager might pre-create instances of Source and/or Sink device interface packages for each attached terminal. An i432 user process needing access to one of these terminals would acquire an AD for a refinement to the needed interface by calling the Terminal_Manager.Get_terminal_interface operation; this operation returns an AD for a refinement of a pre-existing interface package. It is likely, however, that synchronous interface packages for files would be created dynamically, on demand. Thus, an i432 process that needs to perform I/O operations on a particular file would first call the File_Manager.Get_file_interface operation) whose implementation could involve instantiation of the particular file interface package needed (e.g., Source or Sink). The net effect of creating this file interface and returning a refinement for it would be to *open* the specified file for operations of a particular kind. More concretely, the statement sequence:

```
with File_Manager, ... ;
use  File_Manager, ... ;

File_Sink_Instance: File_Sink;      -- Where File_Sink is the
                                    -- sink interface pkg_ref access type
                                    -- for files.

File_Sink_Instance   :=  Get_file_interface(my_file);
```

would open my_file for writing by first creating a synchronous interface (support) package for file sinks and then returning an AD for the appropriate refinement of it; the AD is then assigned to File_Sink_Instance. Subsequently, a call can be made to write into my_file, e.g.,

```
File_Sink_Instance.Write(....);
```

and eventually to close out the file, e.g.,

```
File_Sink_Instance.Close;
```

Note that asynchronous as well as synchronous operations on the opened file can now be invoked. To perform the former, it is first necessary to acquire a reference to the connection created for File_sink. Thus, the statement

```
connection_of_my_file
                := File_Sink_Instance.Get_asynchronous_interface;
```

assigns to connection_of_my_file the reference to be supplied in calls on the Send and Receive operations of the Asynchronous_IO_Interface package. Figure 7-7 illustrates a possible set of relationships that can arise between various user processes, the File_Manager, the interfaces packages, the Peripheral Subsystem Interface, and the AP process (File Server) used to drive an actual disk.

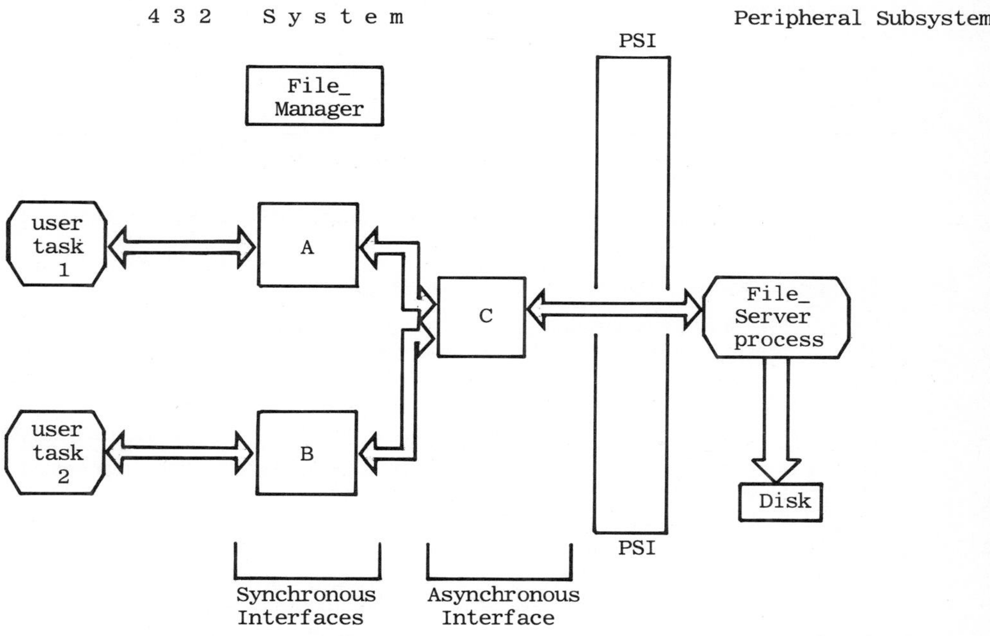

Figure 7-7 Major components involved in setting up and using synchronous file interfaces. User tasks 1 and 2 make calls on the File_Manager package to *open* files on the disk. Opening each file results in creation of a synchronous file interface (interface A for task 1 and interface B for task 2). Each synchronous interface has access to the common asynchronous interface. Read or write calls through A or B are implemented with Send and Receive calls to C. Not shown are the connections and the Request and Reply ports referred to by the connections.

7.3.2. Two Example Uses of Synchronous Device Interfaces

EXAMPLE 1. Display_one_liner is a rudimentary procedure that accepts a reference to a refinement instance of type Terminal_Sink as an argument for use in displaying character strings from a buffer. A skeleton of the subprogram for this procedure is shown in Figure 7-8.

```
use Synchronous_IO_Interfaces;
    . . .

procedure Display_one_liner(
      output_device: in Terminal_Sink;          -- Type Terminal_Sink
                                                -- is defined in Appendix J
    . . .                          )
is
begin
  . . .
  output_device.Write(my_write_buffer, 0, 59); -- Display contents of
                                                -- buffer from offset zero.
                                                -- Width of line is 59 char
  . . .
end Display_one_liner;
```

Figure 7-8 Illustration of generic terminal Write operation.

[A *package refinement access type*, such as Terminal_Sink, is declared using the 432-Ada **package access** type extension. For example,

```
type Terminal_Sink is access package
  --
  -- The set of subprogram specifications representing the
  -- public operations for this abstraction go here.
  --
end Terminal_Sink;
```

In the most general sense, such a declaration can be regarded as a "template" that defines a named refinement (or abstraction) of a device interface; the latter is represented by a package instance that specifies and implements the full set of operations for a specific device type. Similar "package access" declarations are to be found in the specification of the Synchronous_IO_Interfaces found in Appendix J.]

To call Display_one_liner, one must specify, as the argument, an instance of the package refinement access type Terminal_Sink. Default refinement instances of the types Terminal_Source and Terminal_Sink are already provided by iMAX. They are accessible under the names Terminals(i).Source and Terminals(i).Sink. Here *i* is a value of type "interface_range" currently defined as:

```
type interface_range is short_ordinal range 0..5;

  -- (The range values 1..5 correspond to terminals numbered 1..5,
  -- and the value 0 is reserved for future Intel use.)
```

Hence, a valid call might be:

```
Display_one_liner(Terminals(1).Sink);
```

On the other hand, and although not particularly likely in this case, a user is free to substitute a different package body as the required device interface, so long as it has the same specification as that of package refinement access type

Terminal_Sink. (This specification may be found in the iMAX package, Terminal_IO_Interfaces, but, to save space, we do not show it in Appendix J.) For example, in 432-Ada, one may supply the declarations,

```
package Brand_X_Terminal_Support  is
       ...
   pragma refinement(Terminal_Sink);     -- The "Sink view" of
                                         -- Brand_X begins here.
       ...
end Brand_X_Terminal_Support;
  --
  -- Function:
  --   The Brand_X_Terminal_Support package contains the
  --   specifications for all the operations for a terminal of
  --   Brand_X_Terminal_Type. Embedded within this package is the
  --   refinement pragma that marks the beginning of the subsequence
  --   of operations that collectively represent the Terminal_Sink
  --   abstraction.

package body Brand_X_Terminal_Support is ... end Brand_X_Terminal_Support;

Our_Terminal_Sink: constant Terminal_Sink
                         := Terminal_Sink(Brand_X_Terminal_Support);
  -- Our_Terminal_Sink is assigned an AD for the Terminal_Sink
  -- refinement of the package Brand_X_Terminal_Support.
```

In this context, a call on Display_one_liner may specify Our_Terminal_Sink as the operative abstraction of the Brand_X interface; that is:

```
Display_one_liner(Our_Terminal_Sink);
```

The above illustrates how specific refinements of device interfaces may be passed to procedures. We next show how different views of a given device abstraction may be selected dynamically.

EXAMPLE 2. Now consider a procedure, Fancy_display, that expects as an argument a richer device interface than was required by Display_one_liner. Fancy_display, will, among its other duties, issue requests to draw straight lines at various angles, but only when the currently attached output device has the attributes of a graphics terminal. When the attached device is character-oriented only, straight lines are merely simulated by strings of periods, asterisks, or other special characters. (This option produces jagged line approximations, except for verticals and horizontals.)

In this example straight-line approximations are displayed when invoking the Write operation of the device interface (using the ''characters'' view of the device). ''Actual'' straight lines are drawn only when invoking the Draw_line operation of the device interface (using the ''lines'' view of the same interface).

Figure 7-9 shows a skeleton form of Fancy_display. In this example, the local variables chars_output and graphic_output are assigned different abstractions (refinements) of the supplied device interface object through application of Transform_interface. The variable graphics_output gets the abstraction needed for drawing lines and is used only after first checking that the attached device currently has this functionality. This fact is determined by a call on the Interface_description operation of the given interface which returns the query record containing an array of the abstraction names supported by that interface. The reader should have little trouble following the rest of the code in Figure 7-9.

7.4. Structure and Use of the Asynchronous Device Interface

As mentioned at the end of Section 7.2, iMAX provides a standard asynchronous device interface which may be accessed by the user when it is more appropriate to issue I/O requests by sending messages than to issue procedure calls. This interface takes the form of the iMAX package, Asynchronous_IO_Interface, whose specification is given in Appendix J.

The four data-transmission operations of this package, Send, Cond_send, Receive, and Cond_receive, can only be used by specifying an access to a *connection_record*, which is a high-level communication data structure that characterizes the asynchronous I/O channel between the program and the device. A connection_record, whose formal definition is given as follows, includes a request_port, a reply_port and a copy of the device description used in the companion synchronous device interface.

```
type  connection_record  is
  record
    request_port:        port;           -- Port for I/O request messages
    name:                print_name;     -- Identifying name.
    device_description:  query_record;   -- Device-specific information.
    reply_port:          port;           -- Port which may be used as
                                         -- a message reply port.
  end record;
```

Access to such a record is easily, and safely gained via a call on the Get_asynchronous_interface operation in the corresponding synchronous I/O interface package (for the same device).

An asynchronous I/O transaction (request or reply) takes the form of an *I/O_message_record,* whose top-level structure is, formally:

```
type IO_message_record  is
  record
    command_record:   command_record_rep;
    reply_port:       port;
    data_buffer:      buffer_array;
  end record;
```

This record mirrors the structure of a typical I/O request used in driving a hardware device. The contents of the command_record component provides:

```
procedure Fancy_display(
    output_device: Fancy_Sink)      -- Matching argument must be
                                    -- a package instance of Fancy_Sink.
is
  start, len:          integer range 0 ..
                             output_device.interface_description.buffer_length;
  chars_output:        Characters_view;
                                    -- Characters_view is an abstraction
                                    -- capable of writing only character
                                    -- strings.
    . . .
begin
    . . .
  chars_output := output_device.Transform_interface(Characters_view);
                                    -- Extract a new view of the given
                                    -- interface and assign to chars_output.
  chars_output.Write(my_write_buffer, start, len);
                                    -- Display title text line.
    . . .
  if
   -- The attached device has line_drawing capability (check if the
   -- new abstraction is included in output_device.Interface_description
   -- abstractions).
  then
    declare                         -- Block entry.
      graphic_output: Lines_view;   -- Lines_view is an abstraction of
                                    -- Fancy_Sink capable of drawing lines.
    begin
      graphic_output := output_device.Transform_interface(Lines_view);
                                    -- Extract a new view of the given inter-
                                    -- face and assign to graphics_output.
      graphic_output.Draw_line(initial_x, initial_y,
                               final_x,   final_y   );
                                    -- Issue I/O request to draw specified
                                    -- line.
        . . .
    end;
    . . .
  else
    -- Use chars_output abstraction for drawing an approximation for
    -- straight line beginning with (initial_x, initial_y) and
    -- terminating with (final_x, final_y).
  end if;
    . . .
  chars_output.Write(my_write_buffer, start, len);
                                    -- Display another text line.
    . . .
end  Fancy_display;
```

Figure 7-9 Illustrating dynamic selection of different abstractions of a device interface object supplied as an argument to a procedure.

- the order code for read, write, etc.
- an integer message_id, useful for identifying unsuccessful requests so that, upon receipt of error replies, such requests may be noted and perhaps retried
- a reply_code identifying the kind of an error encountered, if any

- an array of records each providing control information for a buffer. This information includes the buffer's current "cursor" index, the buffer's length, etc.

The need for the reply_port requires no motivation here. The data_buffer is an array of one or more buffer references to which the command is to be applied. If a Read command is sent, the buffer(s) are filled according to the input transfer rules for the particular device source. If a Write command is sent, the buffer(s) are emptied, according to the output transfer rules of for the particular device sink. The listing in Appendix J provides the formal description for the data_buffer field and the various definitions on which it is based.

To Send or Receive an I/O request, one merely designates as arguments a connection and an IO_message. The specifications for these two operations of the asynchronous interface are simply:

```
procedure Send(
    c:          connection;
    msg:        IO_message);

procedure Receive(
    c:          connection;
    msg:   out  IO_message);
```

As might be suspected from our discussions in Chapter 5, the Cond_send and Cond_receive operations also require the designation of a boolean variable (success) as an output argument.

It is conceivable that a user would wish to execute I/O transactions using Surrogate Sends and Receives—to avoid anticipated blocking. These less likely operations are not provided in the Asynchronous_IO_Interface. However, once a connection has been established for a device, the programmer is free to use its ports directly, such as by referring to them in Surrogate (or ordinary) Send and Surrogate (or ordinary) Receive operations made available in the iMAX Typed_Ports package. [Readers may wish to refresh their memories by reviewing Section 5.5.]

We close a loop opened in Section 7.1 by reviewing two matters of detail:

a. where messages go to that are sent through the asynchronous interface, and

b. where messages come from that are returned through the asynchronous interface.

Recall that messages are sent to (received from) the IP process whose processor is controlled by the Attached Processor. (That IP processor is named in the device_description component of the connection_record specified in the send or receive operation.)

One may usefully review Figure 7-5 at this point. A server process executing in the AP will be waiting to receive a sent I/O request as a result of having issued a (blocking) RECEIVE order to its slave IP. The RECEIVE order must specify the request_port component named in the interface's connection_record so the IP can "know" where to go to receive the user's I/O request. In due course, the IP process will get an I/O request message from that request_port. A reply message, formulated by an AP process, will be sent by the AP via a SEND order to its IP. In turn, the IP will enqueue this message (as a request) at the reply_port named in the IO_message_record of the I/O request.

One may now ask the following question: When a new device is added to a Peripheral Subsystem or, correspondingly, when a new synchronous interface object is added to the Computational Subsystem, how does this information reach the other subsystem, respectively, that needs to know about these changes? Here is a brief two-part answer:

- Whenever a new physical device is attached to a Peripheral Subsystem, access to that device must come under control of its appropriate type manager. This may require adding a new type manager or informing an existing type manager of additional resources. In either case, it is the governing type manager that is responsible for handing out synchronous interfaces that access the new device. Correspondingly, whenever a new synchronous interface refinement is created, the appropriate system table in the AP referred to in the underlying interface object is also updated so that AP can allocate a new pair of server processes for the new interface refinement instance (or achieve an equivalent effect by communicating appropriate requests directly to the proper device drivers).
- Note that the "business" described in the preceding paragraph goes under the more general heading of *device allocation and deallocation*.

  A device abstraction is just another i432 refinement, and so, when it is created, it becomes available for use by any user process that acquires an Access Descriptor for it. In Section 7.3 we have already noted that control over the distribution of Access Descriptors for device abstractions is the responsibility of the type manager for such objects. An abstraction can safely be removed from the system, that is, deallocated, when there are no longer any Access Descriptors that refer to it. Deallocation may, therefore, be achieved explicitly by the operating system, or implicitly by the garbage collector.

  We do not rule out the possibility that two or more user processes may have concurrent access to the same device interface refinement instance. In that event, however, preventing conflicting use of the corresponding physical device is the responsibility of the applications subsystem designer.

  The problem is no different than preventing conflict over concurrent use of a database. The usual way to solve this problem is to interpose a single Ada server task that acts as an arbiter between the several users and the device abstraction. A device abstraction that is to be shared would probably have an

Open operation defined on it, as well as a Close operation. The arbiter task would then respond to I/O requests by first checking to see whether or not the device (for example, a file, or a line printer), has been Opened to the caller.

The allocation and deallocation of physical devices is dealt with in a similar way within a Peripheral Subsystem. An actual device is accessible only by a device driver process, which is in turn accessible to other AP processes. A physical device becomes accessible to a 432 process, therefore, only after the corresponding driver process has been created and after the specifics of that driver are recorded in the central system table addressable by the AP. The physical device description information that must be recorded in a newly created device abstraction, must be acquired through a secondary transaction with an AP process. (We leave these details to the imagination of the reader.)

7.5. I/O System Assessment

Our primary objective for this section is to put the I/O system, examined thus far, into a broader perspective. We will do this in two ways: first, we consider two high-level questions not yet raised, and second, we will attempt a brief comparison between the structure of the i432 I/O system with today's traditional I/O systems.

We have skirted at least two high-level issues. The first is the matter of deciding how much of the technical material presented on i432 I/O structures and mechanisms should be known to the "ordinary" user. The best answer we can give here is: none at all—provided we may assume that such a user has no need for directly specifying asynchronous I/O operations.

Standard Ada defines the library packages Input_Output and Text_IO. The operations of these packages necessarily present procedural and hence synchronous interfaces. These operations form a rich set on which programmers may base still higher-level (synchronous interfaces). Other language processors would also be expected to be implemented in Ada. One may, therefore, safely assume that most, if not all, users will always rely on some compiler to select and use the appropriate device interfaces made available by iMAX or by other system programmers.

We also assume that readers of this chapter are the exceptions. They either have an intellectual or a practical need to know about the I/O structures and mechanisms discussed thus far.

The other matter skirted thus far is how to decide when synchronous device interfaces are to be preferred over asynchronous interfaces. [How, for example, does the Ada compiler decide which type of interface to use in compiling the subprogram bodies for Read, Write, Get, and Put operations of the library packages, Input_Output and Text_IO?] We can give a partial answer to this question here. The choice, whether for the applications or systems programmer, including compiler writer, will inevitably hinge on anticipated efficiency.

Asynchronous interfaces may well be more efficient for many types of physical devices. However, for "simulated physical devices" like files or pipes (channels between programs), which involve relatively more software than hardware, use of synchronous device interfaces may well be more efficient. A complicating factor is that various influential parameters, such as system loading, new device designs and the like, may, in fact, change over time and alter the balance. Since iMAX provides both types of interfaces for every device, the subsystem designer can be assured of the flexibility needed over the long run.

The i432 I/O system structure mirrors many of the objectives and features provided in other conventional and contemporary systems. An especially important question to ask, therefore, is: In what key way (or ways) does it contrast with, or perhaps surpass, those systems? We provide one response here.

The i432 I/O systems takes full advantage of the underlying object- (and refinement-) based architecture. Device interface objects and their refinements are separate protection domains. That is, each interface object (or refinement) is necessarily created by a call on an appropriate type manager, and hence, can have access to it restricted in a manner agreed to by the object manager. Also, each interface object owns just those local data objects needed to carry out its publicly accessible operations. Because each device interface (or abstraction of it) serves as a separate protected "island", any module that has access rights for an object (or refinement) is free to call on it directly in request of service. No "middleman" module is needed to serve as a reliable switching agent or broker.

In (non-capability-based) conventional systems, the "grain size" of a protected domain is necessarily quite coarse. In most systems, the total address space of a process may be decomposed into only a limited number of protected sub-address spaces, often one. Even in the Multics system, the number of protected addresses spaces within a process is limited to the (relatively small) number of distinguished protection "rings". As a result, there is heavy reliance on "supervisor mode" and on an address space that is accessible only while the processor executes in this mode. Resulting I/O system structures have, therefore, led to a path-critical step of indirection between the maker of an I/O request (i.e., the caller) and the particular device interface object desired as a target.

In these systems, interface objects are usually called DIM's, for device interface modules. An individual DIM is usually not protected. In Multics, for example, a user may compose a DIM. In between the caller and the particular DIM, it is, therefore, essential to place a major interpretation and switching module, access to which is protected. Let us call this the IOCP (for I/O Control Program). Unfortunately, the IOCP is necessarily large and unwieldy.

A call to an operation of a DIM is intercepted by the IOCP, which must validate it by consulting protected system tables. Such tables are also used to determine the address of the desired DIM, and perhaps to perform some translation of the user's call so that it may be "understood" by the target DIM. (The tables, often called "Attach Tables", allow the IOCP to map a user's logical device, or data-stream name, into a particular DIM.)

These verifying, switching, and possible translation functions of the IOCP must be performed on every I/O request (if security is to remain tight). Moreover, as the system grows or changes in configuration, such as when DIMs are changed or when new ones are added, the IOCP must be updated, and this must clearly be done with care. Usually, maintenance on the IOCP requires system shutdown.

The i432 I/O object based structure allows for the elimination of the IOCP and most, if not all, of its functions. The system-wide Attach Table mentioned above is, in the i432 structure, now safely distributed among the separately protected device interface objects as owned device_description records and to tables resident in the various Peripheral Subsystems.

In summary, elimination of the IOCP leads to an important efficiency (and system maintenance) advantage over conventional systems. This advantage arises as a direct consequence of the i432's object-based architecture. We trust that many readers' interests in I/O system architecture, and especially in that of the i432, has now crossed that magical threshold, leading to commitment for further study of this interesting subject, heretofore regarded by many as "too complex to master".

As promised in the opening of this chapter, we are now ready to revisit our portfolio management system to see how some of the i432 I/O facilities may be used with, and perhaps to enhance, our case study information system.

7.6. I/O Operations for the Portfolio Management Information System

In all previous discussions of the portfolio management system, we deferred detailed discussion of input/output. Such postponement is no longer necessary. In this section we first review the structure of Figure 2-5, our "basic plan" for the portfolio management system. We do this expressly to suggest how the input/output operations, implicit for that plan, may be accomplished. In particular, we consider the:

- *login* sequence — that results in a club member being put in touch, through a terminal, with the corresponding Member task.
- *session* interactions — the input/output operations in the *command loop* of Member task.
- *logout* sequence — that results in a disconnect between the member, the corresponding Member task, and the terminal just used.

We then consider one interesting enhancement of the original plan, namely the changes needed to provide on-line, up-to-the-minute, quotations on listed stocks. (Such quotations may be used by members merely for information purposes, or in performing analyses of portfolio holdings. The Club_Portfolio operations, Print_winners, Print_losers, and Print_non_movers fall in this category.)

7.6.1. Terminal Operations

For convenience in this discussion, we regard the Task_Master of the portfolio subsystem as the executive routine that responds to login requests of club-members and that also executes the logout function. Two scenarios are described, according to each of the following two assumptions:

1. Member tasks have been created and activated in advance, one for each member. (We suppose that the Task_Master has created these tasks, but this assumption is not critical.)
2. A Member task is created and activated anew by the Task_Master, each time the corresponding member logs in to a terminal. (In this case, the Member task instance is aborted when the member issues a logout command or when some time-out condition requires termination.)

For all communication between the Task_Master and the terminals, asynchronous device interfaces are used; whereas, for all communication between Member tasks and their respective terminals, it seems sufficient to use synchronous device interfaces. We assume as well that for all communication between the Task_Master and individual Member tasks, the Ada rendezvous mechanism (synchronous communication) is also used (although the reader is free to consider alternative use of explicit message-based communication). In what follows, we also assume that two device interface refinement instances have already been created for each physical terminal on which a member may log in, one a Terminal_Source instance and the other a Terminal_Sink instance. The Task_Master is assumed to hold a copy of the Access Descriptor for each of these terminal interface refinements, enabling it to read from or write to each terminal. We let AD_T_Sink(k) and AD_T_Source(k) represent references for the Terminal_Sink and Terminal_Source refinements for terminal *k*.

Our two companion scenarios begin with the Task_Master issuing an asynchronous read request to each terminal and then entering a polling loop to await the arrival of a reply or receipt of some other message of interest. Each reply message signifies the beginning of a login sequence with a member. (If the sequence is not completed satisfactorily, the Task_Master issues another asynchronous read request to that terminal so as to be receptive to another login attempt.) When a login sequence is completed successfully at terminal k, the

Task_Master performs one of the following two actions (according to whether Scenario 1 or Scenario 2 is operative):

1. (Scenario 1) Issues a Go entry call to the Member task identified in the login sequence, using AD_T_Sink(k) and AD_T_Source(k) as actual parameters, or
2. (Scenario 2) Creates and activates a new Member task and then issues it a Go entry call containing AD_T_Sink(k) and AD_T_Source(k) as actual parameters.

At this point, the club member is connected through terminal *k* to his/her Member task which can proceed with the execution of a series of commands issued from the terminal. The main structure of a Member task is presumed to be a "command loop", repeatedly requesting and then executing a command received from the terminal. To get a command, the Member task issues one or more procedural I/O read requests through T_Source(k), interspersed, as necessary, with procedural I/O write requests issued through T_Sink(k) to assist the member in formulating a correctly-phrased command.

The above command loop is exited upon receipt of a correctly formed logout request. At this point, the Member task will execute one of the following sequences (according to whether Scenario 1 or Scenario 2 holds):

1. (Scenario 1) Nullifies the two references (Access Descriptor copies), AD_T_Sink(k) and AD_T_Source(k), received from Task_Master; then issues a Ready_to_quit task entry call to the Task_Master. By accepting this call, the Task_Master knows that the Member task issuing the call has ceased making Read requests to terminal k. (The **accept** statement may be completed simply as a no op.) The Task_Master then reissues an asynchronous read request to the terminal whose identity was received as an **in** parameter from the Ready_to_quit entry call. The Task_Master now awaits another login request at this terminal.
2. (Scenario 2) Issues a Ready_to_quit task entry call to the Task_Master. Upon acceptance of this call, which would also contain the identity of the terminal on which the quitting Member task has been executing, the Task_Master does the following: aborts the corresponding Member task; writes out a sign-off message on that terminal; and reissues an asynchronous read request to that terminal to await another login request.

Without providing all the program structure details, which the reader may now easily fill in, we have offered a candidate pair of scenarios to show how the device interface objects (and refinements) described in the earlier sections of this chapter can be used in carrying out the base plan of our portfolio management system. Other ways to use the i432 I/O facilities can also be explored, and the reader is invited to do so.

7.6.2. On-Line Connection to the Stock Market

In the basic plan of Figure 2-5, we assumed the existence and accessibility of a library package, named Stock_Mkt_Info. (This package was placed in the **with** list of Club_Portfolio.) We suggested that calls from Club_Portfolio to Stock_Mkt_Info would get current prices of specified stocks, but we gave no hint as to how the stock market data in the latter package would be maintained current.

In Plan 1, we may imagine that "Airlift Specialists, Inc." delivers a floppy disk each morning marked "Market_data". This disk contains the closing market data from the previous day. (Someone is then charged to mount this disk on the proper drive before the first login of a club member on that day.) Of course, a device driver and Source device interface object must be made available for use of this disk.

With Plan 1, it is still necessary to visualize how information would be read off that disk when needed. If the information on the disk is already well structured, so that particular records may be picked out by associative lookup, the problem is made easy. In that event, we can presume that a subprogram local to Stock_Mkt_Info issues the appropriate I/O Read request, and that this subprogram is itself called, when needed, in the course of executing a public operation of Stock_Mkt_Info. That Read request may well use a synchronous device interface, because there is normally nothing else the caller wishes to do until the response is received.

On the other hand, it is more reasonable to assume that information on the disk is stored in a format that requires all of it to be transferred into i432 object space in a form that can be searched efficiently—as part of a lookup operation of Stock_Mkt_Info. Following this tack, some means is required to reinitialize Stock_Mkt_Info on a daily basis, prior to its first use that day by club members. Implied here is the need for a utility program that produces a new instance of Stock_Mkt_Info from a new Mkt_data disk. (This program would be executed by the person who mounts the new disk.)

For Plan 1, we accepted the proposition that Stock_Mkt_Info must be reinitialized daily to provide it with updated market data. For Plan 2 we now suppose that up-to-the-minute wire_service stock market data is available.

To what extent must the structure of Stock_Mkt_Info be changed to take advantage of the wire service? Availability of wire service data implies that Stock_Mkt_data no longer needs to be reinitialized each day. Nor will this package need to own any market data. The wire service itself provides a ''smart'' query service. Hence, the lookup operation within Stock_Mkt_Info needs merely to forward lookup calls in the form expected by the wire service.

In this case, Stock_Mkt_Info will again need access to a Source device interface abstraction having a Read operation. The matching device driver in the Peripheral Subsystem now interfaces to a data communications system. If we assume that the AP or some other processor on the same Peripheral Subsystem bus serves as a network host, then the driver merely sends and receives messages via that network host program.

Again, we have sketched two plans as starting points for implementation of some details implied in the basic program structure given in Figure 2-5. Our immediate aim has been to help the reader relate what has been learned from preceding sections of this chapter to the investment portfolio application selected for this book. Readers will no doubt see other ways to take advantage of i432 I/O facilities, not only for application to our case study, but, more importantly, for application to systems of particular interest to them.

8 PROCESS MANAGEMENT

8.1. Introduction

In this book we describe iMAX interfaces useful for the construction of application-specific operating systems. Each interface serves as a type manager for an important *resource* category, each resource being represented as an i432 object. For example, the Typed_Ports and Extended_Type_Manager interfaces described in preceding chapters are user-accessible facilities for managing Port Objects and Extended Type Objects, respectively. In this chapter we introduce the facility for the management of Process Objects, i.e., iMAX's Process_Manager (PM) interface, which provides users the means for creating and managing processes.

iMAX defines a Process_Manager interface which is simply a template to which each actual process manager will conform. There may be several different implementations of the Process_Manager interface, each providing a different level of process management support. Moreover, within an individual application environment, such as within an executing Ada program, most users can remain indifferent to the nature of process management support provided by the underlying system. This is because the compiler and iMAX ensure that some implementation of Process_Manager can always be referenced correctly by an executing program that needs to spawn and exercise control over other processes, such as Ada tasks.

System programmers can develop their own implementations of the Process_Manager interface, tailored to particular application environments. In this way, an implementer of a particular system can specify the scheduling policies, resource controls, resource accounting, and other services to be exercised over processes within that system. Each instance of Process_Manager also projects a particular set of process management functions onto the processes managed by that instance. Among these functions might be those which create, start, suspend, resume, reschedule, reduce or extend memory resources for, destroy, inspect or adjust the state of, and keep statistics on processes. The system designer determines which classes of programs may use which Process_Manager implementations. For example, a minimal process manager implementation (provided by iMAX) would be used to support processes within iMAX, and the processes which implement a higher level process manager. A system with its own higher level process manager would require all applications programs to use that process manager so they would not circumvent the resource scheduling and accounting policies implemented by it.

The 432-Ada *package refinement* feature illustrated in Chapter 7 provides the ability to implement a specific set of process management services which can then be viewed through a pre-declared general process management interface. Using this feature, the process manager interface is defined as a *package refinement access type*. With this definition, a variable can be declared whose type is this package refinement access type; the value assigned to it references a package instance that is a specific implementation of Process_Manager.

In the remainder of this chapter we examine the Process_Manager interface in greater detail. Section 8.2 discusses the public operations of the Process_Manager package type in the context of the data types on which these operations depend. In reading this material, one may refer to Appendix K which presents the Process_Manager package refinement access type and related type definitions. Section 8.3 sketches different possible implementations of Process_Manager. Section 8.4 summarizes what aspects of process management have and have not been examined in this chapter.

8.2. The Process_Manager Interface

The Process_Manager interface (PM) contains operations to control processes (Figure 8-1) and operations to read and set process attributes (Figure 8-2.)

The control operations can best be understood in terms of the lifecycle of a process, as suggested by the macro-state graph in Figure 8-3. Most control operations appear as arcs on the state graph. The additional arc labeled "system stop" represents automatic action of the underlying system. The term *macro-state* is used because we choose to ignore a number of the details concerning a process when it is in the "executing" state. For example, a process in the executing state may, for scheduling purposes, be either actually in the dispatching mix or kept out of the dispatching mix (by the process manager). A process is said to be in the dispatching mix from the time it is first sent to its Dispatching Port with a new non-zero value for its period count (rescheduled) until its period count has been decremented to zero or until it incurs a fault that cannot be handled. (Thus, a process remains in the mix even if it is blocked on a port or is not running while a fault which it incurred is being handled.)

Each process may have specified for it a notification port and message through which the creator of the process, for example, may be notified of "terminal" events for that process. The notification message is sent to the notification port when the process can no longer execute, e.g., when it is terminated,

Operation	Explanation
Create_process	Creates and returns a new process.
Start	Starts a newly created process or restarts a process from one of several non-executing states.
Suspend	Causes an executing process to be suspended until a later call on Resume.
Resume	Causes a *suspended* process to continue executing.
Destroy	Destroys a process.
Delay_caller	Delays the calling process by a specified amount of time.
Raise_exception	Causes a specified exception to be raised in a process.
Wait_for_process_termination	Waits for a specified process to terminate.

Figure 8-1 Operations of the Process_Manager for controlling a process.

Operation	Explanation
Read_process_info	Returns a copy of the "unchanging" attributes of a process.
Read_process_state	Returns a copy of the "changing" attributes
Read_process_micro_state	Returns a copy of the "changing" attributes of a process including its micro-state.
Set_notification_port_and_message	Sets a notification port and a message for a process.
Set_time_limit	Sets the maximum time a process can execute.
Set_scheduling_info	Sets the parameters: time slice, deadline, and priority.

Figure 8-2 Operations of the Process_Manager for reading and setting process attributes.

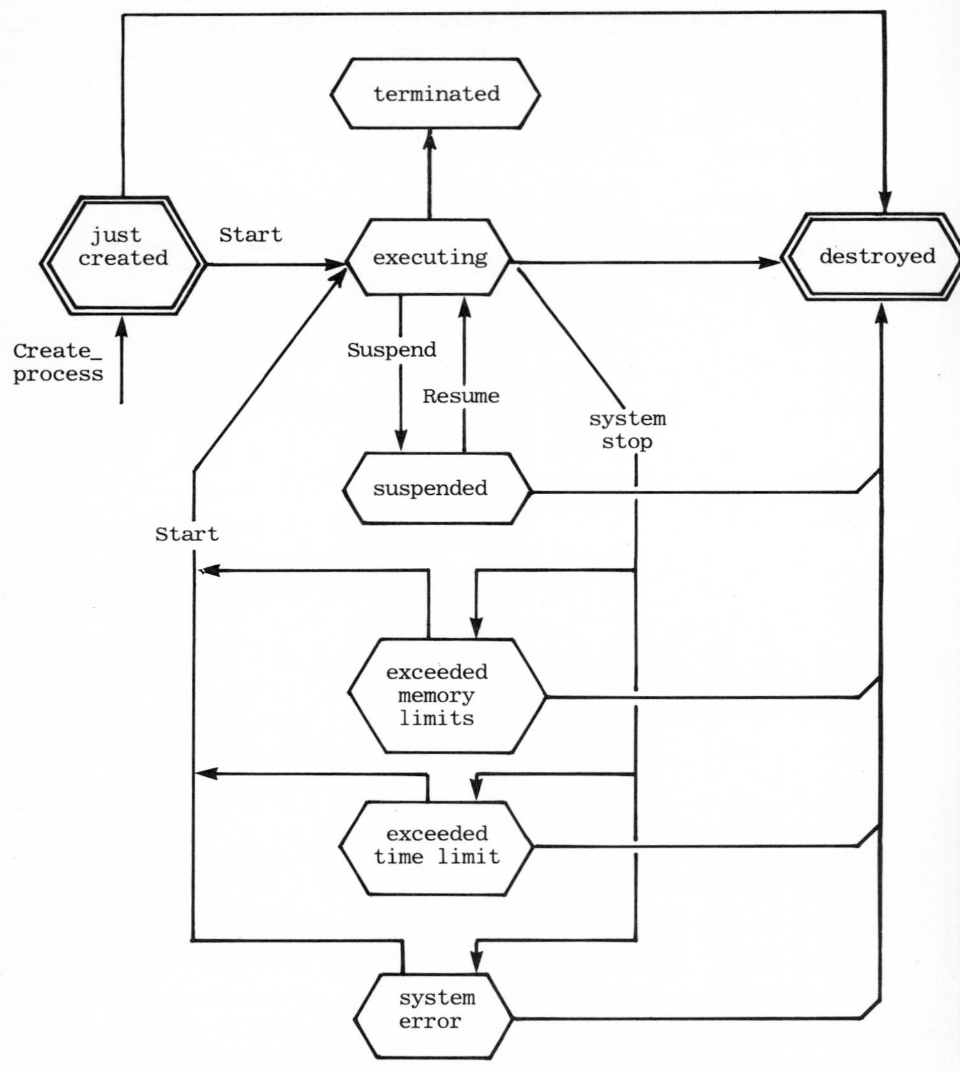

Figure 8-3 Macro-state diagram to explain the lifecycle of a process

destroyed, or removed from the dispatching mix for having exceeded some user-specified limit.

The user-readable attributes of each process are collected in several records, defined in Figure 8-4. A process' fixed attributes are provided in *process_info_rec*; variable attributes (i.e., state information) of a process are provided in two records: *process_state_rec* and *process_micro_state_rec*. The functions, Read_process_info, Read_process_state, and Read_process_micro_state respectively return this information.

```
type process_states is (
  executing,
  just_created,
  suspended,
  exceeded_memory_limit,
  exceeded_time_limit,
  system_error,
  terminated,
  destroyed);

type process_micro_states is (
  not_executing,
  on_processor,
  on_cport,
  on_service_port);

type process_info_rec is
  record                          -- Returned by Read_process_info.
    process_id:               short_ordinal;
    process_globals:          Process_Definitions.process_globals_rep;
    name:                     string;
    notification_port:        iMAX_Definitions.port;
    notification_message:     dynamic_typed;
    time_limit:               time_limit_type;
    scheduling_info:          scheduling_info_rec;
  end record;

type process_state_rec is
  record                          -- Returned by Read_process_state.
    state:                    process_states;
    process_clock:            milliseconds;
  end record;

type process_micro_state_rec is
  record                          -- Returned by Read_process_micro_state
    state:                    process_states;
    micro_state:              process_micro_states;
    process_clock:            milliseconds;
  end record;
```

Figure 8-4 Type definitions for process_states and process_info_rec.

All process attributes, with the exception of process_globals, process_id, and the process state components, can be specified by the user. Some of these attributes can be set unconditionally; others are *advisory* only. For example, the caller can set (and later reset) the notification port and message, but can only set the time_limit and other scheduling parameters in an advisory sense. The underlying implementation can ignore advisory specifications in the event, for example, that processes are to be scheduled not individually, but in job-related groups.

For most process attributes, the implementation of Process_Manager supplies default values, so that the user is not required to specify them at all. The default values of some process attributes may be overridden only in the course of creating a process and cannot be changed thereafter. The name of a process is one such example. Other attributes, such as the notification port and message, may be set only after a process is created; a Set_. . . operation is used for this purpose.

8.2.1. The Create_Process Operation and Its Use

The specification of Create_process is given in Figure 8-5. Although this operation has *eight* parameters, the caller is only required to specify *init_proc* which

```
function Create_process(
    init_proc:               access_initial_proc;
      -- The procedure to execute.
    init_params:             dynamic_typed := null;
      -- Parameters to init_proc.
    name:                    string;
      -- The text name of the process.
    job:                     Jobs_Manager_Types.job := null;
      -- The job in which the caller is executing, i.e., the job
      -- in the caller's process globals.
    heap_sro:                iMAX_Definitions.storage_resource := null;
      -- The sro from which to create the process. This determines
      -- the scope of the process and whether the process is frozen or
      -- normal. Default is the global heap sro in the caller's
      -- process globals.
    init_stack_objtab_size: objtab_size_type := 0;
      -- Initial size of the process stack object table. This is an
      -- advisory parameter, and may be ignored by particular
      -- Process_Manager implementations.
    init_stack_size:         mem_size_type := 0;
      -- Initial size of the process stack allocation block. This is an
      -- advisory parameter, and may be ignored by particular
      -- Process_Manager implementations.
    call_stack_depth:        integer := 0;
      -- Number of contexts to be pre-allocated for this process.
      -- This is an advisory parameter, and may be ignored by particular
      -- Process_Manager implementations.
  return process;  -- Has control_rights.
  --
  -- Function:
  --   A new process is created and returned. The parameter list
  --   includes only those process attributes which can be set only
  --   at process creation time. Default values are provided for
  --   all process attributes except the procedure to execute
  --   (init_proc); this is the only parameter which MUST be specified.
  --   Attributes for which there are no parameters may be changed after
  --   a process has been created (and before it is started, if desired)
  --   by calling one of the Set_... operations.
```

Figure 8-5 Specification of the Create_process function in package access type Process_Manager.

supplies the beginning procedure, i.e., the initial execution environment for the new process.

The dynamic package feature of 432-Ada is used to specify init_proc. An instance of the package access_initial_proc is passed as the init_proc parameter to Create_process. This instance is obtained by instantiating the generic package initial_proc; in this instantiation, the initial procedure to be executed by the new process is given as the generic parameter *main*. Figure 8-6 shows the initial_proc and access_initial_proc specifications from Process_Manager_Types in Appendix K.

```
generic
  with procedure main(             -- Formal generic parameter.
            params: dynamic_typed);
package initial_proc is
  procedure main(
      params: dynamic_typed)
    renames main;
end initial_proc;                  -- End of generic package spec.


type access_initial_proc is access initial_proc;
  -- Declares access_initial_proc to be an instance
  -- of the dynamic package named initial_proc.
```

Figure 8-6 Specification of the generic package *initial_proc* and package access type *access_initial_proc*. The formal parameter of initial_proc is the procedure *main* which itself has one parameter whose type is dynamic_typed.

Figure 8-7 shows an Ada program fragment which creates a process named "Task_Master". The mechanism just described is used to specify Spawn_servers as the initial procedure of the new process.

8.2.2. Other Operations of the Process_Manager Interface and Their Use

The Create_process operation returns an AD with *control_rights* for the created process; no *read* or *write* rights are returned. Depending on the particular process manager implementation, the AD returned from the Create_process operation may or may not also have *suspend_and_resume_rights*. The rights returned by Create_process are *software-defined* type rights. Calls on all other operations in Process_Manager, with the exception of Suspend, Resume, and the Read_. . . operations, must supply an AD with *control_rights* for the specified process. Calls on Suspend and Resume require that the AD for the specified process contain *suspend_and_resume_rights*.

The creator of a process may make ADs for that process accessible to other

```
   ...
use Process_Manager_Types;
   ...

  declare
    use Some_Process_Manager;
     ...

    procedure Spawn_servers(
         server_p: dynamic_typed)
    is begin ...  end;

    initial_environment: access_initial_proc;
  begin
    initial_environment := new initial_proc(init_proc => Spawn_servers);
        -- Create an instance of initial_proc with Spawn_servers as its
        -- one public operation.

    -- Can now make call on Create_process as follows:
    Local_Process_Manager.Create_process(
        init_proc    =>  initial_environment,
        init_params  =>  dynamic_typed(some_server_p),
        name         =>  "Task_Master");    -- Remaining five arguments
                                            -- are defaulted.
  end;
```

Figure 8-7 An Ada program fragment to illustrate a call on Create_process.

agents in a system. If any of these ADs have *control_rights*, the process may be controlled by the agents that have access to them. Alternatively, the creator of a process may remove *control_rights* from such ADs so that other agents may read information about the process but may not perform control operations on it. Similar considerations apply to *suspend_and_resume_rights*. In the simplest case, control operations may be used to start a process and let it execute to completion. Wait_for_process_termination enables an agent to suspend its own operation until some other process has finished executing. To wait for the termination of more than one process (i.e., for all or for some of these to terminate), the more general notification mechanism may be used. (Use of Wait_for_process_termination is specified as mutually exclusive with use of the notification port and message mechanism.) A process may be aborted, no matter what its (macro) state, by a call to Destroy.

Several of the Process_Manager operations, including Destroy, are performed asynchronously with the caller; users may need to be aware of the cause-and-effect time lags involved. Details such as these, and more complete descriptions of all PM operations, including those not mentioned here, are given in the PM interface specifications in Appendix K.

8.3. Different Possible Implementations of the Process_Manager Interface

In the previous section, we described the general Process_Manager interface without reference to specific implementations of that interface. The functionality supported by a given Process_Manager implementation may range from a purely minimal scheme to an arbitrarily rich one. In this section, we examine two of the many possible implementations of Process_Manager, and discuss some of their ramifications.

First, we review the architecture details needed to understand dispatching and scheduling of processes at the lowest level. Recall from Chapter 5 that a process is scheduled by specifying a *service time*, which is the maximum amount of compute time to be used during each of a given number of service periods; the latter is specified as the *period count*. (These values are embedded in the Process Object.) After each (but the last) service period has been completed, the process is reinserted into the request queue of its Dispatching Port in *deadline-within-priority* order. The specified deadline is an integer measure of how long the process may be delayed, relative to other enqueued processes of the same priority. (The *deadline* and *priority* values are maintained in the Process' Carrier Object and are copied into the appropriate request queue entry when a process is reinserted into its Dispatching Port.) The copied deadline values for enqueued processes within a given priority level are updated by the hardware (to reflect the effect of elapsed time) each time another request (process) is inserted into the Dispatching Port. (These detailed hardware operations are described in the i432 Architecture Reference Manual.)

8.3.1. A Simple, Close-to-the-Hardware Implementation

A minimal process management implementation (MPM) might consist merely of allowing its users to create, initialize, and start processes. Suspend, Resume, Raise_exception, and Destroy would likely not be implemented. In this scheme, processes have an infinite time limit (period count) and they must not terminate. (Alternatively, processes could be automatically destroyed if they terminate. This option would probably require MPM to include a service process that would perform the destruction of the processes that terminate.)

Defaults are provided for the process scheduling parameters (time slice or service time, deadline, and priority); users can override the defaults or change the scheduling parameters of an executing process by calling Set_scheduling_parameters. Thus, processes execute entirely under control of the hardware dispatching and scheduling mechanisms. Because they have an infinite period count, created processes would never be sent to their scheduling port, so MPM does not need to include a service process to handle the scheduling port.

Depending on the level of fault handling and memory management in the system, MPM might require its users to specify explicitly some of the optional parameters in the Create_process operation. For example, it might require users to specify the stack and stack object table sizes and the maximum call stack depth so that they would never need to be expanded. (In more sophisticated systems, these parameters would usually be defaulted and the system would expand them as necessary.) The level of memory management support in the system also determines whether MPM processes can be created only during system initialization, or whether they can also be created any time after the system has been initialized.

The most important consequence of a minimal process management implementation is that it implements no scheduling policy on top of the hardware-provided scheduling mechanisms. MPM users must allocate processor resources among themselves in some way to prevent overloading the system. In the next subsection, we examine a possible implementation to address this issue.

8.3.2. Higher-Level Implementations

A much richer Process_Manager implementation, such as for a multi-user time-shared operating system, would dynamically control the amounts of processor (and memory) resources consumed by each user. The optional *job* parameter to Create_process allows Process_Manager implementations to provide policies and services that are based on a characterization of the user on whose behalf a process is created. Individual processes, or those grouped as *jobs*, might be suspended and resumed, examined and given more processor or storage resources if needed, restarted, or destroyed. Usage statistics might be gathered on a per-process or per-job basis.

To facilitate implementation of such a scheme, iMAX provides a comprehensive set of process management primitives assembled in a Process Manager Support package. Figure 8-8 is a graphical outline of this rich implementation scheme. A process is sent to a Scheduler of the High Level PM Implementation whenever it undergoes a change that may affect the Scheduler's treatment of it or of other processes in the system. The agent which sends the process to its Scheduler may be part of a user's thread of control, or may be a service process of PM Support. Based on the states of the processes it receives, the Scheduler may move processes in and out of the mix via operations of PM Support, or may send notification messages to notification ports.

In general, the strategy is to give PM implementers, through the PM Support package, the ability to specify and implement policies in terms of the primitive operations of iMAX and the underlying mechanisms of the architecture. Setting the service time, period count, deadline, and priority of a process are examples of policy specification via the operations of PM Support. Automatic dispatching and other port operations are examples of underlying mechanisms of the architecture.

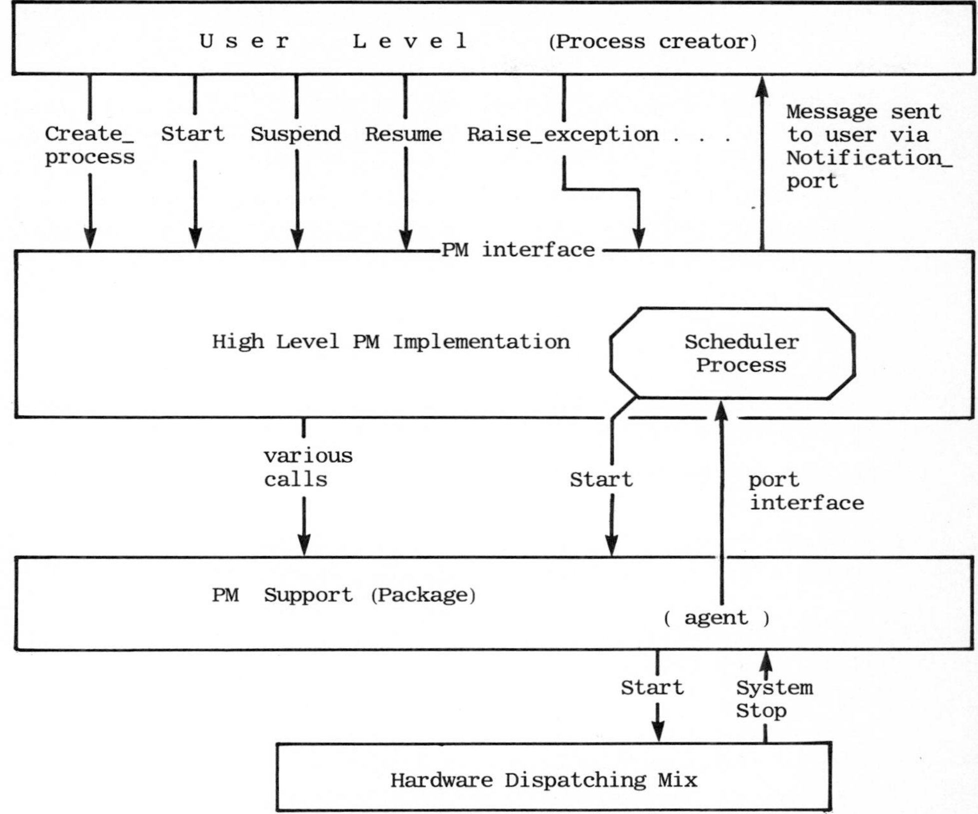

Figure 8-8 Program structures for use of a rich (and hypothetical) Process_Manager interface (PM): High-level view. Its implementation includes an auxiliary Scheduler process. Processes in need of rescheduling or other attention are sent via operations of the Support package to the Scheduler, using the process' *port attribute*. The agent sending a process to the scheduler may either be part of the user's thread of control or a separate process that is instantiated in the Support package.

8.4. Summary

In this chapter we have introduced the reader to some of the major design objectives for process management in the i432 System. iMAX provides a general framework in the form of the package Process_Manager_Types which gives the specification of a Process_Manager interface. An iMAX-supplied implementation of this interface may suffice for many users. Others may wish to implement their own versions of this interface.

We have indicated how individual implementations of this interface can range from one offering minimal functionality to one offering a maximum of sophistication. We have also provided only a general introduction to the use of the Process_Manager interface. What we have not done is examine in detail the structure of a rich implementation of the PM interface. This can be done in a future effort, perhaps by others. We trust, however, that the opportunities to implement a range of process managers tailored to different user needs is now clear. No discussion of the opportunities for process management can be complete, however, without offering a companion introduction to the management of the storage resources for processes. We do this in the next chapter.

9 MEMORY MANAGEMENT

9.1. Introduction

No significant general purpose computer system can function without service facilities for memory management and filing. In preceding chapters we have alluded to the i432 Memory Management and Object Filing services, but have avoided the temptation to discuss these subsystems in detail, reasoning that later was better. We have, however, suggested that these management facilities were as comprehensive as might be found in any of today's commercially available computer systems—truly a requirement if the i432 is to live up to its micro-mainframe "label".

In this chapter we first introduce i432 Memory Management and Object Filing. We then present an overview of the design strategies and some implementation details for Memory Management. We focus especially on those concepts and specifics that i432 subsystem designers and some applications programmers should know. Chapter 10 examines object filing in more detail.

- By *memory management*, we refer to the dynamic allocation and deallocation of storage resources, spanning both primary storage ("main memory"), and a swapping store (typically disc memory).
- By *filing*, we refer to the storing (and retrieving) of information units in (and from) long-term store (secondary memory). We assume all secondary memory structures are tied logically to one i432 System, but may reside at widely separated sites.
- By *object filing*, we refer to the filing of objects that always retain their identity and type even in the filed-away state. Such objects may be periodically brought back to short-term, active status, to participate as long as needed, as

objects in i432 computation structures—and then returned to file status, supplanting older versions in long-term storage.

Objects filed in long term status may have composite structures. Thus, even though no one object may exceed 128KB in length (64KB for data part and 64KB for access part), the size of the composite may be quite large, or may have rich structure, or both. An example of a composite would be the compiled representation of an Ada library-level package. It would consist of a Domain Object and its associated Instruction Objects, Constant Object, and objects representing owned data structures, if any.

[Traditional files, which may be individually much longer than 128KB in length, may also be treated in the framework of the object filing system, much as regular files are routinely accessed, for example, when using *Open*, *Read* or *Write*, and *Close* sequences.]

The totality of object space may be viewed, as in Figure 9-1, to be partitioned into two main parts, *active object space*, and *passive object space*. An object may be created in the active space and later either deleted when it becomes unreachable, or transferred to the passive object space (an ''intelligent'' form of long-term storage'') until needed again. We see that an *active object* is simply one that resides in active address space, while a *passive object* refers to an object residing in passive object space. The transfer of an object from active to passive space is controlled by the object's type manager, with default mechanisms provided for the same purpose in cases where the intent to ''passivate'' an object may be deduced by the system.

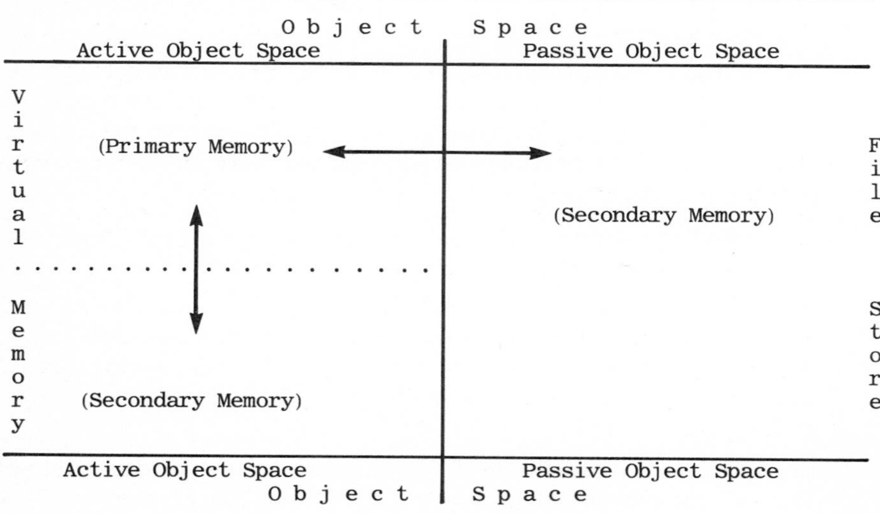

Figure 9-1 The Partition of i432 Object Space.

Transfer from one space to another may be achieved through use of an accessible iMAX interface package. Reference to the contents of a passive object, that is, Read, Write, or Update, may also be achieved by using this same interface. All such operations are accomplished while ensuring the consistency of the affected objects, through explicit use of provided synchronization mechanisms.

These mechanisms permit an object to exist simultaneously in both active and passive object space so that changes to a version in active space may be reflected in passive space under controlled conditions. Use of these mechanisms guarantees data consistency under conditions where two or more processes may be attempting accesses to the same passive object during the same time frame. The same mechanisms protect against system crashes. A full system crash causes loss of the active space but not the passive space. Such a crash need not be catastrophic, therefore, if users periodically update objects in passive space.

Before going further, it is important to stress that the system's storage is actually implemented in two parts, following a "two-space model". To most users, however, storage appears as a single space. The two-space or two-level view of store is more visible to type managers than to most programmers and is certainly invisible to all novice users.

The active object space is itself decomposed into two parts. Active objects may reside in either main memory or secondary memory. The totality of memory comprising the active object space is the *virtual memory* of the i432 system. Active objects in main memory may of course be addressed directly, using the i432 hardware and software discussed in earlier chapters.

An attempt to address an active object that resides in secondary memory results in a detected fault, which invokes the machinery of the i432 Memory Management Subsystem to transfer the referenced object to main memory. This latter facility, usually referred to as a "virtual memory" or "virtual storage system", has become a standard service offered with most minicomputers and with nearly all of today's mainframe systems.

[A brief historical reminder: the modern segmented virtual storage concept is rooted in the Burroughs B5000 system architecture, first announced in 1961 [11]. In that system, storage descriptors hold a hardware-sensed "presence bit" to indicate presence or absence of the target segment in main memory. If the presence bit is false, a hardware segment fault is signalled, invoking the system's software memory management subsystem. There follows an attempt to fetch the object from secondary storage, update the descriptor's presence bit, and return control to the routine that faulted, so that execution may continue as though no segment fault had occurred. (The i432 Object Descriptor has an *allocated* bit that corresponds directly with the B5000's presence bit. In both cases this bit is set by software and sensed by hardware.)

Shifting a B5000 segment from primary to secondary memory is a decision made and executed by software components of the memory management subsystem. Many of today's systems also support recording the nature and frequency of object use. The hardware automatically records some or all of this usage information; in turn, software decisions to transfer segments to secondary memory are based on these usage data. An early example was the GE645 system architecture [44]. Segment descriptors for this system contained "has-been-accessed" and "has-been-written" bits. (Each i432 Object Descriptor also has such bit fields set by the hardware. These are called, respectively, the *accessed* and *altered bits*.

In principle, the early and current virtual memory management systems are qualitatively quite similar. Current systems are more effective, especially because the amount of affordable main memory has increased by more than two orders of magnitude since the early 1960s. The extra space means that more structuring information can be maintained in memory (such as tables and pointers describing the users' information objects.) Moreover, this structuring "overhead" can be better distributed in memory. The result is that more comprehensive algorithms are used for managing primary memory, thus limiting the frequency of swapping to secondary memory.]

In spite of the many significant advances just cited, most current architectures still fail to provide effective support for parallel garbage collection. (Such support is, in fact, a significant architectural feature of the i432, as described at the end of Section 9.2.) A parallel garbage collector can be reclaiming storage objects while other processors execute programs that consume reclaimed space [17].

In conventional systems, execution of the garbage collector algorithm is necessarily mutually exclusive with execution of application programs that rely on an available supply of reclaimed storage blocks. This circumstance leads to interruptions of application programs at unpredicatable points in time when the services of the garbage collector become critical. Because of this problem, real world applications, whose forward progress must not be interrupted for garbage collection, are conventionally programmed to avoid the need for it. All too often, applications programmers have avoided the problem by choosing programming languages (like Fortran, Cobol, and Assembly language) whose semantics do not rely on implicit garbage collection. Unfortunately, choice of such languages has often led to other expenses such as in program maintenance. Effective use of modern high-order languages like Ada implies the need for garbage collection. As a consequence, one can expect to see added pressure applied to system designers for the development of architectures suitable for parallel garbage collection.

With this historical development and commentary as background, we naturally expect a significant degree of maturity in the model and implementation for memory management in the iMAX Operating System—even in the first released versions. For example, parallel effective garbage collection and memory compaction algorithms run, when needed, not only as separate processes, but also on separate processors, in support of programs that generate large numbers of objects having relatively short lifetimes.

The first released version of the iMAX Memory Management provides sophisticated algorithms for management of main (real) memory only. These routines form the nucleus of the virtual memory and object filing algorithms. Our description of the entire Memory Management and Object Filing subsystems are therefore given "bottom-up". First we describe the model for main memory management in Section 9.2. We then describe the design and implementation extensions for virtual memory management (Section 9.3) and object filing (Chapter 10). At the end of Chapter 10, we view the behavior of our portfolio management system as it is expected to operate under the fully-implemented Virtual Memory Management and Object Filing Subsystems.

The first release of iMAX is useful for a variety of applications that can run entirely in main (real) memory—which can be as large as 16MB. (Recall that users are provided with advanced I/O Subsystems as described in Chapter 7.) Conceivably, this first collection of memory management packages will also be useful as a starting base for system designers wishing to extend the operating system to provide their own virtual memory management or filing system, or both. These designers need not wait to use a more comprehensive iMAX release.

We end this introduction by reminding the reader of the close relationship between memory management and process management. Any user, advanced enough to take full advantage of the several iMAX memory management interfaces, will very likely also need to know about and perhaps use the iMAX interface provided for process management which we have already introduced in Chapter 8.

9.2. Management of Main Memory

A set of operating system packages and tasks, hereafter referred to as Memory Management, performs the functions of main memory management. The tasks cooperate to assume not only the responsibility of making the most of the available physical space, a relatively scarce resource, but also to construct and maintain in a consistent state, the mappings of all i432 objects and their components from logical to physical addresses. Memory Management responds to explicit (and implicit) demands for resources needed as processes request creation of objects (and progress from one context to another). Neither the Operating System nor any individual process is required to "know in advance" how many objects, or of what sizes, will be needed for execution. This is, of course, a crucial point. Any initial allocation selected for a process by the system may be extended by Memory Management as needed, up to the limit of the system's available space resources.

To reach this objective, Memory Management constructs and maintains in main memory an elaborate set of private data structures. The overhead of space and processing effort associated with the storage and management of these data structures is not insignificant by standards used for many predecessor systems. However, the increased functionality that is derived is paid for with main storage that has become relatively inexpensive and with extra processing that can be run for the most part concurrently with the execution of users' code.

It makes little sense for us to present a full description of all these internal records and of the governing procedural components of Memory Management. Not only would such a presentation require the space of a small book, but the details presented, which are subject to change, would be of interest mainly to those who wish to construct their own complete operating system. For that audience, specialized literature would be more useful. Instead, we take a subsystem designer's view in explaining Memory Management. The principal data structure one needs to know about for use of these interfaces is the Storage Resource Object. We have discussed the top-level structure of SROs in Chapters 4 and 8. In this section, however, the SRO becomes a focus of attention.

Recall that a Storage Resource Object records the use of one or more blocks of contiguous main memory. Figure 9-2 illustrates some of the details of an SRO that might be used for managing one block of physical memory (called the *allocation block*). This block is represented in the Physical Storage Object (PSO) by a *storage block specifier* consisting of a pair of physical addresses that serve as bounds on the block. The figure is illustrative of the initial condition of a global heap SRO; the PSO for this initial condition defines only a single (very large) block of storage. (Later snapshots of the PSO would show it containing a number of storage block specifiers, each defining a distinct allocation block. These block specifiers are actually linked in a single list and the list is searched in a convenient way each time space for a new object of a given size must be found.)

All *global* heap storage space is drawn from one of two system-wide PSOs, one for the normal global heap SRO and one for the frozen global heap SRO. Each normal (or frozen) *local* heap SRO shares the same system-wide normal (or frozen) PSO. When it is necessary to allocate space for a new object, the i432 uses a "rotate-first-fit" algorithm for selecting the allocation block out of which the object will be created. The header part of the PSO provides the state information needed to apply the rotate-first fit algorithm [35]. The strategy of using one global PSO for essentially all heap allocation system wide assures relatively even distribution of free space and hence minimizes the amount of work required by the compaction algorithm on the rare occasions when it is invoked. Using a global PSO assures that the search will be short, since allocation blocks will generally be large compared with the average size of created objects allocated from them.

A different strategy is used for allocation for stack SROs. The PSO for a stack SRO is not shared with any other SRO. (When a process P is created, its stack SRO is also created, as is the associated PSO. Memory Management initializes the PSO's single storage block specifier to represent an allocation block of size (optionally) specified in the call that creates P. See the init_stack_size parameter in Figure 8-5.)

When an object is created from any kind of SRO, a chunk of available space of the requisite size is allocated and its Object Descriptor is constructed and

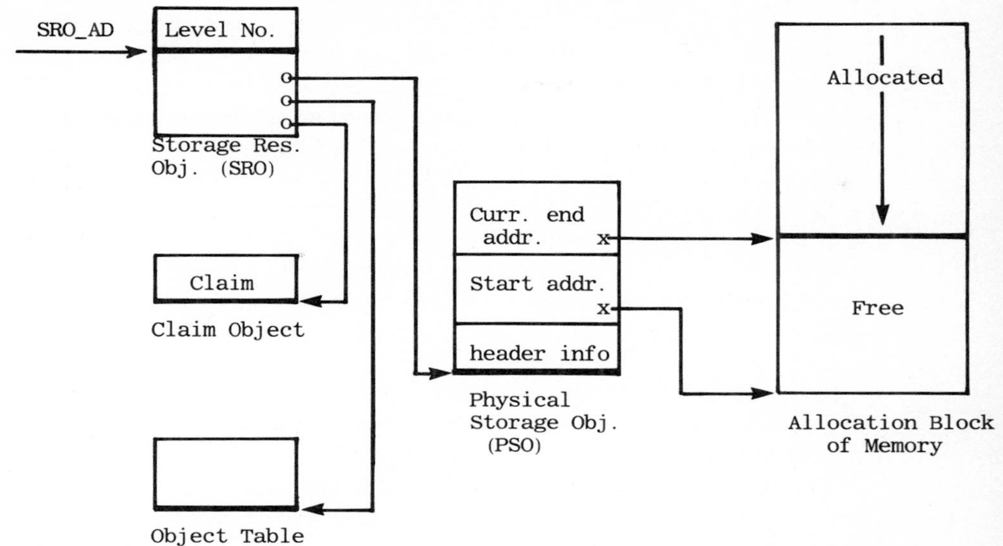

Figure 9-2 Structure of an SRO and the block of physical storage it refers to. An SRO holds Access Descriptors for a Physical Storage Object, an Object Table, and a Claim Object. A PSO may hold one or more *storage block specifiers*, each containing two physical addresses that are bound a block of available space and thus define an allocation block. (The "x" marks an absolute physical address, rather than a logical address or offset.) Although not shown, the Object Table holds Object Descriptors for objects residing in the allocation block of the related PSO. The Claim Object holds an ordinal value representing the current (total) amount of storage space controlled by this SRO.

added to the SRO's Object Table. That descriptor contains a physical address pointing to the base of the allocated chunk as well as the lengths of its data and access parts. A corresponding adjustment is made to the Current End Address component of the affected storage block specifier in the PSO.

For each new object created from an SRO, the allocation block represented by the affected storage block specifier naturally shrinks in size. Any request to create a new object Z whose size exceeds that available from any of the storage block specifiers within a PSO will invoke additional system "machinery" to adjust the PSO so that at least the particular object creation request can succeed. For example, the PSO can be provided a new storage block specifier of sufficient size for allocation of object Z. Alternatively, the allocation block of an existing storage block specifier can be increased by an appropriate amount.

The approach to adjusting the PSO depends on the allocation discipline used. When it is necessary to increase the available resources for a heap SRO, it is sufficient to add to its PSO another storage block specifier representing a disjoint allocation block; however, to facilitate the automatic reclamation space occupied by stacked objects, the PSO for a stack SRO is best managed with a single storage block specifier. In the rare occasions when a stack must be enlarged, it is done primarily by enlarging the allocation block represented by the specifier or, in case the stack SRO uses normal rather than frozen memory, by replacing the specifier with a new one that represents a larger allocation block and *relocating* all the currently stacked objects into the space governed by the new specifier. (The strategy used in the current implementation is to set a fixed size for the initial allocation block of a stack SRO (e.g., 4K bytes); this block is then doubled in size each time it must be enlarged, until some large system-determined upper bound is reached; after this, another storage block specifier containing a second, disjoint allocation block is added to the PSO of the stack SRO.)

The immediate memory resource supplying the space needed for adjustment of PSO storage block specifiers is the so-called *Free List*. (This list is a private data structure maintained by Memory Management and is a list of free-to-use memory blocks sorted in order by base address. Sorting in base address order enables the manager of a Free List to immediately coalescence newly added blocks in the list to adjoining blocks. Actually, two such Free Lists are maintained, one for normal memory and one for frozen memory.) New blocks of memory are added to the Free List whenever an object is reclaimed by the Garbage Collector or whenever local heap objects are automatically deleted by virtue of executing RETURN instructions.

One can imagine ideal conditions in which a dynamic equilibrium might prevail between the rate at which new blocks of free storage (having some size distribution) are added to a Free List F and the rate at which storage blocks (having the same size distribution) are dispensed from allocation blocks of PSOs whose storage block specifiers are ''acquired from'' F. Since a real system can only approach such an equilibrium occasionally, backup mechanisms must be provided when deficiencies arise in the Free List.

- The Garbage Collector process can be requested to find all unreachable objects, entries for which can then be placed on the Free List. (As just mentioned, new blocks added to the Free List are coalesced with adjoining ones.)
- When no block on the Free List is of sufficient size, the Compaction process can be requested to relocate allocated objects until a contiguous free block of sufficient size is formed by ''coalescence''. Note that the compaction algorithm can fail if, after coalescing all of the PSO's allocation blocks, there is still an insufficient amount of free space available.
- Finally, if a virtual memory facility is available, some currently allocated objects can be swapped out to secondary storage, thereby freeing up sufficient main memory.

The i432 Memory Management subsystem utilizes all of these strategies to adjust the equilibrium between the Free List resources and the demands on PSO allocation blocks. The decision strategy used, that is, which of the available mechanisms to invoke when, is made by the iMAX module that manages the Free List in response to a request for a free storage block that is larger than currently available. The decision is based on the size R of the block requested and the current "operating condition" of the Free List. Two key parameters, for example, might describe the operating condition: (a) the total amount of storage S on the Free List and (b) mean free block size F (the ratio of S and the number of free blocks on the list.)

As long as S substantially exceeds R, recourse to a relatively costly replacement algorithm for swapping out selected objects from real memory can probably be avoided. When activated, the Compaction process runs only until a free block of a specified size is obtained or until the ratio F rises above a given threshold, whichever the reason for its activation. The frequency of appeal to the Garbage Collector is a direct function of the kinds of programs being executed. (Thus, executing Ada programs may, and LISP-like programs will definitely, lead to heavy use of the Garbage Collector; by contrast, the Garbage Collector should not be needed at all when executing a mix of Basic, Fortran, and Cobol programs.) Although the interplay between the three space reclamation mechanisms is clearly complex, just the fact that the Memory Management can choose among the three of them at any given time offers, in principle, a degree of flexibility and an opportunity for achieving performance levels that have not been furnished through most previous operating system designs.

The Claim Object component of an SRO, shown in Figure 9-2, denotes an allocation limit for an SRO (either virtual or actual, depending on whether the particular system does or does not support virtual memory). The *claim value* is decremented as objects are allocated from the SRO and incremented when they are later reclaimed by the Garbage Collector. Two or more related SROs may share the same Claim Object, and hence can be managed as a unit. Thus, one claim value may be used to maintain control over allocation from a group of SROs related to a process tree. (We come back to this point in Section 9.3.)

Thus far we have primarily considered the internal structure of SROs and the relationship between its structure and the underlying support of Memory Management. We are now ready to consider, at a higher level, how SROs are used to manage storage resources needed to execute programs. To understand how SROs are used at this level, our starting view is that of an i432 System executing a collection of logically-independent processes. During its "lifetime" each of these processes may spawn a tree of subsidiary (related) processes. We will examine the allocation of objects, as required by the various processes within this picture, the strategies and mechanisms used, and the related low-level services put at the disposal of the systems programmer, should these be needed. We will also examine the strategies and mechanisms used for deallocation of these same objects.

It turns out (by design) that to understand allocation and deallocation of objects, one needs primarily to understand the structure and management of SROs, especially those used within individual process families. To get started, then, we first examine a means for classifying allocated objects according to their expected *lifetimes*. We then examine the relationships among SROs.

We find that, as a process tree grows (and shrinks), so grows (and shrinks) a companion tree structure of SROs—whose use accounts for the dynamic allocation (and deallocation) of process-related objects. Interestingly enough, nearly everything we learn about SROs as used in the management of main memory carries over to the management of virtual memory, which spans main memory and secondary memory.

Three kinds of SROs are found useful, corresponding to three kinds of lifetimes the objects allocated from these SROs will have. These are referred to as:

1. global heap SROs
2. stack SROs
3. local heap SROs

9.2.1. Object Lifetime Strategies

We can speak about an object's *lifetime*, in terms of major events that transpire from the point of its allocation to its deallocation. Strictly speaking, the lifetimes of objects created by processes lie on a continuum, from fleetingly short to "eternal". From a practical point of view, however, object lifetimes fall conveniently into three broad, relatively easily managed categories:

1. An object should live (that is, remain allocated) as long as it is reachable from another reachable object. The lifetime for such an object may be independent of the lifetime of the process that creates it, and is, therefore, allocated from a global heap SRO. Ada library-level packages are represented by i432 objects that fall in this category.

   Reclamation of space for objects allocated from a global heap SRO can occur only via the services of the system's Garbage Collector. (This task can run concurrently with any of the other Memory Management tasks (including the Compaction process), and concurrently with all user tasks.)

2. An object, X, should live only for the duration of an activation of subprogram, P, for which X has been allocated. Several kinds of objects local to a subprogram may need to be created for use during activation of that subprogram. Among these are arrays of records, and records containing arrays of dynamic dimensions that cannot fit into the preallocated Context Object

whose size is fixed. Domain Objects representing Ada packages declared local to a subprogram are also allocated from the stack SRO. These objects are automatically deallocated from that stack SRO (and their space explicitly reclaimed) upon execution of the matching RETURN instruction.

3. An object, X, is allocated while executing in a context, G, but its lifetime is tied to that of a specified predecessor context, C. Falling in this category is any object, X, representing an instance of an Ada **access** type whose declaration is elaborated while the program executes in context C, but which is actually allocated during execution in this or a subsequent context, G as a consequence of either a variable declaration or the evaluation of an *allocator expression*. Object X would be allocated from a local heap SRO created during execution within context C.

   [In the special case where C and G are the same context, instances of type **access** variables, e.g., Extended Type Objects, would still be allocated from a local heap SRO allocated within context C. Note that instances for non-access types declared in an enclosing scope need not be allocated as separate objects from the stack SRO, but may be stored in the local variable or operand stack areas of the current Context Object. This simpler treatment is possible for simple variables, and arrays.]

   Deallocation of object X would occur no later than when Context Object C is deallocated. This event occurs when the subprogram activation, for which Context Object C was constructed, is completed. The dynamic link AD in a Context Object for a subprogram activation that allocates a local heap SRO is always stripped of its *return* rights. Upon executing the RETURN instruction, use of the dynamic link AD induces a fault (raises an exception.) The handler invokes a Memory Management routine which deallocates the local heap SRO and all the objects allocated in it and reclaims all storage associated with the affected local heap SRO. (The choice, whether or not to employ a separate service task to perform this reclamation is an iMAX implementation decision. In principle such a task could execute concurrently with the Garbage Collector and also concurrently with the user program for whom the service is performed.)

   The interim, between the time that object X is created and the point at which context C is deallocated, may be relatively long, in part because the number of contexts intervening between C and G, may be quite large. It is possible that, during this interim, object X may become unreachable. This condition makes the storage for object X a candidate for reclamation by the Garbage Collector and the latter may reclaim it before (perhaps long before) the thread of control exits from context C.

In the case of objects whose lifetimes fall in category one, there can be no special trigger for deallocation and reclamation. Hence, an unreachable object, i.e., garbage, may continue in the allocated state for an indefinite period of time, especially when there is plenty of free space left to be allocated. On the other hand, in the case of objects whose lifetimes fall in category two, the trigger for deallocation can be (and is) keyed to a precisely-defined hardware event, namely execution of a RETURN instruction. Since the frequency of allocation for such objects is high, it is fortunate that their deallocation is assured at the earliest safe time.

We have already suggested that for category three objects (those drawn from local heap SROs) the mechanism guaranteeing their deallocation is intermediate between those used for objects of the first two categories—and so is the response time. Software, namely the compiler, sets up a hardware trigger of the event, and software, namely iMAX, handles the event. The mechanism takes advantage of level numbers associated with objects allocated from local heap SROs. In the remainder of this subsection we explain and illustrate this mechanism.

Associated with a stack SRO is a counter representing the current level number; this counter is incremented and decremented by one during execution of each CALL and RETURN instruction, respectively. When an object Y is created from a stack SRO, it acquires a level number attribute equal to the current level number of the stack SRO from which Y is created. This attribute is represented as a hardware-sensed value in Y's Object Descriptor. When a local heap SRO, H, is created by a process R, the heap H acquires a level number equal to the current level counter in R's stack SRO. Subsequently, all objects allocated from H acquire the same level number as that of H. [Note that level numbers are not the same as *display indices* used in stack architectures to denote the lexical levels. Level numbers represent the length of the dynamic chain whereas display indices represent the length of the static chain.]

The *deallocation semantics* of the RETURN instruction executed in current context C is such that all objects having level numbers equal to or greater than that of context C are deallocated from the stack SRO and then the stack SRO's level counter is decremented by one. Part of these semantics is carried out by software. This is the part having to do with deallocation of a local heap SRO that was allocated and assigned the level number of the current Context Object C; return of control from this context causes (with software intervention) deallocation of the local heap SRO and necessarily of all objects created from it.

Consider the following illustrative scenario:

- Some process, Q, is executing with a Context Object C. Suppose there is now a need to allocate a local heap SRO, so it can be used later for the allocation of objects of, say, **access** type S. As indicated above, this local heap SRO is logically allocated from process Q's stack SRO and is given a level number that is the same as that of Context Object C.
- Subsequent execution within context C may now lead to extensions of the dynamic chain via the generation of contexts for D and then E, all assumed to lie within the scope of **access** type S. (These Context Objects have succes-

sively higher level numbers.) Object instances of type S may, therefore, be created at any point subsequent to the creation of its local heap SRO, during execution within contexts C, D, and E.

- Now consider what happens when the process executes the chain of three RETURN instructions from contexts E, D, and C, respectively. Each execution of a RETURN instruction leads to the deallocation of all objects on the stack SRO having the level number equal to that of the stack SRO. (The stack SRO's level counter is then decremented by one.) The local heap SRO, therefore, remains allocated after executing RETURN instructions from contexts E to D and from D to C, assuring that prior to each RETURN, objects of **access type** S are still accessible from the current and earlier contexts. Such accessibility is, of course, required by Ada visibility rules.
- When the RETURN instruction within context C is executed, however, a fault occurs because the dynamic link in context C has no *return* rights; iMAX intercedes, deallocates the local heap SRO and all the objects allocated from it, and ''fixes'' the dynamic link AD (by reinstating *return* rights) to allow the RETURN instruction to complete without further fault. At this point the hardware proceeds with the deallocation of all other objects allocated from the stack SRO during execution of context C (objects whose level numbers equal the current value of the stack SRO's level counter.) The level counter is then decremented once again and control returns to the context which caused creation of context C.

9.2.2. Prevention of Dangling References

The automatic (and explicit) deallocation mechanisms invoked for objects drawn from stack (and local heap) SROs implies the need for a companion mechanism that prevents the occurrence of accessible Access Descriptors for objects already deallocated. Such *dangling references* must be prevented to ensure the integrity of the system.

The insertion of level numbers in Object Descriptors is the key idea behind the i432 architects' solution to this problem. During execution of every i432 instruction that writes an Access Descriptor, Obj_AD, into the access part of an object, B, the hardware checks that the level number of Obj is less than or equal to that of B. A lifetime-violation fault occurs if this test fails. The effect of this test is to guarantee that objects referenced by Access Descriptors have equal or longer lifetimes than the Objects holding such references.

Translated into higher-level terms, the hardware imposes the following restriction on the transmission of Access Descriptors: If procedure R calls procedure T, then T may not return to R an AD for either T's Context Object, or for any object having the same level number as T's Context Object. In Ada terms, T may not return to its caller an access value for an object whose type is declared immediately within the scope of T.

Note that the converse is not true, since R may safely pass to T, as an input argument, any AD accessible in R's context. This is true, because the object referenced by any such AD is guaranteed to have a longer lifetime than that of T's context.

Note also that all objects created from a global heap SRO have level number values of zero; hence any procedure T is free to return as an output argument, or as a returned value, an Access Descriptor for an object allocated from a global heap SRO. This means that, occasionally, an object that might otherwise be drawn from a local heap SRO must be drawn instead from a global heap SRO. Indeed, code generated by the i432 Ada compiler conforms with the above "conventions", and so no compiled code can generate lifetime-violation faults.

[In truth, the hardware actually offers a way to eliminate the overhead of the level compatibility check. This check is clearly unnecessary when, for example, it is known that the AD being copied into some target object is a reference to a level zero object. Every AD has an *unchecked copy rights* bit. If this bit is set *on*, the level check is bypassed when the AD is copied. Certain iMAX modules take advantage of this escape feature—which should otherwise be used with extreme caution. (Note that the overhead of level checking is always bypassed by the hardware when the target object is the current Context Object. A little thought should convince the reader it is safe to copy any AD into the current Context Object; this is because there can be no shorter-lived object accessible to a process than its own current Context Object.)]

So far, we have looked only at the memory management of a single process. In a later subsection we extend the explanation to full process trees and to forests of such trees that represent logically independent processes. Before doing so, however, we make some additional comments about global heap SROs.

9.2.3. Frozen and Normal Memory

The version of iMAX which operates with main memory only (no virtual memory and no object filing) recognizes two categories of objects having indefinite (level zero) lifetimes. In one category are objects that should never be made inaccessible. Low-level System Objects like Dispatching Ports, Processor Objects, Processor and Process Carriers fall in this category. Such objects are placed in a section of memory named *frozen memory*, governed by the *frozen* global heap SRO. A user, concerned with processing that has "tight" time constraints, may require that the stack SRO for a process be placed in frozen memory and hence allocated from the frozen global heap SRO. (This may be done by using the iMAX interface package called Process_Globals_Definitions.)

Objects not allocated from the frozen global heap SRO are allocated from the *normal* global heap SRO. Recall that an attempt to add a new storage block specifier to the PSO of a normal heap SRO can lead to an attempt by the Compaction process to relocate objects currently allocated from the SRO (so as to create an allocation block of sufficient size from the modified the Free List.) To perform relocation, the Compaction process must have mutually exclusive access to the Object Table of the SRO. During compaction, therefore, all objects allocated from that SRO must perforce be temporarily inaccessible to any other task. As we will see, such inaccessibility may rule out use of normal memory for some processes.

Initially, the management of all of main memory reduces to the management of just two global heap SROs, one for frozen memory and the other for normal memory. When a process is created, it is allocated a stack SRO, which will itself be allocated from one of the above two global heap SROs. The stack SRO's PSO component is also created from the same global heap SRO. Thus,

- If the stack SRO is allocated from normal memory, the stack SRO's allocation block defines a block of normal memory. Hence, objects created from this stack SRO are subject to occasional inaccessibility (on the rare occasions when the Compaction process is relocating objects that were allocated from that stack SRO).
- If the stack SRO is allocated from frozen memory, then the stack SRO's allocation block defines a block of frozen memory. Objects in frozen memory can never be relocated. Hence, all objects created from this stack SRO will remain accessible for the entire life of that process.

The PSO component for a local heap SRO is also the same as that of the governing global heap SRO. Hence, if the local heap SRO is allocated from normal memory, objects created from it are also subject to occasional inaccessibility because the allocation block for a local heap SRO defines a block of normal memory.

The Process Globals Object, first mentioned in Chapter 4, contains an entry called the default_global_heap_SRO. This pointer is preset upon process creation by the process-management component of the operating system to refer to the *normal* global heap SRO, but can be "overridden" by the caller of PM.Create_process, as was suggested in Chapter 8. Also, the iMAX user interface package, Process_Globals_Definitions provides the means for reading or resetting this default value. (We do not include the specification of this package in our Appendix; however, it may be examined by consulting the iMAX 432 Reference Manual (Appendix B).)

9.2.4. SRO Trees that Match Process Trees

Process trees are typically formed in the execution of Ada programs and in programs written in other languages that also provide multitasking semantics. The model developed in Chapter 3 is, therefore, useful. An Ada program begins execution as a single process. The start-up of a new task is represented at a lower level as the creation of an offspring process. Since any Ada task may spawn none, one, or more other tasks, a tree of processes results from these actions. An Ada task may not terminate until all its offspring tasks have terminated (or have been aborted.) Therefore, when an Ada program completes execution, we are assured that all processes, including the root process, have been terminated. Note that if we traverse a path from the root node of this tree to any leaf node, we encounter processes having ever shorter lifetimes.

A simple resource-allocation view may be superimposed over the process view just given. The root process needs storage resources to operate with, and these resources must have longer lifetimes than those of its immediate offspring. This principle is, of course, applied recursively, giving rise to a corresponding tree of SROs having correspondingly shorter lifetimes (higher level numbers).

Logically speaking, the stack SRO provided to the root process serves as the "fund" from which resources are drawn for use by each offspring process. (For those interested, we explain the physical relationships below.) When a task issues an (implicit or explicit) request for the creation of a new task, the resources required for the corresponding offspring process are only logically allocated from a local heap SRO created by the parent.

The physical relationships among nodes of the SRO tree are as follows: All SROs, Object Tables, and PSOs for stack SROs are allocated from the global heap SRO. (The PSO component of the global heap rooting the SRO tree is shared by *all the local heap SROs* in the tree. The Claim Object component of the global heap rooting the SRO tree is shared by *all the heap SROs* in the tree. Thus, as new heap objects are allocated (deallocated) during execution in the process tree, the single claim value is decremented (incremented) appropriately. Note that the claim for a process tree is also charged for the allocation blocks of its stack SROs, but these charges are made *in advance*, i.e., when a stack SRO is created and when it becomes necessary to enlarge its allocation block.

The logical relationships among the SROs of the tree are superposed over these physical allocations by way of software-defined extensions in the SRO itself. These include *parent*, *offspring* and *sibling* references. The use of these references enables iMAX routines to update storage resource relationships in a process tree as individual processes are born, are terminated, or require more resources including more free space or lengthier Object Tables during their lifetimes.

Here we make clear why a local heap SRO is allocated to account for the stack SROs for use of spawned processes. A parent may spawn more than one process while executing in one particular context. Moreover, the order in which the offspring are created and terminated in this context cannot be determined at compile time. Therefore, keeping track of stack SROs associated with activated offspring processes requires a heap management discipline. (The Object Table in the parent process' stack SRO cannot be used to keep track of these processes.)

To be more concrete, suppose a parent process allocates only one local heap SRO when executing in a context D in which one or more offspring processes are created. (The same local heap SRO may also serve for the allocation of object instances for **access** types.) Each process spawned within context D can then be given a stack SRO, that is reachable from this local heap SRO. A parent process cannot return from context D to its caller without first being assured of the demise of each of its offspring. This assurance corresponds to being certain that all stack SROs reachable from all local heap SROs allocated in a given context have been deallocated. Only then can the local heap SRO be safely deallocated along with logical deallocation of the associated Context Object of the parent process. (The rules just stated apply as well when offspring processes become parents for their offspring.)

The important conclusion to be drawn from this lengthy discussion, is that no new lifetime strategies need be introduced when expanding storage resource allocation from a single process to a tree of processes. The same mechanisms introduced in preceding subsections, in particular the level number attributes of allocated objects and constraints over their use, still apply.

Figure 9-3 shows a process tree at a point where six processes coexist. Figure 9-4 illustrates an SRO tree representing a possible snapshot of the resource allocation history for the process tree in the preceding figure.

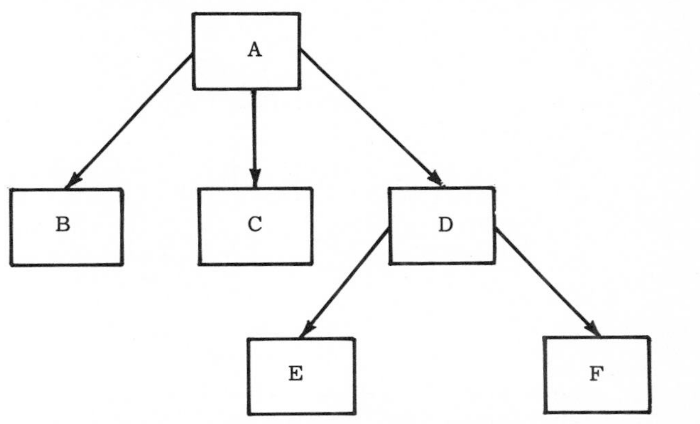

Figure 9-3 A sample process tree. Process A spawns processes B, C, and D. Process D spawns processes E and F.

Figure 9-4 reinforces what we said earlier regarding allocation of local heap SROs for use in spawning processes. In this figure it is assumed that processes B and C are both spawned while process A is executing in the same context (level 5). Stack SROs for these offspring processes are linked as immediate offspring of the same local heap SRO and acquire level numbers (6) that are each one higher than that of the parent local heap SRO. Thereafter, successive contexts for the execution of processes B and C begin with level 6. Later, while executing at level 7, process A spawns process D, using another local heap SRO

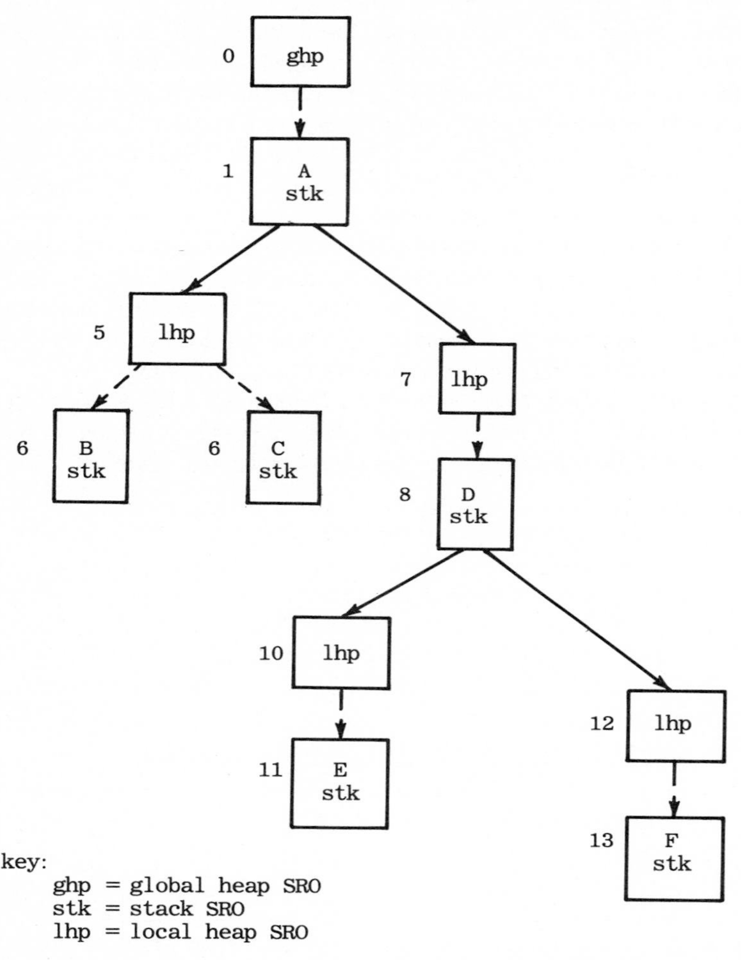

Figure 9-4 A possible SRO tree for the process tree of Figure 9-3. Level numbers are shown to the left of each SRO. Process A spawns B and C while in a context at level 5 and spawns D while in a context at level 7. Two different local heap SROs are used. Process D spawns E and F at levels 10 and 12, respectively. A created local heap SRO has a level number greater than or equal to that of its parent stack SRO, while the level number of a stack SRO is always one greater than that of its parent heap SRO.

(with level 7) to serve as the parent SRO for the stack SRO for D. (The stack SRO for D is given a level number that is one higher, i.e., 8.) The figure then suggests that in later contexts of process D, processes E and F are spawned in a similar way, and following similar level numbering rules. Note that a local heap

SRO may serve simply as a resource-management link between the stack SRO of one process R and the stack SROs of R's offspring processes; it need have no other function.

9.2.5. Some Fine Points

In this subsection, we answer five questions that may well have come up in a first reading of this material. The questions and the answers expand on some of the details we have sketched earlier.

1. Question: How does an executing process acquire more memory resources when there is no more free space in its stack SRO and more is needed? (This question assumes that the claim value for the SRO is not exhausted and that there is still space in the Object Table associated with the SRO. Such problems are examined in answer to the succeeding two questions.)

   ANSWER: Memory Management fields all storage allocation faults, and so is aware of all failing attempts to allocate objects from SROs having insufficient free space. (The hardware senses an attempt to allocate an object from an SRO that would result in a negative value in the Claim Object.) This fault is corrected when it occurs for any kind of SRO. The actual mechanism by which the fault is corrected is somewhat complex; its explanation is made easier by referring to the state transition diagram in Figure 9-5.

   The life cycle of a byte of physical storage begins in an initial ''SRO'' state. It is moved to the ''allocated in use'' state by hardware (object creation).

   - Stack allocated space is returned to the ''SRO'' state by execution of a hardware RETURN instruction.
   - A byte allocated from local heap space may go directly to the ''Free List'' state via a software-induced *return level fault* fielded by iMAX. (This is the fault required to recover space for objects from local heap space on exit from a context level in which the local heap was created.)
   - Other bytes, part of local and global objects, are garbage collected. First, they move to the ''Allocated garbage'' state, meaning they become candidates for reclamation. At some point later, the Garbage Collector process (GCOL) finds such objects and puts them on Memory Management's free list; hence the ''Free List'' state.

     Movement from the Free List to the SRO state occurs whenever Memory Management runs its Compaction algorithm. Compaction first searches SROs for ''depleted'' storage block specifiers, i.e., those having fewer than some (small) number N of free bytes. These specifiers and the space they control are removed from the SRO and placed on the free list. At this point, memory is compacted; in the process the free list may be reorganized. Finally, Compaction searches the free list for large blocks, which are placed in SROs that need them; that is, depleted SROs are "reloaded" with new (additional) resources, i.e., with new storage block specifiers.

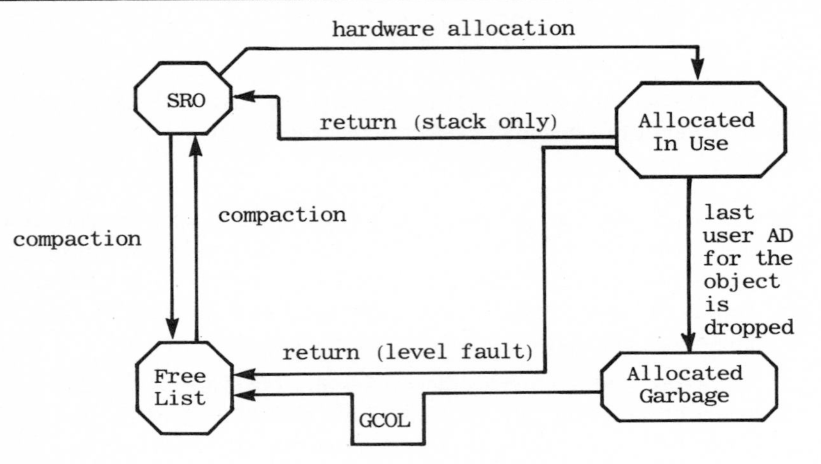

Figure 9-5 States of physical memory in the i432 Memory Management Model.

If more physical space is needed in a stack SRO using frozen memory, then no relocation (compaction) is permitted. Instead, the SRO is given an additional block of free space and its PSO is assigned another storage block specifier containing the additional space. (That specifier is then linked to the previous one(s) in the PSO.)

2. Question: How is *overflow* of an Object Table for a stack or local heap SRO dealt with? Presumably an overflow could occur if there is a need for more Object and Refinement Descriptors for the objects allocated in the SRO than there is room in the associated Object Table.

   ANSWER: The initial size of an Object Table is a constant, determined by the Operating System designers. If this size proves to be too small for some SRO, the resulting fault will invoke the appropriate module of Memory Management to correct the matter. The solution is either to enlarge the Object Table by first relocating the table and then enlarging it, or else to create an "overflow" Object Table. (Since enlargement involves relocation, Object Tables of SROs for frozen storage are expanded only by use of overflow tables. Overflow Object Tables are linked in a list, with the links held in a hidden, system-wide table called the Table of Object Tables. Finding space to enlarge the Object Table or to build an overflow table requires some of the same SRO management steps outlined in our response to the preceding question. So, we need not repeat that explanation.

3. Question: How is *underflow* of the claim value for an SRO tree dealt with? An underflow can occur whenever an already created process in the corresponding process tree needs to expand its SRO Object Table or allocation block, or when a new process and its initial storage resources must be allocated.

   ANSWER: This problem is considered one to be solved by the Process_Manager. For example, the process on whose behalf the claim value underflow is attempted can be sent as a message to its notification port, as discussed in Section 8.1.

4. Question: How are level violations avoided when SENDing messages between processes? A message is sent in the form of an Access Descriptor which is copied into the address space of the receiver. Presumably the sender does not know the level of the context in which the receiver will be executing upon receipt of the message. Moreover, since the message structure itself may contain Access Descriptors for other objects, how can the sender be sure that the receiver will not incur a level violation when attempting to copy any such Access Descriptors.

   ANSWER: In the most general case, level violations can indeed be incurred in transmitting a message from a Sender process, via a Port Object, to a Receiver process. Recall from Chapter 4 that the AD for a sent message is ultimately assigned to the Interprocess Message AD slot in the Context Object of the Receiver process. Also, the Sender must have access to the AD for the Message Object in order to send it. Therefore, if level violations are to be avoided, the lifetime of the Message Object must be comparable to or greater than those of the Sender's Context Object, the Port Object used for transmission, and the Receiver's Context Object. Moreover, if the message is to reach its destination and not be lost en route, the lifetime of the Receiver's Context Object must not end before that of the Sender's Context Object and the lifetime of the Port Object must not end before the message is received. These constraints are expressed in the following two sets of "level relationships":

   (1) level(Message Obj.) <= min(level(Sender's Context Obj.),
   level(Port Obj.),
   level(Receiver's Context Obj.))

   (2) level(Port Object)
   <= level(Receiver's Context Object)
   <= level(Sender's Context Object)

   There is no problem "living with" these constraints so long as all interprocess communication is achieved using ports created from instantiations of the iMAX Typed_Ports package described in Appendix G. Recall that messages enqueued on such ports are instances of access types declared in the same generic package that defines the port itself. Hence, all Message Objects referred to by such access variables are necessarily allocated from the same local heap SRO from which the port itself is created. Therefore, the level of the Port Object is always the same as the level of every Message Object whose AD is enqueued on it. To assure that the remaining constraints are satisfied, it is sufficient that the context in which the instance of Typed_Ports is created is the same as (or is an antecedent of) the context in which the Sender and Receiver Processes are spawned. (A programmer who chooses to use ports created from the iMAX Untyped_Ports package must exercise more care to avoid level-check violations. This tradeoff is not unreasonable.)

5. Question: Thus far, no mention has been made of Process Objects and how they are allocated when a process is created. From what SRO or SROs are Process Objects allocated? How and when are Process Objects deallocated?

   ANSWER: Process Objects (together with their lists of preallocated Context Objects) are allocated from the global heap SRO (frozen or normal). Process Objects retain level zero attributes, however preallocated Context Objects have their levels adjusted when they are logically taken off the "preallocated list" and linked into the dynamic chain. It is essential that Process Objects have level zero so that Process Management routines can manipulate them (and refer to them) without risk of incurring level violations.

   A process P terminates when it executes a RETURN instruction from its root context. By design, this return step induces a return level fault (no *return* rights in the dynamic link). Such a fault causes P's Carrier Object to be enqueued as a request on the Fault Port. The iMAX process serving the Fault Port can access P's Process Object, and through it all of P's Context Objects and other level zero objects, via P's Carrier Object. The iMAX fault handling process is able to invoke the requisite Memory Management routines to reclaim all of P's remaining storage resources.

   [To do its job, Memory Management uses the per-system Table of Object Tables mentioned in the answer to the second question in this series. This table contains a number of useful pieces of information needed to locate the related storage resources of a process. We do not go into further details here.]

9.2.6. The iMAX SRO_Manager Package

A limited but very useful subset of the SRO management functions, described in preceding subsections, is made available to users through the iMAX interface package named SRO_Manager. We give its specification in Appendix L. [A comparable and identically-named package is available for use with the virtual memory management system.]

The SRO_Manager package allows a user to create local heap SROs (from the current stack SRO) and to manage them individually. Typical users are those wishing to design and implement their own interpreters and simulators. (The Access Descriptor for the created local heap SRO is returned with *create* rights, after which the user is free to call for the removal of such rights when passing out copies of this Access Descriptor. Create rights are needed for creating new objects from a heap SRO.)

SRO_Manager does not offer the user the opportunity to create separate stack SROs, since the underlying architecture provides one for each process and there is no way for the underlying architecture to use more than one per process. However, a user is free to call for the creation of objects from either the system-provided stack SRO or from a heap SRO and to use these objects for any explicit purpose, such as for simulating stacks.

In particular, a user may create an object of specified size from any local heap SRO (or from the one global heap SRO) for which an Access Descriptor with create rights can be supplied as an argument. The Create_object (also Create_typed_object) operation applies only to local and global heap SROs. Recall that a user process P can get access to the global heap SRO associated with P by using the iMAX Process_Globals_Definitions interface package.

In addition, a user may call for the creation of ''stack objects'' from the current stack SRO using the Create_stack_object operation. (By *stack objects*, we simply mean objects that will be automatically deallocated upon exit from the context in which they were created.)

A user may also issue calls, for the creation of *refinements* for specified objects created from either the stack SRO or from a heap SRO. Thus, the operation, Create_generic_refinement, whose specification is repeated for convenience in Figure 9-6, allows the user to acquire an Access Descriptor for a refinement of any specifiable object from a heap SRO. The call also specifies the offsets and lengths for the data and access parts of the refinement.

All of the operations of this package are translated into single i432 instructions with the exception of the operation for creating a local heap SRO whose specification is repeated in Figure 9-7.

9.2.7. The Garbage Collector Process, GCOL

As mentioned in the introduction to this chapter, the ability to perform parallel garbage collection effectively is an important i432 System property. The iMAX process GCOL executes Dijkstra's ''On the Fly Garbage Collection'' algorithm [17] in parallel with most other iMAX processes and with all user processes. In this subsection we give a limited overview of the algorithm and of the i432 architectural support on which it is based. A full description of the actual i432 implementation of this algorithm is beyond the scope of interest here.

```
procedure Create_generic_refinement(
    obj:            dynamic_typed;     -- Object to be refined.
    d-offset:       short_ordinal;     -- Data part offset of the
                                       -- refinement in bytes.
    d-length:       short_ordinal;     -- Data part length of the
                                       -- refinement (in bytes) - 1.
    a-offset:       short_ordinal;     -- Access part offset of the
                                       -- refinement (number of AD slots).
    a-length:       short_ordinal;     -- Access part length of the
                                       -- refinement (number of AD slots).
    rtn:        out dynamic_typed;     -- The resulting refinement.
    sro:            storage_resource_with_create := null);
                                       -- SRO for create.
  --
  -- Function:
  --    A heap refinement is created from the specified object,
  --    with data and access parts at specified offsets, each with
  --    with specified lengths. The base type of the created
  --    refinement will be the same as the base type of the
  --    original object. Its system type will be generic.
```

Figure 9-6 Specification for operation to create a refinement of an object created from a local heap SRO.

```
function Create_local_heap
   return storage_resource;      -- AD for an SRO.
   --
   -- Function:
   --    This function creates a local heap SRO.
   --    The lifetime of the created local heap SRO is that of the
   --    Context Object for the caller.
```

Figure 9-7 Specification of the Create_local_heap operation, copied from the iMAX SRO_Management package.

The conceptual framework for this algorithm is as follows: The system is modelled as a set of "mutators" and a "collector", all potentially able to run in parallel. A mutator is a process that acquires (consumes) objects for its use from a pool of free storage and in doing so marks those objects as "in use". When the collector runs through a collection cycle, it performs two scans over all objects that can have been consumed by mutators since the last collection cycle. Each such scan is also called a "marking phase" because during these scans the collector marks the objects encountered in such a way that upon completion of the second scan, it is possible to identify by the marks found on the objects, which are garbage. These objects are then added to the free storage pool. An underlying requirement for the success of the collector algorithm is that the object structure, which may be viewed as a set of directed graphs, can be scanned completely. To accomplish this, there must be for each separate directed graph a distinguished or *root* node from which to pursue the scan of that graph to completion. The collector must have a list of such roots at its disposal. In the i432 implementation, the set of Processor Objects serves, in essence, as the requisite set of root nodes.

Understanding how the algorithm works is also based on understanding the marking scheme used by the mutators and the collector. This scheme requires tri-state marking for each object. Thought of as "colors", these states are *white*, *gray*, and *black*. (This implies that any i432 implementation scheme must provide for a two-bit field for encoding the color of an object. As explained below, these two bits are allocated in the Object and Refinement Descriptors.)

It is assumed at the outset that all free objects are marked *white* and that whenever a mutator acquires a free object, it is automatically marked *black*. Before explaining what the collector does, we note how mutator marking is implemented by the i432 hardware.

Although not previously mentioned, i432 Object (and Refinement) Descriptors contain a hardware-recognized and hardware-manipulated *reclamation bit*. (For reasons to be explained below, this same bit is also referred to in the i432 architecture literature as the *copied bit*.) When an object or a refinement is created by the processor, the reclamation bit in the corresponding Object or Refinement Descriptor, is set true, in effect changing the marking from white to black. Thus, the processor cooperates with any object-consuming process to mark *black* each newly created object (or refinement). Another important point to note about the reclamation bit is that whenever the processor executes a COPY AD instruction to copy an AD for some object T, the reclamation bit in the Object Descriptor for T is set to true. (For purposes of garbage collection, a Refinement Descriptor is regarded as representing an object that has a single AD in its access part, namely the AD for the underlying object. Hence, if COPY AD copies an AD for a refinement R of T, then the reclamation bit in the Refinement Descriptor for R is marked true, which has the effect of marking R black.)

The first marking phase of a parallel collector cycle begins by scanning all such descriptors and resetting their gray bits to white to indicate that all objects referred to by the containing descriptors are potentially garbage when discovered to be unreachable as a result of the second marking phase.

The purpose of the second marking phase is to mark all non-garbage objects *black* so that any remaining objects in the structure that are still *white* are then considered to be garbage. (Note that during the second phase a mutator executing in parallel can mark white objects gray without interfering with the plan of the collector.) The second marking phase begins by first marking *gray* all objects representing root nodes. Then all objects colored *gray* are scanned. For each of these, the object itself is re-colored *black* and all its "successor objects", i.e., all objects, if any, referred to in the access part of the blackened node, are colored *gray*. This scan over all objects colored *gray* is continued until no more *gray* objects can be found. At this point all non-garbage objects have been colored *black* and all objects still *white* are garbage. The Object Tables are scanned once again and the memory spaces for all objects still colored *white* are linked into the Free List.

The i432 Garbage Collector puts itself to sleep at the close of each collector cycle (after first invoking the appropriate module of Memory Management that needs to know the Collector is finished). How frequently the Garbage Collector is reawakened to run again is an issue to be decided by the iMAX implementers. In simple implementations, GCOL can be awakened at equally-spaced intervals of time. In more sophisticated implementations, the sleep period can be determined dynamically on the basis of various performance measures and statistics gathered by the system.

One final note of detail concerns the encoding of the three colors. In the i432 implementation, a second bit in the Descriptor is also reserved for color encoding. This bit is software defined and augments the hardware-defined *reclamation bit*. The particular encoding of the bit pair to represent the three colors, *white*, *gray*, and *black*, although cleverly done, needn't concern us here.

What is important is that the algorithm permits mutators to execute while the collector is in operation. Some garbage created by a mutator while the collector is in operation may be collected in that cycle, but is guaranteed to be collected at latest in the next cycle. The correctness of the algorithm and the implementation also assures that, no non-garbage objects can ever be mistakenly collected as garbage. The frequency at which the collector is run determines how seldom a mutator will run out of objects to consume and be temporarily forced to wait for garbage collection. For many kinds of real-world applications this kind of interruption need never occur.

We have now completed our primary overview of main memory management. In the next section we revisit this design especially to show how it may be generalized to the management of virtual memory.

9.3. Management of Virtual Memory

The model presented for the management of main memory in the i432 is generalized here in two ways. The first form of generalization is to express the management of storage resources for collections of process trees through the mechanism of an MCO or *Memory Controller Object*. The other form of generalization is to extend main memory, i.e., Real Memory, to a Virtual Memory address space that includes Real Memory. When available, either the "Real Memory Only" model or the Virtual Memory model may be used in i432 Systems; both models will be implemented to include the MCO generalization and both models will be implemented with a companion Object Filing System to form a "complete" memory, having both active and passive address spaces.

The whole of memory (real or virtual) memory may be viewed logically as a single data structure which is a collection of *Memory Controller Objects* or *MCOs*, one allocated to each user. A user can be abstractly viewed as a set of jobs (each possibly executing as a process tree). The storage resources needed for this set of jobs are represented as a "forest" of SRO trees, with each being rooted in the same global heap SRO. Hence, an MCO controls the resources implied by such a forest.

An MCO contains several parameters used to control allocations of primary and virtual memory within the resource. Certain usage statistics, and history information (counts of key events) are also maintained in the MCO. These data may be periodically examined and used as a basis for adjusting the control parameters. To simplify our discussions, the mechanism and rationale of the MCO is introduced in the context of the Virtual Memory implementation. (Where appropriate, we point out which MCO parameters have meaning only in the Virtual Memory implementation.)

Two iMAX interfaces are provided. Each provides a different view of memory, one for ordinary users (the SRO_Manager package) and one for privileged users (the MCO_Manager package) who wish to operate directly on MCOs. Some applications subsystem designers fall in the first category. Designers of high-level memory and process managers fall in the latter category.

In order to appreciate the two views of an MCO, we need to learn more about its detailed structure. We could approach this problem bottom-up by first suggesting that an MCO is merely a tree structure of SROs and focus on the management of the individual SROs in the tree and not on the management of the tree as a whole. In a sense, this is what has been done in the preceding section. We pursue this a bit further before proceeding with a top-down view of the MCO.

The concept of the process tree is, of course, independent of the scope of the System's active address space (whether limited to real memory or expanded to a virtual memory). The concept and utility of the SRO tree, matching the process tree, also carries over intact.

Even though the System's virtual address space is much larger than real memory, it is still managed as a scarce resource. Therefore, there is still the need to maintain two Physical Storage Objects (PSOs), one for normal virtual memory and one for frozen virtual memory.

[In the virtual memory system, objects allocated from the frozen global heap SRO are not only non-relocatable but also non-swappable. However, objects allocated from the normal global heap SRO are relocatable and may also be swappable. Whether or not such objects are swappable, and if so at what "frequency", depends on a *resource control parameter* that can be set for the governing MCO.]

The MCO defines one distinct section of virtual memory for the entire collection of independent processes whose resources are drawn from the specified global heap SRO—which serves as the root node of the SRO tree for that MCO.

An example SRO tree controlled by an MCO is depicted in Figure 9-8. Resources for each process tree are rooted in a stack SRO, itself an offspring of the global heap SRO.

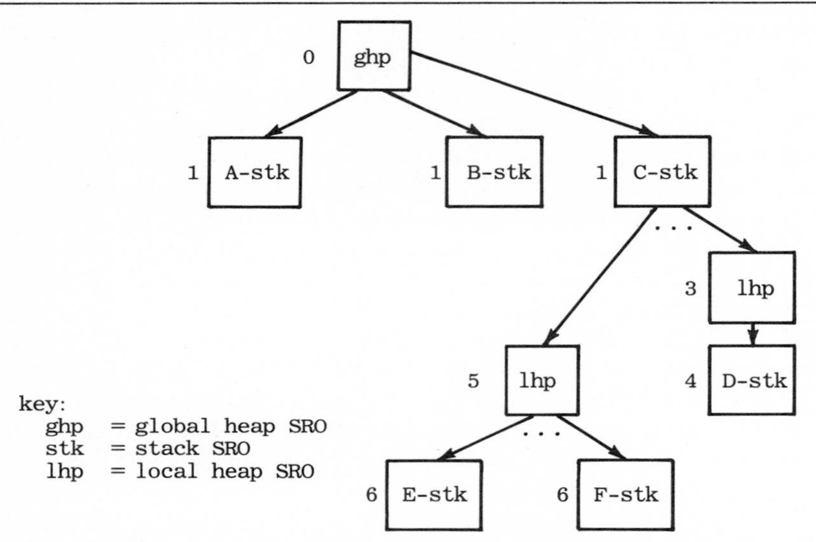

Figure 9-8 Snapshot of an SRO tree for an MCO. The virtual memory for a collection of independent processes, is allocated from the root (global heap) SRO. This figure shows the stack SROs for root processes A, B, and C. Of these, only process C shows offspring (processes D, E, and F).

In Figure 9-8 we illustrate a hypothetical case where a user's SRO tree has at least three co-existent independent processes, A, B, and C. One of these, process C, has some offspring processes, D, E, and F, as evidenced by the stack SROs that have been allocated from local heap SROs rooted in the stack SRO for process C. Since the same lifetime strategies as described in the main memory model carry over here, there should be no surprises upon examining the (hypothetical) level numbers shown in the figure for the various SROs.

As already mentioned, objects created from SROs representing *frozen* memory are themselves allocated from frozen memory. They can never be relocated or swapped out. However, objects created from SROs representing *normal* memory may exist either in primary memory or in swapping store. An object residing in primary memory has the *allocated* bit in its Object Descriptor set to true, and set to false if it either resides in swapping store or is not currently accessible due to some on-going Memory Management operation, such as relocation, which causes objects to be regarded as temporarily "invalid". Relocation may occur when Memory Management determines that compaction is needed to reduce fragmentation in primary normal memory. The object is also subject to being swapped out when free space simply becomes too scarce.

9.3.1. Controlling the Resources of an MCO

An MCO can be created, destroyed, altered, or inspected via calls to the iMAX MCO_Manager package (See Appendix L). A set of three resource control parameter values must be specified in creating an MCO. By studying these three parameters we can learn how a user would be expected to achieve high-level control over the memory resources in an i432 virtual memory system. Setting these control parameters can be done intelligently only if some gathered MCO performance statistics can be made easily accessible to the user. As we will see, these statistics are automatically updated and made accessible to a user having the appropriate type rights to the MCO.

The three resource control parameters are:

- memory type — Determines whether memory management can relocate and swap objects created from the MCO.
- scan rate — Defines the "rate" at which objects created from the MCO are considered for swapping.
- allocation limit — Determines the number of bytes of virtual memory that can be allocated from this MCO without making an explicit call to alter this value.

We have already explained the role played by "memory type" and have suggested the role of "scan rate". If the memory type is normal, then objects belonging to the MCO are relocatable (and can be swapped out if the scan rate is not *never*).

The scan rate parameter has meaning for MCOs used in a Virtual Memory implementations. When the system as a whole needs to locate objects to be swapped out, it scans the list of MCOs in the system, selecting for swapping only objects in MCOs whose scan rates are high enough. More concretely, objects belonging to MCOs with a scan rate of 1 will be considered each time the replacement algorithm passes through memory looking for objects to swap. Objects belonging to MCOs with a swapping rate of 2 will be scanned on every other pass through memory, and so on. In the current implementation there are sixteen rates defined: *asap*, 1, 2, . . . 14, and *never*.

[Setting the rate to *asap* indicates that all objects associated with this MCO are immediately swappable, regardless of reference history; setting the rate to *never* makes the object unswappable. The *ASAP* rate might be chosen for the MCO of some user U under the following scenario: A high-level load controller perceives a thrashing problem. The controller then (a) stops all processes belonging to U and then (b) requests the high-level MCO manager to set U's scan rate to *asap*, thereby expediting the swapping out of objects associated with U.]

If the allocation limit is Lim bytes, then hardware and software combine to guarantee that no more than Lim bytes of memory will be allocated for all the processes created from this MCO. (Lim measures bytes of virtual memory in Virtual Memory implementations and real memory in Real Memory Only implementations.)

The control based on Lim is achieved in a remarkably simple way, as follows: The representation of the MCO includes a reference to a hardware-recognized Claim Object. This Claim Object is assigned a specified allocation limit at MCO creation. Moreover, all SROs in the tree belonging to this MCO have their Claim Object ADs pointing to this "master" Claim Object. Each time an object is allocated from any of these SROs, the MCO Claim Object is automatically adjusted (decremented) by the hardware by the number of bytes allocated for that object. A *storage claim underflow fault* is caused if an attempted allocation would result in a negative storage claim for the affected MCO. When the Garbage Collector reclaims an object belonging to an MCO, the software increments the affected MCO by the number of bytes reclaimed.

The behavior implied by the above type of control can occasionally exhibit unexpected (and indeterminate) "pauses" brought about by the processes of a MCO allocating and deallocating objects faster than the Garbage Collector can reclaim them. That is, unless the Garbage Collector can run, find, and reclaim deallocated objects fast enough, the MCO's claim value may exhibit sporadic underflow conditions which will have no overall effect except on system response. (This phenomenon is possible because in the current implementation the Garbage Collector performs a global function and executes asynchronously with a user's processes.)

9.3.2. Resource Usage Statistics

The MCO_Manager package offers a Read_MCO_statistics function which returns a record containing the current static and dynamic "operating" statistics for a specified MCO. Component values of this record, itemized below, may be examined and used in attempts to dynamically adjust the subsequent performance behavior of the processes whose resources are governed by the MCO.

• storage_claim;	ordinal;	Total of virtual memory yet to be allocated under processor control.
• secondary;	ordinal;	Total virtual memory currently allocated and residing on disk.
• number_of_stack_SROs:	ordinal;	Same as number of active processes under this MCO.
• number_of_heap_SROs:	ordinal;	
• number_of_object_tables:	ordinal;	

- fault_rate: ordinal; Combined missing object fault rate for all processes running under this MCO.

A low-valued fault_rate suggests that the "scan rate" can be reduced (increased in frequency). (The effect of changing the current scan rate can in some cases be noted by observing the relationship between the reported values of *storage_claim* and *secondary*.)

Other feedback information of value to the "MCO controller", whether person or program, includes the reported number of stack SROs, which indicates the number of "living" processes. Performance of certain processes executing under an MCO may well be affected by the total number N of its processes, especially if N represents a large fraction of all the processes currently active in the system; in that event, the user might wish to exercise other controls on the programs themselves (e.g., to suspend, resume, or adjust scheduling parameters of some of the process trees under this MCO, using operations of the Process_Manager interface discussed in Chapter 8).

The specification part of the MCO_Manager package is given in Appendix L. iMAX also provides the lower-level interface to the SRO components of an MCO in an SRO_Manager package similar to the one already described in Section 9.2 but adjusted for use in the virtual memory implementation of SROs. Because the two SRO_Manager packages are so similar, we do not give the virtual memory version in Appendix L. Readers wishing to examine this interface may consult the iMAX 432 Reference Manual.

10 OBJECT FILING

10.1. Introduction

Our introduction to Object Filing for the i432 System was really begun with the disclosure in Section 9.1 that i432 Memory is divided into two distinct spaces, *active object space* and *passive object space*. (See Figure 9-1.) In Chapter 9 we were concerned primarily with management of the active object space. Here we consider the management of the passive space and the interface between the two spaces.

Examining the Object Filing Subsystem design allows us, finally, to view i432 object space top-down. From at least one top-most perspective, the object space appears homogeneous. Objects in active space and objects in passive space are governed by similar accessing and typing rules, structures, and mechanisms. The Object Filing Subsystem provides in software the same architecture for support of object structures, typing, and the consequent protection domains in the passive space as the hardware provides in the active space. (To be sure, as we examine object structures in more detail, there are some semantic differences, but most are inspired by implementation considerations.)

The particular role played by an object tends to determine the object space or spaces in which it resides during its lifetime. An object may be created to live, for example:

- (Case A) entirely in active space, or
- (Case B) entirely in passive space, or
- (Case C) in passive space but may be updated from new versions made active periodically from most recent passive versions, or
- (Case D) in passive space but serves only as a source for versions that enter active space, to live and die there.

From the above examples (which do not form an exhaustive list of the possibilities) we observe that, unlike virtual memory, the same object may exist simultaneously (in different versions) in both spaces. Also bear in mind that objects may be deallocated from either active or passive space. If an object is deallocated from active space, its passive counterpart, if any, survives—and vice versa. We now illustrate each of these four cases:

- Case A. All objects created in active space that are allocated with greater-than-zero level numbers live entirely in active space and are deallocated from that space. They are never transferred to the passive space. (Level-zero objects created in active space need not be "passivated", i.e., put into passive space. Passivation of such objects, as we see later, may be under user control.)
- Case B. Certain objects may be created, initialized and updated directly in the passive space using a sequence of steps bracketed by an *Open* and a *Close* operation. It is possible to prohibit such objects from entering the active space. Objects which may be too costly to activate frequently, such as large directories of other passive objects, are usually treated this way. [The Object Filing Subsystem provides for objects of type "data_file" which may be longer than 128K-bytes; these objects, managed by a separate type manager, are always treated as Case B objects that are never activated.]
- Case C. A Domain Object representing an Ada *owner package* for a small data-base is a good example. As a result of compilation, this object, together with objects holding owned data and the related Instruction Objects, are constructed as a passive composite of individual objects. Its presence in the passive store is recorded in a directory kept in the passive store. When the package is initialized on first use, the corresponding Domain Object is implicitly "activated", meaning a version is placed in active space, where it is updated either during that initialization or as a result of responding to subsequent calls, or both. During each active period, the same Domain Object, identical with respect to identification, type, and structure, exists both as an active object and as a passive object.

  When the process(es) using this owner package terminates execution and there are no more active space Access Descriptors referring to the active Domain Object, it can be transferred to passive space, effectively replacing the older version in an implicit update operation. (Assuring that this "auto-update" takes place is an option that can be specified.) Until needed again in active space, the new version in passive space will be the only extant version of the object. This cycle is repeated for each active period in the life of the Domain Object—until it is explicitly destroyed or implicitly deallocated from the passive object space by a reclamation scheme whose function is analogous to the one used for garbage collection of active space.

[The term "owner package" as used here has the sense defined in Chapter 2. Later we use the term "ownership" in a different sense, namely as an attribute of a reference to a passive-space object. (This attribute is used as a means for the efficient management of the passive object space.) The context in which "owner" appears should resolve any possible ambiguity.]

- Case D. A Domain Object representing an Ada library-level package falls in this category. This Domain Object, as in Case C, is also initially created in passive space and is periodically activated when needed. Here, however, the object is discarded when its period of activation is completed; it is not used to update the passive-space version. Two familiar subcases come to mind.

  1. The Domain Object represents a *transformer package*, such as a mathematical function library package; it has no variable declarations (although its individual subprograms may), and thus has no state that can change while in active space. Hence, the version in passive space never needs updating and will live in passive space until no longer needed (that is, until explicitly or implicitly deallocated.)

     [A program that is given a reference for the transformer package can cause activation of the corresponding Domain Object as a result of a first call on an operation of the package. Thereafter, while the Domain Object remains activated, the public operations of the shared and reentrant Domain Object may be repeatedly invoked by calls from the same or other packages or tasks belonging to the same or independent programs.]
  2. The Domain Object represents a library *owner package*, X. Because X owns data that can be modified during use by a referencing program, a new active space version, i.e., a fresh library copy of X's corresponding Domain Object is created each time a different executing program accesses X. Hence, several active versions of X's Domain Object may coexist in the active object space. (Within a single program, however, X can be shared by two or more processes, but only with care for proper arbitration over access to X's shared data.) Domain Objects for such library packages as X do not need to be saved in passive space. Each new program execution that needs access to X must be guaranteed access to the library package in its initial condition.

Notice that for Cases C and D, by maintaining (possibly older) versions of objects in passive space, a system crash may well leave the active space in an unreliable state but will always leave the passive space undamaged. Therefore, recovery from a system crash is always feasible, provided the secondary storage medium used for the passive space is highly reliable. Also notice that for Case B, where an object lives its entire life in passive space, proper synchronization of multiple (apparently concurrent) attempts to access the passive object, for either reading, initializing, or updating it, can assure users of the system that consistency is preserved. Passive space consistency is also preserved for other classes of objects.

These key design objectives: (1) recoverability from system crashes and (2) consistency preservation, (3) over a space of objects belonging to a wide variety of (user-definable) types, are simple to appreciate conceptually. Object Filing achieves in the i432 implementation, but not without a price paid in the complexity of the required mechanisms needed to accomplish the objectives efficiently.

One may rightly ask, "Do not other commercial systems also achieve the same objectives?" The response is *almost*. Usually, some component of the "triad" is deemphasized or even sacrificed. For example, limiting the emphasis on achieving crash recoverability, as in the IBM System/38 [28, 29], or failure to provide a uniform means for dealing with a variety of object types with concomitant protection domains, as in the Tandem system [5], or both, as in Multics [44], are usually evidenced even in advanced systems.

[Several successful commercial systems provide "one-level" (in our terminology, one-space) stores, in which virtual memory is suuficiently large to serve both as an object store and as a file store. Such systems are vulnerable to crashes in which key references to objects in secondary store are lost from volatile store at crash time, leading to the loss of the entire object space. Such systems must rely on recovery schemes based on the use of backup copies and complex data structures (such as transaction journals) that must be maintained to use these backup copies. In most cases, the quality of the recovery is only as good as the frequency with which backup copies are made.]

This completes our general introduction to the nature of and motivation for object filing. The next section explains some of the problems common to the design of object filing systems and how they are generally met in the i432 subsystem. Section 10.3 examines the user interface to the i432 Object Filing Subsystem, a listing for which is given in Appendix M. Section 10.4 briefly revisits the design of our Portfolio Management application to consider what changes are in order in the light of object filing, while Section 10.5 serves as a short summary of this chapter and of the book as a whole.

10.2. Design Challenges for Object Filling

The designers of any successful object filing system must have solved a collection of challenging implementation problems. In turn, these solutions often hinge on the development of effective mechanisms. This is also true for the i432 Object Filing Subsystem. We introduce some of these problems in this section. In several cases, we explain some of the mechanisms employed in their solutions. Such detail is given primarily where it can help system programmers understand how to take advantage of iMAX's user interface for Object Filing.

10.2.1. Unique Object Identifiers

The number of objects in the System's object space at any one time may never be very large, but certainly the total number of objects created may grow to a very large number over the life of an i432 System. For this reason, a means must be found to generate unique object identifiers (internal names). These identifiers must retain their significance not only over time, but also across significant boundaries of the system.

Thus, to avoid confusion, when an object is deleted from a system its unique identifier (UID) should not be re-used to refer to some object created later. While it exists, an object must retain its identity whether residing in active space or passive space and, if the latter, whether physically residing on one storage device or another, whether connected to one peripheral subsystem or another of the same i432 System, or to a peripheral subsystem of some quite distinct i432 System.

The key to keeping track of objects as they are transferred across the boundary from active to passive space, or vice versa, is the use of unique identifiers. The system maintains an *Active Object Directory* (or AOD) for recording the presence of objects in active space, and a (much larger) *Passive Object Directory* (or POD) for recording the presence of objects in passive space. (The POD itself effectively resides only in the passive space and is subdivided, one per structure.) When an object is activated from the passive address space, an entry for it is created and placed in the AOD. That entry contains the UID for the object and its *Active Access Descriptor*. Correspondingly, when an active object is no longer needed, its entry in the AOD is eliminated. If, however, an active object, no longer needed in the active space, is needed to update its version in the passive space (i.e., needs to be made passive), the appropriate place for it in the passive space is determined by its POD entry. (A UID contains both a logical-device *id* that selects the appropriate POD and a logical address of the object's POD entry, so the mapping from UID to POD entry can be done efficiently.)

Finding ways to generate such unique internal names, to search for objects based on these names, and eventually to delete these names, requires a relatively complex underlying mechanism. A detailed explanation is not appropriate here because, by design, UIDs are not in any way accessible to the user, any more than is the circuitry of the i432 processor. (An explanation is found elsewhere [47].)

10.2.2. Symbolic (Logical) Names for Objects

Objects must not only be uniquely named internally, but they must also have *external symbolic* names. These symbolic names can then be used in the process of linking one component of a program structure to another. (Such external symbolic names are also referred to as *logical names*.) It is important that two or more different objects can have the *same symbolic name*, for example a version of an operating system module and a replacement version. Often, it is the symbolic name of an object that appears in the source program. This name is then preserved by the compiler as a literal constant and may be used as an argument in the activation of a directory search routine when it becomes necessary later to complete a link to the object denoted by that external symbolic name. Two examples come to mind:

1. Suppose some user program (''User_billing'') is activated each week to perform a billing function, and further suppose that User_billing is designed to access a system-supplied library level package named ''Sys_Accounting''. The user properly deserves the assurance that each weekly activation of User_billing will access the latest version of Sys_Accounting. The i432 Object Filing Subsystem is designed to achieve the *dynamic* (symbolic) *linking* of User_billing to Sys_Accounting, and the *dynamic unlinking* of these two modules whenever User_billing is deactivated.

2. Consider two separate i432 Systems S1 and S2. Suppose a user program is represented as a single composite ''A'' in the passive store of S1 (on some storage device.) This device is then dismounted from S1 and mounted on S2. Later, the user activates ''A'' under control of the iMAX version in current use on S2. Object ''A'', when last passivated in S1, was unlinked from the iMAX modules of S1; hence, when activated on S2, it should be dynamically re-linked to the corresponding iMAX modules of S2. These modules are physically (and possibly logically) different from those on S1, but have the same symbolic names as those on S1.

The symmetry of dynamic linking and unlinking is achieved in the i432's Object Filing Subsystem using the mechanism of Link Objects interposed between the referring object and its referent (intended target). A Link Object is a Typed Object (of type ''Link'') that contains the symbolic name of the referent. A POD entry for some referent X that has an associated Link Object will actually point to the Link Object for X rather than to X itself. Calling the Directory Manager to retrieve X by specifying its symbolic name causes the return of a valid Active AD for X. (In the process of obtaining this AD, X's Link Object is said to be ''evaluated''.) Later, an attempt to store this AD for X in some other passive space object Y will result in the storing of a Passive AD for X's Link Object, and not an AD for X itself. This Passive AD is later invalidated as part of the unlinking process that occurs when the referring object is deactivated. (Link Objects are themselves never activated.) A more complete explanation of this mechanism is given elsewhere [47].

[Some earlier filing systems, such as on Multics, introduced dynamic linking via ''link segments'' but lacked the object-based architectural support to make dynamic unlinking practical.]

10.2.3. Composites for Solving the ''Small Object Problem''

Object-based architectures encourage the creation of large numbers of relatively small objects. (Earlier studies on other systems [6, 53] indicate the average size of program components is only two or three hundred bytes). Maintaining small objects in permanent store and repeatedly activating (and deactivating) them one by one in large numbers can incur sizable space and performance penalties.

As suggested in Section 9.1, the solution pursued for the i432 Object Filing Subsystem is to rely on the use of *composites* to minimize these penalties. A composite represents a single logical entity in permanent store. (We discuss some of the details of composites at the end of this subsection.) When a composite must be activated (passivated), the entire group of simple objects that comprise the composite is activated (passivated) as one action.

A composite may be referenced externally only via its *root*. Thus, a user's Working Directory will consist primarily of entries representing composites. A familiar scenario will illustrate how a composite would be referenced:

- John Smith logs on to the System for the purpose of executing the program named "Ours". We assume that Smith has a Working Directory named "J_Smith" and that this directory is searched for a match on the symbolic name "Ours". The matched entry would contain the unique identifier (UID) for the composite representing the program Ours.
- The System will then determine whether or not Ours is currently active; it may be active if some other user who shares Ours happens to be executing it. (Ours is currently active if there is an entry containing its UID in the system-wide Active Object Directory (or AOD). If so, then that entry also contains an active AD for Ours.)
- If Ours is not currently in the active space, then the information found in the directory J_Smith will be used to determine which logical device holds Ours. (For each logical device used for the permanent file store, the System will maintain a directory of passive objects (POD) held on it. The particular POD is accessed directly from an index in the UID and the entry so found will contain the file store address of the root object of Ours).
- An implicit activation procedure then causes the root object of Ours and each of its components to be activated. As each of these is activated, all intra-composite and inter-composite references are converted to active ADs within the objects so activated.

[The following may help explain the above procedure. There is a difference between the activation time of an AD for an object and the activation time of the object itself. The activation of the AD occurs whenever the AD is moved to the active space; an appropriate AOD entry is made, and any links involved are evaluated, etc. However, the object itself still remains in the passive space. Later, when an attempt is made to reference the object using the AD, auto-activation will "copy" the object into the active space. As part of this copying process, any ADs to objects in the composite will be activated by the process just described. In this way, all ADs to objects in the composite will be fully resolved (since all objects in the composite are activated); however, for inter-composite references, the ADs are activated but not the objects to which they refer.]

The passive space versions for some or all of the components of a composite undergoing deactivation may need to be updated. The mechanisms for determining if an object's passive version needs to be updated and how it should be done are discussed in greater detail at the end of this subsection. Briefly, however, the idea is as follows: If the object X is a typed object, then its TDO will be consulted in performing the deactivation of X. X's type manager may have placed in X's TDO a port AD and an AD for a procedure D to be used in passivating X. The port AD is used to send X to a service process P defined by X's type manager, and hence to perform passivation as an asynchronous action. (P will then call the defined passivation procedure to operate on X.) Passivation can also be performed synchronously by invoking the AD for procedure D directly.

10.2.3.1 Additional Details on Composites.

- An important (implementation-driven) design decision is that no component of a composite (other than the root) may be referenced from outside the composite. Hence, the root of a composite has an entry in the Passive Object Directory but its components do not. A composite must be stored in toto on a single logical storage structure.

  Object Filing deals with logical disk structures, not physical devices. A single logical disk structure may actually be composed of several physical disk devices. Alternatively, several logical disk structures can reside on a single physical disk. Object Filing maintains a POD for each of possibly many logical disk structures on the system.

  [The decision to "confine" each composite to a logical structure facilitates efficient transfer of passive information into primary memory, as the transfer of an entire composite can be made in one logically indivisible operation. Since composites can be very large, they are not stored contiguously on disk. Rather, they are broken up into (4KB) chunks, the first containing pointers to the others. A small composite (<4K bytes) is transferable with a single disk operation.]

- A composite passive object comes into existence by stepwise construction, one object at a time, beginning with its root object—which may, of course, contain both data and *Passive Access Descriptors* (PADs). An *action* must be selected and associated with the storing of each PAD in the root object. If the action is "component", the object whose PAD is being stored becomes part of the composite. (Of course, PADs to other composites, either already defined or about to be defined, may also be stored in the root.)

  Suppose, for example, A is the root and B is to be made a component of A's composite. Using appropriate Object Filing operation sequences to be described in a later section (e.g., Open A for writing, . . .), various PADs can be stored in A. In particular, a PAD for B will be stored in A using the "component" action. These representations can then be completed using the appropriate Object Filing operation sequences (e.g., Open B for update, . . .).

If B is to point to other objects that should be part of A's composite, then a similar sequence of Object Filing operations will be performed on B as was performed on A (e.g., Open B for writing, . . .). By selecting the "component" action for a PAD stored in B, the object referred to becomes a component of B's (and thus A's) composite. The definition of a composite proceeds in this recursive fashion, each object in the composite being defined individually after its "parent" is defined.

- The root of a composite and its individual components, are normally made part of active space by a purely implicit mechanism, simply by referencing their contents; the activation occurs automatically, as in the handling of a Virtual Memory fault. As suggested earlier, activation of an object has the effect of creating an entry for the referenced passive object in the Active Object Directory.

[The contents of a passive object can also be transferred to active space explicitly, following a more "primitive" route. For example, let X be an object currently in passive space for which there currently exists no Active AD. First, a Passive Access Descriptor for X, typically obtained by a directory lookup operation, is converted into an Active AD for X. (A side effect of this operation is the creation of an Object Descriptor for X.) With the Active AD, it is possible to open X for reading. Subsequent retrieval operations can then be invoked to copy data and ADs from the passive version of X into any specified destinations of the active space.]

10.2.3.2 Mechanisms for Making Active Objects Passive. We now return to the question raised earlier: "How does the system know what active objects of level-zero should be passivated, and when and how are they passivated?" Here we provide a more detailed answer.

The key design principle is that passivation decisions and actions for a Typed Object are under control of its type manager. In the absence of a passivation subprogram in the type manager, the usual case for type managers written by casual users, system-provided default functions will be applied.

When a Typed Object X is to be subject to Object Filing, the information placed in the TDO (by X's type manager) can include an Access Descriptor for a special port. The port is called a *passivation filter*. If such a port reference is supplied, then X's type manager will also have activated a Passivation Process to receive messages at the port. (In addition to supplying an AD for the passivation filter for X, there may also be deposited in a prespecified slot in X's TDO an AD for an appropriate passivation procedure.) We now indicate how this information is used.

Suppose, for example, the active-space Garbage Collector process has discovered that a certain level-zero object X is no longer reachable. Rather than directly sending an AD for X as a message to Memory Management, indicating that X's space can now be reclaimed, the Garbage Collector first determines (by examining a software-defined bit in X's Object Descriptor) if there currently exists a version of X in passive space. If so, a message to passivate X is sent to the passivation filter. It is assumed that the Passivation Process receiving X has access to a procedure specified by X's type manager which is to be invoked to perform the required passivation operations on X.

In the event that X contains ADs to other (unreachable) typed objects, Y, Z, etc., of different types than X, the Passivation Process may not need to send Y, Z, etc., to their respective filters. Instead, calls can be executed directly on the passivation procedures for Y, Z, etc. Such synchronous action is possible whenever the TDO for one of these objects also contains the AD for the appropriate passivation procedure. If no such procedure reference is supplied in the TDO, then the system supplies a default passivation procedure which updates the passive version of the object before completing the deallocation of the active object.

A special type-specific passivation procedure designed by the type manager is usually used to ensure that objects are in a consistent state before passivation. (When invoked, a passivation procedure can conceivably also gather usage statistics. Thus, billing information can be accumulated, or special purpose messages can be sent to other processes providing them with up-to-date usage information.)

10.2.4. Efficient Management of Passive Object Space

How should passive objects be reclaimed? The i432 designers have recognized certain practical obstacles that prevent efficient and effective garbage collection of passive space using the same type of algorithm employed for the management of active space. We mention here some of the more obvious of these obstacles. Foremost is the matter of I/O overhead. Passive objects may be scattered over a number of different, possibly dismountable, structures. To identify objects that are no longer referenced, it would be necessary to chase chains of Passive Access Descriptors through these objects, perhaps across system sites. Under the best of circumstances, therefore, such action can involve lengthy searches and include numerous lengthy I/O requests. (Passive Access Descriptors will tend to spread through networks of passive objects just as Active Access Descriptors are spread through networks of active objects.) Hence, not only can we expect high I/O overhead, but also too much time may be consumed in freeing up space, allowing unreachable objects to remain too long in the system and perhaps leading to what may be unacceptable operational delays.

The solution adopted is to reduce greatly the number of Passive Access Descriptors that are relevant to the reclamation process that operates over the passive space. This is done by including an *ownership* right in Passive Access Descriptors and by legislating that:

- among all the PADs that can reference a passive space object X, only one PAD can contain *owner* rights for X,
- although PADs without *owner* rights can reference objects on other structures, a PAD with *owner* rights must be on the same structure as the object it references, and
- when an object is no longer reachable by a PAD having *owner* rights, the object becomes reclaimable.

The "single-owner-only" rule can conceivably be restrictive in rare cases, but the implementation tradeoffs strongly favor accepting this restriction. In this scheme each time an unreachable passive space object X is deleted, all other passive space objects referenced from "owner" PADs within X can also be deleted. This approach involves relatively little search overhead. (A more complete discussion of the implementation tradeoffs leading to the single-owner-only scheme is not attempted here.)

10.2.5. Maintaining Consistency of a Collection of Objects across Updates

A major challenge, the fifth and last in the series listed here, is how to maintain the consistency of the entire system object space, given that (a) a crash can occur at a point where an update action on a collection of objects is incomplete and (b) independently executing programs may interfere with one another in the course of updating collections of objects.

The i432 solution to this problem builds on two prior design choices and on the introduction of a third strategy (and mechanism) specific to the solution.

- First, object space is already cleanly divided between active and passive space, so that any crash that occurs while updating active space objects cannot impair the integrity and consistency of the passive space.
- Second, the introduction of composites into the passive space design suggests that the scope of passive space update actions be defined in terms of composites and not in terms of their individual components. Hence, even if there were no way to prevent the introduction of an inconsistency, it should be comparatively easy to isolate the region of inconsistency just to those (probably few) composites that are affected by the update and replace or reconstruct only these objects using available backup information.
- Third, the application of *Atomic Actions* to collections of composites completely prevents partial updating—and hence prevents the introduction of inconsistencies caused either by system crashes or by overlapping query and updating actions. Controlling the references to the passive representations of objects using Atomic Actions serves as a needed synchronizing mechanism among concurrently executing processes that share objects in the passive address space.

At a very high level, an Atomic Action, also called a *Transaction* in iMAX terminology, is nothing more than a framework in which a set of individual interactions with objects in the passive space can be conducted in a controlled way. In particular, if the passive object space is in a consistent state before the Transaction, the passive object space is guaranteed to be in a consistent state at the end of the Transaction. Moreover, by its nature, one Transaction cannot "interfere with" another one. Users who expect to make explicit use of a type manager do not need to know how the Transaction framework is implemented. The users only need to know how to set up and use the Transactions.

The remainder of this subsection elaborates the new concepts and mechanisms needed to understand how the synchronization scheme is implemented. Some readers may wish to skip this discussion on a first reading. We elaborate on the meaning of *Atomic Actions* and in so doing also introduce the concept of *pseudo-temporal environments*. Both of these ideas have recently been studied and extended in proposals by Reed [49, 50] as a basis for synchronizing operations over databases in distributed computing systems. While Reed's proposals are ambitious and unproven in practice, they are applied in the i432 System under circumstances that are carefully restricted, and hence have a much higher probability of becoming a practical success.

An Atomic Action, as defined by Reed [50], "... is a computation that, although composed of primitive computational steps, cannot be decomposed from the point of view of computations outside of the Atomic Action ... The Atomic Action simplifies the task of coping with unplanned concurrency and failure ... Atomic Actions remain atomic in the face of failure; that is, if a failure occurs that prevents the completion of an Atomic Action, the state of all data the Atomic Action has attempted to modify must appear to all other observers to be the state that obtained prior to starting the Atomic Action."

When an i432 program needs to execute a series of (higher-level) operations on one or more passive (composite) objects, the individual operations, and all their substeps are grouped and executed as a single Atomic Action, i.e., a Transaction. This assures that no other program can destructively interfere, or be interfered with in a destructive way, as a result. As we will see shortly, the iMAX Operating System enforces the use of such Atomic Actions on passive objects, since all requests for operations on passive objects must be "filtered" through interface packages.

After any Atomic Action is initiated and before it completes, it may be explicitly aborted by the program that invokes it, or be implicitly aborted as a result of any kind of failure including a time-out or a system crash, without creating a net change to the passive object (or objects) involved in the Atomic Action. An Atomic Action is completed only upon successful execution of a *Commit* operation. This operation puts into effect all the changes produced in the form of tentative new versions of the passive objects involved in that Atomic Action.

The Atomic Action mechanism is successfully implemented by completing all its steps in a distinct section of modelled time (not real time), called *pseudo time*. The recording of events in pseudo time is controlled by a mechanism which Reed has called a *Pseudo Temporal Environment*, or PTE. (Pseudo times are used to replace real time only during Atomic Actions. The use of a PTE assures that all the pseudo times for one Atomic Action fall in an interval that is distinct from all other intervals of pseudo time during which other such Atomic Actions may occur.)

A good way to understand pseudo time is to understand its three key attributes: (We again quote (and paraphrase) from Reed.)

1. A *read* operation from a passive object returns the value written by the latest pseudo-time ordered *write* operation that precedes the *read*.
2. If two steps, A and B, of a computation are ordered such that A precedes B, then, within an Atomic Action, the pseudo time of A is strictly less than the pseudo time of B. (This property ensures that sequential programs still behave the way they would were real-time orderings used.)
3. Pseudo-time orderings correspond to real-time orderings whenever events occur far enough apart in real time. That is, we don't care what pseudo time ordering is assigned to nearly simultaneous events that are not ordered parts of the same computation. We do care that two events, observed to be ordered in the real world, that is, from outside the system, would be ordered in the modelled or pseudo time in the same way.

The pseudo time for an event is determined by generating it from a Pseudo Temporal Environment. It is therefore natural to inquire about PTEs to learn what they are and how they work. However, a little thought suggests that we don't have to know much about PTEs, other than how to use them.

One can think of each PTE as a special clock function that returns pseudo times when requested that fall in a guaranteed-to-be-distinct interval. This "clock" is an abstraction that can be represented as a **private** data type, specified in an Ada package. Of course, the implementation of the PTE data type would be hidden. This is precisely the approach taken in the iMAX Object Filing Subsystem, where a user interface package, Transaction_Manager, is available. Use of this package allows one to acquire Access Descriptors for newly created PTEs upon request. [Reed has provided the details of one example implementation.] In the i432 implementation, PTEs are referenced by access variables of type "transaction".

With the foregoing as the essential background concepts, we are now ready to describe more precisely what a Transaction is and how it is used in the i432

Object Filing Subsystem. Hereafter, we consistently substitute "Transaction" for "Atomic Action".

10.3. Performing Transactions Using the IMAX Interface Packages

To perform a Transaction, two interface packages are used:

- Transaction_Manager — To Create a Transaction, and later to either Abort it or Commit it.
- Passive_Store_Manager — To perform operations such as Update, Passivate, Open, Close, Put, Get, etc., on active and passive versions of objects.

10.3.1. The iMAX Transaction_Manager Package

A user first calls Start_transaction to instantiate a new Transaction and to obtain an AD for it. This Transaction will remain accessible until the user later calls Abort_transaction or Commit_transaction, which cause the specified Transaction to be "decommissioned." (No more pseudo-times will be issued from it.) More importantly, Abort_transaction would be called to cancel the Transaction produced thus far and Commit_transaction would be called to close out the Transaction.

Both Abort_transaction and Commit_transaction also have the effect of *Close*ing out all passive objects that have been *Open*ed for this Transaction by a call to the Passive_Store_Manager. (In particular, objects that were opened for "read" are automatically closed; those opened for "write", however, must have been closed explicitly, else the commit will fail.)

The remaining operation of Transaction_Manager is the function Transaction_info, which returns a record of useful information concerning the specified Transaction. This record includes the Transaction's print name, its state (whether active, committed, or aborted), the time remaining before mandatory abortion, the number of passive objects currently associated with the specified Transaction, and whether or not the specified Transaction is currently *blocked* waiting for an Open operation to succeed. (Open operations are explained in the succeeding subsection.) The specifications for Transaction_Manager are given in Appendix M along with the specifications for Passive_Store_Manager.

10.3.2. The iMAX Passive_Store_Manager Package

The operations of this package can be grouped into two major categories. The first is a simple interface to Object Filing that allows users to explicitly specify how or whether an active space object should be passivated. The remaining operations, which fall into several subcategories, are provided for a user or a type manager that needs to directly manipulate a passive version of an object. Figures 10-1 and 10-2 list the public operations of this package in each of the two major categories.

Operation	Explanation
Update	Makes a specified passive space object agree with its active version.
Reset_active_version	Deletes the specified active version so that the next reference to the object causes a fresh copy to be made from the latest passive space version.

Figure 10-1 Active-version operators of the Passive_Store_Manager package. Both operators allow specification of a Transaction.

The protocol for use of the active-version operators listed in Figure 10-1 requires that the caller either specify a previously created Transaction as an argument or default that argument. In the latter case, Object Filing automatically generates a new Transaction to ''surround'' the active-version operation. For example, the following sequences are functionally equivalent:

```
Start_transaction(my_transaction);
  Update(my_object, my_transaction);
Commit_transaction(my_transaction);
```

and (simply)

```
Update(my_object);
```

A specified passive store object to be Updated must be *known* to the passive space; i.e., either a PAD with *owner* rights exists for the object, or the object is a component of a composite that has been Opened in either write or update mode using the same Transaction. The new passive version that is produced (resulting from Update) is not ''committed'' until the specified Transaction is itself committed.

The procedure Reset_active_version provides the mechanism for explicitly discarding unreachable level-zero active space objects which might otherwise be implicitly passivated via the passivation filter mechanism described in Section 10.2. Thus, the procedure call

```
Passive_Store_Manager.Reset_active_version(my_object, my_transaction);
```

ensures, provided that my_transaction is later committed, that any subsequent reference to my_object will cause it to be restored from its last passive version.

Sub-category	Operation	Explanation
Open and Close	Open	Opens the passive version of an object for read, write, or update. Only one such version can be open for write or update.
	Close	Closes the opened passive version.
Put and Delete	Put_data	Transfers data from an active space object to a passive space object.
	Put_ access_descriptor	Stores a specified AD in a passive space object.
	Put_list_of_ access_descriptors	Stores a specified block of ADs in a passive space object.
	Delete_ access_descriptor	Deletes a specified AD from a passive space object.
	Copy_ access_descriptor	Copies an AD from one passive space object to another.
Get operations	Get_data	Transfers data from a passive space object to an active space object.
	Get_ access_descriptor	Returns a specified AD from a passive space object.
Miscellaneous operations	Get_passive_ definition_info	Returns characteristics and state of a specified passive space object.
	Associate_link	Binds a specified link object to a specified passive space object.
	Set_auto_copy	Changes the "auto_copy" attribute of a passive object's link object.
	Set_not_copyable	Changes the "copyable" attribute of a passive object to false.
	Set_not_activatable	Changes the "activatable" attribute of a passive object to false.

Figure 10-2 Passive space manipulation operators of the Passive_Store_Manager.

(This reset mechanism is particularly useful for compilers that must guarantee the constancy of Domain Objects for library packages, as discussed under Case D, Section 10.1.)

The protocol for using the passive space manipulation operators listed in Figure 10-2 requires that the affected passive versions first be Opened for that type of operation. Thus, the caller first Opens a specified passive object X, for a given access mode, for example

```
handle_1 := Passive_Store_Manager.Open(my_object, write, my_transaction);
```

or

```
handle_2 := Passive_Store_Manager.Open(my_object, update);
```

Opening a passive object returns its *passive_definition*, i.e., a "handle" on a version of the passive object. (The handle is of private type "passive_definition".)

Note that the implementation of Open automatically generates a Transaction for this operation in the event an argument for this optional parameter is not supplied. (There is also a fourth (optional) Open parameter, a time_out value, which the caller can supply. This is the amount of time Open should be allowed to remain blocked before aborting it, in case my_object happens already to be Opened for write or update. Providing the opportunity to supply time_out values on Opens (and on Start_transactions) helps users avoid deadlock. Of course, a malicious user can still specify lengthy time_out values.)

An access mode may have one of the three values listed in the following definition of type open_mode.

```
type open_mode is
  -- The type of access requested in doing an Open operation.
    (read,       -- Only read requests will be permitted on the
                 -- passive definition.

     write,      -- Read and write requests will be permitted on the
                 -- passive definition. A new version is created
                 -- ab initio.

     update);    -- Read and write requests permitted on the
                 -- passive definition.
```

To succeed with an invocation of Open, the caller-supplied reference for the object to be Opened must have rights commensurate with the specified open_mode. For example, the caller's AD must have *read* and *write* rights if the access_mode is "write" or "update"; otherwise, *read* rights are sufficient.

The handle returned by an Open refers to a version of the desired passive object. Each version has associated with it the times it was last opened for reading and for writing.

Executing an Open for "reading" selects the most recent version whose open-for-write time is less than the Transaction time specified in this Open operation. (The current Open request will, however, block if the selected version is (now) being written and if its open-for-writing time is earlier than the Transaction specified in this Open.) Concurrent activations of an Open request for reading of the same same passive space object are permitted. When the last outstanding Open on an older version of a passive object is Closed, that version is deleted.

Executing an Open for ''writing'' will produce a new version. The specified Transaction must, however be later than the open-for-read and open-for-write times (if any) for the most recently committed version. If not, the Object Filing System ''refuses'' this request, since writing values associated with an earlier time would imply that those previously read values, marked by a later time, are erroneous. If the specified Transaction is indeed later than the open time of the most recent version, the Open is permitted, but may be required to wait until the most recent version, if currently Opened, is either committed or aborted. This is because Object Filing assures that Opens for writing may not overlap in time. Blocked Open requests are queued in order of their specified Transactions. (In short, only one Open at a time is allowed for writing into a given passive object. Only after the associated Transaction is either committed or aborted can another Open for writing into the same passive object be permitted.)

A Transaction associated with an Open cannot be committed until all the Opened objects have been closed. The Close operation assures that the corresponding Opened object is in a consistent state and may therefore be installed as a new passive version. Objects that have only been Opened for reading do not have to be explicitly Closed. Failure to invoke the Close operation ''promptly enough'' for an object opened for write or update can cause the current Open to be aborted, as explained in the next paragraph.

Since Open operations may be blocked awaiting completion of other Transactions that involve the same passive definition, the current Open call is allowed to be timed-out. (If the caller fails to specify a time-out argument value, the system will supply a default value.) A Transaction fails, and will be aborted to avoid deadlock, if an Open (or any other step) associated with this Transaction times out.

A Transaction may be used to place an active space object X in passive space that does not currently have a passive version. This is done in steps: first, a Passive AD with *owner* rights for X is stored into some other object that already exists in passive space (using the Put_access_descriptor operation). Next, X is Updated. [A more ''lengthy route'' can be taken. Instead of Updating X, one can instead Open it in write mode. The effect of this Open operation is to create a new passive object of the same size and type as the active space object X. Once the new passive space object has been created in this way, other Put operations (Put_data and Put_access_descriptor) can be called to transfer data values and Access Descriptors into the passive version.]

Once an existing passive object has been Opened for either reading, writing or updating, various other operations may be performed. For example, Put and Get operations may be used, depending on the Open's access-mode. Put operations would be used to assign values to a newly created passive object. Figure 10-3 illustrates the specifications for the operations Put_data.

A similar operation, Put_data_file, can be used to assign values to objects of type data_file. The specification for this operation is not illustrated here because it belongs to a different iMAX interface package. Nevertheless, it seems appropriate to remind the reader that Object Filing also includes management of the non-activatable type data_file, instances of which may be as large as 2**32 bytes. (Note that ordinary passive space objects are *not* expandable; however, passive space data_file objects *are* expandable though they are never activatable.) The corresponding Get operations have nearly identical specifications, except for the intended direction of transfer.

```
procedure Put_data(
    psv_def:     passive_definition; -- An object's passive definition.
    act_buf:     dynamic_typed;      -- Active object containing data.
    psv_disp:    passive_data_segment_displacement := 0;
                                     -- Displacement into "psv_def".
    sz:          active_data_segment_size := -1;
                                     -- Number of bytes to  transfer from
                                     -- "act_buf" to "psv_def". (Default
                                     -- means copy all of "act_buf".)
    act_disp:    active_data_segment_displacement := 0);
                                     -- Displacement into "act_buf".
--
-- Function:
--    Data is transferred from an active object to a passive object.
```

Figure 10-3 Example specification of Put_data operation. Put_data transfers data into a version of a passive object.

A key point to remember about Transactions as implemented in the i432 Object Filing Subsystem is that more than one passive_definition may be opened with the same Transaction. In this way, a user can lock out other processes from accessing a collection of related (composite) objects while the Transaction is in progress. To assure that synchronization works as expected, a Transaction value awarded to a process by Transaction_Manager.Start_transaction should be kept local to the process that requests it. Thus, it would be a mistake for one process to send another a copy of a Transaction reference if both processes might then engage in the same Transaction on the same objects as this joint activity could totally defeat the objective of synchronization.

Before closing this section, we comment on the process of activating passive version objects, in part to give one practical reason why it is not always desirable to allow a passive version object to be activated. The process of activating an object involves the construction of an Object Descriptor for each AD stored in the object. The ''valid'' bit in each such Object Descriptor is set false to indicate that the underlying object is not in main memory and a software-defined bit in the Object Descriptor is set to indicate that a version of this underlying object exists in the passive object space. Copying of the contents of such underlying objects from passive space to active space is then triggered by ensuing ''presence'' faults and accomplished by a fault handling mechanism similar to the one used in virtual memory management. Since the overhead for constructing an Object Descriptor is not insignificant, objects like directories that contain large numbers of Passive ADs are made *non-activatable*. Retrieval, i.e., activation, of individual Passive ADs from such a directory can be done using the Get_access_descriptor operation.

This concludes our all-too-brief overview of the Object Filing Subsystem planned for the i432. It deserves a more complete exposition, but our book is already a long one. Reinforcement of the foregoing discussions can be accomplished by a review of Appendix M. The reader is also directed to the open literature [47] and to the iMAX 432 Reference Manual.

Certainly, the reader should be aware by now that the Object Filing Subsystem will greatly extend the functionality and hence the applicability of the i432 System. When these extensions are in place, a new watershed in commercial operating systems will have been achieved, no doubt inducing other designers to emulate such facilities.

10.4. A Final Glance at the Portfolio Management System

Readers have a surprise in store as we undertake our final inspection of the portfolio management system. It might seem that nothing we have learned in Chapters 9 and 10 need affect the design decisions and options we have considered in preceding chapters. Our new knowledge of i432 Memory Management, either of main memory or the more general virtual memory, seems largely irrelevant to this design. True, the performance of the proposed subsystem may be affected by the amount of main memory available or by the overhead of managing a more general virtual memory, but to any first approximation, it is difficult to see how knowledge of specific performance characteristics vis a vis Memory Management can be significant. And so, only the Object Filing Subsystem is left to consider as possibly relevant.

On the one hand, presence of the Object Filing Subsystem assures the integrity, reliability, and longevity of the portfolio data base. Without Object Filing, our application would be incomplete, unless we were to explicitly include the I/O requests that save (and retrieve) the portfolio data in (and from) long-term store between the end-users' terminal sessions. [The only way to avoid including such steps would be to assure that the portfolio always resides in virtual memory. This approach has some merit, but it does not provide for full insurance against system crashes.] Presence of the underlying Object Filing Subsystem quite fortunately makes the transport of our portfolio to and from long-term store automatic and transparent. Neither the users of the subsystem, nor we, its designers, need be troubled with such matters. Put another way, the underlying Object Filing Subsystem can be said, actually, to complete our design!

Having said all this, we should be ready for the promised surprise. Since the Object Filing Subsystem offers synchronization services as well as ''crash insurance'', we had better reexamine our design to see how much in the way of synchronization mechanism, already built into our design, is actually redundant. In fact a good deal of the task and package structure in the Figures 2-5 and 3-2 ''solutions'' appear in need of reassessment.

Our designs were built on the premise that whenever Ada owner packages can be accessed concurrently by more than one task, arbiter tasks are needed as intermediaries. Apart from whatever other services are rendered by Portfolio_Server in the Figure 2-5 solution, and by both Portfolio_Server and Roster_Server in the Figure 3-2 solution, these server tasks are essentially arbiters. But, they are only needed because Ada semantics provides no guarantee of synchronization over the use of owned data of packages.

Consider this: Each time the Treasurer task (or any other task properly authorized) needs to read or update the portfolio objects, it is necessary only to execute an Atomic Action on those objects. Ordinary Member tasks may also issue read requests of the portfolio objects as Atomic Actions. (Ordinary club members would be barred from opening portfolio objects for writing or updating by being denied the proper rights.) There can be no conflict. The individual Atomic Actions would be encoded as the operations within the Portfolio_Mgr package.

We may now ask, ''Why use arbiter tasks at all in our applications and subsystems programming—if Object Filing eliminates the need for them?'' Two good answers come to mind:

- First, it seems important to be able to design application subsystems like portfolio management so they can run in the absence of Object Filing services—even if only to be able to simulate our design in a ''leaner'' environment, one lacking Object Filing. (Certainly, if it is important to be able to ''port'' an application to another system that lacks certain rich system services, relying on them must be avoided.)
- Second, the synchronization of access to objects provided by Object Filing pertains only to the objects in passive space. Users who want concurrent access to objects in active space must still provide explicit synchronization, such as by use of arbiter tasks. For example, if A were to activate an object X and then B tries to activate X, then A and B would share the same copy; the need for synchronization in this case still remains.

Notice that both responses are arguments for knowing how to accomplish synchronization in at least two different ways. Therefore, readers are invited to learn more about the two Object Filing Subsystem interfaces introduced in the last section and are urged, as an exercise, to redesign our portfolio management system one more time.

10.5. Chapter and Book Summary

We have reached the end of our several studies. At the beginning, we asserted that a proper examination and appreciation of the i432 System would involve a study of the new system's System Implementation Language, its Architecture, and its Operating System. In this book, we have done all three and roughly in this order.

We hope readers who were more interested in the Architecture or in the Operating System did not grow too impatient with the progression we chose, did, more or less, diligently read straight through this book, and can now see why it helps to become familiar with the language Ada—and the model of computation implied by Ada—in order to appreciate the many innovative aspects of the hardware and software design.

The i432 System is not an Ada machine. Most of it was designed independently of Ada, but with a similar semantic model of computation as its basis. Hence, we have not felt it necessary to introduce readers to the entire Ada language. On the other hand, because of its powerful programmer support facilities, including the full Ada language and at least one powerful extension (dynamic packages), the System permits many advanced users of the i432 System to provide their "customers" with a wide variety of other language processors and tailored operating system extensions for the development of end-user applications.

Finally, we hope that the reader has been rewarded in reading this book, as has the writer by writing it, by having acquired both an in-depth perception of, and an enthusiasm for the i432 System and for the creative and productive work of its many designers and implementers. We hope their system proves to be a pronounced success in its primary objective, which—from the start of the venture—has been to offer us a system that helps users to reduce significantly the cost of building and maintaining system and application software.

Appendix A

The iAPX 432—Published Papers

1. S. Zeigler, N. Allegre, R. Johnson, J. Morris, and G. Burns, "Ada for the Intel 432 Microcomputer," IEEE *Computer*, pp. 47–56 (June, 1981).
2. K. C. Kahn and F. J. Pollack, "An Extensible Operating System for the Intel 432," *Proceedings Compcon Spring 1981*, pp. 398–404 (February 1981).
3. S. Ziegler, N. Allegre, D. Coar, R. Johnson, J. Morris, and G. Burns, "The Intel 432 Ada Programming Environment," *Proceedings Compcon Spring 1981*, pp. 405–410 (February 1981).
4. G. W. Cox, W. M. Korwin, K. Lai, and F. J. Pollack, "A Unified Model and Implementation for Interprocess Communication in a Multiprocessor Environment," *Proceedings of the 8th Symposium on Operating System Principles*, (December, 1981).
5. F. J. Pollack, G. W. Cox, D. W. Hammerstrom, K. C. Kahn, K. Lai, and J. R. Rattner, "Supporting Ada Memory Management in the iAPX-432," *Symposium on Architectural Support for Programming Languages and Operating Systems*, (March, 1982).
6. F. J. Pollack, K. C. Kahn, and R. M. Wilkinson, "The iMAX-432 Object Filing System," *Proceedings of the 8th Symposium on Operating System Principles*, (December, 1981).
7. K. C. Kahn, W. M. Corwin, T. D. Dennis, H. D'Hooge, M. R. Gifkins, L. A. Hutchins, and F. J. Pollack, "iMAX: A Multiprocessor Operating System for an Object-Based Computer," *Proceedings of the 8th Symposium on Operating System Principles*, (December, 1981).
8. K. C. Kahn, "A Small-Scale Operating System Foundation for Microprocessor Applications," *Proceedings of the IEEE*, Vol. 66, No. 2, (February, 1978).
9. R. Ebersole, "Designing a High-Performance Bus for a Multiprocessor System," *Phoenix Conference on Computers and Communications*, (May 1982).
10. D. Kinder, "Transparent Multiprocessing Boosts μC Throughput", *Electronic Design News*, (April 15, 1982).
11. R. Kaiser, "The 432 Micromainframe Architecture," *Proceedings of the 35th Conference of the American Institute of Aeronautics and Aerospace*, (September, 1981).
12. R. Johnson, "The Intel iAPX-432: An Architecture for Ada," *Proceedings of the Symposium on High-Level Computer Achitecture*, (October, 1981).
13. H. I. Jacob, "An Architecture for the 80's—The Intel iAPX-432," *Proceedings of Midcon '81*, (November, 1981).
14. J. R. Rattner and W. W. Lattin, "Ada Determines Architecture of 32-bit Microprocessor," *Electronics*, (Feb. 24, 1981).
15. D. Kinder, "Ada, iMAX, and Intel's iAPX 432," *Annual Conference Proceedings for Associazione Italiana Per Il Calcolo Automatico*, (October, 1982).
16. M. J. McGowan, "The Information Management Capabilities of the iAPX 432 Processor," *Computer Technology Review*, (Summer, 1982).
17. K. C. Kahn, "Object-Oriented Languages Tackle Massive Programming Headaches," *Electronics*, (November 17, 1982).

Appendix B

The iAPX 432: *Titles of Manuals and Booklets* published by Intel Corporation, Santa Clara, California

Summaries

1. Intel 432 System Summary: Manager's Perspective
2. iAPX 43201/43202 VLSI General Data Processor Data Sheet
3. iAPX 43203 VLSI Interface Processor Data Sheet
4. System 432/600 32-bit Extensible Computer System Data Sheet
5. iMAX 432 Multifunction Application Executive Data Sheet
6. Intel 432 Cross Development System Data Sheet
7. Intel 432 Asynchronous Communication Link Data Sheet
8. Intel iAPX 43204/43205 Interconnect Data Sheet and Electrical Specification

Technical Manuals for the iAPX 432 Family

9. Introduction to the iAPX 432 Architecture
10. iAPX 432 Object Primer
11. iAPX 432 General Data Processor Architecture Manual (Advance Partial Issue of -002)
12. iAPX 432 Interface Processor Architecture Reference Manual
13. iAPX 432 Interconnect Architecture Reference Manual

Technical Manuals for the Intel 432 Cross Development System

14. Introduction to the Intel 432 Cross Development System
15. Reference Manual for the Ada Programming Language
16. Reference Manual for the Intel 432 Extensions to Ada
17. Intel 432 CDS Ada Support Package User's Guide
18. Intel 432 CDS VAX Host User's Guide
19. Asynchronous Communication Link User's Guide
20. Intel 432 CDS Workstation User's Guide

iMAX 432

21. iMAX 432 Reference Manual

System 432/600

22. System 432/600 System Reference Manual
23. System 432/600 Diagnostic Software User's Guide.
24. System 432/600 Hardware Reference Manual
25. System 432/670 Installation and Maintenance Manual

Appendix C
Stock_Types_And_Constants

```
package Stock_Types_And_Constants is
  --
  -- This package has no body.
  --

  subtype  long_string   is  string(1..30);

  type dollars is new integer;

  type stock_code_pair is
    record
      code:       string(1..4);      -- abbreviation for listed stock
      exch:       string(1..4);      -- abbreviation for stock exchange
    end record;

  type stock_name_info is
    record
      print_name:       long_string;
      stock_code:       stock_code_pair;
    end record;

  type date is
    record
      day:    integer range 1..31;
      month:  integer range 1..12;
      year:   integer range 1900..4000;
    end record;

  type buy_sell_type is (buy, sell);

  type buy_sell_record(buy_sell: buy_sell_type) is
    record
      stock_name:       stock_name_info;
      buy_date:         date;
      num_shares:       integer;
      per_share_price:  dollars;
      commission:       dollars;
      case buy_sell is                  -- record discriminant
       when sell =>                     -- extra data field
        of_buy_date:    date;
       when others =>                   -- no extra field
        null;
      end case;
    end record;
  subtype  purchase_record  is buy_sell_record(buy);
  subtype  sale_record      is buy_sell_record(sell);
end Stock_Types_And_Constants;
```

Generic Queue Manager

```
generic

    type item is private;

package Queue_Mgr is
  type queue  is private;
  null_queue: constant queue;
                              -- A "deferred constant", permitting a user
                              -- express a test to determine if a created
                              -- instance of queue is or is not null
                              -- without actually knowing how "nullness"
                              -- is represented.

  function Create
    return queue;

  procedure Add(
      E:         in     item;
      Q:         in     queue;
      to_front:  in     boolean:= false); -- optional third parameter

  procedure Remove(
      U: out   item;
      Q: in    queue);

  function Is_empty(
      Q: in queue)
    return boolean;

  underflow: exception;   -- raised if Remove
                          -- is passed an empty queue

private
  type queue_element;     -- forward reference

  type queue_element_ptr is access queue_element;

  type queue_element is
    record
      info: item;
      next: queue_element_ptr;
    end record;

  type queue_rep is
    record
      head: queue_element_ptr;
      tail: queue_element_ptr;
    end record;

  type queue is access queue_rep;
  null_queue: constant queue := null; -- Initialization of this
                                          -- constant is hidden.
end Queue_Mgr;
```

Body Part of Generic Queue Manager

```
pragma environment("GenQueMgr.spe");
package body Queue_Mgr is

  function Create
    return queue
  is
  begin
    return new queue_rep(head => null, tail => null);
  end Create;

  procedure Add(
      E:         in     item;
      Q:         in     queue;
      to_front:  in     boolean:= false) -- optional third parameter
  is
    x: queue_element_ptr := new queue_element(info => E, next => null);
  begin
    case to_front is
      when false =>                          -- Put E at tail of queue.
        if Q.tail /= null then               -- queue not empty
          Q.tail.next := x;
        else
          Q.head := x;
        end if;
        Q.tail := x;
      when others =>                         -- Put E at front of queue.
        if Q.tail /= null then               -- queue not empty
          x.next := Q.head;
        else
          Q.tail := x;
        end if;
        Q.head := x;
    end case;
  end Add;

  procedure Remove(
    U: out    item;
    Q: in     queue)
  is
  begin
    if Q.head = null then
      raise Underflow;
    else
      U := Q.head.info;
      if Q.head.next = null then             -- Is Q.head last queue element?
        Q.head := null;
        Q.tail := null;
      else
        Q.head := Q.head.next;
      end if;
    end if;
  end Remove;
```

```
    function Is_empty(
        Q: in queue)
      return boolean
    is
    begin
      return Q.head = null;   -- Return truth value of expression.
    end Is_empty;

  end Queue_Mgr;
```

Purchase_Queue_Mgr

```
  pragma environment("GenQueMgr.bdr","StkTypCon.spr");

  with Queue_Mgr, Stock_Types_And_Constants;

  package Purchase_Queue_Mgr is new Queue_Mgr(
              item    => Stock_Types_And_Constants.purchase_record);
    --
    -- Instantiation of generic Queue_Mgr package to manage purchase queues
    -- formed in portfolio instances by Portfolio_Mgr.
    --
```

Portfolio_Manager specification

```
  pragma environment("PurQueMgr.spr","StkTypCon.spr","StkMktInf.spr");

  with Purchase_Queue_Mgr, Stock_Types_And_Constants, Stock_Mkt_Info;

  package  Portfolio_Mgr  is

    use Purchase_Queue_Mgr, Stock_Types_And_Constants, Stock_Mkt_Info;

    type portfolio_ptr        is private;
    null_portfolio: constant portfolio_ptr; -- A "deferred constant."

    type stocks_held(num : integer) is -- Need to specify num
                                       -- when instantiating this record.
      record
        name:            array (1..num) of stock_name_info;
        num_shares:      array (1..num) of integer;
      end record;

    type stocks_held_ptr is access stocks_held;
                                 -- Used as parameter type in Stock_list.

    type index is range 0..1000;

    type array_of_purchases is
        array (index range <>) of purchase_record;

    type array_of_purchases_ptr is access array_of_purchases;
                                 -- Used as parameter type in
                                 -- History_of_purchases.

    exceeds_holdings:  exception;
```

```
function Create(
    folio_name:    in  long_string)
  return portfolio_ptr;            -- Access made with read,
                                   -- and write writes
                                   -- (No create rights.)
  -- Function:
  --   Creates an instance of type portfolio (allocated from global
  --   heap store) with folio_name as print_name and returns a pointer
  --   (access descriptor) to this instance.

procedure Record_buy(
    folio_ptr:     in  portfolio_ptr;
    buy_info:      in  purchase_record);
  --
  -- Function
  --   Adds new buy transaction to purchase history for this stock.

procedure Record_sell(
    folio_ptr:         in   portfolio_ptr;
    sell_info:         in   sale_record;
    history_underflow: out  boolean);
  --
  -- Function:
  --   Deletes number of shares sold from purchase record in portfolio
  --   for buy_date matching buy date in sell_info. Raises
  --   Exceeds_holdings exception to print an error message if
  --   num_shares exceeds number of shares recorded as purchased on
  --   that date. If not all held shares of that buy_date are sold,
  --   an entry for the residual shares is put back at front of queue.
  --   The recorded commission in the effected purchase_record
  --   is reduced by the ratio of shares retained to shares held before
  --   this sale.
  --   Sets history_underflow true in handling Underflow exception raised
  --   in Purchase_Queue_Mgr.

procedure Number_of_stocks(
    folio_ptr:     in   portfolio_ptr;
    num_stocks:    out  integer);
  --
  -- Function:
  --   Output parameter is number of different stocks currently held
  --   in portfolio accessed by folio_ptr.

procedure Stock_list(
    folio_ptr:     in   portfolio_ptr;
    num_stocks:    out  integer;
    stocks:        out  stocks_held_ptr);
  --
  -- Function:
  --   Returns a reference to a stocks_held record
  --   which is an array of records, each consisting of the
  --   name and number of shares held for a stock
  --   held in portfolio accessed by folio_ptr.
```

```
procedure Shares_and_avg_cost(
    folio_ptr:      in   portfolio_ptr;
    stock_code:     in   stock_code_pair;
    num_shares:     out  integer;
    avg_cost:       out  dollars );
  --
  -- Function:
  --   Output parameters supply number of shares and average cost
  --   per share, including commissions, for stock denoted by given
  --   stock_code in portfolio denoted by folio_ptr.

procedure Num_buys(
    folio_ptr:      in   portfolio_ptr;
    stock_code:     in   stock_code_pair;
    num_purchases:  out  integer);
  --
  -- Function:
  --   Output parameter is number of different purchases for
  --   which stock of given stock_code is currently held in
  --   portfolio denoted by folio_ptr.

procedure History_of_purchases(
    folio_ptr:          in   portfolio_ptr;
    num_purchases:      in   integer;
    stock_code:         in   stock_code_pair;
    purchase_history:   out  array_of_purchases_ptr);
  --
  -- Function:
  --   Output parameter is a reference to an array of purchase
  --   records of length num_purchases for which the stock of the
  --   given stock_code is currently held in portfolio_ptr denoted
  --   by folio_ptr. See Stock_Types_And_Constants for format of a
  --   purchase_record.


function Get_portfolio_name(
    folio_ptr: in portfolio_ptr := null_portfolio)
  return long_string;             -- Name of portfolio.
--
-- Function:
--   If the input parameter folio_ptr corresponds to an existing
--   portfolio, its name is returned; otherwise
--   "No such portfolio^^^^^^^^^^^^" is returned.

private

  type stock_summary;                       -- Forward reference.
  type stock_summary_ptr is access stock_summary;

  type stock_summary is
    record
      stock_name:           stock_name_info :=
                            (print_name => "^^^^^^^^^^^^^^^^^^^^^^^^^^^^^^",
                             stock_code => (code => "^^^^",exch => "^^^^")) ;
      num_shares:           integer := 0;
      avg_cost_per_share:   dollars := 0;
      next:                 stock_summary_ptr := null;
      purchase_history:     Purchase_Queue_Mgr.queue
                                  := Purchase_Queue_Mgr.Create();
    end record;
```

```
   type portfolio;                          -- Forward reference.
   type portfolio_ptr is access portfolio;
   type portfolio is
     record
       portfolio_name:      long_string := "not yet named^^^^^^^^^^^^^^^^^^";
       num_diff_stocks_held: integer := 0;
       stock_list:          stock_summary_ptr := null;
     end record;

   null_portfolio: constant portfolio_ptr := null;

end Portfolio_Mgr;
```

Portfolio_Manager body

```
pragma environment("PrtMgr.spr", "PurQueMgr.spr",
                   "StkTypCon.spr","StkMktInf.spr");

with Portfolio_Mgr, Purchase_Queue_Mgr, Stock_Types_And_Constants,
     Stock_Mkt_Info;

package body Portfolio_Mgr  is  -- Package body begins here


   function Create(
       folio_name:     in  long_string)
     return portfolio_ptr
   is separate;

   procedure Record_buy(
       folio_ptr:      in  portfolio_ptr;
       buy_info:       in  purchase_record)
   is separate;

   procedure Record_sell(
       folio_ptr:          in   portfolio_ptr;
       sell_info:          in   sale_record;
       history_underflow:  out  boolean)
   is separate;

   procedure Number_of_stocks(
       folio_ptr:      in   portfolio_ptr;
       num_stocks:     out  integer)
   is separate;

   procedure Stock_list(
       folio_ptr:      in   portfolio_ptr;
       num_stocks:     out  integer;
       stocks:         out  stocks_held_ptr)
   is separate;

   procedure Shares_and_avg_cost(
       folio_ptr:      in   portfolio_ptr;
       stock_code:     in   stock_code_pair;
       num_shares:     out  integer;
       avg_cost:       out  dollars )
   is separate;
```

```
  procedure Num_buys(
      folio_ptr:      in   portfolio_ptr;
      stock_code:     in   stock_code_pair;
      num_purchases: out   integer)
  is separate;

  procedure History_of_purchases(
      folio_ptr:          in   portfolio_ptr;
      num_purchases:      in   integer;
      stock_code:         in   Stock_code_pair;
      purchase_history: out   Purchase_Queue_Mgr.queue)
  is separate;

  function Get_portfolio_name(
      folio_ptr: in portfolio_ptr := null_portfolio)
    return long_string          -- Name of portfolio.
  is separate;


  -- Locally defined procedures and functions go here:

  function Search_for_stock_code(
      folio_ptr:              in  portfolio_ptr;
      buy_record:             in  purchase_record;
      create_if_not_found:  in  boolean)
    return  stock_summary_ptr;
  is separate;
  --
  -- Function:
  --   Searches portfolio denoted by folio_ptr for presence of stock_code
  --   the same as that given in buy_record. If the stock is found, a
  --   reference to the stock summary for that held stock is returned.
  --   If the stock is not found, the action to be taken depends on the valu
  --   of the input parameter create_if_not_found. If true, a new stock
  --   summary is created, initialized, and added to the portfolio, and a
  --   reference to it is returned. If create_if_not_found is false,
  --   null is returned.
begin
  --
  -- Statements to initalize this package, if needed, go here.
  --
  null;
end Portfolio_Mgr;              -- End of package body.
```

Club_Portfolio specification

```
pragma environment("PrtMgr.spr","TxtIo.spr",
                      "StkTypCon.spr","StkMktInf.spr");

with Portfolio_mgr, Stock_Mkt_Info, Text_IO, Stock_Types_And_Constants;

package Club_Portfolio is

  use Portfolio_Mgr, Stock_Mkt_Info, Text_IO, Stock_Types_And_Constants;

  subtype percent is integer range 0..500;
                                          -- Used in winners, losers and
                                          -- non-movers procedures. See below
```

```
function Print_club_valuation
  return dollars;
  --
  -- Function:
  --   Prints total value of club's portfolio,
  --   based on current market prices.

procedure Print_club_holdings;
  --
  -- Function:
  --   For each held stock, prints:
  --   number of shares held,
  --   average per-share purchase price,
  --   current per-share price,
  --   current value of holdings in this stock.

function Find_stock_code(
    corporate_name: in long_string)
  return stock_code_pair;  -- Returns the standard stock code,
                           -- if any, corresponding to input argument.
  --
  -- Function:
  --   Prints as well as returns the stock code (abbreviation for stock
  --   and exchange where listed.)

procedure Print_individual_stock_summary(
    stock_code:      in stock_code_pair);  -- Standard code for stock.
  --
  -- Function:
  --   Prints summary info on held stock with given stock code
  --   total no. of shares held, this stock, current per-share price and
  --   current value of shares. Also, for each purchase of shares still
  --   held, prints:
  --    purchase date, no. of shares, per-share purchase price,
  --    and commission.

procedure Print_shares_and_value_of_stock(
    stock_code: in stock_code_pair);
  --
  -- Function:
  --   For the given stock_code, prints the number of held shares,
  --   current price per share, and total market value.

procedure Print_average_cost(
    stock_code: in stock_code_pair);
  --
  -- Function:
  --   Prints, for the stock denoted by stock_code, the average cost,
  --   including commissions, of all such stock now held.

procedure Print_winners(
     spread: in percent);   -- Percent deviation.
  --
  -- Function:
  --   Prints list of held stocks for each of which, based on latest
  --   market quotes, the club has a "paper" gain of spread percent
  --   or more over average purchase cost for that stock (including
  --   commission.)
```

```
procedure Print_losers(
     spread: in percent);    -- Percent deviation.
  --
  -- Function:
  --    Analogous with Print_winners.

procedure Print_non_movers(
    spread:  in percent);    -- Percent deviation.
  --
  -- Function:
  --    Lists stocks for which "paper" gain is less than spread. See
  --    description of Print_winners.

procedure Enter_buy(
    purch_date:    in date;
    stock_code:    in stock_code_pair;
    num_shares:    in natural;
    per_sh_price:  in dollars;
    commission:    in dollars);
  --
  -- Function:
  --    Records a buy transaction in club's portfolio.
  --    and provides confirmation copy of response, including
  --    error messages, if any. (Confirmation copy may also go
  --    to an archive file.)

procedure Enter_sell(
    sell_date:     in date;
    stock_code:    in stock_code_pair;
    num_shares:    in natural;
    of_buy_date:   in date;
    sell_commiss:  in dollars); -- Selling commission is not
                                -- recorded in portfolio,
                                -- but used to indicate net gain or
                                -- loss in confirmation copy.
 --
 -- Function:
 --    Records sale of shares bought on of_buy_date. Num_shares held
 --    for this buy date are deleted from the portfolio. A confirmation
 --    copy of this sell transaction is produced, indicating net gain
 --    or loss (and whether long- or short-term) and including error
 --    messages, if any. (Confirmation copy may also go to an archive
 --    file.)
 --

 -- Readers of Chapter 3 should note that this is the place where
 -- the declaration would go for our_portfolio, now appearing in
 -- the body part of this package; also, the specifications
 -- for Create_folio and Delete_folio would be placed
 -- here to revise this package for use with the tasks defined
 -- in Appendixes F and G. To complete this revision, delete the
 -- initialization section of the body part of this package.
 -- These insertions are shown as comments below.

 -- our_portfolio: portfolio_ptr ; -- Declares a variable of type
                                  -- portfolio_ptr which can hold
                                  -- a reference to a portfolio
                                  -- instance.
```

```
  -- function Create_folio(
  --     portfolio_name:   in  long_string;
  --     check:            out boolean)
  --   return portfolio_ptr;

  -- procedure Delete_folio(
  --     portfolio_name:   in  long_string;
  --     check:            out boolean);

end Club_Portfolio;
```

Club_Portfolio body

```
pragma environment("ClbPrt.spr","PrtMgr.spr","TxtIo.spr","StkTypCon.spr",
                   "StkMktInf.spr");

with Club_Portfolio, Portfolio_mgr, Stock_Mkt_Info, Text_IO,
     Stock_Types_And_Constants;

package body  Club_Portfolio  is

  our_portfolio: portfolio_ptr ; -- Declares a variable of type
                                 -- portfolio_ptr which can hold
                                 -- a reference to a portfolio
                                 -- instance.
    -- The above declaration would be moved to the specification part
    -- of this package to modify it for use with the tasks
    -- in Appendixes F and G.

  function Print_club_valuation
    return dollars
  is separate; -- stub

  procedure Print_club_holdings    is separate; -- stub

  function Find_stock_code(
      corporate_name: in long_string)
    return stock_code_pair
  is separate;  -- stub
    -- calls on operation of Stock_Mkt_Info package

  procedure Print_individual_stock_summary(
      stock_code:       in stock_code_pair)
  is separate;  -- stub

  procedure Print_shares_and_value_of_stock(
      stock_code: in stock_code_pair)
  is separate;  -- stub

  procedure Print_average_cost(
      stock_code: in stock_code_pair)
  is separate;  -- stub

  procedure Print_winners(
       spread: in percent)
  is separate;  -- stub
```

```
  procedure Print_losers(
       spread: in percent)
  is separate;  -- stub

  procedure Print_non_movers(
      spread:  in percent)
  is separate;  -- stub

  procedure Enter_buy(
      purch_date:    in date;
      stock_code:    in stock_code_pair;
      num_shares:    in natural;
      per_sh_price: in dollars;
      commission:    in dollars)
  is separate;  -- stub

  procedure Enter_sell(
      sell_date:     in date;
      stock_code:    in stock_code_pair;
      num_shares:    in natural;
      of_buy_date:   in date;
      sell_commiss: in dollars)
  is separate;  -- stub

   -- Insert body parts of Create_folio and Delete_folio here if
   -- revisions for use with tasks in Appendices F and G are made.
   -- These are shown as comments below.

   -- procedure Create_folio(
   --           portfolio_name:  in long_string;
   --           check:           out boolean)
   --   is separate;  -- stub

   -- procedure Delete_folio(
   --           portfolio_name:  in long_string;
   --           check:           out boolean)
   --   is separate;  -- stub

  -- Local declarations (of this package) go here:

  -- package initialization
begin
  our_portfolio := Portfolio_Mgr.Create("Twenty_cousins_club^^^^^^^^^^^");
                                  -- Reference to a newly allocated
                                  -- portfolio instance, named
                                  -- Twenty_cousins_club assigned
                                  -- to our_portfolio.
  -- Above initialization section would be removed when recompiling to
  -- produce revisions for use with tasks defined in Appendices F and G.

end Club_Portfolio;
```

Appendix D

Selected operation bodies for Portfolio_Mgr

```
pragma environment("PrtMgr.bdr","PurQueMgr.spr","StkTypCon.spr",
                   "StkMktInf.spr");


separate(Portfolio_Mgr)               -- Prefix to indicate to the compiler
                                      -- that Portfolio_Mgr is the context
                                      -- in which the following function
                                      -- is to be compiled.

  function Create(
      folio_name: in  long_string)
    return portfolio_ptr
  is
    folio_ptr:  portfolio_ptr;        -- Local reference variable.
  begin
    folio_ptr := new  portfolio;      -- Allocates a new portfolio
                                      -- instance and assigns a reference
                                      -- to folio_ptr.
    folio_ptr.portfolio_name := folio_name;
                                      -- Name now assigned to this portfolio.
    return folio_ptr;
  end Create;



separate(Portfolio_Mgr)               -- Prefix to indicate to the compiler
                                      -- that Portfolio_Mgr is the context
                                      -- in which the following procedure
                                      -- is to be compiled.
  procedure Record_buy(
      folio_ptr:           in  portfolio_ptr;
      buy_info:            in  purchase_record)
  is
    num_diff_stocks :   integer renames folio_ptr.num_diff_stocks_held;
    mark:               stock_summary_ptr;

  begin
    -- Determine, by a call on the local function,
    -- Search_for_stock_code, whether the new purchase is
    -- is for a held stock. If not held, assign a reference to
    -- its stock summary to mark; if not held, create and initialize
    -- a new stock summary and assign a reference to it to mark.

    mark := Search_for_stock_code(folio_ptr,
                                  buy_info.stock_name,
                                  create_if_not_found => true);
```

```
    -- Update the stock summary information.

    mark.avg_cost_per_share := (mark.avg_cost_per_share *
                                   dollars(mark.num_shares)
                                 + buy_info.per_share_price *
                                   dollars(buy_info.num_shares)
                                 + buy_info.commission)

                                / (dollars(mark.num_shares
                                   + buy_info.num_shares));

    mark.num_shares        := mark.num_shares + buy_info.num_shares;

    -- Now add new item to purchase history queue
    Add(buy_info, mark.purchase_history);

  end Record_buy;


separate(Portfolio_Mgr)              -- Prefix to indicate to the compiler
                                     -- that Portfolio_Mgr is the context
                                     -- in which the following procedure
                                     -- is to be compiled.
  procedure Record_sell(
      folio_ptr:           in  portfolio_ptr;
      sell_info:           in  sale_record;
      history_underflow:   out boolean)
  is
    num_diff_stocks:    integer renames folio_ptr.num_diff_stocks_held;
    mark:               stock_summary_ptr;

  begin
    -- Determine, by a call on the local function,
    -- Search_for_stock_code, whether the new purchase is for a
    -- held stock such that the function will return a null
    -- reference value if the stock is not held.
    --
    mark := Search_for_stock_code(folio_ptr,
                                  sell_info.stock_name,
                                  create_if_not_found => false);

    -- Value returned indicates search outcome.
    --
    if mark = null  then             -- No such stock held.
       raise Exceeds_holdings;       -- Exception propagates to caller.

    elsif mark.num_shares < sell_info.num_shares then
      raise Exceeds_holdings;        -- Don't have enough shares to sell.
    else
      -- Remove purchase history records (as many as needed)
      -- representing the holdings that must be sold) for which the
      -- of_buy_date matches that given in sell_info. If not enough
      -- stock held of that of_buy_date, raise Exceeds_holdings.
      -- If there are leftover shares in a purchase record, put the
      -- updated purchase_record back in the queue.
      -- Update values of num_shares and average_cost_per_sh
      -- in the stock_summary record.
      -- Coding to accomplish all this is not included here.
```

```
      null;
    end if;

  exception
    when Underflow =>                -- Raised in activation of
                                     -- Purchase_Queue_Mgr.Remove.
      history_underflow := true;

  end Record_sell;


separate(Portfolio_Mgr)
  function Search_for_stock_code(
      folio_ptr:           in  portfolio_ptr;
      buy_record:          in  purchase_record;
      create_if_not_found: in  boolean)
    return  stock_summary_ptr;
  --
  -- Function:
  --   Searches portfolio denoted by folio_ptr for presence of stock_code
  --   the same as that given in buy_record. If the stock is found, a
  --   reference to the stock summary for that held stock is returned.
  --   If the stock is not found, the action to be taken depends on the value
  --   of the input parameter create_if_not_found. If true, a new stock
  --   summary is created, initialized, and added to the portfolio, and a
  --   reference to it is returned. If create_if_not_found is false,
  --   null is returned.
  is
    cursor : stock_summary_ptr;
  begin
    cursor := folio_ptr.stock_list;
                                     -- Sets cursor to head of stock
                                     -- summary list in portfolio.
    if cursor = null  then           -- Empty portfolio.
      if create_if_not_found = true then
                                     -- Allocate a new stock summary with
                                     -- an initially empty purchase history
                                     -- and add it to the portfolio.
        folio_ptr.stock_list := new stock_summary;

        return folio_ptr.stock_list;
                                     -- Return reference to new stock summary.
      else
        return null;                 -- Return null reference.
      end if;
    else
      loop
        if  cursor.stock_name = buy_record then
                                     -- Found stock_summary.
          return cursor;             -- Return reference to existing
                                     -- stock summary.
        else
          cursor := cursor.next;     -- Advance one link in the chain.
          if cursor = null  then     -- Last stock summary in portfolio.
            if create_if_not_found = true then
                                     -- Allocate a new stock summary with
                                     -- an initially empty purchase history
                                     -- and add it to the end of the portfolio.
```

```
            cursor.next := new stock_summary;
            return cursor.next;   -- Return reference to
                                  -- new stock summary.
          else
            return null;          -- Return null reference.
          end if;
        end if;
      end if;
    end loop;
  end if;
end Search_for_stock_code;


separate(Portfolio_Mgr)

 procedure Stock_list(
     folio_ptr:       in   portfolio_ptr;
     num_stocks:      out  integer;
     stocks:          out  stocks_held_ptr)
 is
   n: integer;
   cursor: stock_summary_ptr;
 begin
  n:= folio_ptr.num_diff_stocks_held;   -- Get value from portfolio.

  if n = 0
    then
      num_stocks:= 0;
      stocks:= null;
    else
      stocks:= new stocks_held(num => n);
                        -- Create an instance of type stocks_held
                        -- whose arrays, name and num_shares,
                        -- are of length n.
      cursor:= folio_ptr.stock_list;
                        -- Initial value of cursor points to
                        -- first stock summary.

      for i in 1 .. n
        loop
          stocks.name(i)        := cursor.stock_name;
          stocks.num_shares(i)  := cursor.num_shares;
                        -- Fill ith slot in each array.

          cursor := cursor.next;
                        -- Advance the cursor.
        end loop;
  end if;
end Stock_list;


separate(Portfolio_Mgr)

 procedure Shares_and_avg_cost(
     folio_ptr:       in   portfolio_ptr;
     stock_code:      in   stock_code_pair;
     num_shares:      out  integer;
     avg_cost:        out  dollars )
```

```
  is
    cursor:          stock_summary_ptr;
  begin
    cursor:= folio_ptr.stock_list;  -- Initialize current_ptr
                                    -- to refer to first stock_summary
                                    -- in the portfolio.
    while cursor /= null  and then
      cursor.stock_name.stock_code /= stock_code loop
        cursor := cursor.next;      -- Advance to next summary.
    end loop;

    if cursor = null  then  -- No such stock
      num_shares := 0;
      avg_cost   := 0;
    else
      num_shares := cursor.num_shares;
      avg_cost   := cursor.avg_cost_per_share;
      end if;
  end Shares_and_avg_cost;
```

Selected operation bodies for Club_Portfolio

```
pragma environment("ClbPrt.bdr","PrtMgr.spr","TxtIo.spr","StkTypCon.spr",
                   "StkMktInf.spr");


separate(Club_Portfolio)              -- Prefix to indicate to the compiler
                                      -- that Club_Portfolio is the context
                                      -- in which the following function
                                      -- is to be compiled.

  function Print_club_valuation
    return dollars
    is
      -- local variable declarations:
      stocks:                stocks_held_ptr;
      num:                   integer;
                             -- Values returned from call on Stock_list.
      check:                 boolean;
      price:                 dollars;
                             -- values returned from call on Find_stock_price
      total_value:           dollars := 0;   -- of the portfolio
      code:                  stock_code_pair;
      no_price:              exception;
    begin
      Portfolio_Mgr.Stock_list(folio_ptr => our_portfolio,
                               num_stocks => num,
                               stocks     => stocks);
      for i in 1 .. num
      loop
        code:= stocks.name.stock_code(i); -- gets next stock_code_pair value
        num:=  stocks.num_shares(i); -- gets next num_shares value
        Stock_Mkt_Info.Find_stock_price(code, price, check);
                               -- get price per share of this stock.
        if not check then raise no_price; end if;
        total_value:= total_value + dollars(num) * price;
      end loop;
```

```
    -- Put(total_value); this kind of put is unimplemented
    return total_value;

    exception
      when no_price => Put("no price for");
                        -- Put(code); this kind of put is unimplemented.
end Print_club_valuation;
```

Appendix E

Member_Ops package, version 1

```
pragma environment("ClbPrt.spr", "StkTypCon.spr");

with Club_Portfolio, Stock_Types_And_Constants;

package Member_Ops is
  use Club_Portfolio, Stock_Types_And_Constants;

  function Print_club_valuation
    return dollars;
    --
    -- Function:
    --   Prints total value of club's portfolio,
    --   based on current market prices.

  procedure Print_club_holdings;
    --
    -- Function:
    --   For each held stock, prints:
    --   number of shares held,
    --   average per-share purchase price,
    --   current per-share price,
    --   current value of holdings in this stock.

  function Find_stock_code(
      corporate_name: in long_string)
    return stock_code_pair;  -- Returns the standard stock code, if any,
                             -- corresponding to the input argument.
    --
    -- Function:
    --   Prints as well as returns the stock code (abbreviation for stock
    --   and exchange where listed.)

  procedure Print_individual_stock_summary(
      stock_code:       in stock_code_pair);    -- standard code for stock
    --
    -- Function:
    --   Prints summary info on held stock with given stock code
    --   total no. of shares held, this stock, current per-share price and
    --   current value of shares. Also, for each purchase of shares still
    --   held, prints:
    --    purchase date, no. of shares, per-share purchase price,
    --    and commission.

  procedure Print_shares_and_value_of_stock(
      stock_code: in stock_code_pair);
    --
    -- Function:
    --   For the given stock_code, prints the number of held shares,
    --   current price per share, and total market value.
```

```
  procedure Print_average_cost(
      stock_code: in stock_code_pair);
    --
    -- Function:
    --   Prints, for the stock denoted by stock_code, the average cost,
    --   including commissions, of all such stock now held.

  procedure Print_winners(
      spread: in percent);    -- Percentage spread.
    --   Prints list of held stocks for each of which, based on latest
    --   market quotes, the club has a "paper" gain of spread percent
    --   or more over average purchase cost for that stock (including
    --   commission.)

  procedure Print_losers(
      spread: in percent);    -- Percentage spread.
    --
    -- Function:
    --   Analogous with Print_winners.

  procedure Print_non_movers(
      spread:  in percent);    -- Percentage spread.
    --
    -- Function:
    --   Lists stocks for which "paper" gain is less than spread. See
    --   description of Print_winners.

end Member_Ops;
```

Member_Ops body part, version 1

```
package body Member_Ops is
  --
  -- The body of each subprogram declaration given here is a call to
  -- the corresponding procedure in Club_Portfolio.

  function Print_club_valuation
    return dollars
    is begin return  Club_Portfolio.Print_club_valuation();  end;

  procedure Print_club_holdings
    is begin  Club_Portfolio.Print_club_holdings;  end;

  function Find_stock_code(
      corporate_name: in long_string)
    return stock_code_pair
    is begin  return Club_Portfolio.Find_stock_code(
                corporate_name);  end;

  procedure Print_individual_stock_summary(
      stock_code:       in stock_code_pair)
    is begin  Club_Portfolio.Print_individual_stock_summary(
                stock_code);  end;
```

```
  procedure Print_shares_and_value_of_stock(
      stock_code: in stock_code_pair)
    is begin  Club_Portfolio.Print_shares_and_value_of_stock(
                  stock_code);  end;

  procedure Print_average_cost(
      stock_code: in stock_code_pair)
    is begin  Club_Portfolio.Print_average_cost(
                  stock_code);  end;

  procedure Print_winners(
       spread: in percent)
    is begin  Club_Portfolio.Print_winners(
                  spread);  end;

  procedure Print_losers(
       spread: in percent)
    is begin  Club_Portfolio.Print_losers(
                  spread);  end;

  procedure Print_non_movers(
      spread:  in percent)
    is begin Club_Portfolio.Print_non_movers(
                 spread);  end;

  -- There are no local declarations here
  -- and no initialization statements are required either.
end Member_Ops;
```

Member_Ops, version 2

```
pragma environment("ClbPrt.spr", "StkTypCon.spr");

with Club_Portfolio, Stock_Types_And_Constants;

package Member_Ops is

  use Club_Portfolio, Stock_Types_And_Constants;
  --
  -- The operations of this package are identical with those
  -- like-named operations in the Club_Portfolio package.
  -- Explanations of these functions are given in that package.

  function Print_club_valuation
    return dollars
    renames  Club_Portfolio.Print_club_valuation;

  procedure Print_club_holdings
    renames  Club_Portfolio.Print_club_holdings;

  function Find_stock_code(
      corporate_name: in long_string)
    return stock_code_pair
    renames  Club_Portfolio.Find_stock_code;

  procedure Print_individual_stock_summary(
      stock_code:       in stock_code_pair)   -- Standard code for stock.
    renames  Club_Portfolio.Print_individual_stock_summary;
```

```
  procedure Print_shares_and_value_of_stock(
      stock_code: in stock_code_pair)
    renames  Club_Portfolio.Print_shares_and_value_of_stock;

  procedure Print_average_cost(
      stock_code: in stock_code_pair)
    renames  Club_Portfolio.Print_average_cost;

  procedure Print_winners(
       spread: in percent)     -- Type percent declared in Club_Portfolio.
    renames  Club_Portfolio.Print_winners;

  procedure Print_losers(
       spread: in percent)
    renames  Club_Portfolio.Print_losers;

  procedure Print_non_movers(
      spread:  in percent)
    renames  Club_Portfolio.Print_non_movers;

end Member_Ops;    -- There is no package body in this case.
```

Appendix F

Roster_Types_And_Constants package may be used with either Figure 2-5 or Figure 3-2

```
package Roster_Types_And_Constants  is

   subtype string_of30  is string(1..30);
   type officers        is (President, Vice_president, Secretary,
                               Treasurer, Member);
                        -- Example of an enumeration type definition.

   type member_record  is
     record
       member_name:     string_of30;
       title:           officers;
       soc_sec_no:      integer  range  000_00_0001..99_999_9999;
                        -- Underscores within an integer literal are
                        -- are ignored by the Ada compiler.
     end record;

    max_num_members:    constant integer := 30;

end Roster_Types_And_Constants;
```

Membership_Roster (owner) package may be used with either Figure 2-5 or Figure 3-2

```
--
pragma environment("RosTypCon.spr",  "TxtIo.spr");

with  Roster_Types_And_Constants, Text_IO;

package Membership_Roster  is

   use Roster_Types_And_Constants, Text_IO;

   type roster  is private;        -- See definition below.

   procedure Lookup_member(
       member_name:  in  string_of30;
       member_info:  out member_record;
       check:        out boolean);
     --
     -- Function:
     --    If a member_record is found whose name component matches
     --    that of the input argument, member_name, then that
     --    member_record is assigned to the output parameter,
     --    member_info, and check is set true;
     --    check is set false if no match is found.
```

```
    procedure List_of_members(
        names_only:    in boolean := true;
        check:         out boolean);
      --
      -- Function:
      --    When the input argument matching names_only is true,
      --    prints the full list of the member names in alphabetical order.
      --    When the names_only value is false, prints the full member_record
      --    for each member, in alphabetical order by member name.
--
-- Requests for membership roster update
--
    procedure Add_new_member(
        my_name:           in  string_of30;
        new_member_name:   in  string_of30;
        new_member_info:   out member_record;
        check:             out boolean);
      --
      -- Function:
      --    If the value of my_name matches the name of the secretary,
      --    if the roster is not already full, and
      --    if the value of new_member_name is not the same as the
      --    name component in any current member's record, a new
      --    member_record is added to the roster with the value of
      --    new_member_info. If successful, check is set true, else
      --    check is set false upon return.

    procedure Update_member(
        my_name:           in  string_of30;
        old_member_name:   in  string_of30;
        old_member_info:   out member_record;
        check:             out boolean);
      --
      -- Function:
      --    If the value of my_name matches the name of the secretary,
      --    and if the value of old_member_name is the same as the
      --    name component in some current member's record, that record
      --    is replaced in the roster with a record whose value is that of
      --    new_member_info. If successful, check is set true, else
      --    check is set false upon return.

    procedure Delete_member(
        my_name:       in  string_of30;
        member_name:   in  string_of30;
        check:         out boolean);
      --
      -- Function:
      --    If the value of my_name matches the name of the secretary,
      --    and if the value of member_name is the same as the
      --    name component in some current member's record, that record
      --    is deleted from the roster. If successful, check is
      --    set true, else check is set false upon return.
private
   type roster is array(1..Max_num_members) of member_record;
     --
     -- An instance of a roster is (assumed to be) instantiated in the
     -- body part of this package.
```

```
end Membership_Roster;

                              Roster_Server task
                    for use with the Figure 2-5 structure
--
task Roster_Server  is           -- The specification part for
                                 -- the Roster_Server task referred to
                                 -- in Figure 3-1

--
-- Title queries
--
  entry Is_President(
      member_name:  in  string_of30;
      check:        out boolean);
    --
    -- Function:
    --   Calls Membership_Roster.Lookup_member to obtain
    --   member's record.
    --   Sets check true if member_name matches that of a member
    --   whose title is President, else returns with check
    --   set to false.

  entry Is_Vice_president(
      member_name:  in  string_of30;
      check:        out boolean);
    --
    -- Function:
    --   Calls Membership_Roster.Lookup_member to obtain
    --   member's record.
    --   Sets check true if member_name matches that of a member
    --   whose title is Vice-president, else returns with check
    --   set to false.

  entry Is_Treasurer(
      member_name:  in  string_of30;
      check:        out boolean);
    --
    -- Function:
    --   Calls Membership_Roster.Lookup_member to obtain
    --   member's record.
    --   Sets check true if member_name matches that of a member
    --   whose title is Treasurer, else returns with check
    --   set to false.

  entry Is_Secretary(
      member_name:  in  string_of30;
      check:        out boolean);
    --
    -- Function:
    --   Calls Membership_Roster.Lookup_member to obtain
    --   member's record.
    --   Sets check true if member_name matches that of a member
    --   whose title is Secretary, else returns with check
    --   set to false.
```

```
--
-- General queries to the roster.
--
  entry Lookup_member(
      member_name:  in  string_of30;
      member_info:  out member_record;
      check:        out boolean);
    --
    -- Function:
    --   Calls Membership_Roster.Lookup_member to acquire copy
    --   of info on a member and sets check true if Lookup
    --   succeeds. Returns with check set to false if
    --   Lookup call "fails".

  entry List_of_members(
      names_only:   in  boolean := true;
      check:        out boolean);
    --
    -- Function:
    --   Calls Membership_Roster.List_of_members to print the
    --   membership roster. If names_only is false, the full
    --   member_record is printed for each member;
    --   otherwise, only member names are printed.
    --   Returns with check set to false if roster is empty;
    --   else returns with check set to true.

--
-- Requests for membership roster update
--
  entry Add_new_member(
      my_name:            in  string_of30;
      new_member_name:    in  string_of30;
      new_member_info:    out member_record;
      check:              out boolean);
    --
    -- Function:
    --   Calls Membership_Roster.Add_new_member to insert info on
    --   a member into the membership roster.
    --   Returns with check false if Add_new_member call "fails";
    --   else returns  with check set to true.
    --   (Can fail if my_name does not match with the name of the
    --   of the Secretary, or if there is already a member of the
    --   given new_member_name in the roster, or if the roster is
    --   already full.)

  entry Update_member(
      my_name:            in  string_of30;
      old_member_name:    in  string_of30;
      old_member_info:    out member_record;
      check:              out boolean);
    --
    -- Function:
    --   Calls Membership_Roster.Update_member to modify info on an
    --   a current ("old") member in the membership roster.
    --   Returns with check false if Update_member call "fails";
    --   else returns with check set to true.
    --   (Can fail if my_name does not match with the name of the
    --   of the Secretary or if there is no such member of the
    --   given old_member_name in the roster.)
```

```
  entry Delete_member(
      my_name:              in string_of30;
      member_name:          in  string_of30;
      check:                out boolean);
    --
    -- Function:
    --   Calls Membership_Roster.Delete_member to delete all info on
    --   a current member in the membership roster.
    --   Returns with check false if Delete_member call "fails";
    --   else returns with check set to true.
    --   (Can fail if there isn't already a member of the given
    --   member_name in the roster.)

end Roster_Server;
```

Portfolio_Server task for use with the Figure 2-5 structure

```
--
task Portfolio_Server is          -- The specification part for
                                  -- the Portfolio_Server task referred to
                                  -- in Figure 3-1
--
-- Portfolio queries
--
  entry Print_club_valuation(
      value:  out dollars);
    --
    -- Function:
    --   Calls the corresponding operation of Club_Portfolio to
    --   print and "return" total value of portfolio instance,
    --   based on current market prices. Note: in Ada, an entry
    --   call may not implicitly return a value.
    --   The value must be returned explicitly, as an in out
    --   or out parameter of the entry.
    --
  entry Print_club_holdings;
    --
    -- Function:
    --   Calls the corresponding operation in Club_Portfolio.

  entry Find_stock_code(
      corporate_name: in  long_string;
      stock_code:     out stock_code_pair);
    --
    -- Function:
    --   Calls the corresponding operation in Club_Portfolio.

  entry Print_individual_stock_summary(
      stock_code:        in stock_code_pair);
    --
    -- Function:
    --   Calls the corresponding operation in Club_Portfolio.
```

```
  entry Print_shares_and_value_of_stock(
      stock_code: in stock_code_pair);
    --
    -- Function:
    --   Calls the corresponding operation in Club_Portfolio.

  entry Print_average_cost(
      stock_code: in stock_code_pair);
    --
    -- Function:
    --   Calls corresponding operation in Club_Portfolio.

  entry Print_winners(
      spread: in percent);    -- Percentage spread.
    --
    -- Function:
    --   Calls the corresponding operation in Club_Portfolio.

  entry Print_losers(
      spread: in percent);    -- Percentage spread.
    --
    -- Function:
    --   Analogous with Print_winners.

  entry Print_non_movers(
      spread:  in percent);   -- Percentage spread.
    --
    -- Function:
    --   Calls the corresponding operation in Club_Portfolio.
--
--
-- Note: All the following entries involve task calls on Roster_Server.
-- The individual membership Roster instance referenced
-- indirectly through Roster_Server is assumed to be created
-- upon initialization of the Membership_Roster package.
--
--
-- Portfolio update requests
--
  entry Enter_buy(
      my_name:       in  string_of30;
      unauthorized:  out boolean;
      purch_date:    in  date;
      stock_code:    in  stock_code_pair;
      num_shares:    in  natural;
      per_sh_price:  in  dollars;
      commission:    in  dollars);
    --
    -- Function:
    --   Determines if member whose name is value of my_name
    --   is authorized to update the Roster. If not, returns
    --   with value of unauthorized still set to true. If yes, sets
    --   unauthorized to false and then calls the corresponding
    --   operation in Club_Portfolio.
```

```
  entry Enter_sell(
      my_name:        in  string_of30;
      unauthorized:   out boolean;
      sell_date:      in  date;
      stock_code:     in  stock_code_pair;
      num_shares:     in  natural;
      of_buy_date:    in  date;
      sell_commiss:   in  dollars); -- Selling commission is not
                                    -- recorded in Roster,
                                    -- but used to indicate net gain or
                                    -- loss in confirmation copy.
    --
    -- Function:
    --   Determines if person whose name is value of my_name
    --   is authorized to update the Roster. If not, returns
    --   with value of unauthorized still set to true. If yes, sets
    --   unauthorized to false and then calls the corresponding
    --   operation in Club_Portfolio.

--
-- Portfolio create and delete requests
--
  entry President_create_folio(
      my_name:          in  string_of30;
      portfolio_name:   in  long_string;
      unauthorized:     out boolean);
    --
    -- Function:
    --   Calls Roster_Server to determine if member whose name
    --   is value of my_name is the current club President.
    --   If not, returns with value of unauthorized still true.
    --   If yes, sets unauthorized to false and then returns after
    --   recording the portfolio name supplied. Creation will not
    --   actually be attempted until a sequence of three creation
    --   requests for the same portfolio name has been received, one
    --   each from the three club officers: President, vice-president
    --   and treasurer.

  entry Vice_president_create_folio(
      my_name:          in  string_of30;
      portfolio_name:   in  long_string;
      unauthorized:     out boolean);
    --
    -- Function:
    --   Request at this entry accepted if and only if the
    --   most recently accepted entry call was for
    --   President_create_folio, and that call was authorized.
    --   Calls Roster_Server to determine if member whose name
    --   is value of my_name is the current club Vice-president.
    --   If not, returns with value of unauthorized set to true.
    --   If yes, sets unauthorized to false and then returns after
    --   recording the portfolio name supplied. Creation will not
    --   actually be attempted until a sequence of three creation
    --   requests for the same portfolio name has been received, one
    --   each from the three club officers: President, vice-president
    --   and treasurer.
```

```
entry Treasurer_create_folio(
    my_name:        in  string_of30;
    portfolio_name: in  long_string;
    unauthorized:   out boolean;
    check:          out boolean);
                        -- If set true, portfolio has been created.
  --
  -- Function:
  --    Request at this entry accepted if and only if the two
  --    most recently accepted entry calls were for
  --    President_create_folio and Vice_president_create_folio
  --    in that order, and if both were authorized calls.
  --    Calls Roster_Server to determine if member whose name
  --    is value of my_name is the current club Treasurer.
  --    If not, returns with value of unauthorized still true.
  --    If yes, sets unauthorized to false. The three supplied
  --    portfolio names are checked. If all are not identical,
  --    a return is executed (with check set to false.)
  --    If they do match, then the Create_folio operation in
  --    Club_Portfolio is called. If this call is successful
  --    (new portfolio created), then check is set true;  return to
  --    Treasurer_create_folio's caller is then executed.

entry President_delete_folio(
    my_name:        in  string_of30;
    portfolio_name: in  long_string;
    unauthorized:   out boolean);
  --
  -- Function:
  --    Calls Roster_Server to determine if member whose name
  --    is value of my_name is the current club President.
  --    If not, returns with value of unauthorized set to true.
  --    If yes, sets unauthorized to false and then returns after
  --    recording the portfolio name supplied. Deletion will not
  --    actually be attempted until a sequence of three deletion
  --    requests for the same portfolio name has been received, one
  --    each from the three club officers: President, vice-president
  --    and treasurer.

entry Vice_president_delete_folio(
    my_name:        in  string_of30;
    portfolio_name: in  long_string;
    unauthorized:   out boolean);
  --
  -- Function:
  --    Request at this entry accepted if and only if the
  --    most recently accepted entry call was for
  --    President_delete_folio, and that call was authorized.
  --    Determines if member whose name is value of my_name
  --    is the current club vice-president.
  --    If not, returns with value of unauthorized set to true.
  --    If yes, sets unauthorized to false and then returns after
  --    recording the portfolio name supplied. Deletion will not
  --    actually be attempted until a sequence of three deletion
  --    requests for the same portfolio name has been received, one
  --    each from the three club officers: President, vice-president
  --    and treasurer.
```

```
entry Treasurer_delete_folio(
    my_name:        in  string_of30;
    portfolio_name: in  long_string;
    unauthorized:   out boolean;
    check:          out boolean);
                       -- If set true, portfolio has been deleted.
  --
  -- Function:
      --   Request at this entry accepted if and only if the two
      --   most recently accepted entry calls were for
      --   President_delete_folio and Vice_president_delete_folio
      --   in that order, and if both were authorized calls.
      --   Calls Roster_Server to determine if member whose name
      --   is value of my_name is the current club Treasurer.
      --   If not, returns with value of unauthorized set to true.
      --   If yes, sets unauthorized to false. The three supplied
      --   portfolio names are checked. If all are not identical,
      --   a return is executed (with check still set to false.)
      --   If they do match, then the Delete_folio operation in
      --   Club_Portfolio is called. If this call is successful
      --   (portfolio deleted), then check is set true;  return to
      --   Treasurer_delete_folio's caller is then executed.
  --
  --
  -- Membership Roster queries
  --
    entry Lookup_member(
        member_name:  in  string_of30;
        member_info:  out member_record;
        check:        out boolean);
      --
      -- Function:
      --   Calls Roster_Server.Lookup_member to acquire copy of
      --   info on a member. Returns with check set to false,
      --   if lookup call "fails" else with check set to true.

    entry List_of_members(
        names_only:   in  boolean:= true;
        check:        out boolean);
      --
      -- Function:
      --   Calls Roster_Server.List_of_members to print the membership
      --   Roster. If names_only is false, the full member_record
      --   is printed for each member and returns with check
      --   set to true; otherwise, only member names
      --   are printed. Returns with check false Portfolio is empty.
  -- Membership Roster updates
  --
    entry Add_new_member(
        my_name:          in  string_of30;
        new_member_name:  in  string_of30;
        new_member_info:  out member_record;
        check:            out boolean);
      --
```

```
    -- Function:
    --    Calls Roster_Server.Add_new_member to insert info on
    --    a member into the membership Roster.
    --    Returns with check false if Add_new_member call "fails";
    --    else returns with check set to true.
    --    (Can fail if my_name does not match with the name of the
    --    of the Secretary or if there is already a member of the
    --    given new_member_name in the Roster, or if the Roster is
    --    already full.)

  entry Update_member(
      my_name:           in  string_of30;
      old_member_name:   in  string_of30;
      old_member_info:   out member_record;
      check:             out boolean);
    --
    -- Function:
    --    Calls Roster_Server.Update_member to modify info on an
    --    a current ("old") member in the membership Roster.
    --    Returns with check false if Update_call "fails";
    --    else returns with check set to true.
    --    (Can fail if my_name does not match with the name of the
    --    of the Secretary or if there is no such member of the
    --    given old_member_name in the Roster.)

  entry Delete_member(
      my_name:       in  string_of30;
      member_name:   in  string_of30;
      check:         out boolean);
    --
    -- Function:
    --    Calls Roster_Server.Delete_member to delete all info on
    --    a current member in the membership Roster.
    --    Returns with check false if Delete_call "fails";
    --    else returns with check set to true.
    --    (Can fail if there isn't already a member of the given
    --    member_name in the Roster.)

end Portfolio_Server;
```

Portfolio_Server body part

```
pragma environment("TskMst2-5.spr","TxtIo.spr","MemRos.spr",
                   "RosTypCon.spr","ClbPrt.spr", "StkTypCon.spr");


separate(Task_Master)                 -- Prefix to indicate to the compiler
                                      -- that Task_Master is the context
                                      -- in which the following task
                                      -- is to be compiled.


task body Portfolio_Server  is


  local_name_1, local_name_2:  string_of30;  -- Used in Create and Delete
                                              -- accepts.
  check_boolean:               boolean;      -- Used in predicates
```

```
begin

  loop

    select
--
-- Accepts for portfolio queries
--
     accept Print_club_valuation(
         value:   out dollars)
     do
       value := Club_Portfolio.Print_club_valuation();
     end Print_club_valuation;

    or

     accept Print_club_holdings
     do
       Club_Portfolio.Print_club_holdings;
     end Print_club_holdings;

    or

     accept Find_stock_code(
         corporate_name: in  long_string;
         stock_code:     out stock_code_pair)
     do
       stock_code :=
        Club_Portfolio.Find_stock_code(corporate_name);
     end Find_stock_code;

    or

     accept Print_individual_stock_summary(
         stock_code:    in stock_code_pair)
     do
       Club_Portfolio.Print_individual_stock_summary(
           stock_code);
     end Print_individual_stock_summary;

    or

     accept Print_shares_and_value_of_stock(



         stock_code: in stock_code_pair)
     do
       Club_Portfolio.Print_shares_and_value_of_stock(stock_code);
     end Print_shares_and_value_of_stock;

    or

     accept Print_average_cost(
         stock_code: in stock_code_pair)
     do
       Club_Portfolio.Print_average_cost(stock_code);
     end Print_average_cost;
```

```
 or

   accept Print_winners(
       spread: in percent)     -- Percentage spread.
   do
     Club_Portfolio.Print_winners(spread);
   end Print_winners;

 or

   accept Print_losers(
       spread: in percent)     -- Percentage spread.
     do
       Club_Portfolio.Print_losers(spread);
     end Print_losers;

   or

     accept  Print_non_movers(
         spread:   in percent)     -- Percentage spread.
     do
       Club_Portfolio.Print_non_movers(spread);
     end Print_non_movers;

   or
--
-- Accepts for Roster update requests
--
     accept  Enter_buy(
         my_name:       in  string_of30;
         unauthorized:  out boolean;
         purch_date:    in  date;
         stock_code:    in  stock_code_pair;
         num_shares:    in  natural;
         per_sh_price:  in  dollars;
         commission:    in  dollars)
     do
       Roster_Server.Is_Treasurer(my_name,check_boolean);
       if check_boolean then
         Club_Portfolio.Enter_buy(purch_date,
                                  stock_code,
                                  num_shares,
                                  per_sh_price,
                                  commission);
         unauthorized := false;
       else
         unauthorized := true;
       end if;
     end Enter_buy;

   or

     accept Enter_sell(
         my_name:       in  string_of30;
         unauthorized:  out boolean;
         sell_date:     in  date;
         stock_code:    in  stock_code_pair;
         num_shares:    in  natural;
         of_buy_date:   in  date;
         sell_commiss:  in  dollars)
```

```
      do
        Roster_Server.Is_Treasurer(my_name, check_boolean);
        if check_boolean then
          Club_Portfolio.Enter_sell(sell_date,
                                    stock_code,
                                    num_shares,
                                    of_buy_date,
                                    sell_commiss);
          unauthorized := false;
        else
          unauthorized := true;
        end if;
      end Enter_sell;

    or

--
-- Roster create and delete requests
--

      accept President_create_folio(
          my_name:        in  string_of30;
          portfolio_name: in  string_of30;
          unauthorized:   out boolean)
      do
        Roster_Server.Is_President(my_name, check_boolean);
        if check_boolean then
          local_name_1 := portfolio_name;   -- Save copy of portfolio_name
                                            -- for checking on subsequent
                                            -- accepts.
          unauthorized := false;
        else
          unauthorized := true;
        end if;
      end President_create_folio;
      --
      -- Sequel of two accepts begins here.
      --
      accept Vice_president_create_folio(
          my_name:        in  string_of30;
          portfolio_name: in  string_of30;
          unauthorized:   out boolean)

      do
        Roster_Server.Is_Vice_president(my_name, check_boolean);
        if check_boolean and local_name_1 = portfolio_name   then
          local_name_2 := portfolio_name;   -- Save copy of portfolio_name
                                            -- for checking on subsequent
                                            -- accept.
          unauthorized := false;
        else
          unauthorized := true;
        end if;
      end Vice_president_create_folio;
```

```
    accept Treasurer_create_folio(
        my_name:        in  string_of30;
        portfolio_name: in  string_of30;
        unauthorized:   out boolean;
        check:          out boolean)
                      -- If set true, portfolio has been created.
  do
    Roster_Server.Is_Treasurer(my_name,check_boolean);
    if check_boolean
        and local_name_1 = portfolio_name
        and local_name_2 = portfolio_name   then
      unauthorized := false;
      Club_Portfolio.Create_folio(portfolio_name, check);
                                  -- Portfolio is created if
                                  -- check is returned with
                                  -- the value, true.
    else
      unauthorized := true;
    end if;
  end Treasurer_Create_folio;
  --
  -- End of sequel (end chain of three accepts).

or

  accept President_delete_folio(
      my_name:        in  string_of30;
      portfolio_name: in  string_of30;
      unauthorized:   out boolean)
  do
    Roster_Server.Is_President(my_name,check_boolean);
    if check_boolean then
      local_name_1 := portfolio_name;  -- Save copy of portfolio_name
                                       -- for checking on subsequent
                                       -- accepts.
      unauthorized := false;
    else
      unauthorized := true;
    end if;
  end President_delete_folio;
  --
  -- Sequel of two accepts begins here.
  --
  accept Vice_president_delete_folio(
      my_name:        in  string_of30;
      portfolio_name: in  string_of30;
      unauthorized:   out boolean)
  do
    Roster_Server.Is_Vice_president(my_name,check_boolean);
    if check_boolean
        and local_name_1 = portfolio_name   then
      local_name_2 := portfolio_name;  -- Save copy of portfolio_name
                                       -- for checking on subsequent
                                       -- accept.
      unauthorized := false;
    else
      unauthorized := true;
    end if;
  end Vice_president_delete_folio;
```

```
     accept Treasurer_delete_folio(
         my_name:           in  string_of30;
         portfolio_name:    in  string_of30;
         unauthorized:      out boolean;
         check:             out boolean)
                            -- If set true, portfolio has been deleted.
     do
       Roster_Server.Is_Treasurer(my_name,check_boolean);
       if check_boolean
           and local_name_1 = portfolio_name
           and local_name_2 = portfolio_name   then
         unauthorized := false;
         Club_Portfolio.Delete_folio(portfolio_name, check);
                                         -- Portfolio is deleted if
                                         -- check is returned with
                                         -- the value, true.
       else
         unauthorized := true;
       end if;
       end Treasurer_delete_folio;
       --
       -- End of sequel (end chain of three accepts).

     or
--
-- Membership Roster query requests
--
       accept Lookup_member(
           member_name:  in  string_of30;
           member_info:  out member_record;
           check:        out boolean)
       do
         Roster_Server.Lookup_member(member_name,
                                          member_info, check);
       end Lookup_member;

     or

       accept List_of_members(
           names_only:   in  boolean := true;
           check:        out boolean)
       do
         Roster_Server.List_of_members(names_only, check);
       end List_of_members;

     or
```

```
--
-- Membership Roster updates
--
        accept Add_new_member(
            my_name:            in  string_of30;
            new_member_name:    in  string_of30;
            new_member_info:    out member_record;
            check:              out boolean)
        do
          Roster_Server.Add_new_member(my_name,
                                      new_member_name,
                                      new_member_info,
                                      check);
        end Add_new_member;

      or

        accept Update_member(
            my_name:            in  string_of30;
            old_member_name:    in  string_of30;
            old_member_info:    out member_record;
            check:              out boolean)
        do
          Roster_Server.Update_member(my_name,
                                     old_member_name,
                                     old_member_info,
                                     check);
        end Update_member;

      or

        accept Delete_member(
            my_name:        in  string_of30;
            member_name:    in  string_of30;



            check:          out boolean)
        do
          Roster_Server.Delete_member(my_name,
                                     member_name,
                                     check);
        end Delete_member;

      end select;

    end loop;

end Portfolio_Server;
```

Appendix G

Roster_Server task for use with the Figure 3-2 structure

```
task Roster_Server  is          -- The specification part for
                                -- the Roster_Server task referred to
                                -- in Figure 3-1

--
-- General queries to the roster.
--
  entry Lookup_member (
      member_name:   in  long_string;
      member_info:   out member_record;
      check:         out boolean);
    --
    -- Function:
    --    Calls Membership_Roster.Lookup_member to acquire copy
    --    for info on a member and sets check true if Lookup
    --    succeeds. Returns with check set to false if
    --    Lookup call "fails", else returns with check set to true.

  entry List_of_members(
      names_only:    in  boolean := true;
      check:         out boolean);
    --
    -- Function:
    --    Calls Membership_Roster.List_of_members to print the
    --    membership roster. If names_only is false, the full
    --    member_record is printed for each member;
    --    otherwise, only member names are printed.
    --    Returns with check set to false if roster is empty;
    --    else returns with check set to true.
--
-- Requests for membership roster update
--
  entry Add_new_member(
      new_member_name:   in  long_string;
      new_member_info:   out member_record;
      check:             out boolean);
    --
    -- Function:
    --    Calls Membership_Roster.Add_new_member to insert info on
    --    a member into the membership roster.
    --    Returns with check false if Add_new_member call "fails";
    --    else returns with check set to true.
    --    (Can fail if there is already a member for the given
    --    new_member_name in the roster, or if the roster is
    --    already full.)
```

```
  entry Update_member(
      old_member_name:  in  long_string;
      old_member_info:  out member_record;
      check:            out boolean);
    --
    -- Function:
    --   Calls Membership_Roster.Update_member to modify info on an
    --   a current ("old") member in the membership roster.
    --   Returns with check false if Update_member call "fails";
    --   else returns with check set to true.
    --   (Fails if there is no such member for the given
    --   old_member_name in the roster.)

  entry Delete_member(
      member_name:  in  long_string;
      check:        out boolean);
    --
    -- Function:
    --   Calls Membership_Roster.Delete_member to delete all info on
    --   a current member in the membership roster.
    --   Returns with check false if Delete_member call "fails";
    --   else returns with check set to true.
    --   (Fails if there isn't already a member for the given
    --   member_name in the roster.)

end Roster_Server;


                         Portfolio_Server task
                for use with the Figure 3-2 structure
--
task Portfolio_Server is         -- The specification part for
                                 -- the Portfolio_Server task referred to
                                 -- in Figure 3-1

--
-- Portfolio queries:
--
  entry Print_club_valuation(
      value:  out dollars);
    --
    -- Function:
    --   Calls the corresponding operation for Club_Portfolio to
    --   print and "return" total value for portfolio instance,
    --   based on current market prices. Note: in Ada, an entry
    --   call may not implicitly return a value.
    --   The value must be returned explicitly, as an in out
    --   or out parameter for the entry.
    --
  entry Print_club_holdings;
    --
    -- Function:
    --   Calls the corresponding operation in Club_Portfolio.

  entry Find_stock_code(
      corporate_name: in  long_string;
      stock_code:     out stock_code_pair);
    --
    -- Function:
    --   Calls the corresponding operation in Club_Portfolio.
```

```
entry Print_individual_stock_summary(
    stock_code:       in stock_code_pair);
  --
  -- Function:
  --   Calls the corresponding operation in Club_Portfolio.

entry Print_shares_and_value_of_stock(
    stock_code: in stock_code_pair);
  --
  -- Function:
  --   Calls the corresponding operation in Club_Portfolio.

entry Print_average_cost(
    stock_code: in stock_code_pair);
  --
  -- Function:
  --   Calls corresponding operation in Club_Portfolio.

entry Print_winners(
     spread: in percent);    -- percentage spread
  --
  -- Function:
  --   Calls the corresponding operation in Club_Portfolio.

entry Print_losers(
     spread: in percent);    -- percentage spread
  --
  -- Function:
  --   Analogous with Print_winners.

entry Print_non_movers(
    spread:  in percent);    -- percentage spread
  --
  -- Function:
  --   Calls the corresponding operation in Club_Portfolio.
--
-- Portfolio update requests:
--
entry Enter_buy(
    purch_date:    in  date;
    stock_code:    in  stock_code_pair;
    num_shares:    in  natural;
    per_sh_price:  in  dollars;
    commission:    in  dollars);
  --
  -- Function:
  --   Calls the corresponding operation in Club_Portfolio.

entry Enter_sell(
    sell_date:     in  date;
    stock_code:    in  stock_code_pair;
    num_shares:    in  natural;
    of_buy_date:   in  date;
    sell_commiss:  in  dollars); -- Selling commission is not
                                 -- recorded in portfolio,
                                 -- but used to indicate net gain or
                                 -- loss in confirmation copy.
  --
  -- Function:
  --   Calls the corresponding operation in Club_Portfolio.
```

```
-- Portfolio create and delete requests:
--
  entry President_create_folio(
      portfolio_name: in  long_string;
      check_point:    out boolean);
    --
    -- Function:
    --   Returns after recording supplied value for portfolio_name
    --   and setting the value for check_point to true.
    --   Creation will not actually be attempted until a sequence
    --   for three creation requests for the same portfolio_name
    --   been received, one each from the three officers: President,
    --   Vice-president, and Treasurer.

  entry Vice_president_create_folio(
      portfolio_name: in  long_string;
      check_point:    out boolean);
    --
    -- Function:
    --   Request at this entry accepted if and only if the
    --   most recently accepted entry call was for
    --   President_create_folio.
    --   Returns after recording supplied value for portfolio_name
    --   and setting the value for check_point to true.
    --   Creation will not actually be attempted until a sequence
    --   for three creation requests for the same portfolio_name
    --   been received, one each from the three officers: President,
    --   Vice-president, and Treasurer.

  entry Treasurer_create_folio(
      portfolio_name: in  long_string;
      check:          out boolean);
                          -- If set true, portfolio has been created.
    --
    -- Function:
    --   Request at this entry accepted if and only if the two
    --   most recently accepted entry calls were for
    --   President_create_folio and Vice_president_create_folio
    --   in that order. The three supplied portfolio names
    --   are now checked. If all are not identical,
    --   a return is executed (with check set to false.)
    --   If they do match, then the Create_folio operation in
    --   Club_Portfolio is called. If this call is successful
    --   (new portfolio created), then check is set true;  return to
    --   Treasurer_create_folio's caller is then executed.

  entry President_delete_folio(
      portfolio_name: in  long_string;
      check_point:    out boolean);

    -- Function:
    --   Returns after recording supplied value for portfolio_name
    --   and setting the value for check_point to true.
    --   Deletion will not actually be attempted until a sequence
    --   for three deletion requests for the same portfolio_name
    --   been received, one each from the three officers: President,
    --   Vice-president, and Treasurer.
```

```
  entry Vice_president_delete_folio(
      portfolio_name: in  long_string;
      check_point:    out boolean);
    --
    -- Function:
    --   Request at this entry accepted if and only if the
    --   most recently accepted entry call was for
    --   President_delete_folio.
    --   Returns after recording supplied value for portfolio_name
    --   and setting the value for check_point to true.
    --   Deletion will not actually be attempted until a sequence
    --   for three deletion requests for the same portfolio_name
    --   been received, one each from the three officers: President,
    --   Vice-president, and Treasurer.

  entry Treasurer_delete_folio(
      portfolio_name: in  long_string;
      check:          out boolean);
                          -- If set true, portfolio has been created.
    --
    -- Function:
    --   Request at this entry accepted if and only if the two
    --   most recently accepted entry calls were for
    --   President_delete_folio and Vice_president_delete_folio
    --   in <that order. The three supplied portfolio names
    --   are now checked. If all are not identical,
    --   a return is executed (with check set to false.)
    --   If they do match, then the Delete_folio operation in
    --   Club_Portfolio is called. If this call is successful
    --   (portfolio deleted), then check is set true;  return to
    --   Treasurer_delete_folio's caller is then executed.

end Portfolio_Server;
```

Portfolio_Server

body part

```
pragma environment("TskMst3-2.spr","ClbPrt.spr", "StkTypCon.spr");

separate(Task_Master)              -- Prefix to indicate to the compiler
                                   -- that Task_Master is the context
                                   -- in which the following task
                                   -- is to be compiled.

task body Portfolio_Server  is

  local_name_1, local_name_2:  long_string;  -- Used in Create and Delete
                                             -- accepts.
```

```
begin

   loop

     select
--
-- Accepts for portfolio queries
--
       accept Print_club_valuation(
           value:   out dollars)
       do
         value := Club_Portfolio.Print_club_valuation();
       end Print_club_valuation;

     or

       accept Print_club_holdings
       do
         Club_Portfolio.Print_club_holdings;
       end Print_club_holdings;

     or

       accept Find_stock_code(
           corporate_name: in  long_string;
           stock_code:     out stock_code_pair)
       do
         stock_code :=
          Club_Portfolio.Find_stock_code(corporate_name);
       end Find_stock_code;

     or

       accept Print_individual_stock_summary(
           stock_code:    in stock_code_pair)
       do
         Club_Portfolio.Print_individual_stock_summary(
             stock_code);
       end Print_individual_stock_summary;

     or

       accept Print_shares_and_value_of_stock(
           stock_code:  in stock_code_pair)
       do
         Club_Portfolio.Print_shares_and_value_of_stock(stock_code);
       end Print_shares_and_value_of_stock;

     or

       accept Print_average_cost(
           stock_code:  in stock_code_pair)
       do
         Club_Portfolio.Print_average_cost(stock_code);
       end Print_average_cost;

     or

       accept Print_winners(
           spread:  in percent)     -- percentage spread
```

```
do
  Club_Portfolio.Print_winners(spread);
end Print_winners;

or

  accept Print_losers(
      spread:  in percent)     -- percentage spread
  do
    Club_Portfolio.Print_losers(spread);
  end Print_losers;

or

  accept  Print_non_movers(
      spread:   in percent)     -- percentage spread
  do




    Club_Portfolio.Print_non_movers(spread);
  end Print_non_movers;

or
--
-- Accepts for portfolio update requests
--
  accept  Enter_buy(
      purch_date:    in  date;
      stock_code:    in  stock_code_pair;
      num_shares:    in  natural;
      per_sh_price:  in  dollars;
      commission:    in  dollars)
  do
      Club_Portfolio.Enter_buy(purch_date,
                               stock_code,
                               num_shares,
                               per_sh_price,
                               commission);
  end Enter_buy;

or

  accept Enter_sell(
      sell_date:     in  date;
      stock_code:    in  stock_code_pair;
      num_shares:    in  natural;
      of_buy_date:   in  date;
      sell_commiss:  in  dollars)
  do
      Club_Portfolio.Enter_sell(sell_date,
                                stock_code,
                                num_shares,
                                of_buy_date,
                                sell_commiss);
  end Enter_sell;

or
```

```
--
-- Portfolio create and delete requests
--

      accept President_create_folio(
          portfolio_name: in  long_string;
          check_point:    out boolean)
      do
          local_name_1 := portfolio_name;   -- Save copy for portfolio_name
                                            -- for checking on subsequent
                                            -- accepts.
          check_point := true;
      end President_create_folio;
      --
      -- Sequel for two accepts begins here.
      --
      accept Vice_president_create_folio(
          portfolio_name: in  long_string;
          check_point:    out boolean)
      do
        if  local_name_1 = portfolio_name   then
          local_name_2 := portfolio_name;   -- Save copy for portfolio_name
                                            -- for checking on subsequent
                                            -- accept.
          check_point := true;
        else
          check_point := false;
        end if;
      end Vice_president_create_folio;
      --
      accept Treasurer_create_folio(
          portfolio_name: in  long_string;
          check:          out boolean)
                        -- If set true, portfolio has been created.
      do
        if      local_name_1 = portfolio_name
            and local_name_2 = portfolio_name   then
          Club_Portfolio.Create_folio(portfolio_name, check);
                                     -- Portfolio is created if
                                     -- check is returned with
                                     -- the value, true.
        end if;
      end Treasurer_Create_folio;
      --
      -- End for sequel (end chain for three accepts).

    or

      accept President_delete_folio(
          portfolio_name: in  long_string;
          check_point:    out boolean)
      do

          local_name_1 := portfolio_name;   -- Save copy for portfolio_name
                                            -- for checking on subsequent
                                            -- accepts.
          check_point := true;
      end President_delete_folio;
```

```
      --
      -- Sequel for two accepts begins here.
      --
      accept Vice_president_delete_folio(
          portfolio_name: in  long_string;
          check_point:    out boolean)
      do
        if  local_name_1 = portfolio_name   then
          local_name_2 := portfolio_name;  -- Save copy for portfolio_name
                                           -- for checking on subsequent
                                           -- accept.
          check_point := true;
        else
          check_point := false;
        end if;
      end Vice_president_delete_folio;
      --
      accept Treasurer_delete_folio(
          portfolio_name: in  long_string;
          check:          out boolean)
                        -- If set true, portfolio has been deleted.
      do
        if      local_name_1 = portfolio_name
            and local_name_2 = portfolio_name   then
          Club_Portfolio.Delete_folio(portfolio_name, check);
                                    -- Portfolio is deleted if
                                    -- check is returned with
                                    -- the value, true.
        end if;
      end Treasurer_delete_folio;
      --
      -- End for sequel (end chain for three accepts).

    end select;

  end loop;

end Portfolio_Server;
```

Appendix H

Package Typed_Ports of the iMAX Operating System

```
with iMAX_Definitions;
package Typed_Ports is
   --
   -- Function:
   --    Typed_Ports consists of three packages which provide the user
   --    with a high level (Ada typed) view of ports, carriers and other
   --    operations.
   --    Private sections are not shown in this Appendix.

   use iMAX_Definitions;


   generic
       type user_message is private;   -- All messages that this package
                                       -- deals with are of this type.
   package Simple_Port_Def is
     --
     -- Function:
     --    This package provides definitions and operations that enable
     --    the user to create ports, and do simple operations on those
     --    ports involving only messages of type "user_message".

   max_message_count:  short_ordinal := 1000; -- Max number of messages
                                              -- in a port's message.
                                              -- queue

   type user_port is private;  -- Ports of this type can only be used
                               -- with type user_message.

   null_user_port: constant user_port;

   type q_discipline is  (
       FIFO,        -- First_in_first_out, also default q_discipline.
       priority);   -- Within same priority, FIFO is used.

   no_send_rights:      exception;
   no_receive_rights:   exception;

   function Has_send_rights(
       prt:  user_port)          -- User_port whose send_rights
                                 -- are to be checked.
     return boolean;             -- Result of inquiry.
     --
     -- Function:
     --    Returns true if the specified port has send rights.
```

```
function Has_receive_rights(
    prt:  user_port)          -- User_port whose receive_rights
                              -- are to be checked.
  return boolean;             -- Result of inquiry.
  --
  -- Function:
  --   Returns true if the specified port has receive rights.

function Create(
    message_count:     short_ordinal range 1 .. max_message_count;
                                                 -- Max number of
                                                 -- messages in the
                                                 -- port's message
                                                 -- queue.
    port_discipline:   q_discipline := FIFO;     -- Organization of
                                                 -- the port's message
                                                 -- queue.
    sro:               storage_resource := null) -- SRO used in the
                                                 -- creation.
  return user_port;                              -- User port that is
                                                 -- created.
  -- Function:
  --   A user_port with the specified message_count and the specified
  --   message queue discipline is created. The SRO used in the
  --   creation defaults to the default_global_heap_SRO.

procedure Send(
    prt:  user_port;          -- Port to which a message is to be sent.
    msg:  user_message);      -- Message that is to be sent.
  --
  -- Function:
  --   The specified user_message is sent to the specified
  --   user_port. In case the send cannot succeed immediately,
  --   the calling process will send_block.

procedure Cond_send(
    prt:  user_port;          -- Port to which a message is to be sent.
    msg:  user_message;       -- Message to be sent.
    suc:  out boolean);       -- True if send succeeded, false otherwise.
  --
  -- Function:
  -- An attempt is made to send the specified message to the
  -- specified port. If the send cannot succeed immediately, then
  -- false will be returned, otherwise true.

procedure Receive(
    prt:  user_port;              -- Port from which a message is to be
                                  -- received.
    msg:  out user_message);      -- Received message.
  --
  -- Function:
  --   A message will be received from the specified user_port. The
  --   calling process will be delayed until the receive succeeds.
```

```
procedure Cond_receive(
   prt:  user_port;           -- Port from which a message is to be
                              -- received.
   msg:  out user_message;    -- Received message, if any.
   suc:  out boolean);        -- True if message was received, false
                              -- otherwise.
  --
  -- Function:
  --   An attempt is made to  receive a message from the specified
  --   user_port. If the receive cannot cusseed immediately, false
  --   be returned. Otherwise true is returned together with the
  --   received message.

end Simple_Port_Def;

generic
    type user_message is private;      -- Type of message as
                                       -- specified by the user.
    type user_carrier_id is private;   -- Type of carrier_id as
                                       -- specified by the user.
package Carrier_Def is
  --
  -- Function:
  --   Definitions and operations on carriers are provided in
  --   this package.

  type user_carrier is private;   -- User_carriers can only carry
                                  -- messages of type user_message.

  function Create(
      id:   user_carrier_id;              -- Carier will have this id
      pri:  short_ordinal := 0;           -- priority.
      sro:  storage_resource := null)     -- SRO used for creation
    return user_carrier;                  -- carrier that is created.
    --
    -- Function:
    --   A user_carrier with the specified id and priority is
    --   created. The SRO used for the creation defaults to the
    --   default_global_heap_SRO of the calling process.

  procedure Get_carrier_message(
      car:  user_carrier;         -- Carrier from which we want to
                                  -- extract a message.
      msg:  out user_message);    -- Message previously received by
                                  -- the carrier.
    --
    -- Function:
    --   The message most recently received by the specified
    --   user_carrier is returned. This operation will null the
    --   message of the user_carrier.

  function Get_carrier_id(
      car:  user_carrier)         -- Carrier whose id is requested.
    return user_carrier_id;       -- Id of the carrier.
    --
    -- Function:
    --   The id of the specified carrier is returned.
```

```
  procedure Set_carrier_priority(
      car_id: user_carrier_id;
      pri:    short_ordinal := 0);
    --
    -- Function:
    --    Sets priority of a carrier specified by "car_id"
    --    to the value given by "pri". If no value for "pri" is
    --    given, the default value, zero, is supplied.

end Carrier_Def;


generic
    type user_port    is private;         -- Port capable of handling
                                          -- user_messages.
    type user_message is private;         -- Type of messages as
                                          -- specified by the user.
    type user_carrier is private;         -- Carrier capable of
                                          -- carrying user_messages.
    type user_carrier_port is private;    -- Port capable of handling
                                          -- user_carriers.
package Surrogate_Port_Def is
  --
  -- Function:
  --    This package contains surrogate port operations.
  --
  -- Note:
  --    It is the programmers' responsibility when instantiating
  --    packages of this generic package, to provide generic
  --    parameters that are in correct relation to one another.


  no_send_rights:        exception;
  no_receive_rights:     exception;
  no_use_rights:         exception;

  procedure Surrogate_send(
      prt:  user_port;              -- Port to which a user_message
                                    -- is to  be sent.
      msg:  user_message;           -- Message that is to be sent.
      car:  user_carrier;           -- Carrier used in surrogate
                                    -- operation.
      dst:  user_carrier_port);     -- Destination port where carrier
                                    -- will be sent (as a message)
                                    -- after the message is sent.
    --
    -- Function:
    --    The specified message will be sent to the specified port.
    --    In cxase the send cannot suceed immediately, then the
    --    specified carrier will block. When eventually the send
    --    succeeds, the carrier will be sent to the specified port.
```

```
    procedure Surrogate_receive(
        prt:  user_port;              -- Port from which a message is
                                      -- to be received.
        car:  user_carrier;           -- Carrier used in surrogate
                                      -- operation.
        dst:  user_carrier_port);     -- Destination port where carrier
                                      -- will be sent (a message)
                                      -- after receiving a message.
     --
     -- Function:
     --    The specified carrier will receive a message from the
     --    specified port. If the receive cannot succeed immediately,
     --    the carrier will block. When eventually the receive
     --    succeeds, the carrier carrying the received message will
     --    be sent to the specified destination port.


  end Surrogate_Port_Def;


end Typed_Ports;
```

Appendix I

Package Extended_Type_Manager of the iMAX Operating System

[AUTHOR'S NOTE: When the manuscript for this book was completed, the iMAX package for this appendix was undergoing revision. The package given here is comparable to but not identical with the actual version used in iMAX.]

```
with Descriptor_Definitions, iMAX_Definitions;
package Extended_Type_Manager is
   --
   -- Function:
   --    This package provides operations for creation and manipulation
   --    of type_definition objects, type definition objects,
   --    and extended_type objects.

   use iMAX_Definitions;

   type rights is range 0 .. 1;

   no_create_rights:     exception;
   no_amplify_rights:    exception;
   type_fault:           exception;


   procedure Create_type(
       len_d: short_ordinal;                  -- TDO data part in bytes.
       len_a: short_ordinal;                  -- TDO access part in 32-bit words.
       sro:   storage_resource := null)       -- SRO used in creation.
       tco:   out type_control;               -- Created Type Control Object.
       tdo:   out type_definition)            -- Created Type Definition Object.
    --
    -- Function:
    --    A type_control object for an Extended Type Object is created
    --    containing an AD for the Type Definition Object also created
    --    in this procedure. The type_definition object is created with
    --    specified lengths for data (len_d) and access (len_a) parts.
    --    The object is created from the specified SRO which defaults
    --    to the default_global_heap_sro.
```

```
function Create_extended_type(
    len_d: short_ordinal;               -- In bytes.
    len_a: short_ordinal;               -- In 32-bit words.
    tco:   type_control;                -- A TCO_AD with create rights.
    sro:   storage_resource := null)    -- SRO used in creation.
  return type_definition;               -- Created Type Definition Object.
  --
  -- Function:
  --   An Extended Type Object is created with specified lengths
  --   for data (len_d) and access (len_a) parts, and with a
  --   specifiedAD for a Type Control Object (tco).
  --   The specified TCO_AD must have create_rights.
  --   If not, a no_create_rights exception is raised.
  --   The object is created from the specified
  --   SRO which defaults to the default_global_heap_sro.


function Retrieve_type_definition(
    ext_type:  extended_type)   -- Extended_type object whose
                                -- type_definition is requested.
  return type_definition;       -- Type_definition of extended_type
                                -- object.
  --
  -- Function:
  --   This function returns an AD for type_definition object
  --   given the specified AD (ext_type) for an Extended Type
  --   Object. The returned type_definition object access
  --   descriptor has no defined type rights but does contain
  --   base rights.


procedure Restrict_rights(
    ext_type:     in out  extended_type;
    type_right_1:         rights := 1;
    type_right_2:         right  := 1;
    type_right_3:         rights := 1;
    delete_rights:        rights := 1;
    unchecked_copy_rights: rights := 1;
    read_rights:          rights := 1;
    write_rights:         rights := 1;
    tco:                  type_control);
  --
  -- Function:
  --   Removes the right(s) from the specified AD for an
  --   Extended Type Object (ext_type). If a particular right
  --   is not specified, it is not removed.

procedure Amplify_rights(
    ext_type:     in out  extended_type;
    tco:                  type_control);   -- With amplify rights.
  --
  -- Function:
  --   Amplifies the right(s) from the specified AD for an
  --   Extended Type Object (ext_type). The specified TCO_AD (tco)
  --   must have amplify rights. If not, a no_create_rights
  --   exception is raised. If the TDO_AD in the specified TCO
  --   does not match the TDO_AD in the specified Extended Type Object,
  --   a type_fault exception is raised.

end Extended_Type_Manager;
```

Appendix J

Package IO_Definitions of the iMAX Operating System

```
with iMAX_Definitions;

package  IO_Definitions  is
  --
  -- Function:
  --   This package contains definitions common to the synchronous and
  --   asynchronous I/O interfaces.
  use  iMAX_Definitions;

  type abstraction_description  is
    record
      abstraction_name: array (1 .. 30) of character;
      abstraction_type: type_description;
    end record;

  type abstractions_array is  array (1 .. 10) of abstraction_description;

  type query_record_rep  is
    record
      device_name:    print_name;          -- Printable device identifier.
      buffer_length:  short_ordinal;       -- Preferred buffer length minus one.
      fixed_length:   boolean;             -- True if "preferred" length
                                           -- is required.
      device_number:  short_ordinal;       -- Unique system device identifier.
      AP_number:      short_ordinal;       -- Controlling attached processor ID.
      abstractions:   abstractions_array;  -- Description of supported
                                           -- abstractions.
    end record;

  type  query_record  is  access  query_record_rep;

end  IO_Definitions;
```

Package Synchronous_IO_Interfaces of the iMAX Operating System

```
with Asynchronous_IO_Interface, iMAX_Definitions,
     IO_Definitions;

package  Synchronous_IO_Interfaces  is
  --
  -- Function:
  --    This package includes definitions of the standard synchronous
  --    I/O interfaces and related types.
  --
  use  IO_Definitions;


  -- Exceptions

  end_of_file:                  exception; -- No more input data.
  transformation_not_allowed: exception; -- Transform_interface was
                                          -- called with an unrecognized
                                          -- new interface type.
  operation_not_allowed:        exception; -- The specified operation is
                                          -- not recognized by the driver
                                          -- or support routine.
  transfer_error:               exception; -- An I/O or protocol error
                                          -- detected during a data transfer.

  subtype xfer_range    is integer range 0 .. 2**16;
                           -- Up to 65,636 bytes can be transferred
                           -- with one operation.

  -- The following set of operations is required of all synchronous I/O
  -- Interfaces.
  --
  --   type Basic_IO_Interface is access package
  --     --
  --     -- Function:
  --     --    This package type defines the minimum synchronous interface.
  --     --    It must be provided for all devices. It includes only routines
  --     --    for determining and changing device interface characteristics
  --     --    and closing the interface.
  --
  --     function Interface_description
  --       return query_record;  -- static interface description
  --
  --     procedure Close;
  --       --
  --       -- Function:
  --       --    This routine renders the interface unusable, after first
  --       --    flushing any buffers and completing any outstanding
  --       --    operations. Any further operations will cause an error.
```

```
--     procedure Reset;
--       --
--       -- Function:
--       --    This routine reintializes the interface. The effect of
--       --    Reset is device-dependent.
--
--
--     function Transform_interface(
--          new_interface_type: type_description) -- type of the new interface
--       return dynamic_typed;
--       --
--       -- Function:
--       --    This routine returns a new, possibly expanded or restricted
--       --    view, of this I/O interface. The transformations allowed can
--       --    be determined by calling Get_Interface_Characteristics.
--
--     function Get_asynchronous_interface
--       return Asynchronous_IO_Interface.connection;
--       --
--       -- Function:
--       --    This function returns a package which implements the standard
--       --    Asynchronous device interface.
--
--   end Basic_IO_Interface;



type  Source  is access package
  --
  -- Function:
  --    This package type defines the synchronous source interface

  -- The following functions and procedures are described in the
  -- Basic_IO_interface package.

  function Interface_description
    return query_record;

  procedure Close;

  procedure Reset;

  function Transform_interface(
       new_interface_type:  type_description) -- type of the new interface
    return dynamic_typed;

  function Get_asynchronous_interface
    return Asynchronous_IO_Interface.connection;

  -- End of basic package.
```

```
  procedure Read(
      data_access:              iMAX_Definitions.dynamic_typed;
                                               -- Access for object
                                               -- containing buffer offset.
      offset:                   xfer_range;    -- Offset of buffer
                                               -- within object.
      requested_length:         xfer_range;    -- Number of bytes
                                               -- to transfer.
      returned_length: out xfer_range);        -- Number of bytes
                                               -- actually transferred.
    --
    -- Function:
    --    This routine does a device dependent read operation, controlled
    --    by the interface characteristics buffer_length and fixed_length.
    --
    --    The number of bytes returned will be less than or equal to that
    --    requested when fixed_length is false. The end_of_file
    --    exception is raised when there is no more data (returned_length
    --    is zero).
    --
    --    The number of bytes returned is a multiple of the preferred
    --    buffer length (buffer_length plus one) when fixed_length is true.
    --    The operation_not_allowed exception is raised if the
    --    requested_length is not at least as large as the preferred
    --    buffer length. The end_of_file exception is raised when there
    --    is no more data (returned_length is zero).

end Source;


type  Sink  is access package
  --
  -- Function:
  --    This package type defines the synchronous sink interface.


  -- The following functions and procedures are described in the
  -- Basic_IO_interface package.

  function Interface_description
    return query_record;

  procedure Close;

  procedure Reset;

  function Transform_interface(
      new_interface_type:  type_description) -- type of the new interface
    return dynamic_typed;

  function Get_asynchronous_interface
    return Asynchronous_IO_Interface.connection;

  -- End of basic package.

  procedure Flush;
    --
    -- Function:
    --    This routine ensures that all previously-written data has
    --    reached the destination device.
```

```
  procedure Write(
      data_access:               iMAX_Definitions.dynamic_typed;
                                  -- Access for object containing buffer.
      offset:                    xfer_range;  -- Offset of buffer
                                              -- within object.
      length:                    xfer_range); -- Number of bytes
                                              -- to transfer.
    --
    -- Function:
    --    This routine does a device dependent write operation.  If
    --    fixed_length is true, the length must be equal to the preferred
    --    buffer length (buffer_length plus one).  (For some interfaces,
    --    a multiple of the preferred buffer length may be allowed.)

end Sink;



type  Store  is access package
  --
  -- Function:
  --    This package type defines the synchronous store.


  -- The following functions and procedures are described
  -- in the Basic_IO_interface package.

  function Interface_description
    return query_record;

  procedure Close;

  procedure Reset;

  function Transform_interface(
      new_interface_type:  type_description) -- type of the new interface
    return dynamic_typed;

  function Get_asynchronous_interface
    return Asynchronous_IO_Interface.connection;

  -- end of basic package

  procedure Flush;
    --
    -- Function:
    --    This routine ensures that all previously written data has
    --    reached the destination device.
```

```
    procedure Read(
        data_access:                read_buff;
        offset:                     xfer_range;
        requested_length:           xfer_range;
        returned_length: out xfer_range);
      --
      -- Function:
      --    This routine does a device dependent read operation, controlled
      --    by the interface characteristics buffer_length and fixed_length.
      --
      --    The number of bytes returned will be less than or equal to that
      --    requested when fixed_length is false. The end_of_file
      --    exception is raised when there is no more data (returned_length
      --    is zero).
      --
      --    The number of bytes returned is a multiple of the preferred
      --    buffer length (buffer_length plus one) when fixed_length is true
      --    The operation_not_allowed exception is raised if the
      --    requested_length is not at least as large as  the preferred
      --    buffer length. The end_of_file exception is raised when there
      --    is no more data (returned_length is zero).


    procedure Write(
        data_access:                iMAX_Definitions.dynamic_typed;
        offset:                     xfer_range;
        length:                     xfer_range);

      --
      -- Function:
      --    This routine does a device dependent write operation. If
      --    fixed_length is true, the length must be equal to the preferred
      --    buffer length (buffer_length plus one). (For some interfaces,
      --    a multiple of the preferred buffer length may be allowed.)

  end Store;

end Synchronous_IO_Interfaces;
```

Package Asynchronous_IO_Interface of the iMAX Operating System

```
with iMAX_Definitions, IO_Definitions;

package  Asynchronous_IO_Interface  is
  --
  -- Function:
  --   This package defines the asynchronous I/O protocol. This protocol
  --   is used between GDP processes and AP device drivers as well as
  --   within the GDP.

  use iMAX_Definitions, IO_Definitions;

  -- The "connection" type, which is the primary type provided by the
  -- Asynchronous_IO_Interface package, is an access to the following
  -- record type. All Asynchronous_IO_Interface operators take a
  -- connection as one parameter.

  type  connection_record  is
    record
      request_port:        port;           -- Port for I/O request messages.
      name:                print_name;     -- Identifying name.
      device_description:  query_record;   -- Device-specific information.
      reply_port:          port;           -- Port which may be used as
                                           -- a message reply port.

    end record;

  type  connection  is  access connection_record;

  -- The representation of an I/O transaction is an access segment with
  -- at least three access descriptors. the first entry is for the
  -- command_record which is a data segment describing the operation to be
  -- performed. The second entry is a reply port for the response message,
  -- and the third and succeeding entries are for data buffers. Since Ada
  -- requires that this structure be declared in reverse order, here is a
  -- picture of what is coming.
  --
```

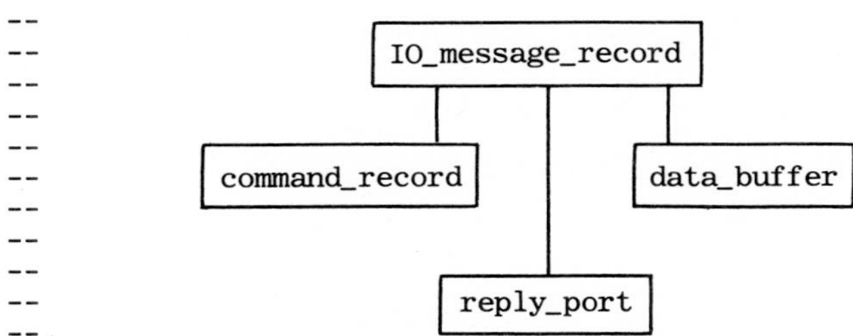

```
type command_value   is  range 0 .. short_ordinal'last;

type error_value     is  range 0 .. short_ordinal'last;

subtype buffer_range is short_ordinal range 1 .. 1;

type buffer_description  is
  record
    offset:              short_ordinal;
    requested_length:    short_ordinal;
    returned_length:     short_ordinal;
  end record;

type  command_record_rep_val  is
  record
    command:             command_value;
    message_id:          short_ordinal;
    reply_code:          error_value;
    buffer_descriptions: array (buffer_range) of buffer_description;
  end record;

type  command_record_rep is access command_record_rep_val;

type  buffer_array is array (buffer_range) of dynamic_typed;

-- I/O command codes
reset:                          constant command_value := 1;
read:                           constant command_value := 2;
write:                          constant command_value := 3;
close:                          constant command_value := 4;
flush:                          constant command_value := 5;
set_device_characteristics:     constant command_value := 6;
get_device_characteristics:     constant command_value := 7;

-- reply codes
success:                        constant command_value := 0;
end_of_file:                    constant command_value := 1;
not_processed:                  constant command_value := 2;
reset_required:                 constant command_value := 3;
invalid_command:                constant command_value := 4;
bad_data_buffer_size:           constant command_value := 5;
invalid_request:                constant command_value := 6;
hard_IO_error:                  constant command_value := 7;
interface_closed:               constant command_value := 8;
reset_returned:                 constant command_value := 9;


type IO_message_record  is
  record
    command_record:   command_record_rep;
    reply_port:       port;
    data_buffer:      buffer_array;
  end record;
```

```
  type  IO_message  is  access  IO_message_record;


  procedure Send(
      c:   connection;
      msg: IO_message);
    --
    -- Function:
    --   This routine sends a message to an I/O device using
    --   the request_port in the connection.

  procedure Receive(
      c:        connection;
      msg: out IO_message);
    --
    -- Function:
    --   This routine receives a reply to an I/O request on the
    --   reply_port in the connection.

  procedure Cond_send(
      c:            connection;
      msg:          IO_message;
      success: out boolean);
    --
    -- Function:
    --   This routine attempts to send an I/O request message to
    --   the request_port in the connection. If the operation succeeds,
    --   success is assigned true. If the port is full and the operation
    --   fails, success is assigned false and the request message is not
    --   sent.

  procedure Cond_receive(
      c:            connection;
      msg:      out IO_message;
      success:  out boolean);
    --
    -- Function:
    --   This routine attempts to receive a reply to an I/O request using
    --   a conditional receive on the reply_port in the connection.

end Asynchronous_IO_Interface;
```

Appendix K

Package Process_Manager_Types of the iMAX Operating System

```
with Process_Globals_Definitions,  iMAX_Definitions
     Descriptor_Definitions;

package Process_Manager_Types  is


  microsec_per_stu: constant := 256;
     -- Length of a system time unit in microseconds.
  subtype milliseconds is integer range 0 .. max_int;

  -- All of the following constants and types related to time
  -- are in units of milliseconds.

  max_time_limit:        constant := 24 * 24* 60 * 60 * 1000;
    -- Maximum time limit is 24 days in milliseconds.
  infinite_time_limit: constant := max_time_limit + 1;
    -- The value "infinite_time_limit" is used to
    -- indicate that the process is to be allowed to run forever.

  subtype time_limit_type is milliseconds range 0 .. infinite_time_limit;

  max_time_slice:        constant := (2**16 - 1) * microsec_per_stu / 1000;
  subtype time_slice_type is milliseconds range 0 .. max_time_slice;

  max_deadline:          constant := (2**14 - 1) * microsec_per_stu / 1000;
  subtype deadline_type   is milliseconds range 0 .. max_deadline;

  type scheduling_info_rec is
    record
      time_slice: time_slice_type;  -- in milliseconds
      deadline:   deadline_type;    -- in milliseconds
      priority:   short_ordinal;
    end record;

    type process_states is (
      executing,
      just_created,
      suspended,
      exceeded_memory_limit,
      exceeded_time_limit,
      system_error,
      terminated,
      destroyed);
```

```
type process_micro_states is (  -- micro state of an executing process
  not_executing,
  on_processor,
  on_cport,
  on_service_port,   -- includes dispatching and delay ports
  in_service);       -- being serviced by iMAX

type process_info_rec is
  --  Those attributes of a process which are either constant, or
  --  changed only by the user, over the lifetime of the process.
  record

    -- The following attributes are constant over the lifetime of
    -- the process.

    process_id:          short_ordinal;
      -- The iMAX-assigned id  of the process.
      -- This is the id used when the process does any locking operations.
    process_globals:     Process_Globals_Definitions.process_globals_rep;
      -- The iMAX-assigned  process globals object of the process.
      -- Compilers generate code which uses iMAX_defined fields in this
      -- object. Users may also define their own fields in this object.
    name:                string;
      -- The user-assigned text name of the process.

    -- The following attributes are defaulted when the process is
    -- created, and may be set by the user.

    notification_port:   iMAX_Definitions.port;
      -- The notification_msg will be conditionally sent to this
      -- notification_port when the process' state becomes
      -- exceeded_memory_limit, exceeded_time_limit, system_error,
      -- terminated, or destroyed. It is the user's responsibility
      -- to ensure that the conditional send will not fail; if the
      -- notification_port is full at the time of the conditional
      -- send, the notification_msg will not be sent.
    notification_msg:    dynamic_typed;
      -- The message to be sent to the notification_port.

    -- The following attributes are defaulted when the process is created
    -- and may be set only in an "advisory" sense. I.e., in setting
    -- them, the user is advising the Process_Manager as to how it
    -- should set them. Particular Process_Manager implementations
    -- may ignore this advice.

    time_limit:          time_limit_type;
      -- The processor time limit for the process.
    scheduling_info:     scheduling_info_rec;
      -- The scheduling parameters for the process.
  end record;

type process_state_rec is
  -- Those attributes of a process which are changed by the system
  -- over the lifetime of the process.
  record
    state:               process_states;
      -- The current state of the process.
    process_clock:       milliseconds;
      -- The current time used by the process in milliseconds.
  end record;
```

```
   type process_micro_state_rec is
     -- Process_state_rec plus micro state.
     record
       state:                  process_states;
        -- The current state of the process.
       micro_state:            process_micro_states;
        -- The current micro state of the process.
       process_clock:          milliseconds;
        -- The current time used by the process in milliseconds.
     end record;

generic
  with procedure main(
           params: dynamic_typed);
package initial_proc is
  procedure main(
      params: dynamic_typed);
    renames main;
end initial_proc;

type access_initial_proc is access initial_proc;

control_rights: constant Descriptor_Definitions.rights :=
                              Descriptor_Definitions.type_right_1;

suspend_and_resume_rights: constant  Descriptor_Definitions.rights :=
                              Descriptor_Definitions.type_right_2;



type Process_Manager is access package
  --
  -- Function:
  --   All operations requiring a process as a parameter, with the
  --   exception of Suspend, Resume, and the Read_... operations,
  --   require the passed process AD to have control_rights .
  --   The operations Suspend and Resume  also  require the passed
  --   process AD to have suspend_and_resume_rights.


  type process_rep is limited private;

  type process is access process_rep;
```

```
function Create_process(
    init_proc:              access_initial_proc;
      -- The procedure to execute.
    init_params:            dynamic_typed := null;
      -- Parameters to init_proc.
    name:                   string;
      -- The text name of the process.
    job:                    Jobs_Manager_Types.job := null;
      -- The job in which the caller is executing, i.e., the job
      -- in the caller's process globals.
    heap_sro:               iMAX_Definitions.storage_resource := null;
      -- The sro from which to create the process. This determines
      -- the scope of the process and whether the process is frozen or
      -- normal. Default is the global heap sro in the caller's
      -- process globals.
    init_stack_objtab_size: integer := 0;
      -- Initial size of the process stack object table. This is an
      -- advisory parameter, and may be ignored by particular
      -- Process_Manager implementations.
    init_stack_size:        integer := 0;
      -- Initial size of the process stack allocation block. This is an
      -- advisory parameter, and may be ignored by particular
      -- Process_Manager implementations.
    call_stack_depth:       integer := 0;
      -- Number of contexts to be pre-allocated for this process.
      -- This is an advisory parameter, and may be ignored by particular
      -- Process_Manager implementations.
  return process;  -- Has control_rights.
  --
  -- Function:
  --    A new process is created and returned. The parameter list
  --    includes only those process attributes which can be set only
  --    at process creation time. Default values are provided for
  --    all process attributes except the procedure to execute
  --    (init_proc); this is the only parameter which MUST be specified.
  --    Attributes for which there are no parameters may be changed after
  --    a process has been created (and before it is started, if desired)
  --    by calling one of the Set_... operations below.

procedure Start(
    prcs: process);
  --
  -- Function:
  --    This procedure serves two purposes: to initially start a newly
  --    created process, and to restart a process which has entered
  --    a state in which it can not execute (for example, when it has
  --    exceeded its memory or processor time limit, or has encountered
  --    an error.)  The passed process must be in a state other than
  --    executing, suspended, or destroyed.

procedure Suspend(
    prcs: process); -- Must have suspend_and_resume_rights.
  --
  -- Function:
  --    The passed process is prevented from executing on a processor
  --    until Resume is called on it. The effect of this call may
  --    be asynchronous, i.e., the process may continue to execute
  --    for a time after Suspend is called.
```

```
procedure Resume(
    prcs: process); -- Must have suspend_and_resume_rights.
  --
  -- Function:
  --    The passed process is continued executing after having had
  --    Suspend called on it.

procedure Destroy(
    prcs: process);
  --
  -- Function:
  --    The passed process is destroyed. The effect of this call may
  --    be asynchronous, i.e., the process may continue to execute for
  --    a time after Destroy is called and before it is actually
  --    destroyed.

procedure Delay_caller(
    time:  milliseconds);
  --
  -- Function:
  --    The calling process is delayed for at least the specified
  --    length of time.

procedure Raise_exception(
    prcs: process;
    e:    System.exception);
  --
  -- Function:
  --    The specified exception is raised in the passed process.
  --    The effect of this call may  be asynchronous, i.e., the
  --    exception may not be raised until some time after
  --    Raise_exception is called.

procedure Wait_for_process_termination;
    prcs: process);
  --
  -- Function:
  --    This procedure is provided for users who do not need the
  --    full generality of the notification port mechanism.
  --    If the notification message and port have already been set,
  --    an exception will be raised. Otherwise, a notification port
  --    will be created, set, and received from, resulting in the
  --    caller blocking until the passed process' state becomes
  --    exceeded_memory_limit, exceeded_time_limit, system_error,
  --    terminated, or destroyed.

function Read_process_info(
    prcs: process)
  return process_info_rec;
  --
  -- Function:
  --    Returns the "unchanging" attributes of the passed process.
```

```
    function Read_process_state(
        prcs: process)
      return process_state_rec;
      --
      -- Function:
      --    Returns the "changing" attributes of the passed process.

    function Read_process_micro_state(
        prcs: process)
      return process_micro_state_rep;
      --
      -- Function:
      --    Returns the "changing" attributes of the passed process,
      --    including the micro state.

    procedure Set_notification_port_and_message;
        prcs: process:
        port: iMAX_Definitions.port;
        msg:  dynamic_typed);
      --
      -- Function:
      --    The notification port and message of the passed process are set.
      --    An exception is raised if a call to Wait_for_process_termination
      --    is currently outstanding on the process.

    procedure Set_time_limit(
        prcs: process;
        lim:  time_limit_type);  -- in milliseconds
      --
      -- Function:
      --    Since time_limit is an advisory parameter, the time limit of
      --    the passed process may or may not be set.

    procedure Set_scheduling_info(
        prcs: process;
        svc:  scheduling_info_rec);
      --
      -- Function:
      --    Since scheduling_info is an advisory parameter, the scheduling
      --    parameters of the passed process may or may not be set.

  end Process_Manager;

end Process_Manager_Types;
```

Appendix L

Package SRO_Manager of the iMAX Operating System

Real Memory Only version

[*Author's note:* The actual iMAX version for this package specifies four additional operations, not given in this appendix. These are:
Create_system_object_from_heap,
Create_system_object_from_stack,
Deallocate_heap_object, and
Read_storage_claim.

```
with iMAX_Definitions;

package SRO_Manager is
  --
  -- Function:
  --   This package provides a low_level interface to memory management.
  --   All but the Create_local_heap function are implemented as
  --   432 instructions. The "heap" allocation instructions take an
  --   optional parameter, i.e., a default SRO. At compile time this
  --   parameter defaults to null, but at run time will default to
  --   the default global heap SRO in the process globals object of
  --   the the executing process. The "stack" allocation intructions
  --   do not need an SRO parameter since the stack SRO is referenced
  --   implicitly.
  --
  use iMAX_Definitions;

  -- Type Rights for SRO Access Descriptors:
  --

  create_rights: constant Descriptor_Definitions.rights :=
                          Descriptor_Definitions.type_right_1;


  procedure Create_object(
      d_length:        short_ordinal;   -- Length of object data part
                                        -- (in bytes) - 1.
      a_length:        short_ordinal    -- Length of object access part
                                        -- (number of AD slots)
      obj:         out object;          -- created object.
      SRO:             storage_resource := null);
                                        -- SRO for create.
    --
    -- Function:
    --   A heap data object of the specified size(s) is created.
    --   If the SRO parameter is defaulted, then the default global
    --   heap SRO in process globals is used for the create.
```

```
procedure Create_generic_refinement(
    obj:          dynamic_typed;     -- Object to be refined.
    d-offset:     short_ordinal;     -- Data part offset of the
                                     -- refinement in bytes.
    d-length:     short_ordinal;     -- Data part length of the
                                     -- refinement (in bytes) - 1.
    a-offset:     short_ordinal;     -- Access part offset of the
                                     -- refinement in bytes.
    a-length:     short_ordinal;     -- Access part length of the
                                     -- refinement (number of AD slots).
    rtn:      out dynamic_typed;     -- The resulting refinement.
    sro:          storage_resource_with_create := null);
                                     -- SRO for create.
  --
  -- Function:
  --   A heap refinement is created from the specified object,
  --   with data and access parts at specified offsets, each with
  --   with specified lengths. The base type of the created
  --   refinement will be the same as the base type of the
  --   original object. Its system type will be generic.

procedure Create_stack_object(
    d_length:       short_ordinal;   -- Length of object data part
                                     -- (in bytes) - 1.
    a_length:       short_ordinal    -- Length of object access part
                                     -- (number of AD slots).
    obj:        out object);         --  Created object.
  --
  -- Function:
  --   A stack object of the specified size(s) is created.

procedure Create_stack_generic_refinement(
    obj:          dynamic_yped;      -- Object to be refined.
    d-offset:     short_ordinal;     -- Data part offset of the
                                     -- refinement in bytes.
    d-length:     short_ordinal;     -- Data part length of the
                                     -- refinement (in bytes) - 1.
    a-offset:     short_ordinal;     -- Access part offset of the
                                     -- refinement in bytes.
    a-length:     short_ordinal;     -- Access part length of the
                                     -- refinement (number of AD slots).
    rtn:      out dynamic_typed;     -- The resulting refinement.

  --
  -- Function:
  --   A stack refinement is created from the specified object,
  --   with data and access parts at specified offsets, each with
  --   with specified lengths. The base type of the created
  --   refinement will be the same as the base type of the
  --   original object. Its system type will be generic.

function Create_local_heap
  return storage_resource;
  --
  -- Function:
  --   This function creates a local heap SRO.
  --   The lifetime of the local heap SRO is that of the current
  --   Context Object of the caller.

end SRO_Manager;
```

Package MCO_Manager of the iMAX Operating System

```
with Descriptor_Definitions, iMAX_Definitions;

package MCO_Manager is
  --
  -- Function:
  --   This package provides operations for creating and destroying
  --   MCOs, reading and adjusting the parameters associated with each
  --   MCO, and reading the usage statistics for each MCO.
  --   The private section for this package is not shown.

  type memory_control_object_rep is limited private;
  type memory_control_object is access memory_control_object_rep;

  asap:  constant := 0;
  never: constant := 0;

  type scan_rate_type is (asap, 1..14, never);
    --
    -- The scan rate determines how often the objects of the MCO are
    -- considered for swapping. This rate in terms of passes through all
    -- MCOs in the system. For each pass only some of the MCOs are
    -- considered.
    --
    --   Scan Rate Value              When MCO Is Scanned
    --         0                      As soon as possible.
    --         1                      Every pass.
    --         2                      Every other pass.
    --         3                      Every third pass.
    --        ...
    --         N                      Every Nth pass.
    --       never                    Never. The MCO is non-swappable.

  type MCO_parameters_type is
    record
      allocation_limit: ordinal;         -- Bytes this MCO can
                                         -- allocate without
                                         -- software intervention.
      frozen:           boolean;         -- Frozen or normal memory.
      scan_rate:        scan_rate_type;  -- Rate objects MCO are
                                         -- considered for swapping.
    end record;
```

```
type MCO_statistics_type is
  record
    storage_claim:          ordinal;     -- Total virtual memory exposed
                                          -- to hardware allocation.
    secondary:              ordinal;     -- Total virtual memory residing
                                          -- on disk.

    number_of_stack_SROs:     ordinal;
    number_of_heap_SROs:      ordinal;
    number_of_object_tables:  ordinal;

    fault rate:               ordinal;   -- Fault rate of this MCO
  end record;

-- Software-defined Type Rights for MCO access descriptors:
--
control_rights:  constant Descriptor_Definitions.rights
                     := Descriptor_Definitions.type_right_1;

function Create(
    MCO_parameters:  MCO_parameters_type)
  return memory_control_object;          -- With control rights.
    --
    -- Function:
    --    This function creates a  new MCO and returns an AD
    --    with control rights for this object. The MCO parameters
    --    determine how much virtual memory can be allocated from
    --    the MCO without software intervention, whether the memory
    --    is frozen or normal, and what scan rate should be used
    --    for objects allocated from this MCO.

procedure Destroy(
    mco: memory_control_object);         -- AD with control rights for
                                          -- the MCO to be destroyed.

  --
  -- Function:
  --    This procedure destroys the MCO specified. It calls Low_Level
  --    Process_Management to destroy any processes living in the MCO
  --    and nulls all Access Descriptors which link the SROs in the
  --    MCO together.
  --
  --    Note:  no globally allocated objects are destroyed.


function Retrieve_global_heap(
    mco:  memory_control_object)         -- AD with control rights
                                          -- for an MCO.
  return iMAX_Definitions.storage_resource;
                                          --  AD for the root SRO.

  --
  -- Function:
  --    This function returns an Access Descriptor for the global heap
  --    SRO which is the root of the SRO tree associated with the MCO.
```

```
    function Read_MCO_parameters(
        mco:  memory_control_object)
      return   MCO_parameters_type;
      --
      -- Function:
      --   This function returns the parameters associated with a MCO.

    procedure Adjust_MCO_allocation_limit(
        mco:          memory_control_object;   -- AD with control rights
                                               -- for MCO to be adjusted.
        adjustment: ordinal;                   -- Amount MCO's allocation
                                               -- limit is to be adjusted.
        increment:  boolean)                   -- true  => increment,
                                               -- false => decrement
      --
      -- Function:
      -- This procedure adjusts a MCO's allocation limit up or down by
      -- the specified amount.

    procedure Adjust_MCO_scan_rate(
        mco:           memory control object;  -- AD with control rights
                                               -- for MCO to be adjusted.
        scan_rate: scan_rate_type)             -- New scan rate.
      --
      -- Function:
      --   This procedure sets the MCO's scan rate to that specified.

    function Read_MCO_statistics(
        mco:  memory_control_object)
      return  MCO_statistics_type;
      --
      -- Function:
      --   This function returns the statistics associated with a MCO.

end MCO_Manager;
```

Appendix M

Package Transaction_Manager of the iMAX Operating System

```
package Transaction_Manager is
  --
  -- Function:
  --    This package manages transactions. These are used to synchronize
  --    access to passive-objects in a manner that maintains
  --    the consistency of a collection of objects.
  --
  --    When a user wants to access one or more passive objects,
  --    she will first start a transaction. This transaction will then be used
  --    in the Open and Update operations for the passive objects that
  --    she wants to access. When she has completed all operations, she will
  --    issue a Commit operation on the transaction. This commits all the
  --    changes she has made, thereby committing new versions for the passive
  --    objects that have been changed. The "commit" operation is
  --    is indivisible, i.e., all changes made or none (e.g., in case of a
  --    system crash). If the user issues an Abort operation, all changes
  --    are forgotten. A time out is associated with a transaction. If this
  --    time expires before the transaction is committed, the transaction
  --    manager will abort the transaction.
  --
  --    The private section for this package is not supplied here.

  type transaction_rec is private;

  type transaction is access transaction_rec;

  type transaction_state is(
              active,              -- Initial state of transaction.
              committed,           -- State after transaction is committed.
              aborted);            -- State after transaction is aborted.

  subtype milliseconds is integer range -1 .. integer'last;
    -- An instance of this type indicates a number of milliseconds.
```

```
type transaction_info_rec is
  -- Returned by Transaction_info.
  record
    pname:      print_name;          -- Print name for this transaction.
    state:      transaction_state;   -- Its state.
    time_left:  milliseconds;        -- Time left until Transaction_Manage
                                     -- will cause an abort.
    num_items:  ordinal;             -- Number of passive object definitio
                                     -- associated with this transaction.
    blocked:    boolean;             -- True if transaction is blocked
                                     -- waiting for an open operation.
  end record;

default_time_out: constant milliseconds := 1000;
                                     -- Default value used in
                                     -- Start_transaction operation.

-- EXCEPTIONS

transaction_not_active:        exception;
  -- The specified transaction is not in the active state.

transaction_already_committed: exception;
  -- The specified transaction has already been committed; abort is
  -- not possible.

-- OPERATIONS

procedure Start_transaction(
    t:          out transaction;         -- The created transaction.
    time_out:       milliseconds := 0;   -- After this time, the transactio
                                         -- will be aborted.
    pname:          print_name := (others => ' ');
                                         -- Name to be associated with this
                                         -- transaction.
  --
  -- Function:
  --   A new transaction is created.
  --   If the specified real-time elapses before a
  --   Commit operation is done on this transaction, the transaction wil
  --   be aborted. If the user does not specify a value for time_out,
  --   the system default value is used.

procedure Commit_transaction(
    t:     transaction);              -- The transaction to be committed.
  --
  -- Function:
  --   The specified transaction is committed and all changes made under
  --   this transaction become commited. The passive object definitions
  --   associated with this transaction must already be closed when
  --   Commit_transaction is called, or the Commit will fail. If the
  --   transaction is in the "abort" state, the exception "transaction_n
  --   active" will be raised. This operation changes the state of the
  --   transaction from "active" to "committed". If the state was alread
  --   committed, this operation is a no-op.
```

```
procedure Abort_transaction(
    t:     transaction);           -- The transaction to be aborted.
  --
  -- Function:
  --   The specified operation is aborted. This implies that the passive
  --   object definitions associated with this transaction resort to their
  --   original state, i.e., the new versions that are being created are
  --   destroyed. If the transaction is in the "committed" state, the
  --   exception "transaction_already_committed" will be raised. This
  --   operation changes the state of the transaction from "active" to
  --   "aborted". If the state was already aborted, this operation is
  --   a no-op.

function Transaction_info(
    t:     transaction)            -- The transaction whose state is to
                                   -- be reported on.

  return transaction_info_rec;     -- Transaction information.
  --
  -- Function:
  --   The information associated with a transaction is returned.
  --   This includes its print_name, state, time remaining, whether it
  --   is blocked, and the number of passive object definitions
  --   associated with the transaction.

end Transaction_Manager;
```

Package Passive_Store_Manager of the iMAX Operating System

```
with Transaction_Manager;
package Passive_Store_Manager is;

  --
  -- Function:
  --    This package provides the interface between Object Filing and
  --    the outside world. It includes the facilities to define, store,
  --    and retrieve passive objects. The operations can be grouped as follo
  --
  --    ACTIVE-VERSION OPERATIONS
  --    -------------------------
  --
  --      These provide the simplest interface to Object Filing, and include
  --      the Update  and Reset_active_version procedures.
  --      These routines take an AD for some active object and change
  --      the correspondence between the current active and passive versions
  --      of the object. These routines can be used without referencing any
  --      of the other facilities provided by this package.
  --
  --      "Update" makes the passive version of the object look like the
  --      current active version of the object.
  --      "Reset_active_version" removes the object from the active
  --      space, but does not change its passive definition; subsequent
  --      references to the object will cause its active version to be restor
  --      from a previously saved passive version.
  --
  --    OPEN and CLOSE
  --    --------------
  --
  --      These routines (and the remainder of this package) are provided for
  --      the user or type manager who needs to directly manipulate the passi
  --      representation of an object. This may be desirable either for
  --      efficiency, or (more importantly) because the object cannot be
  --      represented in the active space.
  --
  --      "Open" is used to make the passive definition of an object availabl
  --      to the user. Further operations (see below) can then be used to
  --      read/write portions of the object. If the object was opened in
  --      write or update mode, "Close" must be used to indicate that the
  --      object is in a consistent state before the stored version of the
  --      passive object is actually changed.
```

```
--  GET, PUT, and DELETE
--  --------------------
--
--    These operations are used to actually manipulate the passive
--    definitions of objects. Such objects must already have been Opened.
--
--    Get operations are used to transfer data or Access Descriptors
--    from passive objects to active objects. Put operations are used to
--    transfer data or Access Descriptors from active objects to passive
--    objects. The Delete operation allows the user to delete an Access
--    Descriptor from the passive representation of an object.
--
--  MISCELLANEOUS
--  -------------
--
--    The routines in this section allow the user to examine and set
--    various attributes pertaining to a particular passive object.
--
--  The private section of this package is not given.

subtype transaction is Transaction_Manager.transaction;

subtype milliseconds is integer range -1 .. integer'last;

type passive_definition_rec is private;

type passive_definition is access passive_definition_rec;

type open_mode is
  -- The type of access requested in doing an Open operation.
    (read,     -- Only read requests will be permitted on passive definition.
     write,    -- Read and write requests permitted on passive definition.
               -- A new version is created ab initio.
     update);  -- Read and write requests permitted on passive definition.

-- The -1 lower bound in  the next two subtypes is used by Get/Put
-- data/Access_Descriptor to specify that the size of the passed buffer
-- is to be used.

subtype access_segment_size is integer range -1 .. 2 ** 14;

subtype active_data_segment_size is integer range -1 .. 2 ** 16;

subtype passive_data_segment_size is
                                     integer range 0 .. integer'last;

subtype access_segment_displacement is
                                     integer range 0 .. 2 ** 14 - 1;

subtype active_data_segment_displacement is
                                     integer range 0 .. 2 ** 16 - 1;

subtype passive_data_segment_displacement is
                                     integer range 0 .. integer'last - 1;
```

```
type passive_definition_info is
  record
    open_mode:          access_mode;
    copyable:           boolean;      -- If true, object can be copied.
    activatable:        boolean;      -- If false, object cannot be activat
    link_associated:    boolean;      -- If true, object has an associated
                                      -- link object.
    link:               boolean;      -- If true, object is a "link" object
    auto_copy:          boolean;      -- Applicable only to "link" objects.
                                      -- If true, storing a passive AD will
                                      -- cause automatic copy of link objec
    sys_type:           system_types;
    psor_type:          processor_types;
    access_length:      access_segment_size;       -- In Access Descriptor
    data_length:        passive_data_segment_size; -- In bytes.
  end record;

type put_ad_action is
  -- Action taken when Access Descriptor is stored in a passive definiti
    (plain,                     -- No action. AD for object with owner
                                -- rights must already exist in some pass
                                -- object.
     owner_if_none,             -- Give AD owner rights if no passive
                                -- descriptor for the object has owner
                                -- rights.
     owner,                     -- Give AD owner rights.
     component,                 -- Store referenced object as a component
                                -- passive object being defined.
     copy_as_owner,             -- Copy referenced composite as a
                                -- distinct object.
     full_copy_as_owner,        -- Copy referenced composite as well as
                                -- composites referenced
                                -- with owner rights. This is applied
                                -- recursively.
     copy_as_component,         -- Same as "copy_as_owner" except referen
                                -- composite is made a component of the
                                -- passive definition being defined.
     full_copy_as_component);   -- Same as "full_copy_as_owner" except
                                -- referenced composites are made compone
                                -- of the passive definition being define

--  EXCEPTIONS

transaction_not_active:   exception
                 renames Transaction_Manager.transaction_not_active;
    -- Specified transaction is not in the active state.

open_timed_out:           exception;
    -- Open operation timed out thereby cancelling the requested operati

no_version_available:     exception;
    -- The specified object version is not available.

object_inaccessible:      exception;
    -- The specified object cannot be accessed, e.g., structure not moun

object_unknown:           exception;
    -- The specified object is unknown; usually, due to the object havin
    -- been destroyed.
```

```
object_lacks_owner:        exception;
    -- No passive object has an AD with owner rights for the object.

read_rights_missing:       exception;
    -- Specified AD for an object lacks read rights.

write_rights_missing:      exception;
    -- Specified AD for an object lacks write rights.

update_illogical:          exception;
    -- Open specified "update" access mode for an object with no passive
    -- definition.

more_owners_not_allowed:   exception;
    -- More passive ADs with owner rights are not permitted.

cannot_be_component:       exception;
    -- The specified object cannot be made a component of the specified
    -- passive definition.

copy_of_object_not_allowed:      exception;
    -- The specified object may not be copied.

bounds_error_on_passive_object:  exception;
    -- The supplied displacement or length would cause an access beyond
    -- the end of the passive object.

bounds_error_on_active_object:   exception;
    -- The supplied displacement or length would cause an access beyond
    -- the end of the active object.

passive_definition_not_open:     exception;
    -- Due to the state of the associated transaction, the specified passive
    -- definition can no longer be used.

delete_rights_missing:           exception;
    -- Specified AD lacks delete rights.

-- OPERATIONS THAT MANIPULATE ACTIVE OBJECT VERSIONS

procedure Update(
    obj:    dynamic_typed;            -- Reference to object that is to be
                                      -- updated in the passive store.
    t:      transaction := null);     -- Transaction that will be associated
                                      -- with updated object version.
  --
  -- Function:
  --   This is the "generic" update procedure for object filing. It is
  --   the standard update procedure for untyped objects. It may also
  --   be called by the type manager for typed objects if no special
  --   semantics are required for object update.
  --
  --   Obj must be "known" to the passive space; either a passive AD
  --   with owner rights must already exist for obj, or obj may
  --   be a component of a composite that has been opened in either write
  --   or update mode using the same transaction. Obj must contain both
  --   read and write rights.
  --
  --   The procedure causes the given object's passive version to agree
  --   with its current active version. The object's passive version that
  --   is produced as a result of the update will not become "committed"
  --   until the specified transaction is committed.
```

```
procedure Reset_active_version(
    obj:     dynamic_typed;                  -- Object affected.

    t:       transaction := null);           -- Transaction associated with the
                                             -- action.
  --
  -- Function:
  --    This procedure is used to return an object to a previously-saved
  --    state. Obj must be "known" to the passive space.
  --    The current active version of the object is deleted so that the ne
  --    reference to the object will cause it to be restored from its last
  --    passive version. Obj must contain both read and write rights.

--   OPEN AND CLOSE OPERATIONS

function Open(
    obj:        dynamic_typed;             -- Reference to the object whose passi
                                           -- definition will be opened.
    mode:       access_mode;               -- Read, write, or update.
    t:          transaction := null;       -- Transaction that will be associated
                                           -- with the returned passive definitio
    time_out: milliseconds := -1);         -- Amount of time Open should block
                                           -- until Open is aborted.
  return passive_definition;
  --
  -- Function:
  --    The passive definition of the referenced object is opened.
  --    The caller's AD must have read and write rights if the specified
  --    access mode is "write" or "update"; otherwise, read rights are
  --    sufficient. If "time_out" is not specified, the system default
  --    is used. Specifying a 0 for "time_out" is a conditional Open.

procedure Close(
    psv_def:  passive_definition); -- Passive definition to be closed.
  --
  -- Function:
  --    Closes the given passive object definition.
```

```
-- PUT AND DELETE OPERATIONS

procedure Put_data(
    psv_def:     passive_definition; -- An object's passive definition.
    act_buf:     dynamic_typed;      -- Active object containing data.
    psv_disp:    passive_data_segment_displacemment := 0;
                             -- Displacement into "psv_def".
    sz:          active_data_segment_size := -1;
                             -- Number of bytes to  transfer from "act_buf"
                             -- to "psv_def". (Default means copy all of
                             -- "act_buf".)
    act_disp:    active_data_segment_displacement := 0);
                             -- Displacement into "act_buf".
--
-- Function:
--   Data is transferred from  an active object to a passive object.

procedure Put_access_descriptor(
    psv_def:          passive_definition; -- A passive definition for an obj.
    AD:               dynamic_typed;      -- An AD that is to be stored in
                                          -- "psv_def".
    action:  in out put_ad_action;        -- Action to be taken in "psv_def".
    disp:             access_segment_displacement := 0);
                                          -- Slot in "psv_def" to store "obj".
  --
  -- Function:
  --   The specified AD is stored in the passive object referenced by
  --   "psv_def" using the specified action. If the put_ad_action is
  --   "owner_if_none", then "action" is set either to "plain" or to
  --   "owner" on output.

procedure Put_list_of_access_descriptors(
    psv_def:        passive_definition; -- A passive definition for an object.
    list:           dynamic_typed;      -- An active object.
    action:         put_ad_action := owner_if_none;
                                        -- Action to be taken with respect
                                        -- to the AD's.
    psv_disp:       passive_access_segment_displacement := 0;
                                        -- The starting slot to store the
                                        -- specified ADs.
    num_of_ads:     access_segment_size := -1;
                                        -- Number of ADs to Put in "psv_def".
                                        -- (Default means store all the ADs.)
    act_disp:       access_segment_displacement := 0);
                                        -- The starting slot to  get the ADs
                                        -- to store in "psv_def".
  --
  -- Function:
  --   The specified ADs are stored in the specified passive object.
  --   This operation is equivalent to doing a sequence of
  --   Put_access_descriptor operations. This operation is provided
  --   as a convenience to the user.
```

```
procedure Delete_access_descriptor(
    psv_def:       passive_definition; -- Passive definition for an object
    disp:          access_segment_displacement);
                                       -- AD to  be deleted.
  --
  -- Function:
  --   The selected AD is deleted from "psv_def". The selected AD
  --   must have delete rights.

procedure Copy_access_descriptor(
    from_psv_def: passive_definition; -- Passive definition for an object.
    from_disp:    access_segment_displacement;
                                      -- Slot in "from_psv_def"
                                      -- containing the AD to be copied.
    to_psv_def:   passive_definition; -- Passive definition for an object.
    to_disp:      access_segment_displacement);
                                      -- Slot in "to_psv_def" where AD
                                      -- should be copied.
    action:       put_ad_action);     -- Action to be taken with
                                      -- respect to the copied AD.
  --
  -- Function:
  --   An AD is copied from one passive definition to the other
  --   using the specified action.

-- GET  OPERATIONS

procedure Get_data(
    psv_def:      passive_definition;   -- An  object's passive definition
    act_buf:      dynamic_typed;        -- Active object containing data.
    psv_disp:     passive_data_segment_displacement := 0;
                                  -- Displacement into passive definition.
    sz:           active_data_segment_size := -1;
                                  -- Number of bytes to transfer to
                                  -- "act_buf" from "psv_def". (Default is
                                  -- size of "act_buf".)
    act_disp:     active_data_segment_displacement := 0);
                                  -- Displacement into "act_buf".
  --
  -- Function:
  --   Data is transferred from a passive object to an active object.

function Get_access_descriptor(
    psv_def:      passive_definition;          -- Passive definition for a
                                               -- object.
    disp:         active_segment_displacement) -- Selects an AD.
  return dynamic_typed;
  --
  -- Function:
  --   The AD at displacement "disp" in the passive object
  --   referenced by "psv_def" is returned.
```

```
-- MISCELLANEOUS: INFORMATION AND SET ATTRIBUTE OPERATIONS:

function Get_passive_definition_info(
    psv_def:        passive_definition)    -- Passive definition for some
                                           -- object.
  return passive_definition_info;
  --
  -- Function:
  --   Information about the object's passive definition is returned.

procedure Associate_link(
    psv_def:        passive_definition;    -- Passive definition for some
                                           -- object.
    link:           dynamic_typed;         -- Reference to a link object.
    action: in out put_ad_action);         -- Action taken with respect to
                                           -- "link".

  --
  -- Function:
  --   The specified link object is associated with the passive object
  --   referenced by "psv_def". To do this association, the passive
  --   object must be opened in "update" or "write" mode.
  --   If put_ad_action is "owner_if_none", then "action"
  --   is set either to "plain" or to "owner" on output.

procedure Set_auto_copy(
    psv_def:        passive_definition;    -- Passive definition for some
                                           -- object.
    auto_copy:      boolean);              -- Value to set to.
  --
  -- Function:
  --   The "autocopy" attribute of the referenced composite link object
  --   is changed. Psv_def must be open for "write" or "update".

procedure Set_not_copyable(
    psv_def:        passive_definition);   -- Passive definition for some
                                           -- object.

  --
  -- Function:
  --   The "copyable" attribute of the referenced composite link object
  --   is changed to false. Psv_def must be open for "write" or "update".

procedure Set_not_activatable(
    psv_def:        passive_definition);   -- Passive definition for some
                                           -- object.

  --
  -- Function:
  --   The "activatable" attribute of the referenced composite link object
  --   is changed to false. Psv_def must be open for "write" or "update".

end Passive_Store_Manager;
```

References

1. ACM. *Proceedings of the 1981 Conference on Functional Programming Languages and Computer Architecture*, ACM, New York, 1981.
2. Department of Defense. *Reference Manual for the Ada Programming Language* Superintendent of Documents, U.S. Government Printing Office, Washington, D.C. 20402, 1980.
3. A. A. Ambler, D. I. Good, J. C. Brown, W. F. Burger, R. M. Cohen, C. G. Hoch, R. E. Wells. Gypsy: A Language for Specification and Implementation of Verifiable Programs, *SIGPLAN Notices* 12(3): 1–10, March, 1977.
4. J. Backus. Can Programming be Liberated from the Von Neumann Style? A functional Style and its Algebra of Programs. *Communications of the ACM* 21(8): 613–641, Aug, 1978.
5. J. F. Bartlett. A NonStop Operating System. In *Eleventh Hawaii Internation Conference on System Sciences*, pages 103–117. January, 1978.
6. A. Batson, S. Ju, D. Wood. Measurements of Segment Size. In *Proceedings of the 2nd Symposium on Operating System Principles*, pages 25–29. ACM, New York, October 1969.
7. G. M. Birtwistle, O. J. Dahl, B. Myhrhaug, K. Nygaard. *Simula Begin*. Auerbach Publishers Inc., Philadelphia, 1973.
8. P. Brinch Hansen. *Operating System Principles*. Prentice-Hall, Englewood Cliffs, New Jersey, 1973.
9. P. Brinch Hansen. The Programming Language Concurrent Pascal. *IEEE Trans. Software Eng. SE-1* (2): 199–207, 1975.
10. D. M. Bulman. Stack Computers: An Introduction. *Computers* 10(5): 18–28, May, 1977.
11. D. M. Bulman. Stack Computers. *Computer* 10(5): 14–16, May, 1977.
12. Burroughs Corporation. *The Descriptor—A definition of the B5000 Information Processing System*. Burroughs Corp, Detroit, Michigan, 1961.
13. J. Cohen. Garbage Collection of Linked Data Structures. *ACM Computing Surveys* 13(3): 341–367, September, 1981.
14. D. C. Cosserat. A Capability Oriented Multi-Processor System for Real-Time Applications. In *Proceedings of the International Conference on Computer Communications*. Infotech, Maidenhead, October, 1972.
15. G. W. Cox, Wm. W. Corwin, K. K. Lai, F. J. Pollack. A Unified Model and Implementation for Interprocess Communication in a Multiprocessor Environment. December, 1981.
16. O. J. Dahl, K. Nygaard. Simula—An Algol-Based Simulation Language. *Communications of the ACM* 9(9), September, 1966.
17. J. B. Dennis, E. C. Van Horn. Programming Semantics for Multiprogrammed Computations. *Communications of the ACM* 9(3): 143–155, March, 1966.
18. E. W. Dijkstra, L. Lamport, A. J. Martin, C. S. Scholten, E. M. F. Steffens. On-the-Fly Garbage Collection: An Exercise in Cooperation. *Communications of teh ACM* 20: 966–975, Novenber, 1978.
19. E. W. Dijkstra. *Programming Languages*. Academic Press, New York, 1968, chapter Cooperating Sequential Processes.
20. R. W. Doran. *High-Level Language Computer Architecture*. Academic Press, New York, 1975, pages 63–108. Chapter: Architecture of Stack Machines.
21. D. M. England. Architectural Features of System 250. In *Infotech State of the Art Report on Operating Systems*. Infotech, "Infotech", 1972.
22. D. M. England. Capability Concept Mechanism and Structure in System 250. In *Proceedings of the International Workshop on Protection in Operating Systems*. INRIA, August, 1974.

23. R. S. Fabry. *A User's View of Capabilities*. Quarterly Report, University of Chicago ICR, November 1967.
24. R. S. Fabry. *Preliminary Description of a Supervisor for a Machine Oriented Around Capabilities*. Quarterly Report, August, 1968.
25. R. S. Fabry. Capability-Based Addressing. *Communications of the ACM* 17(7): 403–412, July, 1974.
26. E. F. Gehringer. Variable-Length Capabilities as a Solution to the Small-Object Problem. In *Proceedings of the 7th Symposium on Operating Systems Principles*. ACM, New York, 1979.
27. R. M. Graham. Protection in an Information Processing Utility. In *CACM*, pages 365–369. ACM, New York, May, 1968.
28. J. V. Guttag. Abstract Data Types and the Development of Data Structures. *Communications of the ACM* 20(6): 396–404, June, 1977.
29. D. Halton. Hardware of the System 250. In *Proceedings of International Switching Symposium. , 1972*.
30. M. E. Houdek, G. R. Mitchell. Translating a Large Virtual Address. *IBM System/38 Technical Developments*. (IBM GSD G580–0237), 1978.
31. M. E. Houdek, F. G. Soltis, R. L. Hoffman. IBM System/38 Support for Capability-Based Addressing. In *Proceedings of the 8th Symposium on Computer Architecture*, pages 341–348. ACM/IEEE, New York, May, 1981.
32. J. K. Iliffe, J. G. Jodeit. A Dynamic Storage Allocation Scheme. *Computer Journal* 5(3): 200–209, October, 1962.
33. J. K. Iliffe. *Basic Machine Principles*. Americal Elsevier Publishing Company, Inc., New York, 1968.
34. J. B. Johnston. The Contour Model of Block Structured Processes. *SIGPLAN Notices* 6(2): 55–82, 1971.
35. A. K. Jones, P. Schwarz. Experience Using Multiprocessor Systems—A Status Report. *ACM Computing Surveys* 12(2): 121–168, June, 1980.
36. K. C. Kahn, Wm. M. Corwin, T. D. Dennis, H. D'Hooge, D. E. Hubka, L. A. Hutchins, J. T. Montague, F. J. Pollack, M. R. Gifkins. iMAX: A Multiprocessor Operating System for an Object-Based Computer. *Proceedings of the 8th Symposium on Operating Systems Principles* 15(5): 127–136, December 1981.
37. D. E. Knuth. *Fundamental Algorithms, The Art of Computer Programming*. Addison-Wesley Publishing Company, Reading, MA, 1968.
38. B. W. Lampson, J. J. Horning, R. L. London, J. G. Mitchel, G. J. Popek. Report on the Programming Language Euclid. *SIGPLAN Notices* 12(2): 1–79, February, 1978.
39. B. W. Lampson, H. E. Sturgis. Reflections on an Operating System Design. *Communications of the ACM* 19(5): 251–265, May, 1976.
40. H. M. Levy. A Comparative Study of Capability-Based Computer architecture. Master's thesis, University of Washington, Dept. of Computer Science, December, 1981.
41. B. H. Liskov, S. N. Zilles. Programming with Abstract Data Types. *SIGPLAN Notices* ACM 9: 50–59, April 1974.
42. B. Liskov, A. Snyder, R. Atkinson, C. Schaffert. Abstraction Mechanisms in CLU. *Communications of the ACM* 20(8): 564–576, August, 1977.
43. Wm. M. McKeeman. *Introduction to Computer Architecture*. SRA, Chicago, 1980, pages 319–382. Chapter 7: Stack Computers.
44. L. P. Meissner, E. I. Organick. *FORTRAN 77*. Addison-Wesley, Reading, MA, 1980.
45. J. G. Mitchell, Wm. Maybury, R. E. Sweet. *Mesa Language Manual* Xerox Palo Alto Research Center, Palo Alto, CA, 1979.
46. G. J. Myers. *Advances in Computer Architecture, 2nd edition*. John Wiley and Sons, New York, 1981.
47. R. M. Needham, R. D. H. Walker. The Cambridge CAP Computer and its Protection System. In *In Proceedings of the 6th Symposium on Operating System Principles*, pages 1–10. ACM/SIGOPS, November, 1977.
48. E. I. Organick. *The Multics System: An Examination of Its Structure*. Massachusetts Institute Technology Press, Cambridge, MA, 1972.
49. E. I. Organick. *Computer System Organization*. Academic Press, New York, 1973.
50. E. I. Organick, A. I. Forsythe, R. P. Plummer. *Programming Language Structures*. Academic Press, New York, 1978.

51. E. J. Pollack, K. C. Kahn, R. M. Wilkinson. The iMAX-432 Object Filing System. In *Proceedings of the 8th Symposium on Operating System Principles*, pages 137–147. ACM, New York, December, 1981. ACM order no. 534810.
52. F. J. Pollack, G. W. Cox, D. W. Hammerstrom, K. C. Kahn, K. K. Lai, J. R. Rattner. Supporting Ada Memory Management in the iAPX-432. In ACM (editor), *Proceedings of Symposium on Architectural Support for Programming Languages and Operating Systems*, pages 117–131. ACM-SIGPLAN, New York, March-April, 1982.
53. D. P. Reed. *Naming and Synchronization in a Decentralized Computer System*. PhD thesis, M.I.T. Dept. of Electrical Engineering and Computer Science, September, 1978. Also available as an M.I.T. Laboratory for Computer Science Technical REport TR-205.
54. D. P. Reed. Implementing Atomic Actions on Decentralized Data. December, 1979. Preprints of Proceedings of the 7th Symposium on Operating System Principles, ACM, New York.
55. D. P. Reed, L. Svobodova. SWALLOW: A Distributed Data Storage System for a Local Network in Zurich, Switzerland. *International Workshop on Local Networks*, August, 1980.
56. J. M. Saltzer. *Traffic Control in a Multiplexed Computer System*. PhD thesis, M.I.T., Dept. Electrical Engineering, May, 1966. Also Project MAC Tech. Rept. TR-30, July 1966, 79 pp.
57. M. Satyanarayanan. A Study of File Sizes and Functional Lifetimes. In *Proceedings of the 8th Symposium on Operating Systems Principles*, pages 96–108. ACM, New York, December, 1981.
58. M. Shaw. Research Directions in Abstract Data Structures. *SIGPLAN Notices* 8(2): 66–70, March, 1976.
59. D. P. Siewiorek, R. S. Swarz. *The Theory and Practice of Reliable System Design*. Digital Equipment Press, Bedford, MA, 1982. Chapter 18: Design Methodology for High Reliability Systems: The Intel 432, coauthored with David Johnson.
60. M. J. Spier, E. I. Organick. The Multics Interprocess Communication Facility. In *Proceedings of the 2nd Symposium on Operating System Principles*. ACM, New York, October, 1969. Reprinted in Freeman, ed., Software Systems Principles A Survey, pages 133–152, 1975 Chicago, SRA.
61. M. J. Spier, T. N. Hastings, D. N. Cutler. An Experimental Implementation of the Kernel/Domain Architecture. *ACM Operating Systems Review* 7(4): 8–21, October, 1973. Also, Proceedings of the 4th Symposium on Operating Systems Principles.
62. M. J. Spier. A Model Implementation for Protective Domains. *International Journal of Computer and Information Sciences* 2(3): 201–229.
63. M. V. Wilkes. *Time-Sharing Computer Systems*. American Elsevier, New York, 1968.
64. M. V. Wilkes, R. M. Needham. *The Cambridge CAP Computer and its Operating System*. North Holland, New York, 1979.
65. M. V. Wilkes. Hardware Support for Memory Protection: Capability Implementations. In *Proceedings Symposium on Architectural Support for Programming Languages and Operating Systems*. pages 107–116. ACM, New York, March-April, 1982.
66. N. Wirth. Modula: A Language for Modular Programming. *Software: Practice and Experience* 7(1): 3–35, January, 1977.
67. Wm. A. Wulf. *Alphard: Toward a Language to Support Structured Programs*. Technical Report, Carnegie-Mellon University, Computer Science Dept., 1974.
68. Wm. A. Wulf, E. Cohen, Wm. Corwin, A. Jones, R. Levin, C. Pierson, F. Pollack. Hydra: The Kernel of a Multiprocessor Operating System. *Communications of the ACM* 16(6): 337–345, June, 1974.
69. Wm. A. Wulf, R. Levin, S. P. Harbison. *HYDRA/C.mmp: An Experimental Computer System*. McGraw-Hill Book Company, New York, 1981.

INDEX